Web Scalability for Startup Engineers

About the Author

Artur Ejsmont is a passionate software engineer and agile leader, currently working for Yahoo! in Sydney. Artur has been working with web applications for over 10 years with a lot of focus on agile, startup-like environments; he loves the Lean Startup model. Artur has worked on websites serving 1M+ pages per hour, both in Europe and Australia. He has also served as a university lecturer and is passionate about sharing his knowledge with others. Artur actively contributes to the tech community as a technical writer, blogger, and public speaker.

About the Technical Editors

Bill Wilder is CTO at Finomial Corporation, an occasional conference speaker, an inconsistent blogger, and leader (since 2009) of Boston Azure. He is recognized by Microsoft as an Azure MVP and is the author of the book *Cloud Architecture Patterns* (O'Reilly Media, 2012). He can be found on Twitter @codingoutloud.

TJ Wilder is a college student in his junior year at the University of Massachusetts at Amherst, majoring in computer science with a minor in mathematics. He has been programming since he was 12 but has taken occasional breaks since then to eat, sleep, and sing. Having interned at DraftKings.com when it was a startup, he looks forward to putting the book's advice to work in more startups in the future.

Dr. Danny Coward is a chief architect and web architect at Oracle. Coward is the sole spec lead for the Java API for Web Sockets for Java EE and Java SE/JavaFX and sole author of the WebSocket technical documentation at Oracle. Coward's work leading WebSocket at Oracle make him the leading expert on Java WebSocket programming. Coward has a decade of experience as a Java developer, where he now seeks to direct and simplify complex technologies to fulfill business objectives. Coward has specialized experience in all aspects of Java software—from Java ME to Java EE to the founding of the JavaFX technology.

Web Scalability for Startup Engineers

Tips & Techniques for Scaling Your Web Application

Artur Ejsmont

New York   Chicago   San Francisco
Athens   London   Madrid   Mexico City
Milan   New Delhi   Singapore   Sydney   Toronto

Cataloging-in-Publication Data is on file with the Library of Congress

McGraw-Hill Education books are available at special quantity discounts to use as premiums and sales promotions, or for use in corporate training programs. To contact a representative, please visit the Contact Us pages at www.mhprofessional.com.

Web Scalability for Startup Engineers: Tips & Techniques for Scaling Your Web Application

1234567890   DOC DOC   1098765

ISBN   978-0-07-184365-2
MHID   0-07-184365-5

Sponsoring Editor Brandi Shailer	**Proofreader** Paul Tyler
Editorial Supervisor Patty Mon	**Indexer** Jack Lewis
Project Manager Kritika Kaushik, Cenveo® Publisher Services	**Production Supervisor** Jean Bodeaux
Technical Editors Bill Wilder, TJ Wilder, Danny Coward	**Composition** Cenveo Publisher Services
	Illustration Cenveo Publisher Services
Copy Editor Lisa McCoy	**Art Director, Cover** Jeff Weeks
	Cover Designer Jeff Weeks

I dedicate this book to all of you passionate geeks.
The future of mankind is truly in your hands now.

Contents at a Glance

Contents

Acknowledgments

I would like to thank Bill Wilder, TJ Wilder, Danny Coward, and Brandi Shailer for all of their feedback and help when working on this book. I would also like to thank Dion Beetson, Craig Penfold, Jackie Reses, Venkatesh Kanchan, Marcelo Maidana, Kristian Kauper, Christof Mueller, Ścibór Sobieski, Mariusz Jarocki, Andrzej Nowakowski, my friends, and my family for supporting and inspiring me over the last 35 years. I would not be who I am today without them.

Introduction

In the coming years, businesses will need to store, transfer, and process increasingly large amounts of data. This will happen mainly due to the exponential growth of technology and our increasing dependency on it. As a result of this wave, the demand for engineers who are able to build scalable systems is going to increase as well.

The initial idea for the book came to me when I realized that most engineers either know a lot about scalability or nothing at all. I realized that there is not enough literature on the subject and that there is no easy way for engineers working in smaller companies to "get to the next level" in terms of understanding scalability. With this in mind, I set out a goal of writing a book that would help people understand the bigger picture and create awareness of how software architecture and the infrastructure work together to promote scalability.

I think of this book as a roadmap for readers to use in their journey to web application scalability. I present both a high-level perspective and a deep dive into important aspects to give real-world advice. There are too many technologies to go through everything in detail, but it is possible to explain concepts and basic rules and showcase selected platforms.

Chapter 1: Core Concepts

The first chapter of this book provides an introduction to the concepts of scalability and a very high-level overview of the book. In this chapter, I propose different stages of web application evolution in terms of scalability as a way to gradually introduce various concepts. I also present an overview of the infrastructure and architecture of a scalable web application.

Chapter 2: Principles of Good Software Design

In this chapter, I discuss different design principles and considerations that are necessary to build flexible and scalable systems. I start with the broadest concepts, like simplicity and coupling, and then discuss some object-oriented design principles, like single responsibility and dependency injection. Finally, I move to design concepts directly related to scalability, like functional partitioning, data partitioning, and self-healing.

Chapter 3: Building the Front-End Layer

In this chapter, I focus on parts of the infrastructure that are directly interacting with the client's software, like web browsers or mobile apps. I explain in-depth ways of handling state in the front-end layer. Then I discuss different components of a scalable front end, like load balancers, proxies, and content delivery networks. Finally, I discuss auto-scaling and different deployment scenarios.

Chapter 4: Web Services

In this chapter, I discuss the benefits and drawbacks of different web service architectures. I explain design principles and go into details of scalability techniques in the context of REST-ful APIs.

Chapter 5: Data Layer

In this chapter, I explain core scalability techniques. I discuss techniques relevant to relational databases like MySQL, but also spend a lot of time discussing NoSQL data stores like Cassandra. Throughout the chapter I explain in detail concepts such as data partitioning (aka sharding), replication, and eventual consistency. I also compare different data layer topologies and challenges related to each of the techniques.

Chapter 6: Caching

In this chapter, I focus on caching, which is one of the key strategies of scalability and high performance. Throughout the chapter I explain in detail HTTP-based caching, different types of HTTP caches, and techniques of scaling HTTP caches. I then describe object caches and common ways of scaling them out. Finally, I spend some time explaining caching best practices, which should help you make better decisions and prioritize your efforts more efficiently when implementing caching.

Chapter 7: Asynchronous Processing

In this chapter, I explain the increasingly popular subjects of messaging and event-driven architecture. I begin by explaining the concepts and benefits of asynchronous processing and how to leverage message brokers to scale web applications. Then, I highlight some of the challenges and pitfalls you may expect when working with asynchronous systems. Finally, I briefly compare some of the most popular messaging platforms to help you choose the best tool for the job.

Chapter 8: Searching for Data

In this chapter, I focus on the wider problem of searching for data. Searching for data is closely related to data stores, and as your data sets grow, it becomes increasingly important to optimize the way you search for and access data. I begin by explaining how different types of indexes work. I then spend some time discussing data modeling, which helps scalability, and how you can think of data modeling in NoSQL data stores like Cassandra. Finally, I provide an introduction to search engines and how they can be used in the context of a web application.

Chapter 9: Other Dimensions of Scalability

In the final chapter of this book, I describe other concepts necessary to scale your throughput, managing yourself better and growing your team. I begin by emphasizing the role of automation as the key technique of increasing engineering efficiency. I discuss topics such as automated testing, deployments, monitoring, and alerting. I then share my own experiences and observations related to project management, which should help you survive in a startup. Finally, I reflect on the challenges of growing agile teams.

Intended Audience

I wrote this book with software engineers, engineering managers, DevOps, and system engineers in mind. The book may be challenging for university students, but it should be understandable for any mid-level and even junior engineer.

I assume readers have a basic understanding of how web applications are built and how related technologies work together. Reading this book does not require you to have knowledge of any particular technology stack like Java, PHP, JavaScript, C#, or Ruby because scalability is a universal challenge in web development. I do assume that readers understand how the HTTP protocol works and that they have basic knowledge of IP networking, HTML, and client-server software development concepts.

Core Concepts

tartups face extreme amounts of uncertainty. To build a successful startup, you must be as flexible as possible. You also need to be resourceful and adapt quickly to changing conditions. These extreme requirements put on the software teams make scalability even more important and challenging than in slowly changing businesses. Things that can take an entire year in a corporate environment may need to happen in just a matter of weeks in a startup. If you are successful and lucky, you may need to scale your capacity up tenfold in a matter of weeks, just to have to scale back down a few months later.

Scalability is a difficult matter for any engineer, and it presents special challenges in the startup environment. As such, leveraging the work done by major players in this space, including Amazon, Azure, and Google clouds, can reduce the overall scope of your work and allow you to focus on addressing your specific needs. As we discuss scalability concepts in the book, we'll also look at some of the services you can apply to address each challenge. Understanding scalability is best approached gradually, and to that end, I'll keep things simple to begin with by focusing on the core concepts from a high level. Anyone with a basic understanding of web application development should feel comfortable diving into the book. As we move forward, I'll take a deeper dive into details of each concept. For now, it's important to establish three main pillars of scalability: what it is and how it evolves, what it looks like in a large-scale application, and what its application architecture looks like.

To fully grasp the concepts in this chapter, it may be worth revisiting it after you've read the entire book. At first, some concepts may seem quite abstract, but you'll find everything comes together nicely as you more fully understand the big picture. This chapter contains a number of diagrams as well. These diagrams often carry much more information than you may notice at first glance. Getting comfortable with drawing infrastructure and architecture diagrams will not only help you get the most out of this book, but may also help you during your next job interview.

What Is Scalability?

Before we dive into the core concepts, let's make sure we are approaching scalability with a unified definition. You're likely reading this book because you want to enable your web applications to scale—or to scale more efficiently. But what does it mean to scale?

Scalability is an ability to adjust the capacity of the system to cost-efficiently fulfill the demands. Scalability usually means an ability to handle more users, clients, data, transactions, or requests without affecting the user experience. It is important to remember that scalability should allow us to scale down as much as scale up and that scaling should be relatively cheap and quick to do.

The ability to scale is measured in different dimensions, as we may need to scale in different ways. Most scalability issues can be boiled down to just a few measurements:

▶ **Handling more data**   This is one of the most common challenges. As your business grows and becomes more popular, you will be handling more and more data. You will have to efficiently handle more user accounts, more products, more location data, and more pieces of digital content. Processing more data puts pressure on your system, as data needs to be sorted, searched through, read from disks, written to disks, and sent over the network. Especially today, with the growing popularity of big data analytics, companies become greedier and greedier about storing ever-growing amounts of data without ever deleting it.

▶ **Handling higher concurrency levels**   Concurrency measures how many clients your system can serve at the same time. If you are building a web-based application, concurrency means how many users can use your application at the same time without affecting their user experience. Concurrency is difficult, as your servers have a limited amount of central processing units (CPUs) and execution threads. It is even more difficult, as you may need to synchronize parallel execution of your code to ensure consistency of your data. Higher concurrency means more open connections, more active threads, more messages being processed at the same time, and more CPU context switches.

▶ **Handling higher interaction rates**   The third dimension of scalability is the rate of interactions between your system and your clients. It is related to concurrency, but is a slightly different dimension. The rate of interactions measures how often your clients exchange information with your servers. For example, if you are building a website, your clients would navigate from page to page every 15 to 120 seconds. If you are building a multiplayer mobile game, however, you may need to exchange messages multiple times per second. The rate of interactions can be higher or lower independently of the amount of concurrent users, and it depends more on the type of the application you are building. The main challenge related to the interaction rate is latency. As your interactions rate grows, you need to be able to serve responses quicker, which requires faster reads/writes and often drives requirements for higher concurrency levels.

The scalability of your system will usually be defined by the combination of these three requirements. Scaling down is usually less important than the ability to scale up, but reducing waste and inefficiencies is an important factor nonetheless, especially so for startups, where every investment may become a waste as business requirements change.

As you have probably noticed, scalability is related to performance, but it is not the same thing. Performance measures how long it takes to process a request or to perform a certain task, whereas scalability measures how much we can grow (or shrink).

For example, if you had 100 concurrent users, with each user sending a request, on average, once every 5 seconds, you would end up with a throughput requirement of 20 requests per second. Performance would decide how much time you need to serve these 20 requests per second, and scalability would decide how many more users you can handle and how many more requests they can send without degrading the user experience.

Finally, scalability of a software product may be constrained by how many engineers can be working on the system. As your system grows, you will need to consider organizational scalability as well; otherwise, you will not be able to make changes or adapt quickly enough. Even though organizational scalability may seem unrelated to technology, it actually may be limited by the architecture and design of your system. If your system is very tightly interconnected, you may struggle to scale your engineering team, as everyone will work on the same codebase. Growing a single engineering team above 8 to 15 people becomes inefficient, as the communication overhead grows exponentially as the team size grows.[40]

HINT

To fully appreciate how scalability affects startups, try to assume a more business-oriented perspective. Ask yourself, "What are the constraints that could prevent our business from growing?" It is not just about raw throughput; it involves development processes, teams, and code structure. I will explore these aspects of scalability in more detail in Chapter 9 of this book.

Evolution from a Single Server to a Global Audience

As a young engineer I used to build web applications that were hosted on a single server, and this is probably how most of us get started. During my career I have worked for different companies and I have witnessed applications in different scalability evolution stages. Before we go deeper into scalability, I would like to present some of these evolution stages to better explain how you go from a single server sitting under your desk to thousands of servers spread all over the world.

I will keep it at a very high level here, as I will go into more detail in later chapters. Discussing evolution stages will also allow me to introduce different concepts and gradually move toward more complex topics. Keep in mind that many of the scalability evolution stages presented here can only work if you plan for them from the beginning. In most cases, a real-world system would not evolve exactly in this way, as it would likely need to be rewritten a couple of times. Most of the time, a system is designed and born in a particular evolution stage and remains in it for its lifetime, or manages to move up one or two steps on the ladder before reaching its architectural limits.

HINT

Avoid full application rewrites at all costs,[45] especially if you work in a startup. Rewrites always take much longer than you initially expect and are much more difficult than initially anticipated. Based on my experience, you end up with a similar mess just two years later.

Single-Server Configuration

Let's begin with a single-server setup, as it is the simplest configuration possible and this is how many small projects get started. In this scenario, I assume that your entire application runs on a single machine. Figure 1-1 shows how all the traffic for every user request is handled by the same server. Usually, the Domain Name System (DNS) server is used as a paid service provided by the hosting company and is not running on your own server. In this scenario, users connect to the DNS to obtain the Internet Protocol (IP) address of the server where your website is hosted. Once the IP address is obtained, they send Hypertext Transfer Protocol (HTTP) requests directly to your web server.

Since your setup consists of only one machine, it needs to perform all the duties necessary to make your application run. It may have a database management system running (like MySQL or Postgres), as well as serving images and dynamic content from within your application.

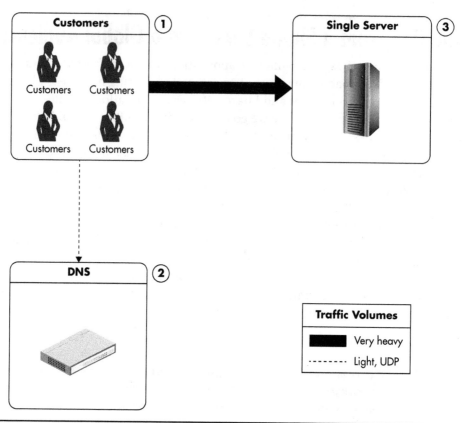

Figure 1-1   *Single-server configuration*

Figure 1-1 shows the distribution of traffic in a single-server configuration. Clients would first connect to the DNS server to resolve the IP address of your domain, and then they would start requesting multiple resources from your web server. Any web pages, images, Cascading Style Sheet (CSS) files, and videos have to be generated or served by your server, and all of the traffic and processing will have to be handled by your single machine. I use different weights of arrows on the diagram to indicate the proportion of traffic coming to each component.

An application like this would be typical of a simple company website with a product catalog, a blog, a forum, or a self-service web application. Small websites may not even need a dedicated server and can often be hosted on a virtual private server (VPS) or on shared hosting.

Virtual private server is a term used by hosting providers to describe a virtual machine for rent. When you purchase a VPS instance, it is hosted together with other VPS instances on a shared host machine. VPS behaves as a regular server—you have your own operating system and full privileges. VPS is cheaper than a dedicated server, as multiple instances can exist at the same time on the same physical machine. VPS is a good starting point, as it is cheap and can usually be upgraded instantly (you can add more random access memory [RAM] and CPU power with a click of a button).

Shared hosting is the cheapest hosting solution, where you purchase a user account without administrative privileges. Your account is installed on a server together with many other customers' accounts. It is a good starting point for the smallest websites or landing pages, but it is too limiting so it is not a recommended option.

For sites with low traffic, a single-server configuration may be enough to handle the requests made by clients. There are many reasons, though, why this configuration is not going to take you far scalability-wise:

▶ Your user base grows, thereby increasing traffic. Each user creates additional load on the servers, and serving each user consumes more resources, including memory, CPU time, and disk input/output (I/O).

▶ Your database grows as you continue to add more data. As this happens, your database queries begin to slow down due to the extra CPU, memory, and I/O requirements.

▶ You extend your system by adding new functionality, which makes user interactions require more system resources.

▶ You experience any combination of these factors.

Making the Server Stronger: Scaling Vertically

Once your application reaches the limits of your server (due to increase in traffic, amount of data processed, or concurrency levels), you must decide how to scale. There are two different types of scaling: vertical and horizontal. I will be covering both techniques in this book, but since vertical scalability is conceptually simpler and it is more common in this evolution stage, let's look at it first.

> *Vertical scalability* is accomplished by upgrading the hardware and/or network throughput. It is often the simplest solution for short-term scalability, as it does not require architectural changes to your application. If you are running your server with 8GB of memory, it is easy to upgrade to 32GB or even 128GB by just replacing the hardware. You do not have to modify the way your application works or add any abstraction layers to support this way of scaling. If you are hosting your application on virtual servers, scaling vertically may be as easy as a few clicks to order an upgrade of your virtual server instance to a more powerful one.

There are a number of ways to scale vertically:

▶ Adding more I/O capacity by adding more hard drives in Redundant Array of Independent Disks (RAID) arrays. I/O throughput and disk saturation are the main bottlenecks in database servers. Adding more drives and setting up a RAID array can help to distribute reads and writes across more devices. In recent years, RAID 10 has become especially popular, as it gives both redundancy and increased throughput. From an application perspective, a RAID array looks like a single volume, but underneath it is a collection of drives sharing the reads and writes.

▶ Improving I/O access times by switching to solid-state drives (SSDs). Solid-state drives are becoming more and more popular as the technology matures and prices continue to fall. Random reads and writes using SSDs are between 10 and 100 times faster, depending on benchmark methodology. By replacing disks you can decrease I/O wait times in your application. Unfortunately, sequential reads and writes are not much faster and you will not see such a massive performance increase in real-world applications. In fact, most open-source databases (like MySQL) optimize data structures and algorithms to allow more sequential disk operations rather than depending on random access I/O. Some data stores, such as Cassandra, go even further, using solely sequential I/O for all writes and most reads, making SSD even less attractive.

▶ Reducing I/O operations by increasing RAM. (Even 128GB RAM is affordable nowadays if you are hosting your application on your own dedicated hardware.) Adding more memory means more space for the file system cache and more working memory for the applications. Memory size is especially important for efficiency of database servers.

▶ Improving network throughput by upgrading network interfaces or installing additional ones. If your server is streaming a lot of video/media content, you may need to upgrade your network provider's connection or even upgrade your network adapters to allow greater throughput.

▶ Switching to servers with more processors or more virtual cores. Servers with 12 and even 24 threads (virtual cores) are affordable enough to be a reasonable scaling option. The more CPUs and virtual cores, the more processes that can be executing at the same time. Your system becomes faster, not only because processes do not have to share the CPU, but also because the operating system will have to perform fewer context switches to execute multiple processes on the same core.

Vertical scalability is a great option, especially for very small applications or if you can afford the hardware upgrades. The practical simplicity of vertical scaling is its main advantage, as you do not have to rearchitect anything. Unfortunately, vertical scaling comes with some serious limitations, the main one being cost. Vertical scalability becomes extremely expensive beyond a certain point.[43]

Figure 1-2 shows the approximate relationship of price per capacity unit and the total capacity needed. It shows that you can scale up relatively cheaply first, but beyond a certain point, adding more capacity becomes extremely expensive. For example, getting 128GB of RAM (as of this writing) could cost you $3,000, but doubling that to 256GB could cost you $18,000, which is much more than double the 128GB price.

The second biggest issue with vertical scalability is that it actually has hard limits. No matter how much money you may be willing to spend, it is not possible to continually add memory. Similar limits apply to CPU speed, number of cores per server, and hard drive speed. Simply put, at a certain point, no hardware is available that could support further growth.

Finally, operating system design or the application itself may prevent you from scaling vertically beyond a certain point. For example, you will not be able to keep adding CPUs to keep scaling MySQL infinitely, due to increasing lock contention (especially if you use an older MySQL storage engine called MyISAM).

Then price per unit begins to grow very rapidly

Sweet spot

Price per capacity unit

Price grows linearly at start, double capacity = double price

Extra capacity needed

Figure 1-2   *Cost of scalability unit*

Locks are used to synchronize access between execution threads to shared resources like memory or files. *Lock contention* is a performance bottleneck caused by inefficient lock management. Operations performed very often should have fine-grained locks; otherwise, your application may spend most of its time waiting for locks to be released. Once you hit a lock contention bottleneck, adding more CPU cores does not increase the overall throughput.

High-performance open-source and commercial applications should scale onto dozens of cores; however, it is worth checking the limitations of your application before purchasing the hardware. Homegrown applications are usually much more vulnerable to lock contention, as efficient lock management is a complex task requiring a lot of experience and fine-tuning. In extreme cases, adding more cores may yield no benefits at all if the application was not designed with high concurrency in mind.

As you can see in Figure 1-3, vertical scalability does not affect system architecture in any way. You can scale vertically each of our servers, network connections, or

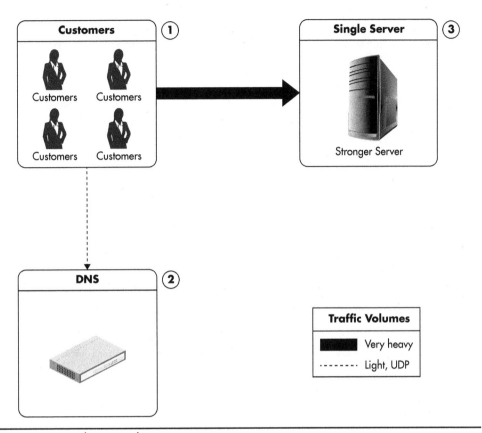

Figure 1-3   *Single server, but stronger*

routers without needing to modify your code or rearchitecting anything. All you need to do is replace a piece of hardware with a stronger or faster piece of hardware.

Isolation of Services

Vertical scalability is not the only option at this early stage of evolution. Another simple solution is moving different parts of the system to separate physical servers by installing each type of service on a separate physical machine. In this context, a service is an application like a web server (for example, Apache) or a database engine (for example, MySQL). This gives your web server and your database a separate, dedicated machine. In the same manner, you can deploy other services like File Transfer Protocol (FTP), DNS, cache, and others, each on a dedicated physical machine. Isolating services to separate servers is just a slight evolution from a single-server setup. It does not take you very far, however, as once you deploy each service type on a separate machine, you have no room to grow.

Cache is a server/service focused on reducing the latency and resources needed to generate the result by serving previously generated content. Caching is a very important technique for scalability. I will discuss caching in detail in Chapter 6.

Figure 1-4 shows a high-level infrastructure view with each service deployed to a separate machine. This still looks similar to a single-server setup, but it slowly

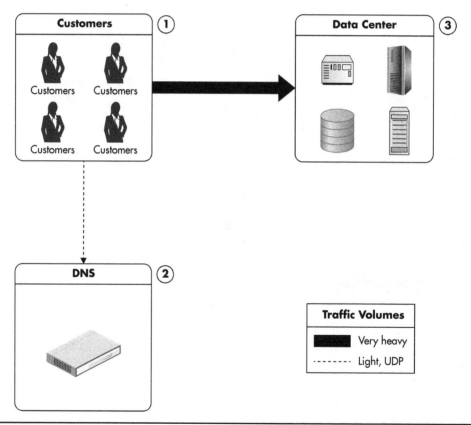

Figure 1-4 *Configuration with separate services residing on different servers*

increases the number of servers that can share the load. Servers are usually hosted in a third-party data center. They are often VPS, rented hardware, or collocated servers. I represent the data center here as a set of servers dedicated to different functions. Each server has a certain role, such as web server, database server, FTP, or cache. I will discuss the details of data center layout later in this chapter.

Isolation of services is a great next step for a single-server setup, as you can distribute the load among more machines than before and scale each of them vertically as needed. This is a common configuration among small websites and web development agencies. Agencies will often host many tiny websites for different clients on shared web servers. A bigger client with a more popular website would move to a separate web server and a separate database. This allows an agency to balance the load between applications of their clients and better utilize resources, keeping each of the web applications simple and fairly monolithic.

In a similar way to agencies hosting customers' websites on separate machines, you can divide your web application into smaller independent pieces and host them on separate machines. For example, if you had an administrative console where customers can manage their accounts, you could isolate it into a separate web application and then host it on a separate machine.

HINT

The core concept behind isolation of services is that you should try to split your monolithic web application into a set of distinct functional parts and host them independently. The process of dividing a system based on functionality to scale it independently is called functional partitioning.

Figure 1-5 shows a scenario in which a web application uses functional partitioning to distribute the load among even more servers. Each part of the application would typically use a different subdomain so that traffic would be directed to it based simply on the IP address of the web server. Note that different partitions may have different servers installed, and they may also have different vertical scalability needs. The more flexibility we have in scaling each part of the system, the better.

Content Delivery Network: Scalability for Static Content

As applications grow and get more customers, it becomes beneficial to offload some of the traffic to a third-party content delivery network (CDN) service.

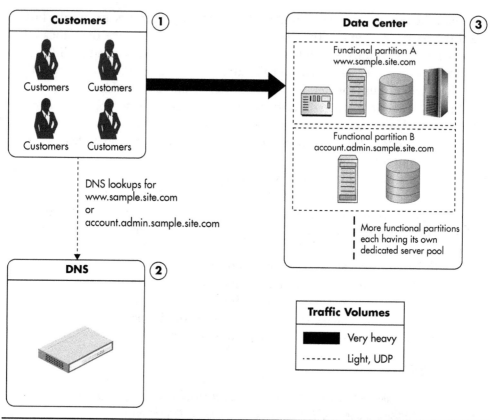

Figure 1-5 *Configuration showing functional partitioning of the application*

A *content delivery network* is a hosted service that takes care of global distribution of static files like images, JavaScript, CSS, and videos. It works as an HTTP proxy. Clients that need to download images, JavaScript, CSS, or videos connect to one of the servers owned by the CDN provider instead of your servers. If the CDN server does not have the requested content yet, it asks your server for it and caches it from then on. Once the file is cached by the CDN, subsequent clients are served without contacting your servers at all.

By integrating your web application with a CDN provider, you can significantly reduce the amount of bandwidth your servers need. You will also need fewer web servers to serve your web application's static content. Finally, your clients may benefit from better resource locality, as CDN providers are usually global companies with data centers located all around the world. If your data center is located in North America, clients connecting from Europe would experience higher latencies. In such case, using CDN would also speed up page load times for these customers, as CDN would serve static content from the closest data center.

Figure 1-6 shows a web application integrated with a CDN provider. Clients first connect to the DNS server. Then, they request pages from your servers and load additional resources, such as images, CSS, and videos, from your CDN provider. As a result, your servers and networks have to deal with reduced traffic, and since CDNs solve a specific problem, they can optimize the way they serve the content cheaper than you could. I will explain CDN in more detail in Chapter 6.

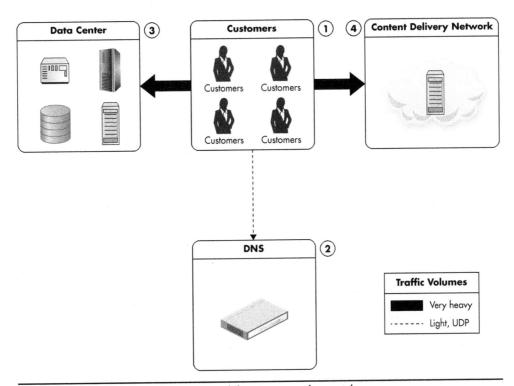

Figure 1-6   *Integration with a content delivery network provider*

The important thing to note here is that this is the first time I mentioned scaling using a third-party service. We did not have to add more servers or learn how to scale HTTP proxies. We simply used the third-party service and relied on its ability to scale. Even though it may seem like "cheating in the scalability game," it is a powerful strategy, especially for startups in their early stages of development, who cannot afford significant time or money investments.

Distributing the Traffic: Horizontal Scalability

All of the evolution stages discussed so far were rather simple modifications to the single-server configuration. Horizontal scalability, on the other hand, is much harder to achieve and in most cases it has to be considered before the application is built. In some rare cases, it can be "added" later on by modifying the architecture of the application, but it usually requires significant development effort. I will describe different horizontal scalability techniques throughout this book, but for now, let's think of it as running each component on multiple servers and being able to add more servers whenever necessary. Systems that are truly horizontally scalable do not need strong servers—quite the opposite; they usually run on lots and lots of cheap "commodity" servers rather than a few powerful machines.

Horizontal scalability is accomplished by a number of methods to allow increased capacity by adding more servers. Horizontal scalability is considered the holy grail of scalability, as it overcomes the increasing cost of capacity unit associated with scaling by buying ever-stronger hardware. In addition, when scaling horizontally you can always add more servers—you never reach a hard limit, as is the case with vertical scalability.

Figure 1-7 shows a simplified comparison of costs related to horizontal and vertical scalability. The dashed line represents costs of vertical scalability, and the solid line represents horizontal scalability.

Horizontal scalability technologies often pay off at the later stage. Initially they tend to cost more because they are more complex and require more work. Sometimes they cost more because you need more servers for the most basic

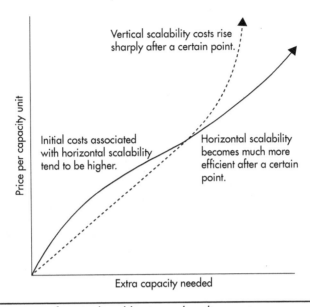

Figure 1-7   *Comparison of vertical and horizontal scaling costs*

setup, and other times it is because you need more experienced engineers to build and operate them. The important thing to note is that once you pass a certain point of necessary capacity, horizontal scalability becomes a better strategy. Using horizontal scalability, you avoid the high prices of top-tier hardware and you also avoid hitting the vertical scalability ceiling (where there is no more powerful hardware).

It is also worth noting that scaling horizontally using third-party services like CDN is not only cost effective, but often pretty much transparent. The more traffic you generate, the more you are charged by the provider, but the cost per capacity unit remains constant. That means that doubling your request rate will just cost you twice as much. It gets even better, as for some services, price per unit decreases as you scale up. For example, Amazon CloudFront charges $0.12 per GB for the first 10TB of transferred data, but then decreases the price to $0.08 per GB.

HINT

Cloud service providers are able to charge lower rates for higher-traffic clients because their overheads of maintenance, integration, and customer care are lower per capacity unit when dealing with high-traffic sites.

Let's quickly review the high-level infrastructure overview of the evolution so far. Once we start deploying different parts of the system onto different servers and adding some horizontal scalability, our high-level diagram may look something like Figure 1-8.

The thing that distinguishes horizontally scalable systems from the previous evolution stages is that each server role in our data center can be scaled by adding more servers. That can usually be implemented in stages of partially horizontal scalability, where some services scale horizontally and others do not. As I mentioned before, achieving true horizontal scalability is usually difficult and expensive. Therefore, systems should start by scaling horizontally in areas where it is the easiest to achieve, like web servers and caches, and then tackle the more difficult areas, like databases or other persistence stores.

At this stage of evolution, some applications would also use a round-robin DNS service to distribute traffic among web servers. Round-robin DNS is not the only way to distribute traffic among multiple web servers; we will consider different alternatives in detail in Chapter 3.

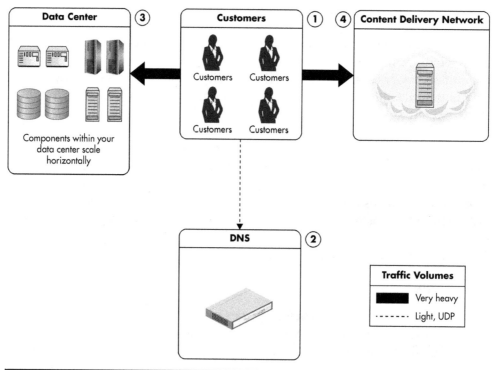

Figure 1-8 *Multiple servers dedicated to each role*

Round-robin DNS is a DNS server feature allowing you to resolve a single domain name to one of many IP addresses. The regular DNS server takes a domain name, like ejsmont.org, and resolves it to a single IP address, like 173.236.152.169. Thus, round-robin DNS allows you to map the domain name to multiple IP addresses, each IP pointing to a different machine. Then, each time a client asks for the name resolution, DNS responds with one of the IP addresses. The goal is to direct traffic from each client to one of the web servers—different clients may be connected to different servers without realizing it. Once a client receives an IP address, it will only communicate with the selected server.

Scalability for a Global Audience

The largest of websites reach the final evolution stage, which is scalability for a global audience. Once you serve millions of users spread across the globe, you will require more than a single data center. A single data center can host plenty of servers, but it causes clients located on other continents to receive a degraded user experience. Having more than one data center will also allow you to plan for rare outage events (for example, caused by a storm, flood, or fire).

Scaling for a global audience requires a few more tricks and poses a few more challenges. One of the additions to our configuration is the use of geoDNS service.

GeoDNS is a DNS service that allows domain names to be resolved to IP addresses based on the location of the customer. Regular DNS servers receive a domain name, like yahoo.com, and resolve it to an IP address, like 206.190.36.45. GeoDNS behaves the same way from the client's perspective. However, it may serve different IP addresses based on the location of the client. A client connecting from Europe may get a different IP address than the client connecting from Australia. As a result, clients from both Europe and Australia could connect to the web servers hosted closer to their location. In short, the goal is to direct the customer to the closest data center to minimize network latency.

Another extension of the infrastructure is to host multiple edge-cache servers located around the world to reduce the network latency even further. The use of edge-cache servers depends on the nature of your application. Edge-cache servers are most efficient when they act as simple reverse proxy servers caching entire pages, but they can be extended to provide other services as well.

> *Edge cache* is a HTTP cache server located near the customer, allowing the customer to partially cache the HTTP traffic. Requests from the customer's browser go to the edge-cache server. The server can then decide to serve the page from the cache, or it can decide to assemble the missing pieces of the page by sending background requests to your web servers. It can also decide that the page is uncacheable and delegate fully to your web servers. Edge-cache servers can serve entire pages or cache fragments of HTTP responses.

Figure 1-9 shows a high-level diagram with multiple data centers serving requests from clients located in different parts of the world. In this scenario, users located in Europe would resolve your domain name to an IP address of one of your European edge servers. They would then be served results from the cache or from one of your application servers. They would also load static files, such as CSS or JavaScript files, using your CDN provider, and since most CDN providers have data centers located in multiple countries, these files would be served from the closest data center as well. In a similar way, users from North America would be directed to American edge-cache servers and their static files would be served from the American CDN data center. As your application grows even further, you may want to divide your main data center into multiple data centers and host each of them closer to your audience. By having your data stores and all of your application components closer to your users, you save on latency and network costs.

Now that we have discussed the wider application ecosystem and the infrastructure at a very high level, let's look at how a single data center might support scalability.

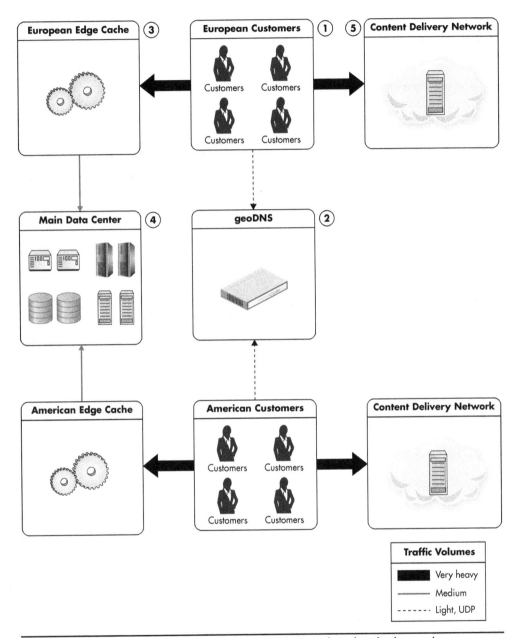

Figure 1-9   *Customers from different locations are served via local edge caches.*

Overview of a Data Center Infrastructure

Let's now turn to the different technologies used in modern web applications. As with the previous section, we'll take a deeper dive into these topics throughout the book, but I first want to lay out the overall communication flow and functions of each technology type.

Figure 1-10 shows a high-level overview of the communication flow starting from the user's machine and continuing all the way throughout different layers of the infrastructure. It is one of the most important diagrams in this book, as it shows you all of the key components that you need to be familiar with to design and implement scalable web applications. You can think of it as a reference diagram, as we will come back to different parts of it in different chapters. In fact, the structure of this book was designed to align closely to the structure of a data center, with each area of responsibility being covered by different chapters of the book.

Many of the components shown serve a specialized function and can be added or removed independently. However, it is common to see all of the components working together in large-scale applications. Let's take a closer look at each component.

The Front Line

The front line is the first part of our web stack. It is a set of components that users' devices interact with directly. Parts of the front line may reside inside of our data center or outside of it, depending on the details of the configuration and third-party services used. These components do not have any business logic, and their main purpose is to increase the capacity and allow scalability.

Going from the top, clients' requests go to the geoDNS server to resolve the domain names. DNS decides which data center is the closest to the client and responds with an IP address of a corresponding load balancer (2).

> A *load balancer* is a software or hardware component that distributes traffic coming to a single IP address over multiple servers, which are hidden behind the load balancer. Load balancers are used to share the load evenly among multiple servers and to allow dynamic addition and removal of machines. Since clients can only see the load balancer, web servers can be added at any time without service disruption.

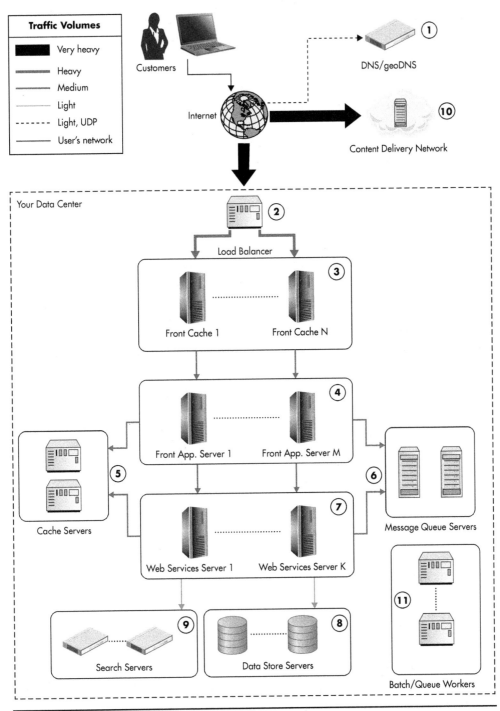

Figure 1-10 *High-level overview of the data center infrastructure*

Web traffic from the Internet is usually directed to a single IP address of a strong hardware load balancer. It then gets distributed evenly over to front cache servers (3) or directly over front-end web application servers (4). Front cache servers are optional; they can be deployed in remote locations outside of the data center or skipped altogether. In some cases it may be beneficial to have a layer of front-end cache servers to reduce the amount of load put on the rest of the infrastructure.

It is common to use third-party services as load balancers, CDN, and reverse proxy servers; in such cases this layer may be hosted entirely by third-party providers. We'll take a closer look at the benefits and drawbacks of scaling them using third parties in Chapter 3.

Web Application Layer

The second layer of our stack is the web application layer. It consists of web application servers (4) responsible for generating the actual HTML of our web application and handling clients' HTTP requests. These machines would often use a lightweight (PHP, Java, Ruby, Groovy, etc.) web framework with a minimal amount of business logic, since the main responsibility of these servers is to render the user interface. All the web application layer is supposed to do is handle the user interactions and translate them to internal web services calls. The simpler and "dumber" the web application layer, the better. By pushing most of your business logic to web services, you allow more reuse and reduce the number of changes needed, since the presentation layer is the one that changes most often.

Web application servers are usually easy to scale since they should be completely stateless. If developed in a stateless manner, adding more capacity is as simple as adding more servers to the load balancer pool. I will discuss the web application layer together with the frontline layer in Chapter 3.

Web Services Layer

The third layer of our stack consists of web services (7). It is a critical layer, as it contains most of our application logic. We keep front-end servers simple and free of business logic since we want to decouple the presentation layer from the business logic. By creating web services, we also make it easier to create functional partitions. We can create web services specializing in certain functionality and scale them independently. For example, in an e-commerce web application, you could have a product catalog service and a user profile service, each providing very different types of functionality and each having very different scalability needs.

The communication protocol used between front-end applications and web services is usually Representational State Transfer (REST) or Simple Object Access Protocol (SOAP) over HTTP. Depending on the implementation, web services should be relatively simple to scale. As long as we keep them stateless, scaling horizontally is as easy as adding more machines to the pool, as it is the deeper data layers that are more challenging to scale.

In recent years, integration between web applications has become much more popular, and it is a common practice to expose web services to third parties and directly to customers. That is why web services are often deployed in parallel to front-end application servers rather than hidden behind them, as shown in Figure 1-10.

I will discuss the web services layer in detail in Chapter 4. For now, let's think of web services as the core of our application and a way to isolate functionality into separate subsystems to allow independent development and scalability.

Additional Components

Since both front-end servers (4) and web services (7) should be stateless, web applications often deploy additional components, such as object caches (5) and message queues (6).

Object cache servers are used by both front-end application servers and web services to reduce the load put on the data stores and speed up responses by storing partially precomputed results. Cache servers will be covered in detail in Chapter 6.

Message queues are used to postpone some of the processing to a later stage and to delegate work to queue worker machines (11). Messages are often sent to message queues from both front-end applications and web service machines, and they are processed by dedicated queue worker machines. Sometimes web applications also have clusters of batch-processing servers or jobs running on schedule (controlled by cron). These machines (11) are not involved in generating responses to users' requests; they are offline job-processing servers providing features like asynchronous notifications, order fulfillment, and other high-latency functions. Message queues and queue workers are covered further in Chapter 7.

Data Persistence Layer

Finally, we come to the data persistence layer (8) and (9). This is usually the most difficult layer to scale horizontally, so we'll spend a lot of time discussing different scaling strategies and horizontal scalability options in that layer. This is also an area of rapid development of new technologies labeled as *big data* and *NoSQL*, as increasing amounts of data need to be stored and processed, regardless of their source and form.

The data layer has become increasingly more exciting in the past ten years, and the days of a single monolithic SQL database are gone. As Martin Fowler says, it is an era of polyglot persistence, where multiple data stores are used by the same company to leverage their unique benefits and to allow better scalability. We'll look further at these technologies in Chapters 5 and 8.

In the last five years, search engines became popular due to their rich feature set and existence of good open-source projects. I present them as a separate type of component, as they have different characteristics than the rest of the persistence stores, and I believe it is important to be familiar with them.

Data Center Infrastructure

By having so many different platforms in our infrastructure, we have increased the complexity multiple times since our single-server setup. What we have achieved is the ability to share the load among multiple servers. Each component in Figure 1-10 has a certain function and should help to scale your application for millions of users.

The layered structure of the components is deliberate and helps to reduce the load on the slower components. You can see that traffic coming to the load balancer is split equally over all front-end cache servers. Since some requests are "cache hits," traffic is reduced and only part of it reaches front-end servers (4). Here, application-level cache (5) and message queues (6) help reduce the traffic even further so that even fewer requests reach back-end web services (7). The web service can use message queues and cache servers as well. Finally, only if necessary, the web services layer contacts search engines and the main data store to read/write the necessary information. By adding easily scalable layers on top of the data layer, we can scale the overall system in a more cost-effective way.

It is very important to remember that it is not necessary to have all of these components present in order to be able to scale. Instead, use as few technologies as possible, because adding each new technology adds complexity and increases maintenance costs. Having more components may be more exciting, but it makes releases, maintenance, and recovery procedures much more difficult. If all your application needs is a simple search functionality page, maybe having front-end servers and a search engine cluster is all you need to scale. If you can scale each layer by adding more servers and you get all of the business features working, then why bother using all of the extra components? We'll continue to look back to Figure 1-10 as we cover the components in further detail.

Overview of the Application Architecture

So far, we've looked at the infrastructure and scalability evolution stages. Let's now take a high-level look at the application itself.

The application architecture should not revolve around a framework or any particular technology. Architecture is not about Java, PHP, PostgreSQL, or even database schema. Architecture should evolve around the business model. There are some great books written on domain-driven design and software architecture[1-3] that can help you get familiar with best practices of software design. To follow these best practices, we put business logic in the center of our architecture. It is the business requirements that drive every other decision. Without the right model and the right business logic, our databases, message queues, and web frameworks are useless.

Moreover, it is irrelevant if the application is a social networking website, a pharmaceutical service, or a gambling app—it will always have some business needs and a domain model. By putting that model in the center of our architecture, we make sure that other components surrounding it serve the business, not the other way around. By placing technology first, we may get a great Rails application, but it may not be a great pharmaceutical application.[t1]

> *A domain model* is created to represent the core functionality of the application in the words of business people, not technical people. The domain model explains key terms, actors, and operations, without caring about technical implementation. The domain model of an automated teller machine (ATM) would mention things like cash, account, debit, credit, authentication, security policies, etc. At the same time, the domain model would be oblivious to hardware and software implementation of the problem. The domain model is a tool to create our mental picture of the business problems that our application is supposed to solve.

Figure 1-11 shows a simplified representation of how application components can be laid out. This already assumes that users use our system as a single application, but internally, our application is broken down into multiple (highly autonomous) web services.

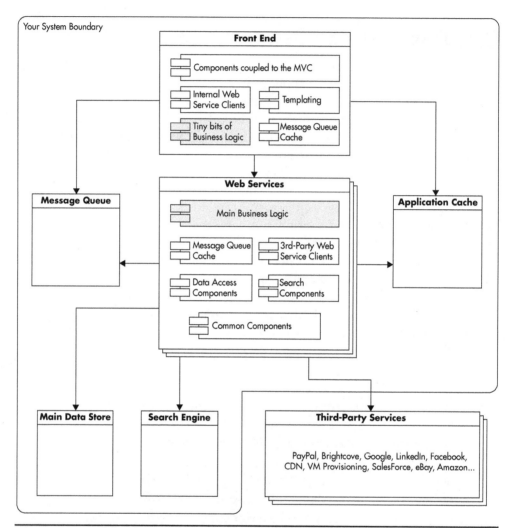

Figure 1-11   *High-level view of an application architecture*

Let's discuss each area of the diagram presented on Figure 1-11 in more detail in the following sections.

Front End

Similar to the way we discussed the infrastructure diagrams, let's take it from the top and look at Figure 1-11 from the point of the client's request. Keep in mind that the center of the architecture lives in the main business logic, but for the sake of simplicity, let's start with the front-end components.

The front end should have a single responsibility of becoming the user interface. The user can be interacting with the application via web pages, mobile applications, or web service calls. No matter what the actual delivery mechanism is, the front-end application should be the layer translating between the public interface and internal service calls. The front end should be considered as "skin," or a plugin of the application, and as something used to present the functionality of the system to customers. It should not be considered a heart or the center of the system. In general, the front end should stay as "dumb" as possible.

By keeping the front end "dumb," we will be able to reuse more of the business logic. Since the logic will live only in the web services layer, we avoid the risk of coupling it with our presentation logic. We will also be able to scale front-end servers independently, as they will not need to perform complex processing or share much state, but may be exposed to high concurrency challenges.

Front-end code will be closely coupled to templates and the web framework of our choice (for example, Spring, Rails, Symfony). It will be constrained by the user interface, user experience requirements, and the web technologies used. Front-end applications will have to be developed in a way that will allow communication over HTTP, including AJAX and web sessions. By hiding that within the front-end layer, we can keep our services layer simpler and focused solely on the business logic, not on the presentation and web-specific technologies.

Templating, web flows, and AJAX are all specific problems. Keeping them separated from your main business logic allows for fast and independent changes. Having the front end developed as a separate application within our system gives us another advantage: we can use a different technology stack to develop it. It is not unreasonable to use one technology to develop web services and a different one to develop the front-end application. As an example, you could develop the front end using Groovy, PHP, or Ruby, and web services could be developed in pure Java.

HINT

You can think of a front-end application as a plugin that can be removed, rewritten in a different programming language, and plugged back in. You should also be able to remove the "HTTP"-based front-end and plug in a "mobile application" front end or a "command line" front end. This attitude allows you to keep more options open and to make sure you decouple the front end from the core of the business logic.

The front end should not be aware of any databases or third-party services. Projects that allow business logic in the front-end code suffer from low code reuse and high complexity.

Finally, allow front-end components to send events to message queues and use cache back ends, as they are both important tools in increasing the speed and scaling out. Whenever we can cache an entire HTML page or an HTML fragment, we save much more processing time than caching just the database query that was used to render this HTML.

Web Services

"SOAs are like snowflakes—no two are alike." –David Linthicum

Web services are where most of the processing has to happen, and also the place where most of the business logic should live. Figure 1-11 shows a stack of web services in a central part of the application architecture. This approach is often called a service-oriented architecture (SOA). Unfortunately, SOA is a fairly overloaded term, so you may get a different definition, depending on who you speak with about it.

> *Service-oriented architecture (SOA)* is architecture centered on loosely coupled and highly autonomous services focused on solving business needs. In SOA, it is preferred that all the services have clearly defined contracts and use the same communication protocols. I don't consider SOAP, REST, JSON, or XML in the definition of SOA, as they are implementation details. It does not matter what technology you use or what protocols are involved as long as your services are loosely coupled and specialized in solving a narrow set of business needs. I will explain coupling and best design principles in the next chapter.

HINT

Watch out for similar acronyms: SOA (service-oriented architecture) and SOAP (which originally was an acronym of Simple Object Access Protocol). Although these two can be seen together, SOA is an architecture style and SOAP is a set of technologies used to define, discover, and use web services. You can have SOA without SOAP, and you can also use SOAP in other architecture styles.

I encourage you to learn more about SOA by reading some of the recommended texts,[31,33,20] but remember that SOA is not an answer to all problems and other architecture styles exist, including layered architecture, hexagonal architecture, and event-driven architecture. You may see these applied in different systems.

A multilayer architecture is a way to divide functionality into a set of layers. Components in the lower layers expose an application programming interface (API) that can be consumed by clients residing in the layers above, but you can never allow lower layers to depend on the functionality provided by the upper layers. A good example of layered architecture is an operating system and its components, as shown in Figure 1-12. Here, you have hardware, device drivers, operating system kernel, operating system libraries, third-party libraries, and third-party applications. Each layer is consuming services provided by the layers below, but never vice versa. Another good example is the TCP/IP programming stack, where each layer adds functionality and depends on the contract provided by the layer below.

Layers enforce structure and reduce coupling as components in the lower layers become simpler and less coupled with the rest of the system. It also allows us to replace components in lower layers as long as they fulfill the same API. An important side effect of layered architecture is increased stability as you go deeper

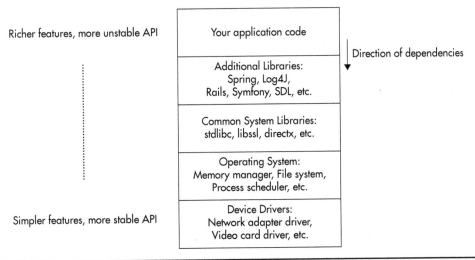

Figure 1-12 *Example of a multilayered architecture*

into the layers. You can change the API of upper layers freely since few things depend on them. On the other hand, changing the API of lower layers may be expensive because there may be a lot of code that depends on the existing API.

> *Hexagonal architecture* assumes that the business logic is in the center of the architecture and all the interactions with the data stores, clients, and other systems are equal. There is a contract between the business logic and every nonbusiness logic component, but there is no distinction between the layers above and below.

In hexagonal architecture, users interacting with the application are no different from the database system that the application interacts with. They both reside outside of the application business logic and both deserve a strict contract. By defining these boundaries, you can then replace the person with an automated test driver or replace the database with a different storage engine without affecting the core of the system.

> *Event-driven architecture* (EDA) is, simply put, a different way of thinking about actions. Event-driven architecture, as the name implies, is about reacting to events that have already happened. Traditional architecture is about responding to requests and requesting work to be done. In a traditional programming model we think of ourselves as a person requesting something to be done, for example, createUserAccount(). We typically expect this operation to be performed while we are waiting for a result, and once we get the result, we continue our processing. In the event-driven model, we don't wait for things to be done. Whenever we have to interact with other components, we announce things that have already happened and proceed with our own processing. Analogous to the previous example, we could announce an event UserAccountFormSubmitted. This mental shift leads to many interesting implications. Figure 1-13 shows the difference in interaction models. We'll look more closely at EDA in more detail in Chapter 7.

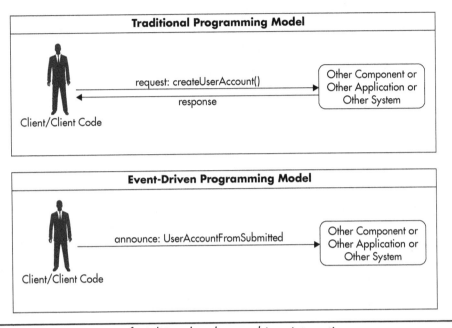

Figure 1-13   *Comparison of traditional and event-driven interactions*

No matter the actual architecture style of the system, all architectures will provide a benefit from being divided into smaller independent functional units. The purpose is to build higher abstractions that hide complexity, limit dependencies, allow you to scale each part independently, and make parallel development of each part practical.

> ### HINT
>
> *Think of the web services layer as a set of highly autonomous applications, where each web service becomes an application itself. Web services may depend on each other, but the less they depend on each other, the better. A higher level of abstraction provided by services allows you to see the entire system and still understand it. Each service hides the details of its implementation and presents a simplified, high-level API.*

Ideally, each web service would be fully independent. Figure 1-14 shows a hypothetical portfolio of web services belonging to an e-commerce platform. In this example, the text analysis service could be an independent service able to detect the meaning of articles based solely on their content. Such a service would not require user data or assistance from any other services; it would be fully independent.

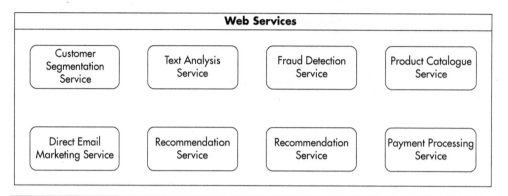

Figure 1-14 *Conceptual view of services in the web services layer*

Unfortunately, it is usually impossible to isolate all services like this. Most times, there will be some dependencies between different services. For example, a customer segmentation service could be a service based on user activity, and social network data produces a customer profile. To assign users to different customer segments, we may need to integrate this service with main user data, activity history, and third-party services. The customer segmentation service would most likely be coupled to services other than the text analysis service.

No matter what the implementation of your web services, don't forget their main purpose: to solve business needs.

Supporting Technologies

Figure 1-11 shows web services surrounded by a few smaller boxes labeled message queue, application cache, main data store, and search engine. These are isolated since they are usually implemented in different technologies, and most often they are third-party software products configured to work with our system. Because they are third-party technologies, they can be treated as black boxes in the context of architecture.

Notice that the database (main data store) is simply a little box in the corner of the diagram. This is because the data store is just a piece of technology; it is an implementation detail. From the application architecture point of view, the data store is something that lets us write and read data. We do not care how many servers it needs; how it deals with scalability, replication, or fault tolerance; or even how it persists data.

> **HINT**
>
> *Think of the data store as you think of caches, search engines, and message queues — as plug-and-play extensions. If you decide to switch to a different persistence store or to exchange your caching back ends, you should be able to do it by replacing the connectivity components, leaving the overall architecture intact.*

By abstracting the data store, you also free your mind from using MySQL or another database engine. If the application logic has different requirements, consider a NoSQL data store or an in-memory solution. Remember, the data store is not the central piece of the architecture, and it should not dictate the way your system evolves.

Finally, I decided to include third-party services in the architecture diagram to highlight their importance. Nowadays computer systems do not operate in a vacuum; large systems often have integrations with literally dozens of external systems and often critically depend on their functionality. Third-party services are outside of our control, so they are put outside of our system boundary. Since we do not have control over them, we cannot expect them to function well, not have bugs, or scale as fast as we would wish. Isolating third-party services by providing a layer of indirection is a good way to minimize the risk and our dependency on their availability.

Summary

Architecture is the perspective of the software designer; infrastructure is the perspective of the system engineer. Each perspective shows a different view of the same problem—building scalable software. After reading this chapter, you should be able to draw a high-level picture of how the architecture and the infrastructure come together to support the scalability of a web application. This high-level view will be important as we begin to drill into the details of each component.

As you can see, scalability is not an easy topic. It touches on many aspects of software design and architecture, and it requires broad knowledge of many different technologies. Scalability can only be tamed once you understand how all the pieces come together, what their roles are, and what their strong points and weak points are. To design scalable web applications is to understand the impact of the architecture, infrastructure, technologies, algorithms, and true business needs. Let's now move forward to principles of good software design, as this is a prerequisite to building scalable web applications.

Principles of Good Software Design

M any of the scalability issues encountered in real-world projects can be boiled down to violations of core design principles. Software design principles are more abstract and more general than scalability itself, but they lay down a solid foundation for building scalable software.

Some of the principles presented in this chapter are related to object-oriented design and others related directly to scalability, but most of them are more abstract and universal, allowing you to apply them in different ways. A skilled software craftsperson should understand both good and bad software design practices, starting with what drives the reasoning behind design decisions. Let's get started with understanding some of those decisions now.

Simplicity

"Make things as simple as possible, but no simpler." –Albert Einstein

The most important principle is keeping things *simple.* Simplicity should be your northern star, your compass, and your long-term commitment. Keeping software simple is difficult because it is inherently relative. There is no standardized measurement of simplicity, so when you judge what is simpler, you need to first ask yourself for whom and when. For example, is it simpler for you or for your clients? Is it simpler for you to do now or maintain in the future?

Simplicity is not about using shortcuts and creating the quickest solution to the problem at hand. It is about what would be the easiest way for another software engineer to use your solution in the future. It is also about being able to comprehend the system as it grows larger and more complex. The lessons of simplicity often come from experience with different applications, using different frameworks and languages. Revisiting code you have written, identifying complexity, and looking for solutions to simplify is the first step to learn from your own mistakes. Over time you develop sensitivity and an ability to quickly judge which solution is simpler in the long run. If you have an opportunity to find a mentor or work closely with people who value simplicity, you will make much faster progress in this area. There are four basic steps to start promoting simplicity within your products. Let's take a look at each in more detail.

Hide Complexity and Build Abstractions

Hiding complexity and building abstractions is one of the best ways to promote simplicity. As your system grows, you will not be able to build a mental picture of the entire system because it will have too many details. Human working memory has limited space—either you see the whole system without much detail or you see all the details of a very narrow part of the system. To make software simple is to allow this mental zoom in and zoom out. As your system grows, it cannot and will not all be simple, so you have to strive for local simplicity.

> *Local simplicity* is achieved by ensuring that you can look at any single class, module, or application and quickly understand what its purpose is and how it works. When you look at a class, you should be able to quickly understand how it works without knowing all the details of how other remote parts of the system work. You should only have to comprehend the class at hand to fully understand its behavior. When you look at a module, you should be able to disregard the methods and think of the module as a set of classes. Zooming out even more, when you look at the application, you should be able to identify key modules and their higher-level functions, but without the need to know the classes' details. Finally, when you look at the entire system, you should be able to see only your top-level applications and identify their responsibilities without having to care about how they fulfill them.

Let's consider an abstract example as shown in Figure 2-1, where circles represent classes/interfaces. When you work on a class or an interface, you look

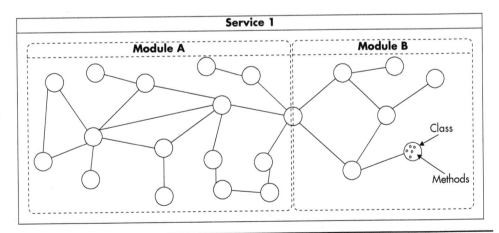

Figure 2-1   *Levels of abstraction*

at the circle and its contents. You may also need to look at its neighbors since each edge represents dependencies on another class or interface. In this way, complexity is not about how many nodes you have in your network, but how many edges you have between your nodes, with nodes being classes and edges being dependencies on one another. A good general rule is that no class should depend on more than a few other interfaces or classes.

To build local simplicity, you also need to separate functionality into modules, so once you look at the higher level of abstraction, you need not be worried about how modules perform their duties, but how they interact. If you look at Figure 2-1 on the higher level, you can disregard details of each module and focus on its interactions. In this case, the interactions between Module A and Module B are reduced to a single public interface that is visible to both modules.

In large and complex systems you will need to add another layer of abstraction where you create separate services. Each service becomes responsible for a subset of functionality hiding its complexity and exposing an even higher level of abstraction.

Avoid Overengineering

The second practice promoting simplicity is to deliberately avoid the urge to overengineer. Engineers love challenges and puzzles, and they love the challenge of building complex software. When you try to predict every possible use case and every edge case, you lose focus on the most common use cases. In such a situation you can easily follow the urge of solving every problem imaginable and end up overengineering, which is building a solution that is much more complex than is really necessary.

Good design allows you to add more details and features later on, but does not require you to build a massive solution up front. Beginning with a reasonable level of abstraction and iterating over it gives better results than trying to predict the future and build everything that might be needed later on.

The Java community used to be notorious for their overengineering of the simplest things. Fortunately in recent years, frameworks like Spring and dynamic languages built on top of the Java Virtual Machine (e.g., Groovy) show the right vision. Engineers have to care about simplicity and the most common scenarios, not building imaginary systems that no one can ever use or understand.

> ### HINT
> *If you like to solve puzzles, ask yourself this question each time you design a piece of software: "Can this be any simpler and still allow flexibility in the future?" Building software that is simple to understand and proves to be extensible can give a great deal of satisfaction.*

Overengineering usually happens when people try to do the right thing, but choose the wrong perspective or assume too much about future needs. I encourage you to ask yourself "What tradeoffs am I making here?" or "Will I really need this?" and work closely with the business stakeholders to better understand the biggest risks and unknowns. Otherwise, you may spend a lot of time following dogmas and building solutions that no one will ever need. Most of the principles covered in this chapter come with some cost, and it is your responsibility to define the line between the right amount of complexity and overengineering. It is a difficult role and there is almost no black and white—it is a game of tradeoffs played entirely in shades of gray.

Try Test-Driven Development

Adopting a test-driven development (TDD) methodology will also promote simplicity. You do not have to follow it all the time—practicing TDD for just a few months should be long enough to give you a new perspective.

Test-driven development is a set of practices where engineers write tests first and then implement the actual functionality. It is a radical approach, but worth experiencing. The main benefits are that there is no code without unit tests and there is no "spare" code. Since developers write tests first, they would not add unnecessary functionality, as it would require them to write tests for it as well. In addition, tests can be used as a type of documentation, as they show you how the code was meant to be used and what the expected behavior was.

As a side effect of experiencing the test-first methodology, engineers go through an important mental shift. It forces them to assume the client's point of view first, which helps them to create much cleaner and simpler interfaces. Since you have to write your test first, you have to imagine how would you use the component you are about to build. To write tests, you assume the viewpoint of the client code using your component, rather than focusing on the internal implementation of it. This slight difference in approach results in greatly improved code design and application programming interface (API) simplicity.

> **_HINT_**
>
> _When you design code, whether using TDD or not, think about it from the perspective of your client. Put yourself in the shoes of a new developer who joined your team and started using your interface. What methods would they want to call, what parameters would they want to pass, and what response would they expect to be returned? When you think about it from this perspective, you ensure that clients can interact easily with your code._

Learn from Models of Simplicity in Software Design

Simplicity can sometimes go unnoticed or be misinterpreted as a lack of complexity. When things fall into place naturally, when there is no difficulty in adapting the system or understanding it, you have probably witnessed well-crafted simplicity. It is a great experience to realize that a system you are working on is well designed. Whenever you find this quality, analyze it and look for patterns. Grails, Hadoop, and the Google Maps API are a few models of simplicity and great places for further study. Try analyzing these frameworks:

▶ **Grails** Grails is a web framework for the Groovy language modeled on Rails (a Ruby web framework). Grails is a great example of how simplicity can become transparent. As you study the framework and begin using it, you realize that everything has been taken care of. You see how things work as expected and how extending functionality seems effortless. You also realize that you cannot imagine it being much simpler. Grails is a masterpiece of making a developer's life easy. Read _Grails in Action_[22] and _Spring Recipes_[14] to learn more.

▶ **Hadoop** Get familiar with the MapReduce paradigm and the Hadoop platform. Hadoop is a great piece of open-source technology helping to process petabytes of data. It is a large and very complex platform, but it hides most of its complexity from developers. All that developers have to learn is an incredibly simple programming API. When you get to know Hadoop better, you realize how many difficult problems it solves and how simple it makes it for developers to process almost infinite amounts of data. To get a basic understanding of MapReduce and Hadoop, I recommend reading the original MapReduce white paper[w1] and _Hadoop in Action_.[23]

▶ **Google Maps API** Explore the Google Maps API. There are few APIs that I admire as much as Google Maps. Over the years the API has changed, but it is still a great example of a flexible API that solves complex problems in extremely simple ways. If all you need is a map with a single marker, you can get it done in an hour, including the time for creating API keys. As you dig deeper you find more and more amazing features, like overlays, user interface (UI) customizations, and map styles, all fitting perfectly into place.

As you read through this chapter, you will see more design principles promoting simplicity. Simplicity is the underlying value that helps you scale your systems. Without simplicity, engineers will not be able to comprehend the code, and without understanding your software, you cannot sustain growth. Remember, especially at scale, it is always better to design something that is simple and works than something sophisticated and broken.

Loose Coupling

The second most important design principle is to keep coupling between parts of your system as low as necessary.

> *Coupling* is a measure of how much two components know about and depend on one another. The higher the coupling, the stronger the dependency. *Loose coupling* refers to a situation where different components know as little as necessary about each other, whereas no coupling between components means that they are completely unaware of each other's existence.

Keeping coupling low in your system is important for the health of the system and ability to scale, as well as your team morale. Let's go through some of the effects of low and high coupling:

▶ High coupling means that changing a single piece of code requires you to inspect in detail multiple parts of the system. The higher the overall coupling, the more unexpected the dependencies and higher chance of introducing bugs. Suppose you introduce a change to the user authentication process and you realize that you need to refactor five different modules because they all depend on the internal implementation of the authentication process. Sound familiar? Low coupling would allow you to introduce these changes without the risk of breaking other parts of the system.

▶ Low coupling promotes keeping complexity localized. By having parts of your system decoupled, multiple engineers can work on them independently. As a result, you will be able to scale your company by hiring more engineers, since no one has to know the entire system in full detail to make "local" changes.

▶ Decoupling on a higher level can mean having multiple applications, with each one focused on a narrow functionality. You can then scale each application separately depending on its needs. Some applications need more central processing units (CPU), whereas others need input/output (I/O) throughput or memory. By decoupling parts of your system, you can provide them with more adequate hardware and better scalability.

Promoting Loose Coupling

The single most important practice promoting loose coupling is to carefully manage your dependencies. This general guideline applies to dependencies between classes, modules, and applications.

Figure 2-2 shows how classes, modules, and applications are laid out within a system. A system is the whole—it contains everything: all of the applications you develop and all the software you use in your environments. Applications are the highest level of abstraction within the system, and they serve highest-level functions. You might use an application for accounting, asset management, or file storage.

Within an application you have one or more modules that implement finer, more granular features. Since applications are often developed and deployed by different teams, modules (like credit card processing, Portable Document File [PDF] rendering, or File Transfer Protocol [FTP] interfacing) should be independent enough for multiple teams to work on them in parallel. If you do not feel confident in another team taking ownership of a certain module, it is likely too tightly coupled with the rest of the application.

Finally, your modules consist of classes, which are the smallest units of abstraction. A class should have a single purpose and no more than a few screens of code. I will talk more about single responsibility later in this chapter.

In object-oriented languages like Java, C#, or PHP you can promote low coupling by correct use of public, protected, and private keywords. You want to declare as many methods as private/protected as possible. The reason for this approach is that the more methods you make private, the more logic remains hidden from the outside world. Hiding details is a great way to reduce coupling and promote simplicity. The less access other classes have to your class, the less aware they are of how the class does its job. Private methods can be refactored

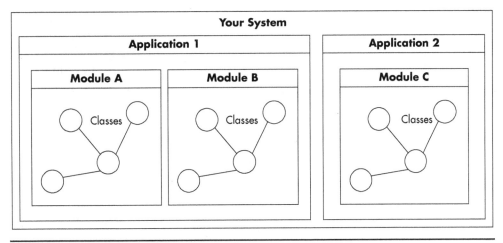

Figure 2-2   *Parts of the system*

and modified easily, as you know that they can only be called by the same class. This way, the complexity is localized and you do not have to search far to find out what could potentially break. Exposing many public methods, on the other hand, increases a chance of external code using them. Once a method is public, you cannot assume that no one is using it anymore and you have to search carefully throughout the application.

> ### HINT
>
> *When writing code, be stingy. Share only the absolute minimum of information and functionality that satisfies the requirements. Sharing too much too early increases coupling and makes changes more difficult in the future. This applies to every level of abstraction, whether class, module, or application.*

To reduce coupling on the higher levels of abstraction, you want to reduce the contact surface area between parts of your system. Loose coupling should let you replace or refactor each element of the system without major work on the rest of the system. Finding the balance between decoupling and overengineering is a fine art, and engineers often disagree on the necessary level of abstraction. You can use diagrams to help you make these decisions (tradeoffs) more easily. When you draw a diagram of your application, the contact surface area is determined by the number of dependencies that cross boundaries of two elements of your diagram. Figure 2-3 shows two examples: a highly coupled application and a loosely coupled one.

As you can see in Figure 2-3, a highly coupled application can make it difficult to modify or refactor its parts without affecting remaining modules. In addition, modules know about each other's structure and access their parts directly. The second example shows modules that have more privacy. To reduce the contact surface area, public functionality of module B was isolated to a small subset and explicitly made public. Another important thing to notice is that the second application does not have circular dependency between modules. Module A can be removed or refactored without affecting module B, as module B does not depend on module A at all.

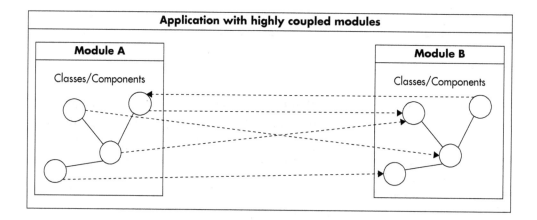

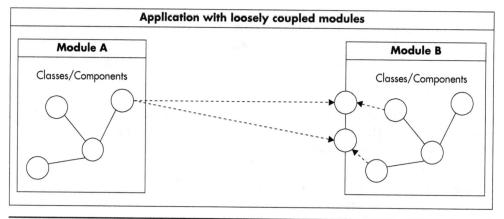

Figure 2-3   *Comparison of high and low coupling*

Avoiding Unnecessary Coupling

On the other side of the spectrum, there are practices that increase coupling. A great example of unnecessary coupling is the practice of exposing all the private properties using public getters and setters. It is a trend that originated many years ago around Java Beans. The idea of providing getters and setters came from the need to build generic code manipulation tools and integrated development environments (IDEs). Unfortunately, this practice was completely misunderstood by the wider community. Something that was meant to allow IDE integration became a bad habit replicated across other platforms and languages.

When you work with object-oriented languages like Java or PHP, creating a new class should not begin by adding public getters and setters for all of your class members. This breaks encapsulation and invites coupling. It is a much better approach to start with private methods and make them protected or public only when really necessary. Different languages give you different ways of achieving the same goals—the point to remember is to hide as much as you can and expose as little as possible.

Another common example of unnecessary coupling is when clients of a module or class need to invoke methods in a particular order for the work to be done correctly. Sometimes there are valid reasons for it, but more often it is caused by bad API design, such as the existence of initialization functions. Clients of your class/module should not have to know how you expect them to use your code. They should be able to use the public interface in any way they want. If you force your clients to know how the API is supposed to be used, you are increasing the coupling, because now not only are the method signatures part of the contact surface area, but also the order in which they should be used.

Finally, allowing circular dependencies between layers of your application, modules, or classes is a bad coupling practice. It is quite easy to notice and relatively easy to avoid once you are aware of the danger of circular dependencies. Usually, drawing a diagram of your system is enough to expose circular dependencies, which is a key reason I recommend using diagrams in your design process. A diagram of a well-designed module should look more like a tree (directed acyclic graph) rather than a social network graph.

Models of Loose Coupling

Understanding loose coupling takes a lot of practice. Fortunately, as with simplicity, you can gain a lot of experience by reading code and analyzing systems built by other people.

A good example of loose coupling is the design of Unix command-line programs and their use of pipes. Whenever a process is created in a Unix system, it automatically gets three open files that it can read from and/or write to (called standard output, standard input, and standard error). The files are not necessarily actual files; they can be virtual file handlers pointing to a terminal, a network socket, a file on a hard drive, or a pipe connecting to another process. The Unix system exposes a very simple API to read from and write to files. All you get is just a few simple functions. The operating system hides from the program the real nature of the file handler. Whether it is a real file or a network socket, the program can read and write to it in the same way. That allows Unix command-line programs like grep, sed, awk, and sort to perform a specific function and be connected using pipes to perform much more complex tasks. I personally believe that Unix file handling is a genius solution and a great example of a "framework" promoting loose coupling between programs.

Another good example of loose coupling is Simple Logging Facade for Java (SLF4J). I strongly encourage you to have a look at its structure and compare it to Log4J and Java Logging API. SLF4J acts as a layer of indirection, isolating complexity of implementation from the users of the logging interface. It also exposes a much simpler and cleaner API that can be understood within minutes.

Loose coupling is one of the most fundamental principles of building flexible software. I highly encourage you to prioritize creating loosely coupled modules. I also encourage reading some of the books discussing coupling from different perspectives.[1,2,5,10,12,14,22,27,31]

Don't Repeat Yourself (DRY)

"I think one of the most valuable rules is avoid duplication. Once and only once, is the Extreme Programming phrase." –Martin Fowler

Repeating yourself implies that you are undertaking the same activity multiple times. There are many areas in your software engineering life where this can be applied, from the code you write in your applications, to repetitive testing before each code release, to your company operations as a whole.

> **HINT**
>
> If you are doing the same thing over and over again, chances are that you are wasting your life away. Instead of doing the same thing multiple times, you could be doing something cool like building new features or thinking of better solutions for your customers' needs. Try to agree with your team and your boss on some basic rules to avoid repetitiveness—for example, that duplicated code fails code review and every new class needs to come with automated tests.

There are a number of reasons developers repeatedly waste time:

▶ **Following an inefficient process**   This can occur in the release cycle, the way new features are designed, sign-offs, or meetings and it is where continuous improvement can bring you great benefits. Use feedback, introduce incremental change, and repeat. It is common for teams to be aware of wasted time but still fail to do anything about it. Whenever you hear, "This is just how we do it" or "We have always done it this way," it is most likely an inefficient process and an opportunity for change.

▶ **Lack of automation**   You waste time deploying manually, compiling, testing, building, configuring development machines, provisioning servers, and documenting APIs. At first it feels like a simple task, but with time it gets more and more complex and time consuming. Before you know it, your entire day is spent deploying code and testing releases, with virtually no time devoted to building new features. The burden of increased manual work is very easily missed, as it builds up in tiny increments. Try to automate your builds and deployments from day one, as they will only get more complicated as you go along.

▶ **Not invented here, also known as reinventing the wheel**   This is often a problem arising from writing code before considering the reuse of existing code. It is a pattern of behavior especially common among younger engineers, who enjoy implementing things that are easily available (in-house or in open-source world). Good examples are implementing hashing functions, sorting, b-trees, Model View Controller (MVC) frameworks, or database abstraction layers. Even though you are not literally repeating yourself, you are still wasting time because you could use tools and libraries that others have built before you. Any time I am about to write a generic library I search online first and usually there are a few good open-source alternatives available.

▶ **Copy/paste programming**   Imagine that you have existing code that does a similar thing to what you are about to develop. To save some time, you copy and paste a large chunk of code and then modify it just a little bit. Now you have two copies of similar code to maintain and apply changes to. After some time, you realize that every change you make has to be applied in multiple parts of the system and that bugs often recur as fixes are not applied to all copies of the affected code. Try to get your team to commit to some rules, such as "we never copy and paste code." That should give everyone authority to point out duplication during code reviews and create some positive peer pressure.

▶ **"I won't need it again so let's just hack it quickly" solutions**   You will sometimes approach a problem that seems isolated in nature. You think, "I will never need this code again; I'll just hack it." In time, the problem occurs again and you have to work with the code that was hacked together as a one-off script. The problem now is that the code is not documented, unit tested, or properly designed. Even worse, other engineers can come along and copy/paste the hacked-together solution as a base for their own one-off scripts.

Copy and Paste Programming

Copy and paste programming is such a common problem that I believe it needs a few more words. Applications face this issue because developers usually do not realize that the more code you write, the more expensive it becomes to support and maintain the application. Copying and pasting results in more code within your application. More code results in higher maintenance costs—an exponentially growing technical backlog. Changes to applications with code duplication require modifications to all copies, tracking differences between copies, and regression testing all of the copy-pasted code. Since complexity rises exponentially with the number of lines of code, copy and pasting is actually an expensive strategy. In fact, copy-paste programming is such a serious problem that people spend their careers researching ways to deal with it. White papers[w2–w5] published by the National Aeronautics and Space Administration (NASA) show that 10 percent to 25 percent of large systems' codebase is a result of copy-paste programming.

Dealing with code duplication can be frustrating, but there is nothing that patient refactoring can't fix. A good first step is to search through the codebase and document every occurrence of the duplicated functionality. Once you have done this, you should have a better understanding of what components are affected and how to refactor them. Think about creating abstract classes or extracting repetitive pieces of code into separate, more generic components. Both composition and inheritance are your friends in battling repetitive code.

Another good way to deal with copy-paste programming is the use of design patterns and shared libraries. A design pattern is an abstract way of solving a common problem. Design patterns are solutions on a software design level. They can be applied to different systems and different subject matters. They are concerned with structuring object-oriented code, dependencies, and interactions, not with particular business problems. A design pattern could suggest how to structure objects in a module, but it would not dictate what algorithms to use or how business features should work. Design patterns are out of the scope of this book, but you can learn more through a number of books[1,7,10,36,18] to get more familiar with most common patterns.

You can also employ web services to combat duplication on higher levels of abstraction. Instead of building the same functionality into each application you develop, it is often a good idea to create a service and reuse it across the company. I will talk more about benefits of web services in Chapter 4.

> **HINT**
>
> *Prevent future repetition by making the most common use cases the easiest. For example, if your library provides 20 functions, only 5 of which will be used 80 percent of the time, keep these 5 operations as easy to use as possible. Things that are easy to use tend to be reused. If using your library is the easiest way to get things done, everyone will use your library. If using your library is difficult, you will end up with duplication or hacks.*

Coding to Contract

Coding to contract, or coding to interface, is another great design principle. Coding to contract is primarily about decoupling clients from providers. By creating explicit contracts, you extract the things that clients are allowed to see and depend upon. Decoupling parts of your system and isolating changes is a key benefit discussed earlier in the chapter.

> A *contract* is a set of rules that the provider of the functionality agrees to fulfill. It defines a set of things that clients of the code may assume and depend upon. It dictates how a piece of software can be used and what functionality is available, but does not require clients to know how this functionality is implemented.

The term "contract" means different things in different contexts. When I talk about methods in object-oriented programming, the contract is the signature of the method. It defines what the expected parameters are and what the expected result is. A contract does not specify how the result is produced, as this is an implementation detail that you should not worry about when you look at the contract. When I talk about classes, a contract is the public interface of the class.

It consists of all the accessible methods and their signatures. Going further up the abstraction layers, the contract of a module includes all the publicly available classes/interfaces and their public method signatures. As you can see, the higher the level of abstraction, the more complex and broader a contract may get. Finally, in the context of an application, contract usually means some form of a web service API specification.

As I already mentioned, the contract helps in decoupling clients from providers. As long as you keep the contract intact, clients and providers can be modified independently. This in turn makes your code changes more isolated and thus simpler. When designing your code, create explicit contracts whenever possible. You should also depend on the contracts instead of implementations whenever you can.

Figure 2-4 shows how a contract separates clients from the providers. Provider 1 and Provider 2 could be two alternative implementations of the same contract. Each provider could be a separate module, and since they both fulfill the same

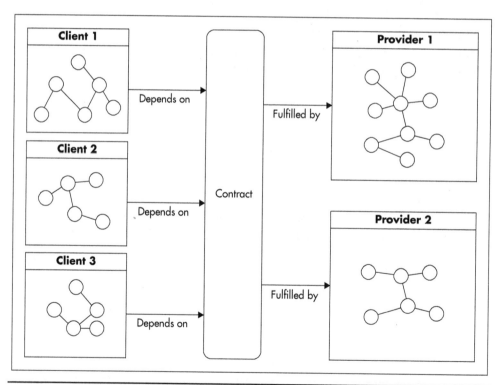

Figure 2-4 *Clients decoupled from providers*

contract, clients can use either without needing direct knowledge of which implementation is being used. Any code that fulfills the contract is equally good in the eyes of the client, making refactoring, unit testing, and changes to the implementation much simpler.

> ### HINT
>
> *To make coding to contract easier, think of the contract as an actual legal document. When people agree to do something in a legally binding document, they become much more sensitive to details, as they may be liable if specific stipulations are not met. A similar situation happens in software design. Every part of the contract that is loose increases future liability. As a provider, exposing more than necessary increases your future costs because any time you want to make a change, you will need to renegotiate the contract with all of your clients (propagating the change throughout the system).*

When designing a class, first consider what functionality your clients really need and then define the minimal interface as the contract. Finally, implement the code fulfilling the contract. Deal with libraries and web services in the same way. Whenever you expose a web service API, be explicit and careful about what you expose to your clients. Make it easy to add features and publish more data when needed, but start with as simple a contract as possible.

To illustrate the power of coding to contract, let's have a look at the Hypertext Transfer Protocol (HTTP) protocols. HTTP is implemented by different applications using different programming languages on different platforms, and yet, it is one of the most popular protocols ever developed. Some of the clients of the HTTP contract are web browsers like Firefox and Chrome. Their implementations vary and their updates are released on different schedules by different organizations. Providers, on the other hand, are mainly web servers like Apache, Internet Information Services (IIS), or Tomcat. Their code is also implemented in different technologies by different organizations and deployed independently all around the world. What is even more exciting is that there are other technologies implementing the HTTP contract that many people have never even heard of. For example, web cache servers like Varnish and Squid implement the HTTP protocol as both clients and providers. Figure 2-5 shows how clients and providers become decoupled by the HTTP contract.

Despite the complexity of the ecosystem and all the applications involved, HTTP provides flexibility of independent implementation changes and transparent provider replacement. HTTP is a beautiful example of decoupling by contract, as all that these applications have in common is that they implement or depend upon the same contract.

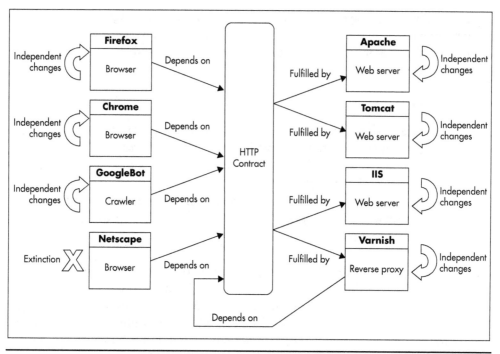

Figure 2-5 *HTTP contract decouples implementations*

Draw Diagrams

"You know what architecture really is? It is an art of drawing lines. With an interesting rule that once you have drawn a line all the dependencies that cross that line point in the same direction." –Robert C. Martin

Drawing diagrams is a must-have skill for every architect and technical leader. Diagrams summarize knowledge, and they truly are worth a thousand words. With diagrams, you document the system, share knowledge, and help yourself fully understand your own designs. Many engineers do not design their code up front and skip diagrams in favor of getting straight into the code. I have watched people do it, and I was doing the very same thing myself. Especially with the adoption of agile practices and lean startup methodologies, there is not much time for up-front designs, but that does not mean there should be none at all.

HINT

If you find it difficult to draw diagrams, you can start by drawing diagrams to document what you have already built. It is easier to draw diagrams of applications and features that you have already built and that you understand well. Once you get more comfortable with different diagram types, try to draw as you code. Flesh out class interfaces by looking at them from the client's point of view, attempt to write high-level unit tests for these interfaces, and draw some simple diagram sketches. By assuming the client's point of view and drawing simple diagrams at the same time, you will validate your own design and discover flaws before the code is even written. Once you're more comfortable with diagrams, attempt to do more up-front design. Don't get discouraged if you find it difficult to design up front. It is not an easy task to switch from code first to design first, so be prepared that it may take months or years before you get completely comfortable with the process.

Imagine you want to design a circuit breaker component. A circuit breaker is a design pattern that can be used to increase robustness of your system and protect it from failures of other components (or third-party systems). It allows your code to check if an external component is available before attempting to perform an action. Listings 2-1 and 2-2 and Figures 2-6 and 2-7 show how the component could be designed. You begin with a draft of the main interface (Listing 2-1) and then validate the interface by drafting some client code (Listing 2-2). This could be a unit test or just a draft of code that doesn't have to compile. At this stage, just make sure that the interface you create is clear and easy to use. Once you flesh out the main use cases, support the design with a sequence diagram showing how clients interact with the circuit breaker, as seen in Figure 2-6. Finally, sketch out the class diagram, as in Figure 2-7, to ensure you did not break design principles and that the structure is sound.

Listing 2-1   *Quick draft of the interface you are designing*

```
interface Zend_CircuitBreaker_Interface
{
    public function isAvailable($serviceName);
    public function reportFailure($serviceName);
    public function reportSuccess($serviceName);
}
```

Listing 2-2 *Draft of the client code*

```
$userProfile = null;
if( $cb->isAvailable("UserProfileService") ){
    try{
        $userProfile = $userProfileService->loadProfileOrWhatever();
        $cb->reportSuccess("UserProfileService");
    }catch( UserProfileServiceConnectionException $e ){
        $cb->reportFailure("UserProfileService");
    }catch( Exception $e ){
        // service is available, but error occurred
    }
}
if( $profile === null ){
    // handle the error in some graceful way
    // display 'System maintenance, you can't login right now.' message
}
```

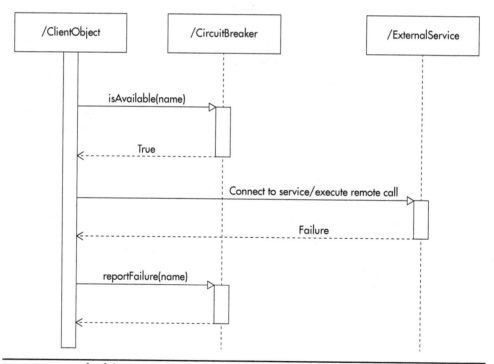

Figure 2-6 *Draft of the sequence diagram drawn while designing the interface*

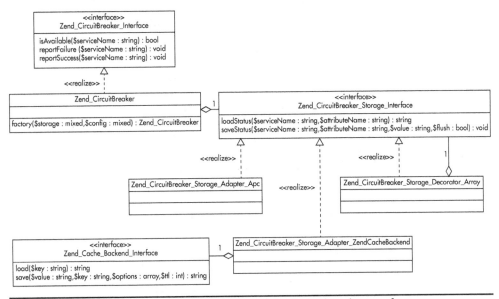

Figure 2-7   *Draft of the class diagram drawn while designing the interface*

I believe that following this simple design process is like taking the up-front design into the startup world. You benefit from the diagrams because you can see the design from different angles. At the same time, you reduce the risk of creating an unrealistic design and getting very far into it before having a chance to validate it.

Three types of diagrams are especially useful in documenting and understanding large-scale systems: use case, class, and module diagrams. The more your company scales up and the bigger your teams get, the more you benefit from having these diagrams. Let's have a look at each diagram type in more detail.

Use Case Diagrams

A use case diagram is a simplified map defining who the users of the system are and what operations they need to perform. Use case diagrams are not concerned with technical solutions, but with business requirements and are a great way to distill key facts about both new features and those business requirements. When you document a new feature, support it with a simple use case diagram. Use case diagrams contain actors represented by humanoid icons, actions that actors perform, and a high-level structure of how different operations relate to each other. Use case diagrams may also show communication with external systems, such as a remote web service API or a task scheduler. Do not include too many details about requirements. Keep it simple so the diagram maintains readability and clarity. By leaving use case diagrams at a high level, you can distill key operations and business processes without drowning in an ocean of details.

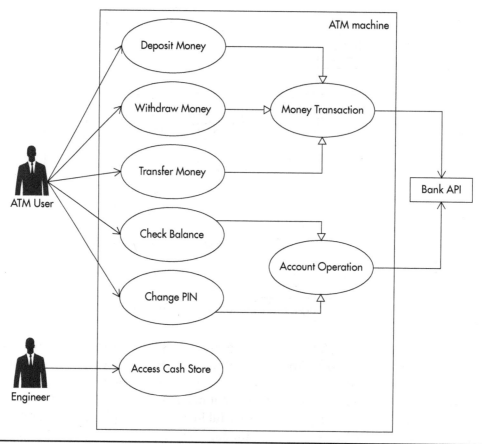

Figure 2-8 *Simple ATM use case diagram*

Figure 2-8 shows an example of a simple use case diagram with a hypothetical automated teller machine (ATM) application. Even though an ATM machine involves many details related to authentication, security, and transaction processing, you focus only on what users of the ATM should be able to accomplish. From this perspective, it is not important to know the ordering of the buttons on the screen or what the ATM does to implement each feature. You only see a high-level overview of the requirements that will help to define the final contract and show the intent of the ATM system.

Class Diagrams

Class diagrams present the structure of individual modules. A class diagram typically includes interfaces, classes, key method names, and relationships between different elements. Class diagrams are good for visualizing coupling, as each class becomes a node of the diagram and each dependency becomes a line. By drawing a class diagram, you see immediately which classes are highly coupled with the rest of the module and which are more independent. Simply watch how many lines are connected to each node to judge how many dependencies the node includes. Class diagrams are the best tools to visualize a module's structure with its classes, interfaces, and their interdependencies.

Figure 2-9 shows a simple example of a class diagram. The key elements here are interfaces and classes, with their most important methods and dependencies represented by different types of lines. In this case, you have two implementations of the EmailService. The first one delivers e-mails instantly, using a Simple Mail

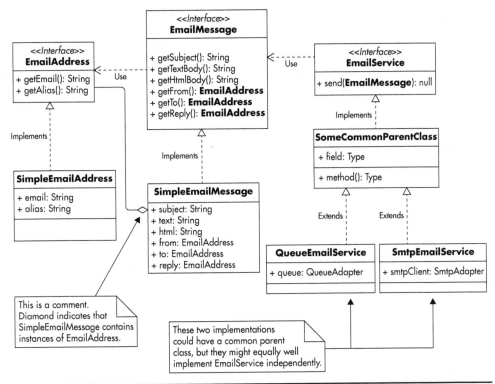

Figure 2-9   *Simple e-mail module class diagram*

Transport Protocol (SMTP) protocol adapter, and the second one adds e-mails to an e-mail queue for delayed delivery.

The EmailService interface is also a good example of the benefits of coding to contract. Whoever depends on the EmailService interface could send e-mails using either SMTP or queue-based implementations without having to know how the e-mails are actually delivered.

Interfaces should only depend on other interfaces and never on concrete classes. Classes, on the other hand, should depend on interfaces as much as possible.

Module Diagrams

The module diagram is similar to a class diagram because it displays structure and dependencies. The only difference between module and class diagrams is that module diagrams focus on the higher level of abstraction. Module diagrams represent the zoom-out view of the code, with less depth but more surface area. Instead of looking at classes and interfaces, module diagrams focus on relationships between larger parts of the system. You use module diagrams to show high-level dependencies and interactions between a module and its direct neighbors of the dependency graph. A module can be a package or any logical part of the application responsible for a certain functionality.

Figure 2-10 shows an example of a module diagram focusing on a hypothetical PaymentService with its relations to other parts of the application that may be relevant to the payment functionality. Module diagrams usually focus on parts of the application that are relevant to the functionality being documented while ignoring other irrelevant pieces. As your system grows larger, it is better to create a few module diagrams, each focusing around certain functionality, rather than including everything on a single diagram. Ideally, each diagram should be simple enough so you could remember and re-create it in your mind.

Be creative and don't worry whether you "draw it correctly" or not. Practice in making your diagrams understandable is more important than perfection and following notation standards. Learn more about Unified Modeling Language (UML) and design patterns by consulting sources.[1,7,10] I also recommend ArgoUML as a desktop UML diagram drawing tool. It is an open-source Java application that can be used across your company without uploading your software designs into the cloud. If you prefer cloud-based solutions and online collaboration, try draw.io, a free and easy-to-use online service integrated with Google Drive. Draw.io is my preferred tool, and almost all of the diagrams in this book were created using it.

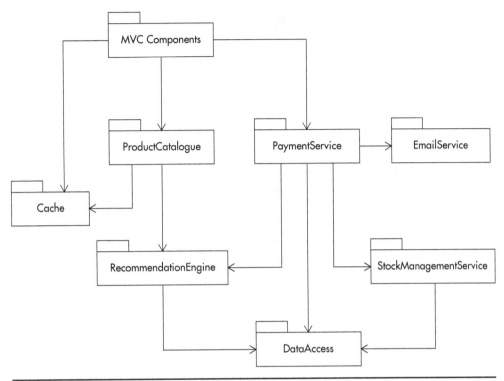

Figure 2-10   *Module diagram focused on PaymentService*

Single Responsibility

Single responsibility is a powerful way to reduce the complexity of your code. At its core, the single-responsibility principle states that your classes should have one single responsibility and no more. Single responsibility reduces coupling; increases simplicity; and makes it easier to refactor, reuse, and unit test your code—all core principles discussed so far. Following this principle will result in producing small and simple classes that can be easily refactored and reused.

In the short term, it may be easier to simply keep adding methods to an existing class, regardless if the new functionality is within the responsibility of the class or not. However, after months of work, you will notice that your classes become large and closely coupled with each other. You will see them interacting with each other in unexpected ways and doing many unrelated things. At the same time, the size of each class will make it hard to fully understand its behavior and its role. This is when complexity rises sharply with every new line of code.

Promoting Single Responsibility

There are no hard-and-fast metrics that define whether your class is following the single-responsibility principle, but there are some guidelines that can help:

▶ Keep class length below two to four screens of code.

▶ Ensure that a class depends on no more than five other interfaces/classes.

▶ Ensure that a class has a specific goal/purpose.

▶ Summarize the responsibility of the class in a single sentence and put it in a comment on top of the class name. If you find it hard to summarize the class responsibility, it usually means that your class does more than one thing.

If your class breaks any of these guidelines, it is a good indicator that you may need to revisit and potentially refactor it.

On the higher level of abstraction, you should partition your functionality across modules to avoid overlaps. You would do it in a similar way as with classes—try to summarize responsibility of a module or an application in one or two sentences, just on a higher level. For example, you could say, "File Store is an application allowing clients to upload files and manage their metadata, and it also allows clients to find files based on complex searches." This makes the application's purpose clear. Limit its scope and isolate it from the rest of the system using an explicit interface (for example, a web service definition).

Examples of Single Responsibility

To keep things simple, let's take validation of an e-mail address as an example. If you place your validation logic directly in the code that creates user accounts, you will not be able to reuse it in a different context. You will have to either copy-paste the validation code or create an awkward dependency between classes that should not know about each other, both of which break core principles of good software design. Having validation logic separated into a distinct class would let you reuse it in multiple places and have only a single implementation. If you need to modify the validation logic at a later date, you will only need to refactor a single class. For example, you may need to add support for UTF-8 encoded Unicode characters in domain names. Having a single class responsible for e-mail validation should make the change isolated and much simpler than if validation logic was spread across different classes. As a side effect of the single-responsibility principle, you will likely end up with much more testable code. Since classes have less logic and fewer dependencies, it will be easier to test them in isolation. A good way to explore single responsibility further is to research some of the design patterns such as strategy, iterator, proxy, and adapter.[5,7] It can also help to read more about domain-driven design[2] and good software design.[1,37]

Open-Closed Principle

"Good architecture maximizes the number of decisions not made." –Robert C. Martin

The open-closed principle is about creating code that does not have to be modified when requirements change or when new use cases arise. Open-closed stands for "open for extension and closed for modification." Any time we create code with the intent to extend it in the future without the need to modify it, we say we apply the open-closed principle. As Robert C. Martin advocates, the open-closed principle allows us to leave more options available and delay decisions about the details; it also reduces the need to change existing code. The prime objective of this principle is to increase flexibility of your software and make future changes cheaper.

This is best explained with an example. Consider a sorting algorithm where you need to sort an array of Employee objects based on employee names. In the most basic implementation, you could include the sorting algorithm itself and all necessary code in a single class, EmployeeArraySorter, as shown in Figure 2-11. You would expose just a single method, allowing the sort of an array of Employee objects, and announce that the feature is complete. Even though it solves the problem, it is not very flexible; it is actually a very fixed implementation. Since all of the code lives together in a single class, you have very little ability to extend it or add new features without changing the existing code. If you had a new requirement to sort an array of City objects based on their population, you may not be able to reuse the existing sorting class. You would be faced with a dilemma—do you extend the EmployeeArraySorter to do something completely unrelated to its original design, or do you copy-paste the class and add the necessary modifications? Luckily you have a third option, which is to refactor the solution and make it open-closed compliant.

The open-closed solution requires you to break down the sorting problem into a set of smaller problems. Each of these tasks can then vary independently without affecting the reusability of remaining components. You can have a single interface that compares two objects called Comparator and another interface that performs a sorting algorithm called Sorter. Sorter would then use instances of

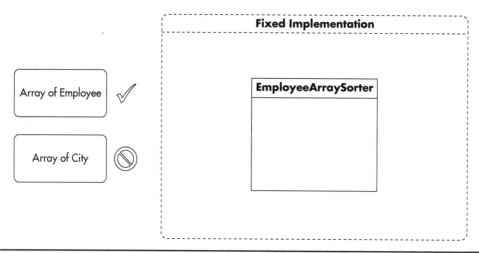

Figure 2-11   *Fixed implementation*

Comparator and an array to do the actual sorting. Figure 2-12 shows how it might look. Note that this implementation is similar to the Java Comparator API.

Using this approach makes reusing existing code easier. For example, to change sorting fields or types of sorted objects, you just add a new Comparator implementation that would have almost no code in it. You do not need to

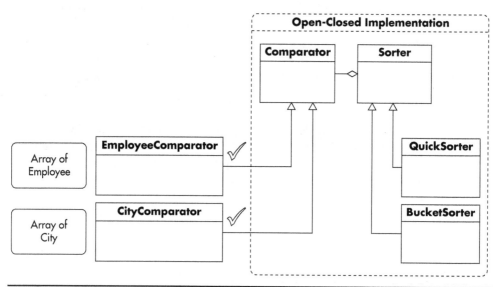

Figure 2-12   *Open-closed implementation*

change any code that lives in "the dotted box" in Figure 2-12. If you wanted to change the sorting algorithm itself, you would not have to modify Comparators or other clients of the Sorter implementation. You would only need to create a new implementation of the Sorter interface. By allowing parts of the solution to change independently, you reduce the scope of changes necessary. You also allow extensions that do not require modification of the existing code.

Other good examples of the open-closed principle are MVC frameworks. These frameworks have dominated web development partially due to their simple and extensible nature. If you think about it, how often have you needed to modify the MVC component within a framework? If the framework is well architected, the answer should be "never." However, you have the ability to extend the MVC components by adding new routes, intercepting requests, returning different responses, and overriding default behaviors. You do not have to modify the existing framework code to be able to extend its original functionality, and that is the open-closed principle in action.

As with other design principles, begin by familiarizing and exposing yourself to various frameworks that promote the open-closed principle. Experiencing different approaches is an effective way to get started and will help you see differences and recurring patterns. For example, open-closed is beautifully done in the Spring MVC framework for the Java language. Users have great flexibility to modify the default behavior without ever modifying the framework, yet the client code does not have to be coupled to the framework. By using annotations and conventions, most of your classes do not even have to know about the existence of the Spring framework at all!

Dependency Injection

We have already discussed dependencies in this chapter, as it is one of the most important topics when it comes to coupling and complexity. Dependency injection is a simple technique that reduces coupling and promotes the open-closed principle. Dependency injection provides references to objects that the class depends on, instead of allowing the class to gather the dependencies itself. At its core, dependency injection is about knowing as little as possible. It allows classes to "not know" how their dependencies are assembled, where they come from, or what actual implementations are fulfilling their contracts. It seems like a subtle change from pull to push, but it has a great impact on the flexibility of software design.

Let's consider an analogy comparing a class implementing dependency injection to a CD player.[L34] All that a CD player knows is the interface of a compact disc.

It knows how to read the tracks, how music is encoded, and what optical parameters of the laser are necessary to read the contents of the CD. The compact disc inserted into the CD player is a dependency, and without it a CD player is unable to work correctly. By pushing the responsibility of finding dependencies onto its users, a CD player can remain "dumb." At the same time, a CD player is more reusable, as it does not have to know every title ever burned on CD or every combination of songs in all the compilation albums ever made. Instead of knowing all possible CDs or assembling them magically itself, the CD player depends on you (the client) to provide a readable instance of a CD. As soon as you satisfy the dependency with an instance of a compact disc, the CD player can operate.

As an additional benefit, the CD player can be used with different nonstandard implementations of a compact disc. You can insert a cleaning disc or a testing disc with specially crafted malformed tracks, allowing you to test different failure scenarios.

Figure 2-13 shows how an overburdened CD player might look. It could have a hardcoded list of known CDs, and any time you wanted to play a new disc you would need to make changes to its code.

Now let's look at the implementation of the same CD player using dependency injection. Figure 2-14 shows how a typical CD player operates. It does not know

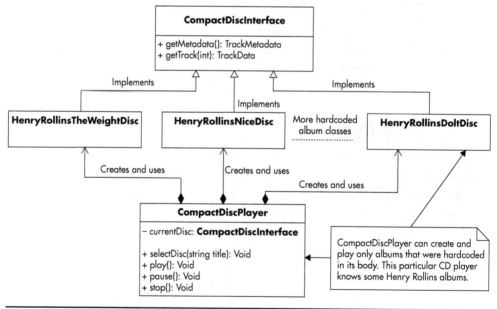

Figure 2-13 *CD player without dependency injection*

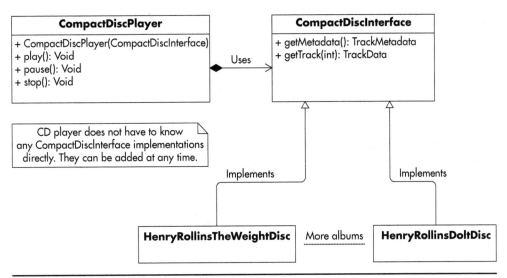

Figure 2-14   *CD player using dependency injection*

anything about discs themselves; it depends on its clients to provide it with a functional instance of a compact disc. This way, you keep the implementation opened for changes (allow new discs) but closed for modification (CD player never has to change).

In practice, dependency injection can be summarized as not using the "new" keyword in your classes and demanding instances of your dependencies to be provided to your class by its clients. Listing 2-3 shows an example of a constructor-based dependency injection in Java. Using this approach, as soon as the instance is created, it is fully functional; there are no additional expectations on what has to happen for the CD player instance to work. The responsibility of gathering all the dependencies can be pushed out of the class itself, making it simpler, more reusable, and testable.

Listing 2-3   *Example of constructor-based dependency injection*

```
class CompactDiscPlayer {
    private CompactDisc cd;
    public function CompactDiscPlayer(CompactDisc cd){
        this.cd = cd;
    }
    // other methods and business logic
}
```

When used well, dependency injection reduces local complexity of the class and makes it dumber, which is a good thing. Without knowing who the provider of the contract is or how to get an instance of it, our class can focus on its single responsibility. The code of the class becomes simpler, and it requires less understanding of the rest of the system to modify and unit test the class. It may seem like you will end up with the same code, just in a different place, but this is exactly the purpose. By removing the assembly code from your classes, you make them more independent, reusable, and testable. Dependency injection is a practice that has been promoted for many years within the object-oriented programming (OOP) community. Given that dependency injection does not require use of any framework, I recommend getting familiar with the Spring framework or Grails framework as great examples of dependency injection in practice.[w76,1,14,22,7]

Inversion of Control (IOC)

Dependency injection is an important principle and a subclass of a broader principle called inversion of control. Dependency injection is limited to object creation and assembly of its dependencies. Inversion of control, on the other hand, is a more generic idea and can be applied to different problems on different levels of abstraction.

> *Inversion of control* (IOC) is a method of removing responsibilities from a class to make it simpler and less coupled to the rest of the system. At its core, inversion of control is not having to know who will create and use your objects, how, or when. It is about being as dumb and oblivious as possible, as having to know less is a good thing for software design.

IOC is heavily used by several frameworks, including Spring, Symfony, Rails, and even Java EE containers. Instead of you being in control of creating instances of your objects and invoking methods, you become the creator of plugins or extensions to the framework. The IOC framework will look at the web request and figure out which classes should be instantiated and which components should be delegated to.

IOC is also referred to as "the Hollywood principle" because the subject of IOC is being told, "Don't call us, we will call you." In practice, this means your classes do not have to know when their instances are created, who is using them, or how their dependencies are put together. Your classes are plugins, and some external force will decide how and when they should be used.

Imagine you wanted to build an entire web application in pure Java without any web framework. No web server, no frameworks, no API. Just Java. To accomplish such a complex task, you would need to write a lot of code yourself. Even if you decided to use some third-party libraries, you need to control the entire application flow. By using a web framework, you reduce the complexity of your own code. Not only do you reduce the amount of code that has to be written, but you also reduce the amount of things that developers have to know. All you have to learn is how to hook into the framework, which will create instances of your classes. The framework will call your methods when requests arrive and handle default behavior and control the execution flow from extension point to extension point.

Figure 2-15 illustrates a web application written in pure Java (no frameworks). In this case, a large chunk of the application would focus on talking to the external world. The application would have to be responsible for things like opening network sockets, logging to files, connecting to external systems, managing threads, and parsing messages. Your application has to control almost everything, which implies that you will have to be aware of most of these things.

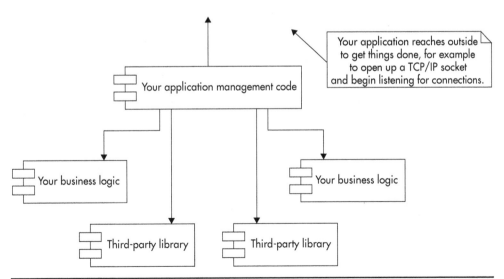

Figure 2-15   *Web application written in pure Java, no IOC framework*

If you used an IOC framework, your application might look more like Figure 2-16. Not only can the framework take away a lot of responsibilities, but now our application does not even have to know about most of these things that happen. Even though all the same things need to happen, they can happen outside of our application code. This does not change the overall complexity of the system, but it does reduce the local complexity of your application.

Inversion of control is a universal concept. You can create an inversion of control framework for any type of application, and it does not have to be related to MVC or web requests. Components of a good IOC framework include the following:

▶ You can create plugins for your framework.

▶ Each plugin is independent and can be added or removed at any point in time.

▶ Your framework can auto-detect these plugins, or there is a way of configuring which plugin should be used and how.

▶ Your framework defines the interface for each plugin type and it is not coupled to plugins themselves.

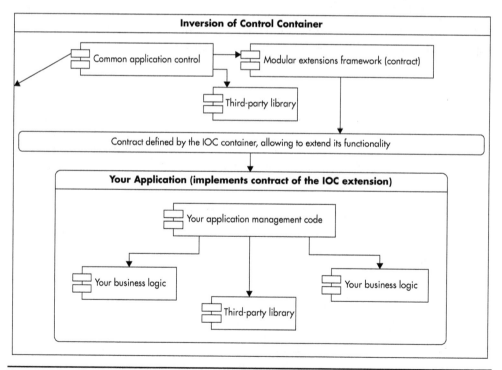

Figure 2-16   *The same web application within an IOC container*

HINT

Writing code for an IOC framework is like keeping fish in a fish tank. You can have many fish in a tank and they can have some autonomy, but they live in a larger world that is out of their control. You decide what the environment in the tank is and when fish get fed. You are the IOC framework, and your fish are your plugins, living in a protective bubble of not knowing.

Designing for Scale

Designing for scale is a difficult art, and each technique described in this section comes with some costs. As an engineer, you need to make careful tradeoffs between endless scalability and the practicality of each solution. To make sure you do not overengineer by preparing for scale that you will never need, you should first carefully estimate the most realistic scalability needs of your system and design accordingly.

HINT

To put it into perspective, many startups fail and thus never need to design for scale at all. (Depending on the source of statistics, you could say that up to 90 percent of all startups fail.) Most startups that succeed moderately have limited scalability needs (the following 9 percent of all startups). Only a very limited number of companies ever grow to the size that requires horizontal scalability (the remaining 1 percent).

In a similar way to the design principles discussed so far, tackling complexity and coupling, there are a few principles that help design scalable systems. As you learn more about scalability, you may realize that many of the scalability solutions can be boiled down to three basic design techniques:

▶ **Adding more clones**   Adding indistinguishable components

▶ **Functional partitioning**   Dividing the system into smaller subsystems based on functionality

▶ **Data partitioning**   Keeping a subset of the data on each machine

Each of these techniques offers different benefits and introduces different costs. It is worth becoming more familiar with each of them to be able to design scalable systems efficiently. Let's discuss each of these techniques in more detail using an example. Imagine you are building a web application that would let people manage their eBay auction bids. Users would create accounts and allow your application to bid on their behalf. Nice and simple.

Adding More Clones

If you are building a system from scratch, the easiest and most common scaling strategy is to design it in a way that would allow you to scale it out by simply adding more clones. A *clone* here is an exact copy of a component or a server. Any time you look at two clones, they have to be interchangeable and each of them needs to be equally qualified to serve an incoming request. In other words, you should be able to send each request to a random clone and get a correct result.

Using our example of an eBay bidding application, as your application grows in popularity, you will need to scale all of the components of your application. As mentioned in Chapter 1, you can either upgrade your existing servers (scale vertically) or add more servers to your setup to distribute the load (scale horizontally). Scaling by adding clones works great in the case of web servers, so let's consider it first. Figure 2-17 shows a single web server setup with the eBay bidding application deployed on it.

To scale by adding clones, your goal is to have a set of perfectly interchangeable web servers and distribute the load equally among them all. In this setup, the load (web requests) is usually distributed among clones using a load balancer. Ideally, whenever the load balancer receives a request, it should be able to send it to any of the servers without needing to know where the previous request went. Figure 2-18 shows the same application scaled by adding clones.

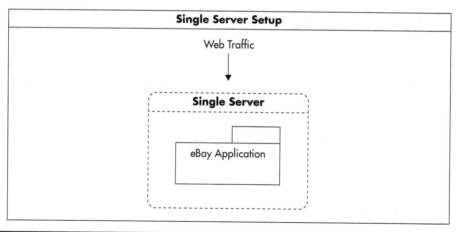

Figure 2-17 *Single-server setup*

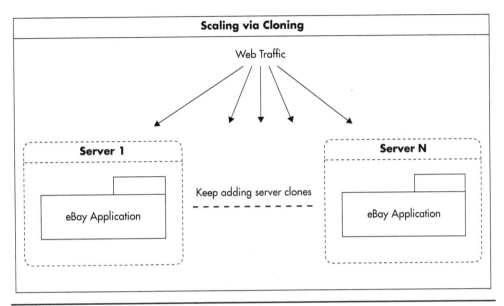

Figure 2-18   *Scaling out by adding clones*

To scale by adding clones, you need to pay close attention to where you keep the application state and how you propagate state changes among your clones. Scaling by adding clones works best for stateless services, as there is no state to synchronize. If your web services are stateless, then a brand-new server is exactly the same as a server that is already serving requests. In such a case, you can increase capacity by simply adding more servers to the load balancer pool. (*Stateless service* is a term used to indicate that a service does not depend on the local state, so processing requests does not affect the way the service behaves. No particular instance needs to be used to get the correct result. I will discuss stateless services in more detail in Chapter 3 and Chapter 4.) Note that scaling by adding clones of the same thing is not reserved for stateless services. In fact, databases have been scaling out using this technique for years through the use of replication. I will explain replication and scaling by adding clones in the context of databases in Chapter 5.

Scaling via adding clones is like a hospital's emergency room unit. If you had the budget to hire numerous equally trained doctors and purchase more operating room space and equipment, you could easily increase the overall number of emergency patients processed. Equally skilled doctors are equally well suited for treating any patient who is unlucky enough to have an emergency.

Scaling by adding clones is the easiest and cheapest technique to implement in your web layer. If you follow front-end and web services layer best practices presented later in Chapters 3 and 4, you will be able to scale most of your stack using this technique. The main challenge with scaling by adding clones is that it is difficult to scale stateful servers this way, as you need to find ways to synchronize their state to make them interchangeable.

Functional Partitioning

The second primary scalability strategy is functional partitioning. It is fairly universal and applicable across different levels of abstraction. The main thought behind the functional partitioning technique is to look for parts of the system focused on a specific functionality and create independent subsystems out of them.

In the context of infrastructure, functional partitioning is the isolation of different server roles. You divide your data centers into different server types. You have your object cache servers, message queue servers, queue workers, web servers, data store engines, and load balancers. Each of these components could be built into the main application, but over the years, engineers realized that a better solution is to isolate different functions into independent subsystems. Think of functional partitioning as a different way to scale your hospital. Instead of hiring more and more generic doctors, you can start hiring specialists in each area and providing specialized equipment for different types of operating rooms. Emergencies of different types may require different tools, different techniques, and different experience on behalf of the doctor.

In a more advanced form, functional partitioning is dividing a system into self-sufficient applications. It is applied most often in the web services layer, and it is one of the key practices of service-oriented architecture (SOA). Going back to the example of the eBay bidding application, if you had a web services layer, you could create a set of highly decoupled web services handling different parts of functionality. These services could then have their logical resources like data stores, queues, and caches. Figure 2-19 shows such a scenario where functionality was split into a profile service and a scheduling service. Depending on specific needs, these services could share underlying infrastructure like data store servers or they could be hosted separately. By giving your services more autonomy, you promote coding to contract and allow each service to make independent decisions as to what components are required and what the best way to scale them out is.

Functional partitioning is most often applied on a low level, where you break your application down into modules and deploy different types of software to different servers (for example, databases on different servers than web services).

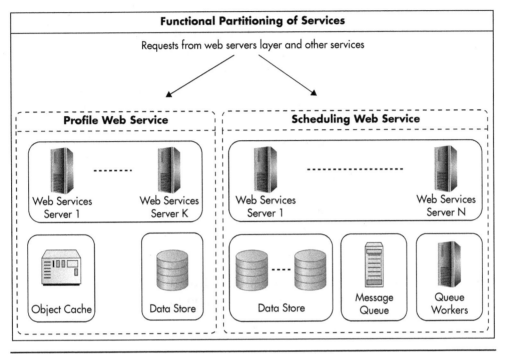

Figure 2-19 *Functional partitioning*

In larger companies, it is also common to use functional partitioning on a higher level of abstraction by creating independent services. In such cases, you can split your monolithic application into a set of smaller functional services. Additional benefits of such division is the ability to have multiple teams working in parallel on independent codebases and gaining more flexibility in scaling each service, as different services have different scalability needs.

There are numerous benefits of functional partitioning, but there are also a few drawbacks. Functional partitions are independent and usually require more management and effort to start with. There is also a limited number of functional partitions that you can come up with, limiting your ability to scale using this technique. After all, you can't keep rewriting your application and keep dividing it into smaller and smaller web services to scale endlessly.

Data Partitioning

The third main scaling strategy is to partition the data to keep subsets of it on each machine instead of cloning the entire data set onto each machine. This is also a manifestation of the share-nothing principle, as each server has its own subset of data, which it can control independently. Share nothing is an architectural principle where each node is fully autonomous. As a result, each node can make its own decisions about its state without the need to propagate state changes to its peers. Not sharing state means there is no data synchronization, no need for locking, and that failures can be isolated because nodes do not depend on one another.

To illustrate further, let's again look at the eBay bidding application. To recap, I scaled it in one way by adding more web servers (adding clones) and then I scaled it in a different way by splitting the web services layer into two independent services. This gave me two different types of scalability. But there is one more way I can scale it out: by distributing the load based on the data itself. A good example of such partitioning is splitting the data stored in the object cache of the profile web service from Figure 2-19.

To scale the object cache, I could add more clones, but then I would need to synchronize all of the state changes between all of my servers. Alternatively, I could look for further functional partitioning opportunities. I could try to cache web service responses on one cache server and database query results on another server. Neither of these approaches seems very attractive in this case, though, as they would not let me scale very far. A better way out would be to create a mapping between the cache key of the cached object and the cache server responsible for that key. Figure 2-20 shows how such mapping could be implemented.

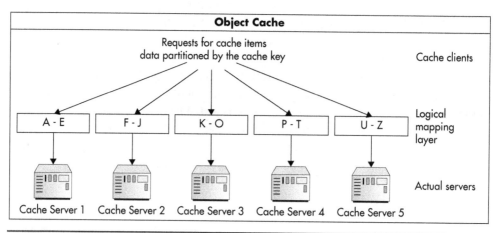

Figure 2-20 *Data partitioning*

Figure 2-20 shows a simplistic approach where I distribute cached objects among cache servers based on the first letter of the cache key. In practice, applications use more sophisticated ways of partitioning the data, but the concept remains the same. Each server gets a subset of the data for which it is solely responsible. By having less data on each server, I can process it faster and store more of it in memory. Finally, if I had to increase the capacity even further, I could add more servers and modify the mapping to redistribute the data.

Think back to the hospital analogy. If your hospital was providing scheduled visits to see your specialists, you would probably have to scale your specialists by using data partitioning. After all, you can't have your patients see a different doctor every time they come for a visit. You could get around the problem by logging the doctor's name on each patient's card. By using a registry of which patient is treated by which doctor, your front desk staff could easily schedule appointments with the correct doctors.

Data partitioning, applied correctly with scaling by adding clones, effectively allows for endless scalability. If you partition your data correctly, you can always add more users, handle more parallel connections, collect more data, and deploy your system onto more servers. Unfortunately, data partitioning is also the most complex and expensive technique. The biggest challenge that data partitioning introduces is the fact that you need to be able to locate the partition on which the data lives before sending queries to the servers and that queries spanning multiple partitions may become very inefficient and difficult to implement.

I will discuss data partitioning in more detail in Chapter 5, as it is one of the key scaling techniques in modern data stores. You can also read more about adding clones, functional partitioning and data partitioning.[27,41,w34,w35]

Design for Self-Healing

"Any sufficiently large system is in a constant state of partial failure." –Justin Sheehy

The final design principle in this chapter is designing software for high availability and self-healing. A system is considered to be available as long as it performs its functions as expected from the client's perspective. It does not matter if the system is experiencing internal partial failure as long as it does not affect the behavior that clients depend on. In other words, you want to make your system appear as if all of its components were functioning perfectly even when things break and during maintenance times.

> A *highly available system* is a system that is expected to be available to its clients most of the time. There is no absolute measurement of high availability, as different systems have different business requirements. Instead of defining an absolute measure of high availability, systems are measured in the "number of nines." We say a system with 2 nines is available 99 percent of the time, translating to roughly 3.5 days of outage per year (365 days * 0.01 = 3.65 days). In comparison, a system with availability of 5 nines would be available 99.999 percent of the time, which makes it unavailable only five minutes per year.

As you can imagine, different business scenarios will have different outage tolerances. The main point to remember is that the larger your system gets, the higher the chance of failure. If you need to contact five web services and each of them connects to three data stores, you are depending on 15 components. Whenever any of these components fails, you may become unavailable, unless you can handle failures gracefully or fail over transparently.

As you scale out, failures become a much more frequent occurrence. Running 1,000 servers can easily give you a few failing servers every single day.[w58] To make matters even worse, there are other reasons for failures, such as power outages, network failures, and human errors. Operating at scale magnifies these issues so that failure must be considered a norm, not a special condition. When designing for high availability, you need to hope for the best but prepare for the worst, always thinking about what else can fail and in what order.

One of the most exciting examples of such a high-availability mindset is a system developed at Netflix called Chaos Monkey. Netflix reliability engineers decided that the best way to prove that the system can handle failures is to actually cause them on an ongoing basis and observe how the system responds. Chaos Monkey is a service that runs during office hours and kills random components of the Netflix infrastructure. It may seem like a completely absurd idea that a company would risk outages this way, but what it really does is prove that their system is able to handle any type of failure.

Another similar example of the high-availability mindset is a concept called Crash-Only.[w57] Advocates of the Crash-Only approach say that the system should always be ready to crash, and whenever it reboots, it should be able to continue to work without human interaction. This means that the system needs to be able to detect its failure, fix the broken data if necessary, and start work as normal, whether it is serving requests, processing queue messages, or doing any other type of work. Following this practice, CouchDB, a popular open-source data store, does not even provide any shutdown functionality. If you want to stop a CouchDB instance, you just have to terminate it.

What better way to prove that your system can handle failures than make it fail every day? I have witnessed many outages caused by the fact that there was some component that kept local server state or could not handle network timeouts properly. Continuously testing different failure scenarios is a great way to improve the resilience of your system and promote high availability. In practice, ensuring high availability is mainly about removing single points of failure and graceful failover.

> *Single point of failure* is any piece of infrastructure that is necessary for the system to work properly. An example of a single point of failure can be a Domain Name System (DNS) server, if you have only one. It can also be a database master server or a file storage server.

A simple way to identify single points of failure is to draw your data center diagram with every single device (routers, servers, switches, etc.) and ask yourself what would happen if you shut them down one at a time. Once you identify your single points of failure, you need to decide with your business team whether it is a good investment to put redundancy in place. In some cases, it will be easy and cheap; in other cases, it may be very difficult or expensive. Especially if the system was not designed with high availability in mind, you may need to carefully consider your tradeoffs.

Redundancy is having more than one copy of each piece of data or each component of the infrastructure. Should one of the copies fail, your system can use the remaining clones to serve clients' requests. Systems that are not redundant need special attention, and it is a best practice to prepare a disaster recovery plan (sometimes called a business continuity plan) with recovery procedures for all critical pieces of infrastructure.

Finally, if you had a system that was highly available and fully fault tolerant, you may want to implement self-healing. Self-healing is a property going beyond graceful failure handling; it is the ability to detect and fix problems automatically without human intervention. Self-healing systems are a holy grail of web operations, but they are much more difficult and expensive to build than it sounds.

To give you an example of self-healing, consider failure handling in Cassandra, which is an open-source data store. In Cassandra, a data node failure is handled transparently by the system. Once the cluster recognizes node failure, it stops any new requests from being routed to the failed node. The only time when clients may be failing is during the failure recognition phase. Once the node is blacklisted as failed, clients can still read and write data as usual, as remaining nodes in the cluster provide redundancy for all of the data stored on the failed node. Whenever the failed node comes back online, it is brought up to speed with the data it missed and the system continues as if nothing happened.

In the same way, replacing a dead node with a brand-new, blank node does not require system administrators to reconstruct the data from backup, as is often necessary in relational database engines. Adding a new empty data node causes the Cassandra cluster to synchronize the data so that over time the newly added machine is fully up to date. When a system can detect its own partial failure, prevent unavailability, and fully fix itself as soon as possible, you have a self-healing system. Minimizing the mean time to recovery and automating the repair process is what self-healing is all about.

> *Mean time to recovery* is one of the key components of the availability equation. The faster you can detect, react to, and repair, the higher your availability becomes. Availability is actually measured as mean time to failure / (mean time to failure + mean time to recovery). By reducing the time to recovery, you can increase your availability, even if the failure rate is out of your control. This may be the case when using cloud hosting services like Amazon Web Services (AWS), as cloud providers use cheaper hardware, trading low failure rates for low price. In such an environment, you need to focus on mean time to recovery, as mean time to failure is something you cannot control.

I highly recommend learning more about high availability, monitoring, and self-healing systems as your scalability experience advances. A number of great sources exist for further study.[w35,w4,w7,w1,w15,w18,w27,w36,w39,w42] In Chapter 5, we'll return to high availability to describe different storage engines and their properties.

Summary

Whether you are a software engineer, architect, team lead, or an engineering manager, it is important to understand design principles. Software engineering is all about making informed decisions, creating value for the business, and preparing for the future. Remember: design principles are your northern star, your compass. They give you direction and they increase your chances of being successful, but ultimately, you have to decide which approach is best for your system.

As a software engineer or architect, your job is to provide solutions that are the best fit for your business under constraints of limited money, time, and knowledge about the future. If you take your role seriously, you need to keep an open mind and try to consider different points of view. The "cleanest" solution is not always the best if it takes more time to develop or if it introduces unnecessary management costs. For example, the line between decoupling and overengineering is very fine. It is your job to watch out for these temptations and not become biased toward the coolest solution imaginable. Your business needs to make informed tradeoffs between scalability, flexibility, high availability, costs, and time to market. I will discuss tradeoffs that you need to learn to make more often in the last chapter of this book.

Remain pragmatic. Don't be afraid to break the rules, if you really believe it is the best thing for your business or for your software. Every system is different and every company has different needs, and you may find yourself working in a very different context than other engineers. There is no single good way to build scalable software, but first learn your craft, learn your tools, and look for reasons to drive your decisions. The principles laid out in this chapter are a good start on your path to quality software design.

CHAPTER 3

Building the Front-End Layer

T he front-end layer spans multiple components. It includes the client (usually a web browser), network components between the client and your data center, and parts of your data center that respond directly to clients' connections. The front end is your first line of defense, and its components are the ones receiving the most traffic. Every user interaction, every connection, and every response has to go through the front-end layer in one form or another. This in turn causes the front-end layer to have the highest throughput and concurrency rate demands, making its scalability critical. Luckily, a well-designed front end scales relatively easily, and it is also where caching can give you the highest returns.

Front-end applications built with scale in mind are mostly stateless; they depend heavily on caching; and, most importantly, they allow horizontal scalability by simply adding more hardware.

Before we dive in, it's important to understand the different approaches to building web applications. Most of today's websites are built as traditional multipage web applications, single-page applications (SPAs), or hybrids of these two approaches.

▶ **Traditional multipage web applications**   These are websites where clicking a link or a button initiates a new web request and results in the browser reloading an entire page with the response received from the server. This was the model used when the World Wide Web was created and when there was no JavaScript, no AJAX, and no HTML5. Despite the fact that this model is two decades old, you could still build scalable websites using it (mainly for its simplicity).

▶ **Single-page applications (SPAs)**   These execute the most business logic in the browser, more so than either hybrid or traditional applications. These applications are built mainly in JavaScript, with web servers often reduced to providing a data application programming interface (API) and a security layer. In this model, any time you perform an action in the user interface (like clicking a link or typing some text), JavaScript code may initiate asynchronous calls to the server to load/save data. Based on the response received, JavaScript code replaces parts of the user interface. The SPA model has become more popular in recent years with frameworks like AngularJS and mobile app frameworks like Sencha Touch and Ionic, but it is still much less popular than the hybrid model. The main benefit of SPAs is a richer user interface, but users may also benefit from a smaller network footprint and lower latencies between user interactions.

▶ **Hybrid applications**   This is the way most of the modern web applications are built. As the name implies, these applications are a hybrid of traditional multipage web applications and SPAs. Some interactions cause a full page load, and others initiate only partial view updates using AJAX. Adopting AJAX and keeping the overarching multipage structure give developers a lot of flexibility. This allows building a rich user interface, but at the same time provides search engine optimization (SEO) friendliness, deep linking, and relative simplicity.

Most of the recommendations and components presented in this chapter are applicable to all three models, but we'll focus primarily on the common hybrid and traditional models. If you decide to develop a pure SPA, you may have significantly different deployment and caching needs, which are beyond the scope of this book.

Managing State

"The key to efficiently utilizing resources is stateless autonomous compute nodes."
                                                                    –Bill Wilder

Carefully managing state is the most important aspect of scaling the front end of your web application. If you lay a good foundation by removing all of the state from your front-end servers, you will be able to scale your front-end layer by simply adding more clones. We'll first look at the differences between stateless and stateful services and then briefly discuss how to deal with different types of state.

> *Statelessness* is a property of a service, server, or object indicating that it does not hold any data (state). As a consequence, statelessness makes instances of the same type interchangeable, allowing better scalability. By not having any data, service instances are identical from the client's point of view. Instead of holding data themselves, stateless services delegate to external services any time that client's state needs to be accessed.

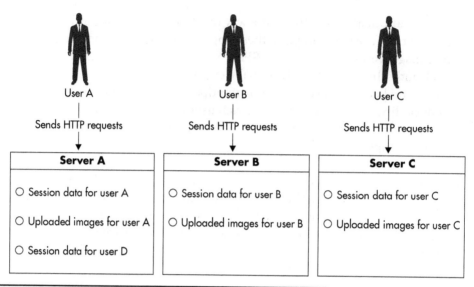

Figure 3-1 *Stateful server*

Figure 3-1 shows an abstract diagram of a stateful web application server. Server instance A holds information that other instances (B and C) cannot access. It could be user session data, local files, local memory state, or even locks. In the context of stateful vs. stateless, state is any information that would have to be synchronized between servers to make them identical. Let's consider Figure 3-2 to see how a stateless server could handle a client's state. In this case, servers A, B, and C are identical, and all of the state is kept outside of their boundaries. They are interchangeable because they are all capable of reaching the client's data.

To better understand the difference between stateful and stateless service, let's consider an analogy to different ways you can order drinks in a pub. When you go to a large pub, it is common to see multiple bars located on different floors or in different corners of the pub. In this analogy, a pub is a website, a bar is a server, and an act of ordering a drink is a web request.

If you pay with cash, you can walk up to any of the bars, order a drink, pay, and simply walk away. There are no additional steps necessary to perform this transaction. The bartender does not need to know who you are, and you can enjoy the services of any bartender at any one of the bars. From the bartender's point of view, it also does not matter how many people are in the pub at the same time, as it does not affect the process of serving drinks. He or she may get more orders, but orders do not affect each other. This is how you would interact with a stateless service.

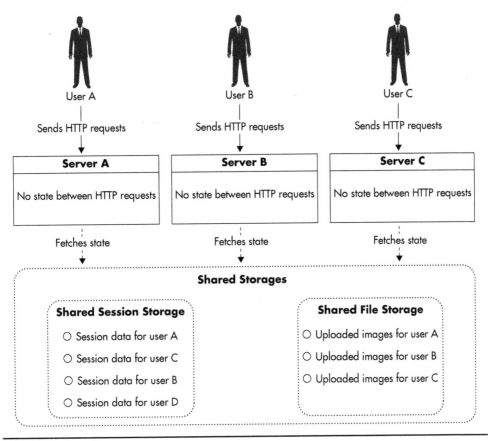

Figure 3-2 *Stateless server*

If you decide to put your drinks on a tab, your transactions look very different. First, you need to initiate your tab by giving a bartender your credit card. Then, any time you want to order a drink, you need to go to the bar where your credit card is and ask for the drink to be put on your tab. You do not have the freedom of moving around the pub and using other bars, as they do not know who you are. You also need to remember to collect your card at the end of the night. From a bartender's point of view, putting drinks on a tab is also more challenging, as the bartender needs to locate the correct tab for each order. The more open tabs he or she has, the more challenging it becomes to find the right tab for each order. This is how you interact with a stateful service.

The key difference between stateful and stateless services is that instances of a stateless service are fully interchangeable and clients can use any of the instances without seeing any difference in behavior. Stateful services, on the other hand, keep some "knowledge" between requests, which is not available to every instance of the service. Whenever clients want to use a stateful service, they need to stick to the selected instance to prevent any side effects.

Let's now have a look at the most common types of state stored in the front-end layer and how to deal with them.

Managing HTTP Sessions

Hypertext Transfer Protocol (HTTP) sessions are used all over the Web. In fact, when you visit a website, your requests will typically be part of an HTTP session. Since the HTTP protocol is stateless itself, web applications developed techniques to create a concept of a session on top of HTTP so that servers could recognize multiple requests from the same user as parts of a more complex and longer lasting sequence (the user session).

From a technical point of view, sessions are implemented using cookies. Figure 3-3 shows a simplified sequence of events. When a user sends a request

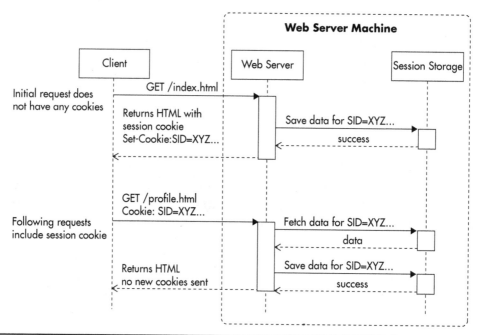

Figure 3-3 *Establishing an HTTP session*

to the web server without a session cookie, the server can decide to start a new session by sending a response with a new session cookie header. The HTTP contract says that all cookies that are still active need to be included in all consecutive calls.

By using cookies, the server can now recognize which requests are part of the same sequence of events. Even if multiple browsers connected to the web server from the same IP address, cookies allow the web server to figure out which requests belong to a particular user. This in turn allows implementation of user login functionality and other similar features.

When you log in to a website, a web application would usually store your user identifier and additional data in the web session scope. The web framework or the application container would then be responsible for storing the web session scope "somewhere" so that data stored in the web session scope would be available to the web application on each HTTP request. In the case of Java, a web session scope would usually be stored in the memory of the web application container; in the case of PHP, it would use files stored on the web server by default. The key thing to observe here is that any data you put into the session should be stored outside of the web server itself to be available from any web server. There are three common ways to solve this problem:

- ▶ Store session state in cookies
- ▶ Delegate the session storage to an external data store
- ▶ Use a load balancer that supports sticky sessions

If you decide to store session data in cookies, the situation is fairly simple. In your application, use session scope as normal; then just before sending a response to the client, your framework serializes the session data, encrypts it, and includes it in the response headers as a new value of the session data cookie. The main advantage in this approach is that you do not have to store the session state anywhere in your data center. The entire session state is being handed to your web servers with every web request, thus making your application stateless in the context of the HTTP session. Figure 3-4 shows how session data is passed around in this case.

The only practical challenge that you face when using cookies for session storage is that session storage becomes expensive. Cookies are sent by the browser with every single request, regardless of the type of resource being requested. As a result, all requests within the same cookie domain will have session storage appended as part of the request. Browsers will have to include entire session data, even when downloading images or Cascading Style Sheet (CSS) files, or sending AJAX requests.

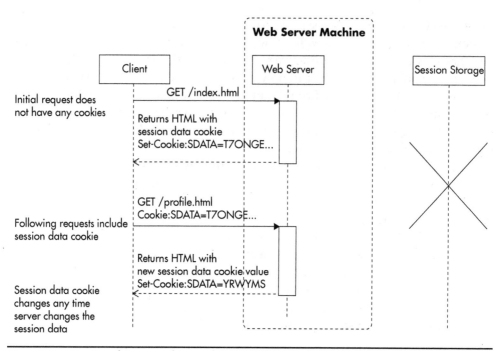

Figure 3-4 *Session data stored in cookies*

Using cookies for session data storage works very well as long as you can keep your data minimal. If all you need to keep in session scope is user ID or some security token, you will benefit from the simplicity and speed of this solution. Unfortunately, if you are not careful, adding more data to the session scope can quickly grow into kilobytes, making web requests much slower, especially on mobile devices. The cost of cookie-based session storage is also amplified by the fact that encrypting serialized data and then Base64 encoding increases the overall byte count by one third, so that 1KB of session scope data becomes 1.3KB of additional data transferred with each web request and each web response.

The second alternative approach is to store session data in a dedicated data store. In this case, your web application would take the session identifier from the web request and then load session data from an external data store. At the end of the web request life cycle, just before a response is sent back to the user, the application would serialize the session data and save it back in the data store. In this model, the web server does not hold any of the session data between web requests, which makes it stateless in the context of an HTTP session. Figure 3-5 shows how session data is stored in this scenario.

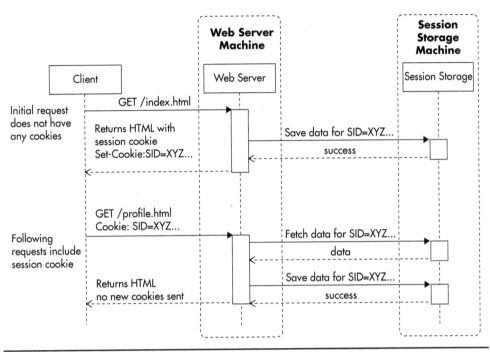

Figure 3-5   *Session data stored in distributed data store*

Many data stores are suitable for this use case, for example, Memcached, Redis, DynamoDB, or Cassandra. The only requirement here is to have very low latency on get-by-key and put-by-key operations. It is best if your data store provides automatic scalability, but even if you had to do data partitioning yourself in the application layer, it is not a problem, as sessions can be partitioned by the session ID itself. We'll look further at data partitioning in Chapter 5, but for now, let's assume that the horizontal scalability of session storage is not a difficult problem, and it can be solved by the data store itself or by simple data partitioning.

If you are developing your front-end web application in Java JVM–based languages (Groovy, Scala, Java), you also have the alternative of using object-clustering technologies like Teracotta for your session storage. Terracotta allows for transparent object access from multiple machines by introducing synchronization, distributed locking, and consistency guarantees. From the front-end scalability point of view, it is just another means to the same end—you need to make all of your web servers identical to allow auto-scaling and horizontal scalability by adding clones.

Finally, you can handle session state by doing nothing in the application layer and pushing the responsibility onto the load balancer. In this model, the load balancer needs to be able to inspect the headers of the request to make sure that requests with the same session cookie always go to the server that initially issued the cookie. Figure 3-6 shows one possible implementation of sticky session.[L18–L19] In this case, any time a new client sends a request, the load balancer assigns the client to a particular web server and injects a new load balancer cookie into the response, allowing the load balancer to keep track of which user is assigned to which server.

Even if it may seem like a good solution, sticky sessions break the fundamental principle of statelessness, and I recommend avoiding them. Once you allow your

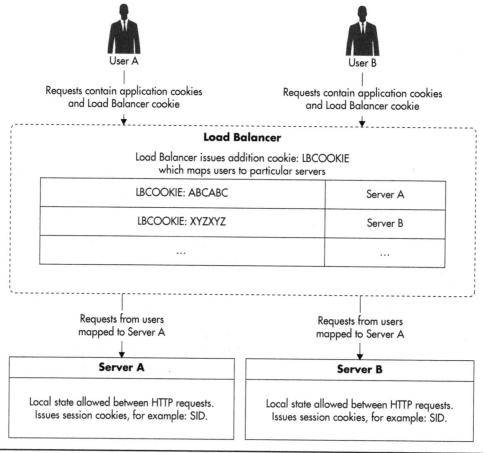

Figure 3-6   *Sticky session based on an additional cookie*

web servers to be unique, by storing any local state, you lose flexibility. You will not be able to restart, decommission, or safely auto-scale web servers without braking users' sessions because their session data will be bound to a single physical machine. In addition, you create a dangerous precedence with sticky sessions. If it is okay to store session data on web servers, maybe it is also okay to store some other state there? If you can do one, you can do the other. Sticky session support of a load balancer can then hide underlying design issues rather than helping you scale your application. Instead, keep all session scope data in cookies or store session data in a shared object store accessible from all web server instances.

Managing Files

The second most common type of state in web applications for front-end servers is file storage. There are two types of files to pay attention to:

▶ User-generated content being uploaded to your servers

▶ Files generated by your system that need to be downloaded by the user

The most common use case is to allow users to upload files and then share or access them. A decade ago, websites rarely allowed users to upload images, but the norm has shifted as people share more images and videos and engage with media-rich social profiles, forcing more and more web applications to manage user-generated files without sacrificing scalability. The flip side of this use case is letting users download files generated by your system. Whether reports, invoices, videos, or images, your system may need to create files for your users and generate uniform resource locators (URLs) to download them. In some cases, you can get away with generating files on the fly and avoid storing them, but in many cases, you will need to store the files in their exact form to ensure they will never change. For example, you don't want the contents of an invoice to change once you release a new version of your code.

Each of these use cases may require files to be available publicly or privately by selected users. Public files are like photos on social media—anyone can download them. Private files, on the other hand, are like invoices, reports, or private messages—they should be accessible only by selected users.

Whether you are hosting your application on Amazon or not, you can consider using Simple Storage Service (S3) or Azure Blob Storage as the distributed file storage for your files. They are relatively cheap and a good fit in the early stages of development, when it may not make sense to store all files internally on your own infrastructure. No matter how you store your files, you should always try to use a content delivery network (CDN) provider to deliver public files to your end users. By setting a long expiration policy on public files, you will allow CDN to cache them effectively forever. This way, the original servers hosting these files will receive less traffic, thereby making them easier to scale. Figure 3-7 shows how public files can be stored and accessed via CDN.

If your user-uploaded content is not meant to be publicly available, all file download requests will have to go to your front-end web application servers rather than being served directly by CDN. Figure 3-8 shows an example of such configuration. A web request for a file is sent to one of the front-end web application servers; the application checks a user's permissions and either allows or denies access to the file. If access is granted, the application downloads the file from the shared file storage and sends it to the client.

If you are hosting your application on the Amazon infrastructure, there is no better solution than uploading files to Amazon S3. Whether you are serving public or private files, you can store them in S3 to make sure your front-end servers are stateless. S3 supports the concept of private and public buckets so that files may be accessible publicly or they may be available only to your application servers.

When you need to serve public files, you simply put them into a public S3 bucket. In such case, S3 provides transparent high availability and scalability, and you do not have to worry about anything; it scales for you. You simply have to upload user files to S3 and keep reference to the public URL and file location in your database in case you needed to delete or update it in the future.

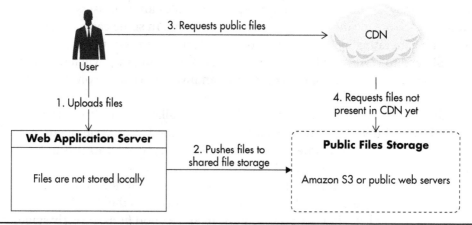

Figure 3-7 *Distributed storage and delivery of public files*

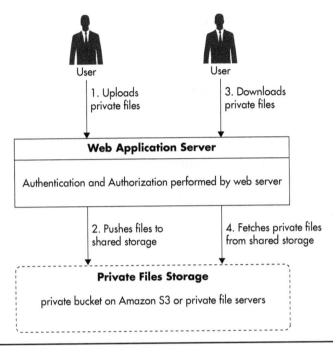

Figure 3-8 *Storage and delivery of private files*

When you need to serve private files, you still store them in S3, but you use a private bucket. A private bucket has the same high-availability and high-scalability capabilities, but it is not open to public access. If you want to serve a private file, you will need to download it to your front-end web application server, as in Figure 3-8.

If you are unable to use cloud-based file storage like S3 or Azure Blob Storage, you will have to build your own file storage and delivery solution. You could look for open-source components, but you will most likely need to build and integrate the system yourself, which can be a considerable amount of work. If you need to store a lot of files but you do not need a lot of throughput, you can use regular file servers with Redundant Array of Independent Disks (RAID) controllers used for redundancy and distribute files among your file servers. Depending on the configuration, each of your file servers may have from a few terabytes to as much as a few dozen terabytes of storage space. You will then also need to think about high-availability issues, as redundancy on a drive level may not satisfy your needs (to achieve true high availability, you need to store each file on multiple physical servers to be able to survive certain types of server failures). The situation becomes even more complex if you need to perform a lot of concurrent reads and writes on the same files. Then you may need to partition a larger number of smaller file servers or use solid-state disks (SSDs) to provide higher throughput and lower random access times.

If you need to scale the file storage yourself, consider partitioning your files by uploading them to a randomly selected server and then storing the location of the file in the metadata database. As you need more servers, you can then use weighted random server selection, which allows you to specify the percentage of new files written to each node. High availability can be achieved by hardware RAID controllers, or if you need higher redundancy levels, by simple file replication. You can either make your application copy each file to two servers at the same time or use something as simple as rsync to keep each of your "master" file servers in sync with the slave.

Building simple file storage is relatively easy, but making it truly scalable and highly available is a much more complex task requiring both time and money. Instead of doing it all by yourself, try to opt for an "out of the box," open-source data store to store your files. For example, MongoDB allows you to store files within a MongoDB cluster by using GridFS. GridFS is an extension built into MongoDB that splits files into smaller chunks and stores them inside MongoDB collections as if they were regular documents. The benefit of such an approach is that you only need to scale one system, and you can leverage partitioning and replication provided by MongoDB instead of implementing your own. You can find similar solutions for other NoSQL data stores, like Astyanax Chunked Object Store released as open source by Netflix. It uses Cassandra as the underlying data store, which allows you to leverage Cassandra's core features like transparent partitioning, redundancy, and failover. It then adds file storage–specific features on top of Cassandra's data model. For example, it optimizes access by randomizing the download order of chunks to avoid hotspots within your cluster.

HINT

Remember that distributed file storage is a complex problem. Where possible, stick with a third-party provider like S3 first. When cloud-based storage is not an option, opt for a data store as a relatively cheap alternative. It may add some performance overhead, but it allows you to build your application faster and reduce the maintenance cost. Only when none of these options work should you consider building a file service from scratch. If you decide to build, be sure to learn more about distributed file systems like Google File System (GFS),[w44] Hadoop Distributed File System (HDFS),[w58] ClusterFS,[w61,L15] and fully distributed and fault-tolerant design.

Managing Other Types of State

A few more types of state can sneak into your application and prevent you from scaling, including local server cache, application in-memory state, and resource locks. Front-end applications often need to cache data to increase performance and reduce load on web services and the data layer. I will discuss caching in more detail in Chapter 6.

A good example of an application that could be sensitive to cache inconsistencies is a real-time bidding application. If you were building an e-commerce website showing auctions in real time and you wanted to cache auction data to improve performance, you could be required to invalidate all of the copies of the cached auction object any time the price changes. If you stored these cache objects in the memory of your web servers, it could become extremely difficult to coordinate such cache invalidation. In such cases, you should cache objects using a shared object cache so there is only one copy of each object and it could be invalidated more easily.

Figure 3-9 shows a scenario where multiple servers end up having different versions of the same object, leading to dangerous pricing inconsistencies. Luckily, not all use cases are sensitive to cache inconsistency. For example, if you were building an online blogging platform like tumblr.com, you could cache user

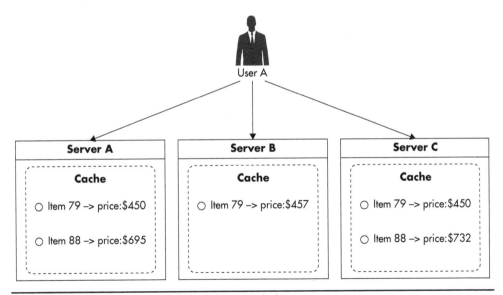

Figure 3-9 *Multiple copies of the same cached object*

names and their follower counts on web servers to speed up the rendering time of their posts. In such a case, users might see different follower counts based on which web server they access, but it would not be a problem if your business was happy to accept such a minor data inconsistency.

The last common example of server state is resource locks. Locks are used to prevent race conditions and to synchronize access to shared resources. In some cases, people would use locks in the front-end layer to guarantee exclusive access to some resources. Unfortunately, for this to work you need to use a distributed locks system. Throughout the years I have seen a few applications that were supposed to be horizontally scalable, but used local locks to synchronize access to shared resources. Unfortunately, this could never work correctly, as locks would be locked independently on each web server without any synchronization. Instead of trying to share locks on web servers, you should "push" the state out of the application servers similar to the way you did it for HTTP session data and file storage.

To show how local locks could prevent you from scaling out, let's consider a web application that manages users' eBay bids. If you developed it to run on a single web server, you could use local locks to synchronize the bidding of each auction. This way, only one thread/process would ever work on a single auction at the same time. Figure 3-10 shows how such a deployment might look.

If you then tried to clone your server and run two independent instances, you would end up with a deployment similar to that shown in Figure 3-11. In this case, locks would not work as expected, as you could have two concurrently running threads, one on Server A and another on Server B, both modifying the same eBay auction without ever realizing that there was another process working on the same data.

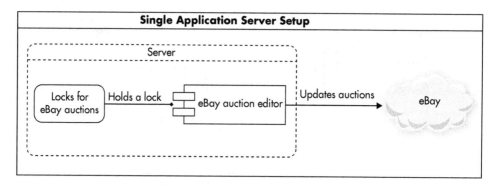

Figure 3-10   *Single server using local resource locks*

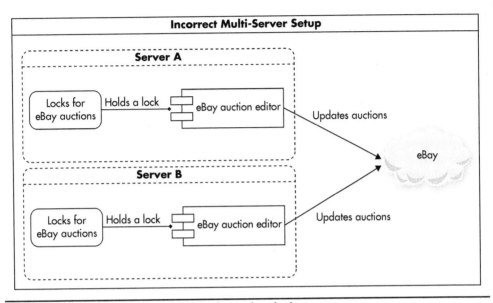

Figure 3-11   *Two clones using local/independent locks*

To avoid this issue you can use a combination of functional partitioning and scaling out using clones. First, you remove locking functionality from the application code and create an independent service from it. Then, use your new shared lock service on all of your web application servers to share locks globally. This way, your web servers do not hold local state (in the context of locks) and can be cloned, replaced, or shut down independently. Figure 3-12 shows how such a deployment might look.

This is actually a common way of scaling out. You isolate a piece of functionality that requires a globally available state, remove it from the application, and create a new independent service encapsulating this functionality. Since the functionality is much more narrow and specialized, it is usually easier to scale out, and it also hides the shared state behind a layer of abstraction from the rest of the system.

The potential downside of this approach is increased latency, as the application needs to perform remote calls to accomplish what used to be a local operation. It can also lead to increased complexity as you end up with more components to manage, scale, and maintain.

The way you implement distributed locking depends mainly on the programming language you choose. If you are developing in Java, I would recommend using Zookeeper with Curator library developed by Netflix.[47,L16–L17] Zookeeper is often

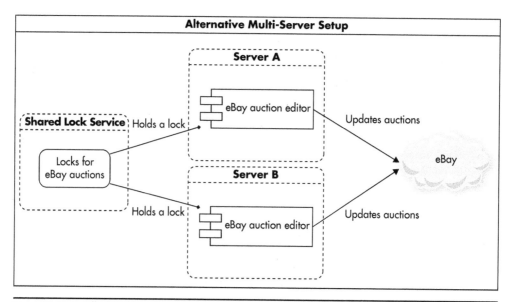

Figure 3-12   *All clones using shared lock management service*

used for distributed locking, application configuration management, leader election, and run-time cluster membership information.

If you are using scripting languages like PHP or Ruby, you may want to use a simpler lock implementation based on atomic operations of NoSQL data stores. For example, locks can be easily implemented using an add operation in Memcached (an in-memory cache engine). Listing 3-1 shows a draft of such simple distributed locking logic. It is not as sophisticated as Zookeeper, as you can't get notifications when a lock gets released, but it is often a good enough solution that can be scaled with ease. Other storage engines usually provide similar atomic primitives, and I have seen locks implemented using Redis, Memcached, and SQL databases like MySQL and PostgreSQL.

Listing 3-1   *Draft of a simple distributed lock implementation using Memcached*

```
$cache->add('lockName', '1', $timeoutInSeconds);
if ($cache->getResultCode() == Memcached::RES_NOTSTORED) {
    // some other process has the lock
}else{
    // I got the lock
}
```

In short, keep all your web servers stateless, both front-end web and web service servers. Keeping servers stateless will let you scale them easily by adding more clones. In the next section, we will explore each front-end component in detail, see their impact on scalability, and discuss how to leverage statelessness of front-end servers to scale them automatically.

Components of the Scalable Front End

Let's now look at the scalability impact of each component on the front-end infrastructure and see what technologies can be used in each area. Figure 3-13 shows a high-level overview of the key components most commonly found in the front-end layer.

As seen in Figure 3-13, the front-end layer includes components like web servers, load balancers, Domain Name System (DNS), reverse proxies, and CDN.

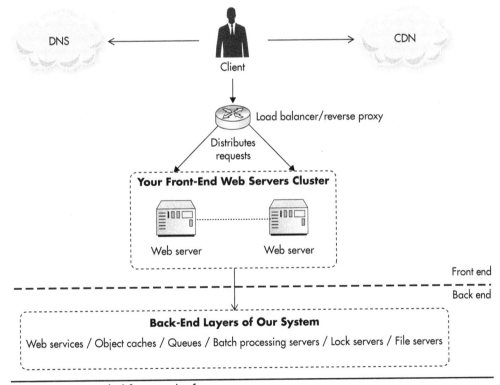

Figure 3-13   *Detailed front-end infrastructure*

Components in the front-end layer are mainly responsible for rendering the user interface and handling connections initiated directly by the user. Let's discuss each component in more detail.

DNS

Domain Name System (DNS) is the first component that your clients talk to when they want to visit your website. No matter if you are hosting a website or a web service (for example, for your mobile app), your clients need to find your server's IP address before they can connect to it. In essence, DNS is used to resolve domain names like ejsmont.org to IP addresses like 173.236.152.169.

In almost all cases, I would recommend using a third-party hosted service instead of deploying your own DNS infrastructure. I would consider hosting my own DNS servers only if I had extremely specialized needs. For example, if I worked for a web hosting company and I needed to support DNS entries for thousands of domains, I might consider hosting my own DNS servers to gain flexibility and save money on the hosted service itself. There are dozens of large DNS hosting companies, which are cheap, reliable, and scale well, so finding a good provider should not be a problem.

If you are hosting your system on Amazon, the best choice is to use Amazon Route 53 service, which is a hosted DNS service integrated closely with other Amazon services. The main advantage of using Route 53 is that it is seamlessly integrated with the Amazon ecosystem. You can easily configure it using the same user interface that you use for other Amazon services. It integrates with other key components, such as an Elastic Load Balancer, and you can configure it entirely using a remote web service API.

If your startup grows much larger, you can also use latency-based routing of Route 53 to direct your clients to the "closest" data center. If you were hosting your servers in multiple Amazon regions (multiple data centers), your clients would actually benefit from establishing a connection to a region that is closer to their location. Route 53 allows you to do that easily using latency-based routing.[L20–L21] It works similar to geoDNS mentioned in Chapter 1, but the data center is selected based on the latency measurement rather than location of the client. When you think about it, this technique is even more robust than geoDNS, as measurements can change over time depending on network congestion, outages, and routing patterns.

Any time a client tries to resolve a domain name to an IP address, it connects to a Route 53 DNS server near its location (Amazon has over 50 edge locations all over the world[L22]). Then, based on the lowest network latency, the Route 53 server responds with an IP address of one of your load balancers (depending on which region is "closer" to the user). Figure 3-14 shows how such routing is performed.

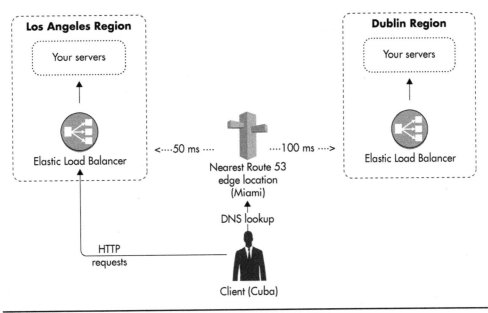

Figure 3-14   *Route 53 latency-based routing*

You can see in this diagram that the application has been deployed in two Amazon regions: one in Europe and another in North America. In such a setup, clients connecting from Cuba would get the IP address of either the European region or North American region, depending on the network latency to each of them.

If you are not hosting your servers on Amazon, there are plenty of providers from which to choose, including easydns.com, dnsmadeeasy.com, dnsimple.com, and dyn.com. Each offers a similar level of service, latencies, and uptime guarantees,[L23–L24] and switching to a different provider is usually an easy task, so selecting a DNS provider should not be a major concern.

Load Balancers

Once your clients resolve your domain name to an IP address using a DNS service, they will need to connect to that IP to request the page or web service endpoint. I strongly recommend using load balancers as the entry point to your data center, as they will allow you to scale more easily and make changes to your infrastructure without negatively affecting your customers.

In the old days, when load balancers were less common and more expensive, DNS was sometimes used to distribute traffic over more than one web server. Figure 3-15 shows how such a round-robin DNS setup might look like.

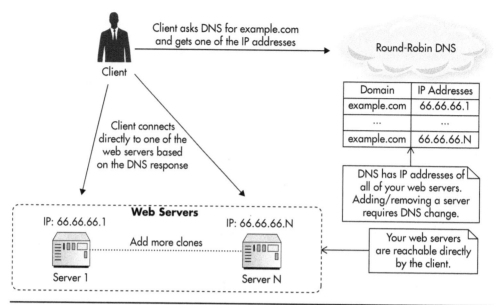

Figure 3-15   *DNS round-robin–based load balancing*

There are a few problems with the round-robin DNS approach, with the biggest issue being that it is not transparent to the clients. You cannot remove a server out of rotation because clients might have its IP address cached. You cannot add a server to increase capacity either, because clients who already have resolved the domain name will keep connecting to the same server (they can cache your DNS records for as long as the Time to Live policy allows). Using round-robin DNS to distribute traffic directly to your web servers makes server management and failure recovery much more complicated, and I would advise against using this strategy in production.

Instead, put a load balancer between your web servers and their clients, as shown in Figure 3-16. In this configuration, all the traffic between web servers and their clients is routed through the load balancer. By doing so, the structure of your data center and current server responsibilities are hidden from your clients.

There are some important benefits to using a load balancer:

▶ **Hidden server maintenance**   You can take a web server out or the load balancer pool, wait for all active connections to "drain," and then safely shut down the web server without affecting even a single client. You can use this method to perform "rolling updates" and deploy new software across the cluster without any downtime.

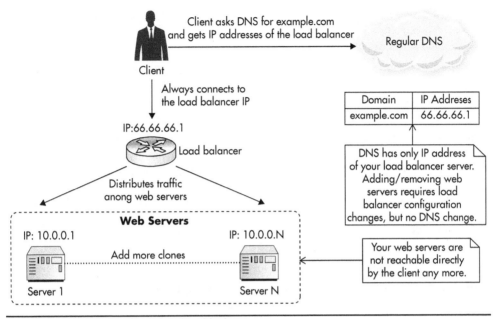

Figure 3-16   *Deployment with a load balancer*

▶ **Seamlessly increase capacity**   You can add more web servers at any time without your clients ever realizing it. As soon as you add a new server, it can start receiving connections; there is no propagation delay as when you use DNS-based load balancing.

▶ **Efficient failure management**   Web server failures can be handled quickly by simply taking a faulty web server out of the load balancer pool. Even if provisioning a new web server takes time, you can quickly remove a broken instance out of the load balancer pool, so that new connections would not be distributed to that faulty machine.

▶ **Automated scaling**   If you are on cloud-based hosting with the ability to configure auto-scaling (like Amazon, Open Stack, or Rackspace), you can add and remove web servers throughout the day to best adapt to the traffic. By having a load balancer, you can do it automatically, without causing any downtime or negatively impacting your customers. I will explain auto-scaling later in this chapter.

▶ **Effective resource management**   You can use Secure Sockets Layer (SSL) offloading to reduce the resources your web servers need. *SSL offloading,* sometimes also called *SSL termination*, is a load balancer feature allowing you to handle all SSL encryption/decryption work on the load balancer and use unencrypted connections internally. I recommend using SSL offloading any time you can get away with it from a security compliance point of view.

As you can see, using a load balancer as the entry point to your data center has a lot of benefits. Load balancers are popular, and there are many good options from which to choose. Because every system is different, it is hard to recommend a particular technology without knowing the details of the application, but there are three broad solution types that fit most of today's systems. Let's quickly go through each of these options and discuss available technologies.

Load Balancer as a Hosted Service

If, as with many startups, you are hosting your application on Amazon EC2 or Azure, I strongly recommend using their hosted load balancer services rather than deploying your own load balancers. One example of such a service is Elastic Load Balancer (ELB) offered by Amazon. ELB is a "load balancer as a service," which is hosted, scaled, and managed by Amazon. All you have to do to start using it is to configure it via the web console and point it to a group of EC2 instances. Some benefits of ELB include the following:

▶ ELB is the cheapest and simplest solution to start with, as you have one fewer component to manage and scale.

▶ ELB scales transparently, so you do not have to worry about the load balancer becoming the bottleneck.

▶ ELB has built-in high availability, so you do not have to worry about ELB becoming a single point of failure. If you decide to install your own load balancers, make sure that you have automatic failover and a hot standby load balancer ready to pick up the load in case the primary load balancer fails.

▶ ELB is cost effective with minimal up-front costs. You pay for what you use, and there is no initial charge for setting up an ELB instance.

▶ ELB integrates with auto-scaling and allows for automatic EC2 instance replacement in case of web server failures. I will describe auto-scaling groups later in this section.

▶ ELB can perform SSL termination, so connections coming from ELB to your web servers are HTTP, not HTTPS (Hypertext Transfer Protocol over SSL). This can significantly reduce the resources needed by your EC2 instances, as you would not need to run the SSL web server at all.

▶ ELB supports graceful back-end server termination by use of the connection draining feature. This lets you take a web server out of the load balancer pool without terminating existing connections. You can take the server out of the pool, wait for existing clients to disconnect, and safely shut down the instance without ever affecting any of the clients.

▶ ELB can be fully managed using Amazon SDK so that you can automate load balancer configuration changes any way you wish. For example, you can automate deployments across multiple machines so that instances are automatically taken out of the load balancer pool during code deployment.

As you can see, ELB is a strong candidate. Amazon managed to build a lot of features into ELB over the years, making it even more attractive than it used to be. There is only one significant reason why ELB may not be suitable for your application:

▶ ELB needs some time to "warm up" and scale out. If you get sudden spikes in traffic that require doubling capacity in a matter of seconds or minutes, ELB may be too slow for you. ELB is great at auto-scaling itself, but if your traffic spikes are sudden, it may not be able to scale fast enough. In such cases, some of your clients may receive HTTP 503 error responses until ELB scales out to be able to handle the incoming traffic.

In addition to publicly facing load balancers, some cloud providers, like Amazon and Azure, allow you to configure their load balancers internally as well. Figure 3-17 shows an example of an internal load balancer. In this deployment scenario you put a load balancer between your front-end servers and your internal services. If all web service requests sent from front-end servers go through an internal load balancer, you gain all the benefits of a load balancer deeper in your stack. You can easily add servers to increase capacity, you can remove machines from the load balancer during maintenance, you can distribute requests among multiple machines, and you can provide automatic failure recovery because the load balancer can remove broken hosts from the pool automatically.

Self-Managed Software-Based Load Balancer

If you are hosted on a cloud provider that does not have a load balancer service or does not meet your requirements, you may want to use one of the open-source (software-based) load balancers. You can use either a reverse proxy like Nginx or a specialized open-source load balancer product like HAProxy. More options are available on the market, but these two are by far the most popular.

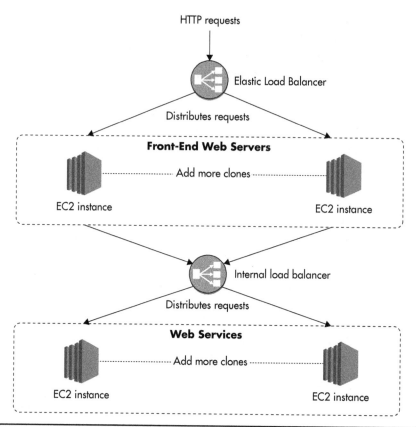

HTTP requests

Elastic Load Balancer

Distributes requests

Front-End Web Servers

.... Add more clones ....

EC2 instance   EC2 instance

Internal load balancer

Distributes requests

Web Services

.... Add more clones ....

EC2 instance   EC2 instance

Figure 3-17   *Internal load balancer*

The main advantage of Nginx is that it is also a reverse HTTP proxy, so it can cache HTTP responses from your servers. This quality makes it a great candidate for an internal web service load balancer, as shown in Figure 3-17. Not only can you scale out your web service layer by adding more servers to the Nginx pool, but you can also benefit greatly from its caching capabilities, reducing the resources needed on the web services layer. I will talk more about these benefits in Chapter 4 and Chapter 6. For now, just know that Nginx is a very good candidate for a reverse proxy/load balancer.

HAProxy, on the other hand, is simpler in design than Nginx, as it is just a load balancer. It can be configured as either a layer 4 or layer 7 load balancer. When HAProxy is set up to be a layer 4 proxy, it does not inspect higher-level protocols and it depends solely on TCP/IP headers to distribute the traffic. This, in turn, allows HAProxy to be a load balancer for any protocol, not just HTTP/HTTPS.

You can use HAProxy to distribute traffic for services like cache servers, message queues, or databases. HAProxy can also be configured as a layer 7 proxy, in which case it supports sticky sessions and SSL termination, but needs more resources to be able to inspect and track HTTP-specific information. The fact that HAProxy is simpler in design makes it perform slightly better than Nginx, especially when configured as a layer 4 load balancer. Finally, HAProxy has built-in high-availability support (HAProxy stands for High Availability Proxy), which makes it more resilient to failures and simplifies failure recovery.

In both cases, whether you use Nginx or HAProxy, you will need to scale the load balancer yourself. You are most likely going to reach the capacity limit by having too many concurrent connections or by having too many requests per second being sent to the load balancer. Luckily, both Nginx and HAProxy can forward thousands of requests per second for thousands of concurrent clients before reaching the capacity limit. This should be enough for most applications, so you should be able to run your web application on a single load balancer (with a hot standby) for a long time.

When you do reach the limits of your load balancer capacity, you can scale out by deploying multiple load balancers under distinct public IP addresses and distributing traffic among them via a round-robin DNS. Figure 3-18 shows how you could scale software-based load balancers beyond a single machine using this technique.

As you can see, there is nothing complicated about this approach. As long as your load balancers are interchangeable and your web servers are stateless, you can keep adding more load balancers to scale horizontally. Having multiple load balancers is more complex to manage, as deployments and configuration changes may need to span multiple load balancers, but it is still a relatively simple way to scale out.

It is acceptable to use round-robin DNS pointing to multiple load balancers (rather than web servers) because you will never have any business logic on your load balancers. You will not have to redeploy or upgrade your load balancers as often as you would with your web servers, and load balancers are much less likely to fail due to a bug.

Hardware Load Balancer

Finally, on the high end of the scale, you have hardware load balancers. If you are hosting a high-traffic website in your own physical data center, you should consider a dedicated hardware load balancer. Devices like Big-IP from F5 or Netscaler from Citrix support very rich feature sets and provide much higher

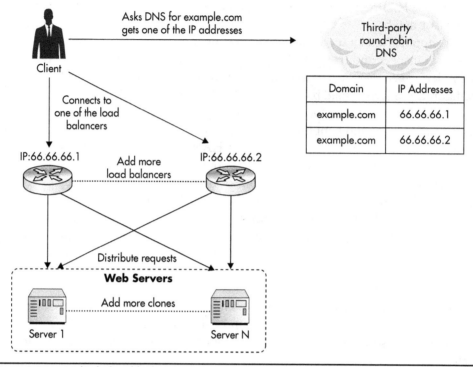

Figure 3-18 *Multiple load balancers*

capacity than software-based load balancers. By having hardware load balancers, you mainly benefit from high throughput, extremely low latencies, and consistent performance. Hardware load balancers are highly optimized to do their job, and having them installed over a low-latency network makes a big difference. They can often handle hundreds of thousands or even millions of concurrent clients, making it much easier to scale vertically.[L25–L26]

The obvious downside of hardware load balancers is their high purchase cost. Hardware load balancer prices start from a few thousand dollars (for a very low-end device) and go as high as over 100,000 dollars per device. Another challenge with hardware load balancers is that they usually require specialized training, and it is harder to find people with the work experience necessary to operate them. Nonetheless, if you are hosting a high-traffic website on your own hardware and you can afford it, a hardware load balancer is the best way to go.

I believe that load balancer as a service will become more popular in the coming years. It is a fairly generic solution, and it is needed by most web infrastructures, so cloud hosting platforms will not be complete without offering a load balancing service anymore. In fact, hosting providers other than Amazon already offer load balancing as a service; you have Azure Load Balancer with support of both internal and external load balancing, Cloud Load Balancers at Rackspace, and LbaaS at Open Stack. So even if you are not hosting your infrastructure on Amazon, it is worth checking whether your hosting provider has a load balancer as a service solution. Scaling through their service might be cheaper and simpler to start with. As your company grows, or when you have specialized use cases, you can switch to your own solution.

Web Servers

As I mentioned before, front-end servers should not have much business logic and they should be treated as a presentation and web service results aggregation layer rather than the core of your system. I will talk more about the benefits of having web services in Chapter 4, but for now let's assume that front-end web servers should not contain business logic, but delegate to web services to perform the actual work.

Because the front end is mainly about handling user interactions, rendering views, and processing user input, it makes sense to use technologies that are good at these tasks. I would recommend dynamic languages like PHP, Python, Groovy, Ruby, or even JavaScript (Node.js) for the front-end web application development, rather than using pure Java or C or a constraining framework like Java EE, JSF, or CGI. You want your technology stack to make common front-end problems simple to solve. For example, you need to make it cheap and easy to take care of SEO, AJAX, internationalization, and daily template changes. It is beneficial to have the same technology stack across all of your layers, as it allows for easier code reuse and requires your team to master fewer technologies. Having said that, it is not uncommon to see different technologies used on the front-end servers and back-end servers of the same system, as different layers may face different challenges and may benefit from a different architectural style.

Once you select your language and framework, you will need to select the actual web server on which to run your application. Luckily, from the scalability point of view, it does not matter much which language you choose and which web server are you running on. As long as your front-end web servers are truly stateless, you can always scale out horizontally by simply adding more servers.

> *Node.js* is a run-time environment and a set of components allowing developers to use JavaScript on the web server side. It is a fairly new technology (development began in 2009) and it is surrounded by a lot of buzz due to some exciting concepts used in Node.js that help maximize throughout. It performs exceptionally well in use cases where the web application needs to maintain open connections with tens or hundreds of thousands of concurrent clients without much communication happening for long periods of time, or with small packets of data exchanged between the client and server. In such applications, a single machine running a Node.js server may support orders of magnitude more clients than other technologies might be able to.

Some will argue that web server choice makes a big difference and that Node.js can handle hundreds of thousands of concurrent connections, whereas Apache will crash and burn on a couple thousand. My answer to that is *yes* and *no*. Yes, it is true that for some use cases one technology may scale much better than another, but on the other hand, it does not matter in the end, as I am talking about horizontal scalability of the entire cluster rather than vertical scalability of a single machine. Worry more about big-picture horizontal scaling from day one rather than focusing on specialized use cases. For some applications, like a chat room, instant notification feature, or a back end for an interactive multiplayer game, it makes more sense to use Node.js rather than Apache or Tomcat, but for the other 98 percent of the use cases, it may be simpler and cheaper to develop in Groovy, Python, PHP, or Ruby, as they have much larger and more mature ecosystems built around them.

There are simply too many choices on the market to fully recommend a particular web server or development stack. It all comes down to the experience you have within the team and personal preferences. Do some research before committing to a particular stack and a web server, but as I mentioned before, no matter what web server you choose, the most important thing for your scalability is to keep your front-end machines stateless.

> ### HINT
>
> *When doing research before choosing your stack, steer away from assumptions and take all benchmarks with a grain of salt. Benchmarks are like political polls; their results always depend on who prepared them. Always assume that there was some agenda behind a benchmark. To gain value from a benchmark, understand what was measured, how was it done, and under what conditions. Finally, pay attention to the graphs, as there are surprisingly many ways in which we may be deceived.*[L27–L28]

Caching

Caching is one of the most important techniques when it comes to scaling the front end of your web application. Instead of trying to add more servers or make them respond faster to clients' requests, use caching to avoid having to serve these requests in the first place. In fact, caching is so critical to the scalability of web applications that Chapter 6 is dedicated to it. To avoid repeating parts of that deeper dive, let's just highlight a few components relevant to the front-end layer of your application here.

One of the first things you should do is integrate a CDN. We'll cover the details of setup in Chapter 6. On a high level, you can use a CDN to proxy all of the web requests coming to your web servers, or you can use it solely for static files like images, CSS, and JavaScript files.

If you decide to serve all of your traffic via the CDN, you may be able to leverage it to cache entire pages and even AJAX responses. For some web application types, you can serve most of your traffic from the CDN cache, resulting in less load on your servers and better response times.

Unfortunately, not all web applications can use CDN to effectively cache entire pages. The more personalized your content is and the more dynamic the nature of your web application, the harder it becomes to cache entire HTTP responses. In such cases, you may be better off deploying your own reverse proxy servers to gain more control over what is cached and for how long. Most common alternatives for it are reverse proxies like Varnish and Nginx, which we'll cover in Chapter 6.

Another way to use caching in the front-end layer is to store data directly in the browser. Modern browsers supporting the web storage specification let you store significant amounts of data (megabytes). This is especially useful when developing web applications for mobile clients or SPAs, as you want to minimize the number of web requests necessary to update the user interface. By using local browser storage from your JavaScript code, you can provide a much smoother user experience, reducing the load on your web servers at the same time.

Finally, if requests cannot be satisfied from the browser caches or reverse proxies, your web servers will need to serve them and generate the responses. In such cases, you may still be able to cache fragments of your responses in an object cache. Most web applications can benefit from a shared object cache like Redis or Memcached. In fact, many startups managed to scale to millions of daily users by beefing up their Memcached clusters. Some of the best examples of scaling using Memcached are Facebook,[w62] Pinterest,[L31] Reddit,[L32] and Tumblr.[L33]

Auto-Scaling

Auto-scaling is a technique of automating your infrastructure so that new virtual servers would be added or removed from your clusters depending on the volume of traffic and server load. Scalability is not just about scaling out; it is also about the ability to scale down, mainly to save cost. Auto-scaling is a technique rather than a component of your front-end infrastructure, but it brings great benefits and is especially easy to implement in the front-end layer of a web stack.

To better understand why it is important to automate scaling of your stack, look at Figure 3-19. It is not important here what metric is shown in the graph, but what the weekly pattern of the load put on the infrastructure is (the graph shows data from a free ISP monitoring tool). The key feature is that traffic changes significantly throughout the day, and it may also be significantly different on the weekends. Rather than having to add and remove virtual machines manually,

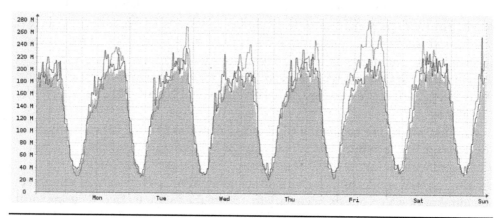

Figure 3-19   *Common infrastructure utilization pattern*

it is better to automate the process so that your system "knows" how to monitor its own condition and scale up or down respectively. Depending on your traffic patterns, using auto-scaling can save you as much as 25 percent or even 50 percent of your overall web server hosting costs. It can also help you handle unexpected spikes in traffic without any human interaction.

The easiest way to implement auto-scaling is to use the hosting provider's auto-scaling tools. Check whether your hosting provider offers auto-scaling functionality before trying to implement your own. Amazon was the first cloud hosting company that implemented auto-scaling as a service, and they are still the leader in that area, but other providers like Rackspace and Azure now provide auto-scaling functionality as part of their cloud hosting suite as well. To better understand how auto-scaling works and what components are involved, let's have a look at an example using Amazon.

First, to be able to configure auto-scaling, you will need to use Amazon EC2 (Elastic Compute Cloud) instances for your web servers. When you use auto-scaling, servers may be added or removed at any time of the day. Auto-scaling can take out any instance at any point in time, so you cannot store any data on your web servers, or at least make sure that any data stored on web servers is disposable (like a cache). Shutting down a web server should not cause any users to be logged out or receive a broken user experience.

Before you can create EC2 instances automatically, you will have to create a web server image (Amazon Machine Image [AMI]) and configure it to be able to bootstrap itself and join the cluster automatically. To do so, everything that is needed for a new EC2 instance to become a fully functional web server must be in the AMI file itself, passed in by AMI launch parameters, or fetched from a remote data store. Amazon allows server images to take bootstrap parameters so you can create a new instance and tell it what cluster it belongs to or what the role of the server is. You can also use Amazon storage services, like SimpleDB, to store bootstrap configuration for EC2 instances, so any time a new EC2 instance is started using a particular AMI image, it will be able to load the necessary configuration from the shared data store and configure itself to become a fully functional web server.

Next, you can create an auto-scaling group to define scaling policies. An auto-scaling group is the logical representation of your web server cluster and it can have policies like "add 2 servers when CPU utilization is over 80 percent" or "set minimum server count to 4 every day at 9 A.M." Amazon has a powerful policy framework, allowing you to schedule scaling events and set multiple thresholds for different system metrics collected by Cloud Watch (a hosted service used to gather system-level metrics).

When you create an auto-scaling group, you can also decide to use Amazon ELB. If you decide to do that, new instances added to the auto-scaling group will be automatically added to the load balancer pool as soon as they complete bootstrapping. This way, Amazon auto-scaling can launch new instances, add them to the load balancer, monitor cluster metrics coming from Cloud Watch, and based on the policies, add or remove further server instances. Figure 3-20 shows how Amazon auto-scaling works. Auto-scaling controls all of the instances within the auto-scaling group and updates ELB any time servers are added or removed from the cluster.

Auto-scaling is in some ways similar to self-healing, explained in Chapter 2, as you make your system handle difficulties without human interaction. No matter how many servers you have or when traffic spikes occur, your network engineers will not have to monitor the load or react to changing conditions. Your system will able to adjust its infrastructure depending on the current conditions and provide a good user experience (peak) in a cost-effective manner (trough).

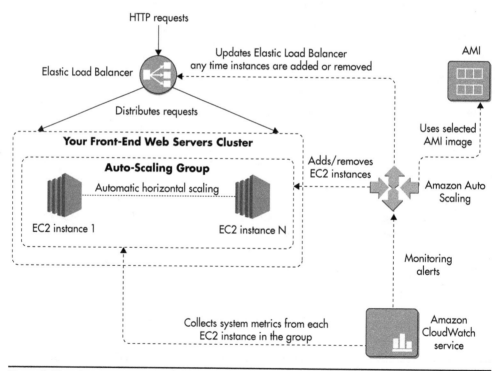

Figure 3-20 *Amazon auto-scaling*

Deployment Examples

Finally, let's put it all together and see two different deployment scenarios: a web application hosted entirely on Amazon and one hosted in a private data center on dedicated hardware. Naturally, these are just blueprints and many of the components included here are optional and may be scaled down depending on your particular system needs.

AWS Scenario

There is a lot of value in additional services provided by Amazon. If your company is a young startup, you really need to be able to get up and running fast. For young startups, every day may be the difference between success and failure, as uncertainty is colossal and resources are sparse. Figure 3-21 shows a blueprint of a typical Amazon web application deployment with web services and data storage layers removed for simplicity.

Just by looking at the diagram, you can see that Amazon is a full stack-hosting company. They thought of pretty much everything a scalable web application might need. As a result, the only components that you are responsible for in Figure 3-21 are your EC2 instances. Even there, however, Amazon can detect EC2 instance failures, shut down the broken servers, and create a new one based on the auto-scaling needs.

In the example in Figure 3-21, the application uses Route 53 as the DNS. Since Route 53 provides high availability and scalability out of the box, you will not need to worry about managing or scaling the DNS. Further down the stack, web requests hit the ELB, where you can implement SSL offloading and round-robin traffic distribution to your auto-scaling group. In this case, you do not have to worry about scalability or high availability of the load balancer either, as ELB provides them out of the box.

When requests finally hit your web servers (EC2 instances), web servers use the web services layer, caches, queues, and shared data stores to render the response. To avoid storing any local state, all files (public and private) are stored in S3. Public files are served directly from S3, and private files are returned by your web servers, but they are still stored on S3 for scalability and high availability.

On its way back to the client, responses may be cached in CloudFront. Since not every application would benefit from CloudFront, this component is optional. You could deliver public content directly from S3 without going through CloudFront with a similar effect. S3 and CloudFront both provide high scalability and high availability as part of the service. In addition, they also speed up your response times by having edge servers hosted all around the world.

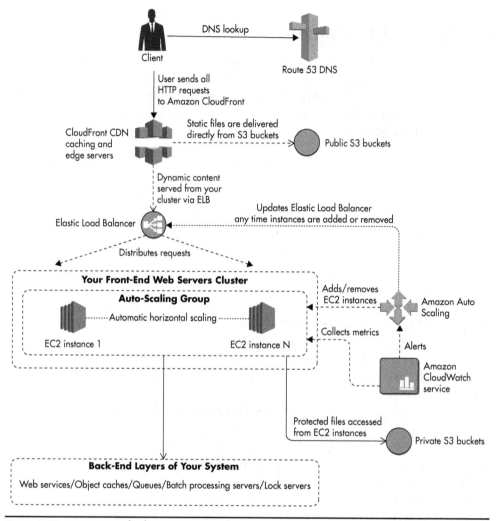

Figure 3-21 *Amazon deployment example*

As you can see, there are a lot of components in this deployment, but most of them are hosted services. When you think of it, that is a huge amount of features and a load off your mind. Just ten years ago, I wouldn't have dreamed of being able to scale, deploy, and develop so quickly simply by using third-party platforms.

If you are a small startup on its way up, consider leveraging Amazon to help you scale. You should be able to use it at least until you get your product right and enough cash in the bank to be able to afford building custom solutions for all these problems. Amazon is very cost efficient for small companies that need to deal with a lot of uncertainty, as there is virtually no up-front cost. As you become larger and richer, priorities often change and it may become much more attractive to host your systems on your own hardware.

Private Data Center

The second deployment scenario is based on dedicated hardware in a physical data center. In this configuration, the only services that you could easily offload to third parties are DNS and CDN. Some people use Amazon S3 for file storage even when hosting on their own infrastructure, but it is not a very common practice.

Even though hosting on bare metal forces you to manage much more yourself, there are considerable benefits of dedicated hardware. The most significant reasons for hosting on your own hardware are

▶   You may require more predictable latencies and throughput. Hosting on your own hardware lets you achieve submillisecond server-to-server round trips.

▶   Hardware servers are much more powerful than virtual servers. You will need many fewer machines when migrating from the cloud to bare hardware.

▶   Buying servers up front is expensive when you are a small company, but once your network engineering team grows and you are managing over a hundred servers, it may become cheaper to have your own servers rather than renting "compute units." Some things, like random access memory (RAM), input-output (I/O) operation, and SSD drives, are still very expensive in the cloud when compared to regular servers. In general, vertical scaling is more effective when done using your own hardware.

▶   Some companies need to conform to strict security or legal requirements. For example, some gambling jurisdictions require companies to host all of their servers within a particular location—in such a case, hardware is a necessity, not an option.

Figure 3-22 shows an example of a private data center deployment. I would still recommend using third-party DNS and CND providers, but the rest of the stack would have to be managed by your own team.

In similar fashion to Amazon deployment, requests first hit the load balancer; in this case it would be a hardware device: HAProxy or Nginx. If you decide that you need another layer of caching, you may use Nginx as the load balancer or put a layer of reverse proxy servers between your load balancer and your web

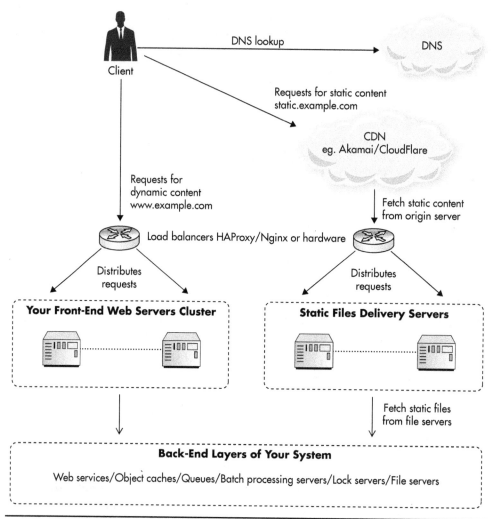

DNS lookup

DNS

Client

Requests for static content
static.example.com

CDN
eg. Akamai/CloudFlare

Requests for
dynamic content
www.example.com

Fetch static content
from origin server

Load balancers HAProxy/Nginx or hardware

Distributes
requests

Distributes
requests

Your Front-End Web Servers Cluster

Static Files Delivery Servers

Fetch static files
from file servers

Back-End Layers of Your System

Web services/Object caches/Queues/Batch processing servers/Lock servers/File servers

Figure 3-22 *Private data center deployment*

servers. This way, you can cache entire HTTP responses. The only thing inhibiting vertical scaling for your load balancer is the price per device. In such a case, you may implement the round-robin solution to distribute traffic over multiple load balancers.

Since you cannot provision hardware servers on demand, you would not be able to implement auto-scaling and you would need to coordinate and plan scale-out events more carefully. Adding hardware can take weeks, or in some bureaucratic companies even months, so plan your capacity carefully, as you will not be able to handle traffic spikes by adding new machines with the click of a button. Even when you host on your own hardware, I would still strongly recommend building your web applications in a stateless fashion. This way, even if you cannot automate the scaling process, you can still perform it quickly and avoid horizontal scalability roadblocks.

When hosting on your own hardware, you will also need to choose how to deploy your shared file storage. The file store solution depends mainly on the throughput and data size, and I already presented a few options earlier in this chapter. I prefer solutions where the application does not have to know how files are stored and replicated. Depending on the budget and requirements, you can use anything from a simple File Transfer Protocol (FTP) server to a more sophisticated solution like Storage Area Network (SAN) or NoSQL data stores.

No matter which file storage solution you choose, you will need to be able to serve these files via a CDN. When hosting on S3, public buckets become automatically available over HTTP, so you can just point the CDN to them. In case of a private data center, you will need to put a layer of web servers in front of your file storage to allow public access to your files via the CDN.

As you can see, the components of the infrastructure and underlying principles of the architecture remain the same—the only pieces that change are the technologies used to achieve the same goals. I believe that it is much cheaper and quicker to get started by hosting on the cloud, and then once you grow large enough you can consider moving to a private data center.

Summary

The front end is usually one of the key areas requiring high scalability, as it needs to sustain the highest levels of concurrency and request rates. Luckily, if designed well, it can be a relatively easy area to scale, as it has the least amount of state that needs to be managed (replicated or synchronized).

I would strongly recommend reading some more books and articles focusing on the technologies mentioned in this chapter. There are some great books on caching, load balancers, and general front-end optimization techniques.[8,48–49] I would also recommend reading a little bit on modern web frameworks like Spring[14] or Grails,[22,34] as they promote good web application architecture. Finally, I would recommend getting more familiar with cloud hosting.[29,w34–w36,w38]

Web Services

Careful design of the web services layer is critical because if you decide to use web services, this is where most of your business logic will live. Before you jump into implementation of your web services, it is important to consider whether you need them in the first place and what tradeoffs you are willing to make. There are many benefits that come with web services, such as promoting reuse and higher levels of abstraction, but there are also some drawbacks associated with them, such as higher up-front development costs and increased complexity.

To help you make these decisions, I will discuss different approaches to designing and developing web services together with some of their benefits and costs. I will also cover scalability considerations and some best practices of building scalable web services. Before we get into details of how to scale web services, let's first have a look at different design approaches.

Designing Web Services

Initially, web applications were built using simple, monolithic architecture. At this time, all of the interactions were done using Hypertext Markup Language (HTML) and JavaScript over Hypertext Transfer Protocol (HTTP). Beginning in the mid-2000s, it became increasingly popular to expose alternative ways to interact with web applications by providing different types of application programming interfaces (APIs). This allowed companies to integrate their systems and collaborate on the Web. As the Web got bigger, the need for integration and reuse grew with it, making APIs even more popular. The most recent significant driver for API adoption came in the late 2000s with a massive mobile development wave. Suddenly, everybody wanted a mobile app and it became clear that in many cases, a mobile app was just another user interface to the same data and to the same functions that the existing web applications already had. The popularity of mobile applications helped APIs become a first-class citizen of web development. Let's now have a look at different ways of designing APIs.

Web Services as an Alternative Presentation Layer

Arguably the oldest approach to developing web services in the context of web applications is to build the web application first and then add web services as an alternative interface to it. In this model, your web application is a single unit with extensions built on top of it to allow programmatic access to your data and functionality without the need to process HTML and JavaScript.

To explain it better, let's consider an example. If you were building a hotel-booking website, you would first implement the front end (HTML views with some AJAX and Cascading Style Sheets [CSS]) and your business logic (usually back-end code running within some Model View Controller framework). Your website would then allow users to do the usual things like searching for hotels, checking availability, and booking hotel rooms.

After the core functionality was complete, you would then add web services to your web application when a particular need arose. For example, a few months after your product was live, you wanted to integrate with a partner company and allow them to promote your hotels. Then as part of the integration effort you would design and implement web services, allowing your partner to perform certain operations, for example, searching for hotels based on price and availability. Figure 4-1 shows how such a system might look.

As you can see in Figure 4-1, your web application is developed, deployed, and executed as a single unit. It does not mean that you cannot have multiple servers running the exact same copy of the application. It just means that they

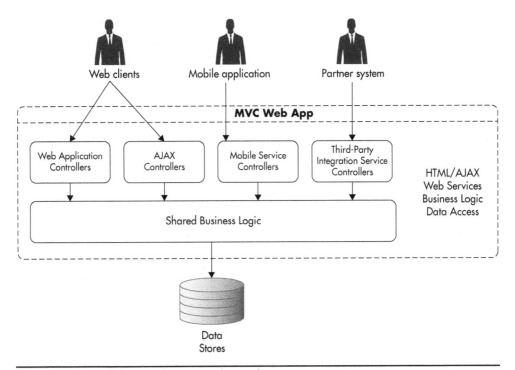

Figure 4-1   *Monolithic application with a web service extension*

all run the same codebase in its entirety and that there is no distinction between presentation and service layers. In fact, there is no distinct web services layer in this approach, as web services are part of a single monolithic application.

Web applications like this would usually be developed using a Model View Controller framework (like Symfony, Rails, or SpringMVC), and web services would be implemented as a set of additional controllers and views, allowing clients to interact with your system without having to go through the complexity of HTML/AJAX interactions.

Although you could argue that this approach is immature or even obsolete, I believe that there are still valid reasons for using it in some situations. The main benefit of this approach is that you can add features and make changes to your code at very high speed, especially in early phases of development. Not having APIs reduces the number of components, layers, and the overall complexity of the system, which makes it easier to work with. If you do not have any customers yet, you do not know whether your business model will work, and if you are trying to get the early minimum viable product out the door, you may benefit from a lightweight approach like this.

The second important benefit of this approach is that you defer implementation of any web service code until you have proven that your product works and that it is worth further development. Although you can develop web services very efficiently nowadays, they still add to the up-front cost. For example, when using a monolithic approach, you can simply use your native objects anywhere in your code by passing them around rather than having to add new web service functionality. Managing web service contracts and debugging issues can be very time consuming, making the difference between success and failure of your early project.

Finally, not every web application needs an API, and designing every web application with a distinct web services layer may be just unnecessary overengineering.

On the other hand, for all but the simplest of systems, the monolithic approach is the worst option from a scalability and long-term maintenance point of view. By having all of the code in a single application, you now have to develop and host it all together. It may not be a problem when you have a team of four engineers all working together in a single room, but it becomes very difficult to keep growing such a system past a single engineering team, as everyone needs to understand the whole system and make changes to the same codebase.

As your application grows in size and goes through more and more changes, the flexibility of making quick, ad hoc changes becomes less important. In turn, the separation of concerns and building higher levels of abstraction become much more important. You need to use your judgment and make tradeoffs between the two depending on your situation.

If you decide to use the monolithic approach, you need to be cautious of its potential future costs, like the need for major refactoring or rewrites. As I explained in Chapter 2, keeping coupling under control and functional partitioning are important things to consider when designing for scale. Luckily, the monolithic approach is not the only way to design your applications. Let's have a look at the opposite end of the spectrum now: the API-first approach.

API-First Approach

The term *API-first design* is relatively new, and different people may define it slightly differently. I would argue that API-first implies designing and building your API contract first and then building clients consuming that API and the actual implementation of the web service. I would say it does not matter whether you develop clients first or the API implementation first as long as you have the API contract defined beforehand.

The concept of API-first came about as a solution to the problem of multiple user interfaces. It is common nowadays for a company to have a mobile application, a desktop website, a mobile website, and a need to integrate with third parties by giving them programmatic access to the functionality and data of their system.

Figure 4-2 shows how your system might look if you decided to implement each of these use cases separately. You would likely end up with multiple implementations of the same logic spread across different parts of your system. Since your web application, mobile client, and your partners each have slightly different needs, it feels natural to satisfy each of the use cases by providing slightly different interfaces. Before you realize it, you will have duplicate code spread across all of your controllers. You then face the challenge of supporting all of these implementations and applying changes and fixes to each of them separately. An alternative approach to that problem is to create a layer of web services that encapsulates most of the business logic and hides complexity behind a single API contract. Figure 4-3 shows how your application might look when using an API-first approach.

In this scenario, all of your clients use the same API interface when talking to your web application. There are a few important benefits to this approach. By having a single web service with all of the business logic, you only need to maintain one copy of that code. That in turn means that you need to modify less code when making changes, since you can make changes to the web service alone rather than having to apply these changes to all of the clients.

It is also important to note that most of the complexity and business logic have been pushed away from the client code and into the web services layer. This, in turn,

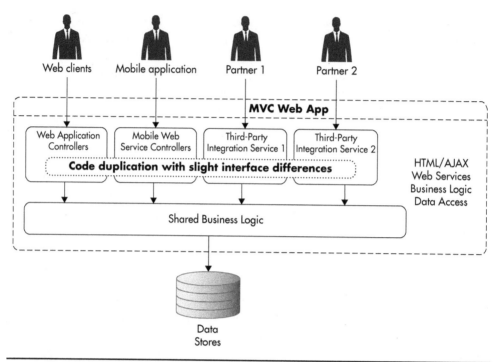

Figure 4-2 *Application with multiple clients and code duplication*

makes developing and changing clients much easier, as they do not have to be concerned with business rules or databases—all they need to do is know how to use a simplified interface of the API.

Having an API can also make it easier to scale your system, as you can use functional partitioning and divide your web services layer into a set of smaller independent web services. By having a higher layer of abstraction, you can decouple your clients from the internals of your web services. This decoupling helps make the system easier to understand, as you can work on the client without the need to understand how the service is implemented, and vice versa— you can work on the web service without worrying how clients are implemented or what do they do with the features your API exposes.

From a scalability point of view, having a separation of concerns helps in scaling clients and services independently. It also allows you to share the load among more servers, as different services can then use different technologies and be hosted independently to better fit their needs.

Unfortunately, the API-first approach is usually much more difficult in practice than it might sound. To make sure you do not overengineer and still provide all

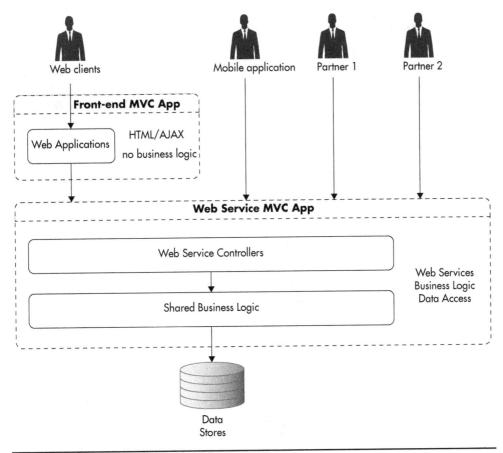

Figure 4-3   *API-first application with multiple clients*

of the functionality needed by your clients, you may need to spend much more time designing and researching your future use cases. No matter how much you try, you still take a risk of implementing too much or designing too restrictively. That is mainly because when you are designing your API first, you may not have enough information about the future clients' needs.

API-first should not be a mantra. Some applications will benefit from it; others will not. I believe one could generalize and say that API-first is better suited for more mature systems and more stable companies than it is for early-phase startups. Developing in this way may be a cleaner way to build software, but it requires more planning, knowledge about your final requirements, and engineering resources, as it takes more experience to design a scalable web service and make it flexible at the same time.

Pragmatic Approach

Rather than following one strategy to build every application you see, I would recommend a more pragmatic approach that is a combination of the two others. I would recommend thinking of the web services layer and service-oriented architecture from day one, but implementing it only when you see that it is truly necessary.

That means that when you see a use case that can be easily isolated into a separate web service and that will most likely require multiple clients performing the same type of functionality, then you should consider building a web service for it. On the other hand, when you are just testing the waters with very loosely defined requirements, you may be better off by starting small and learning quickly rather than investing too much upfront.

To give you an example of how you could judge that, let's consider an example. If I were to implement a web app for a brand-new startup—let's say I was building yet another improved selfie-editing website—I would prefer to get a prototype in front of my users as soon as possible. I would prefer to start testing the concept in a matter of weeks rather than going through detailed design, modeling, and implementation of my web services and clients. The reason is that most of these brilliant startup ideas are illusions. Once you put your product in front of the user, you realize that they don't need it at all or, in the best-case scenario, they need something slightly different, which now you need to cater to. Until you have proven that people are willing to pay their hard-earned cash for what you are about to build, you are taking a risk of wasting time and overengineering.

On the other hand, if I was working in a startup with a few million dollars in funding or a product with a strong paying user base and I had to implement a new supporting product, I might go for the API-first approach. For example, if I was working on an e-commerce website and I had to build a product recommendation engine for an existing shopping cart website, it might be a better choice to hide that complexity behind a web service and start with an API-first approach. By having more stability and faith in my business's decisions, it would be more important for me to make sure I can maintain and scale my products rather than learn and fail fast. By having recommendation logic encapsulated in the web service, I could provide a simple API and easily integrate these features into my existing website. In addition, it would not matter whether my original website was built with an API-first approach or not, as it would be a client of my service. As long as I can build a fairly decoupled recommendation web service, I do not care how my clients are structured.

Unfortunately, if you go for that hybrid approach, you are in for a game of tradeoffs and self-doubt—either you risk overengineering or you make a mess. As a result of that mixed approach, you are likely going to end up with a combination of tightly coupled small web applications of little business value and a set of web services fulfilling more significant and well-defined needs. Ideally, over time as your company becomes more mature, you can phase out all of the little "messy" prototypes and gradually move toward service-oriented architecture. It may work out well, but it may also become a bit of a mess as you go along. I know that it might sound strange, but trying to take constraints into consideration and making the best decision based on your current knowledge seems like the winning strategy for startups rather than following a single strict rule.

When designing web services, you will also need to choose your architectural style by choosing a type of web service that you want to implement. Let's have a look at the options available to you.

Types of Web Services

Design and some of the implementation details of web services tend to be a topic of heated debate. I would like to encourage you to keep an open mind to alternatives and reject dogmas as much as it is possible. In that spirit, I would like to discuss two main architectural styles of web services. As we discuss each of the types, I will go into some benefits and drawbacks when it comes to scalability and speed of development, but I would prefer if you made your own judgment as to which style is more suitable for your web application. Let's have a look at the function-centric architectural style first.

Function-Centric Services

Function-centric web services originated a long time ago—in fact, they go as far back as the early 1980s. The concept of the function-centric approach is to be able to call functions' or objects' methods on remote machines without the need to know how these functions or objects are implemented, in what languages are they written, or what architecture are they running on.

A simple way of thinking about function-centric web services is to imagine that anywhere in your code you could call a function (any function). As a result of that function call, your arguments and all the data needed to execute that function would be serialized and sent over the network to a machine that is supposed to execute it. After reaching the remote server, the data would be converted back to the native formats used by that machine, the function would be invoked, and then results would be serialized back to the network abstraction format. Then the result would be sent to your server and unserialized to your native machine formats so that your code could continue working without ever knowing that the function was executed on a remote machine.

In theory, that sounds fantastic; in practice, that was much more difficult to implement across programming languages, central processing unit (CPU) architectures, and run-time environments, as everyone had to agree on a strict and precise way of passing arguments, converting values, and handling errors. In addition, you had to deal with all sorts of new challenges, like resource locking, security, network latencies, concurrency, and contracts upgrades.

There were a few types of function-centric technologies, like Common Object Request Broker Architecture (CORBA), Extensible Markup Language – Remote Procedure Call (XML-RPC), Distributed Component Object Model (DCOM), and Simple Object Access Protocol (SOAP), all focusing on client code being able to invoke a function implemented on a remote machine, but after years of development and standardization processes, SOAP became the dominant technology. It was partially due to its extensibility and partially due to the fact that it was backed by some of the biggest technology companies at the time like IBM, Oracle, Sun, BEA, and Microsoft.

The most common implementation of SOAP is to use XML to describe and encode messages and the HTTP protocol to transport requests and responses between clients and servers. One of most important features of SOAP was that it allowed web services to be discovered and the integration code to be generated based on contract descriptors themselves.

Figure 4-4 shows how integration using SOAP might look. First, the web service provider exposes a set of XML resources, such as Web Service Definition Language (WSDL) files describing methods and endpoints available and definition of data structures being exchanged using XML Schema Definition (XSD) files. These resources become the contract of the web service, and they contain all the information necessary to be able to generate the client code and use the web service. For example, if you developed in Java, you would use special tools and libraries to download the contract and produce the native Java client library. The output would be a set of Java classes, which could then be compiled and used within your application. Behind the scenes, these classes would delegate to SOAP libraries encapsulating all of the data serialization, authentication, routing, and error handling. Your client code would not have to know that it uses a remote web service; it would simply use the Java library that was generated based on the web service contract (WSDL and XSD files).

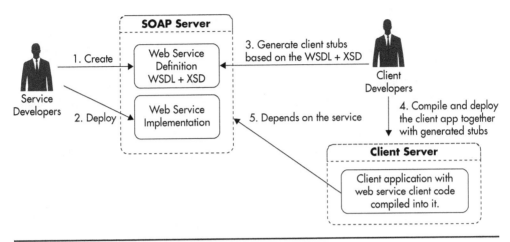

Figure 4-4   *SOAP integration flow*

Another important feature of the initial SOAP design was its extensibility. Over the years, literally dozens of additional specifications were created, allowing for integration of higher-level features like transactions, support for multiphase commits, and different forms of authentication and encryption. In fact, there were so many of these specifications that people began referring to them as ws-* specifications (from their names like ws-context, ws-coordination, ws-federation, ws-trust, and ws-security). Unfortunately, that richness of features came at a cost of reduced interoperability. Integration between different development stacks became more difficult, as different providers had different levels of support for different versions of ws-* specifications.

In particular, people who worked in the web development space and used dynamic languages like PHP, Ruby, Perl, or even Python found it difficult to integrate with SOAP web services. Developing client code in these technologies was usually possible, but often ran into integration issues. Developing SOAP web services using these technologies was simply not practical, as they did not get the support or funding necessary to develop needed tooling and libraries. Arguably, web technologies were excluded from the SOAP world because none of the giants would implement or support it. As a result, the Web needed an alternative to SOAP to allow integration that was easier and cheaper to implement. This, in turn, led to JavaScript Object Notation (JSON)–based Representational State Transfer (REST) services gaining popularity.

The interoperability and usability of SOAP can be a concern in some situations, but something even more important to consider in the context of scalability is the fact that you cannot use HTTP-level caching with SOAP. SOAP requests are issued by sending XML documents, where request parameters and method names are contained in the XML document itself. Since the uniform resource locator (URL) does not contain all of the information needed to perform the remote procedure call, the response cannot be cached on the HTTP layer based on the URL alone. This in turn makes SOAP much less scalable in applications where the web service response could be cached by a reverse proxy.

Another serious issue with SOAP when it comes to scalability is that some of the additional ws-* specifications introduce state into the web service protocol, making it stateful. In theory, you could implement a stateless SOAP web service using just the bare minimum of SOAP-related specifications, but in practice, companies often want to use more than that. As soon as you begin supporting things like transactions or secure conversation, you forfeit the ability to treat your web service machines as stateless clones and distribute requests among them.

Although SOAP comes with high complexity and some scalability drawbacks, I learned to respect and like it to some degree. I believe that having a strict contract and ability to discover data types and functions adds significant value in corporate enthronements. If you had to integrate closely with enterprises like banks or insurance companies, you might benefit from SOAP's advanced security and distributed computing features. On the other hand, I do not think that SOAP is a good technology to develop scalable web services, especially if you work for a startup. SOAP is no longer dominant, and if you are not forced into using it, you probably have little reason to do so, as its complexity and development overhead will slow you down significantly.

Luckily there is an alternative to SOAP. Let's have a closer look at it now.

Resource-Centric Services

An alternative approach to developing web services focuses around the concept of a *resource* rather than a *function*. In function-centric web services, each function can take arbitrary arguments and produce arbitrary values; in resource-centric web services, each resource can be treated as a type of object, and there are only a few operations that can be performed on these objects (you can create, delete, update, and fetch them). You model your resources in any way you wish, but you interact with them in more standardized ways.

REST is an example of a resource-oriented architectural style that was developed in the early 2000s. Since then, it became the de facto standard of web application integration due to its simplicity and lightweight development model.

To understand better how you can model resources using REST, let's consider an example of an online music website where users can search for music and create public playlists to listen to their favorite songs and share them with their friends. If you were to host such a service, you might want to expose a REST API to allow clients to search for songs and manage playlists. You could then create a "playlists" resource to allow users to create, fetch, and update their lists and a set of additional resources for each list and each song within a list.

It is important to note that REST services use URLs to uniquely identify resources. Once you know the URL of a resource, you need to decide which of the HTTP methods you want to use. Table 4-1 shows the meaning of each HTTP method when applied to the "playlists" resource of a particular user. In general, the GET method is used to fetch information about a resource or its children, the PUT method is used to replace an entire resource or a list by providing a replacement, POST is used to update a resource or add an entry, and DELETE is used to remove objects.

Whenever you create a new playlist using the POST request to /playlists/324 resource, you create a new playlist for user 324. The newly created list also becomes available via GET requests sent to the same resource as /playlists/324 is a parent resource for user's playlists. Table 4-2 shows how you could interact with the

Example URL: http://example.org/playlists/324

HTTP Method	Resulting Behavior
GET	Fetch list of URLs of playlists created by the user 324
PUT	Replace entire collection of playlists for that user (you submit a collection of lists)
POST	Create a new list by posting the name of the list
DELETE	Delete all lists of user 324

Table 4-1   *HTTP Methods Available for the Playlists Resource*

Example URL: http://example.org/playlists/324/my-favs	
HTTP Method	**Resulting Behavior**
GET	Fetch list of URLs of all the songs that were added to "my-favs" list by user 324
PUT	Replace entire "my-favs" playlist (you submit a collection of song URLs)
POST	Add a song to the playlist (you submit the URL of the song to be added to "my-favs")
DELETE	Delete an entire "my-favs" playlist

Table 4-2   *HTTP Methods Available for the Selected Playlist Resource*

/playlists/324/my-favs resource representing a custom music playlist called "my-favs" created by the user 324.

The API could also expose additional resources—each representing a song, an album, or an artist—to allow clients to fetch additional metadata. As you can see in Table 4-3, not all methods have to be supported by each resource, as in some cases there may be no way to perform a certain operation. Table 4-3 shows how you could manage individual songs in users' playlists.

REST services do not have to use JSON, but it is a de facto standard on the Web. It became popular due to its simplicity, compact form, and better readability than XML. Listing 4-1 shows how a web service response might look when you requested a playlist entry using a GET method.

Example URL: http://example.org/playlists/324 /my-favs/41121	
HTTP Method	**Resulting Behavior**
GET	Fetch metadata of a playlist entry (that could be author, streaming URL, length, or genre)
PUT	Add song 41121 to the "my-favs" list if not present yet
POST	**Not supported for this endpoint**
DELETE	Remove song 41121 from the playlist

Table 4-3   *HTTP Methods Available for Playlist Member Resource*

Listing 4-1   *Response to GET http://example.org/playlists/324/my-favs/678632*

```
{
    "SongID": "678632",
    "Name": "James Arthur - Young",
    "AlbumURL": "http://example.org/albums/53944",
    "AlbumName": "Unknown",
    "ArtistURL": "http://example.org/artists/1176",
    "ArtistName": "James Arthur",
    "Duration": "165"
}
```

If you wanted to compare REST to SOAP, there are a few important things that stand out. First of all, since you only have four HTTP methods to work with, the structure of REST web services is usually predictable, which also makes it easy to work with. Once you have seen a few REST services, learning to use a new REST API becomes a quick and simple task. If you compare it to SOAP service development, you will find that every web service uses a different set of conventions, standards, and ws-* specifications, making it more challenging to integrate.

From the web service publishers' perspective, REST is more lightweight than SOAP because all you need to do is create an online wiki with definitions of resources, HTTP methods applicable to each resource, and some request/response examples showing the data model. You can implement the actual REST resources using any web stack, as very little functionality needs to be supported by the REST framework (or a container). It's basically just an HTTP server with a routing mechanism to map URL patterns to your code. An additional benefit of REST over SOAP is that you will not have to manage the ever-more-complex API contract artifacts like WSDL and XSD files.

From a client point of view, integration with REST service has both drawbacks and benefits. Clients will not be able to auto-generate the client code or discover the web service behavior, which is a drawback. But at the same time, REST services are much less strict, allowing nonbreaking changes to be released to the server side without the need to recompile and redeploy the clients. Another common way to go around the problem of discoverability is for the service provider to build and share client libraries for common languages. This way, client code needs to be written only once and then can be reused by multiple customers/partners. Obviously, this approach puts more burden on the service provider, but allows you to reduce onboarding friction and create even better abstraction than auto-generated code would.

From a security point of view, REST services are much less sophisticated than SOAP. To allow authorized access to REST resources, web services usually require authentication to be performed before using the API. The client would first authenticate (often using OAuth 2) and then provide the authentication token in HTTP headers of each consecutive request. REST services also depend on transport layer security provided by HTTPS (HTTP over TLS Transport Layer Security) rather than implementing their own message encryption mechanisms. These tradeoffs make REST simpler to implement across web development platforms, but it also makes it harder to integrate with enterprises where you need advanced features like exactly-once delivery semantics.

From a scalability point of view, an important benefit of REST web services like the example discussed earlier in this section is that it is stateless and all public operations performed using the GET method can be cached transparently by HTTP caches. The URL of the REST request is all that is needed to route the request, so GET requests can be cached by any HTTP cache between the client and the service. That allows traffic for the most popular resources to be offloaded onto reverse proxies, significantly reducing the load put on your web services and data stores.

As you can probably see, REST is not clearly better than SOAP; it does not replace or deprecate SOAP either—it is just an alternative. From an enterprise perspective, REST may not be mature, strict, and feature rich enough. From a startup perspective, SOAP may be too difficult, strict, and cumbersome to work with. It really depends on the details of your application and your integration needs. Having said that, if all you need is to expose a web service to your mobile clients and some third-party websites, REST is probably a better way to go if you are a web startup, as it is much easier to get started with and it integrates better with web technologies no matter what stack you and your clients are developing on.

Since we have discussed types of web services and different approaches to designing them, let's now spend some time looking at how to scale them.

Scaling REST Web Services

To be able to scale your web services layer, you will most often depend on two scalability techniques described in Chapter 2. You will want to slice your web services layer into smaller functional pieces, and you will also want to scale by adding clones. Well-designed REST web services will allow you to use both of these techniques.

Keeping Service Machines Stateless

Similar to the front-end layer of your application, you need to carefully deal with application state in your web services. The most scalable approach is to make all of your web service machines stateless. That means you need to push all of the shared state out of your web service machines onto shared data stores like object caches, databases, and message queues. Making web service machines stateless gives you a few important advantages:

▶ You can distribute traffic among your web service machines on a per-request basis. You can deploy a load balancer between your web services and their clients, and each request can be sent to any of the available web service machines. Being able to distribute requests in a round-robin fashion allows for better load distribution and more flexibility.

▶ Since each web service request can be served by any of the web service machines, you can take service machines out of the load balancer pool as soon as they crash. Most of the modern load balancers support heartbeat checks to make sure that web service machines serving the traffic are available. As soon as a machine crashes or experiences some other type of failure, the load balancer will remove that host from the load-balancing pool, reducing the capacity of the cluster, but preventing clients from timing out or failing to get responses.

▶ By having stateless web service machines, you can restart and decommission servers at any point in time without worrying about affecting your clients. For example, if you want to shut down a server for maintenance, you need to take that machine out of the load balancer pool. Most load balancers support graceful removal of hosts, so new connections from clients are not sent to that server any more, but existing connections are not terminated to prevent client-side errors. After removing the host from the pool, you need to wait for all of your open connections to be closed by your clients, which can take a minute or two, and then you can safely shut down the machine without affecting even a single web service request.

▶ Similar to decommissioning, you will be able to perform zero-downtime updates of your web services. You can roll out your changes to one server at a time by taking it out of rotation, upgrading, and then putting it back into rotation. If your software does not allow you to run two different versions at the same time, you can deploy to an alternative stack and switch all of the traffic at once on the load balancer level. No matter what way you choose, stateless web services mean easy maintenance.

▶ By removing all of the application state from your web services, you will be able to scale your web services layer by simply adding more clones. All you need to do is add more machines to the load balancer pool to be able to support more concurrent connections, perform more network I/O, and compute more responses (CPU time). The only assumption here is that your data persistence layer needs to be able to scale horizontally, but we will cover that in Chapter 5.

▶ If you are using a cloud hosting service that supports auto-scaling load balancers like Amazon Elastic Load Balancer or Azure Load Balancer, you can implement auto-scaling of your web services cluster in the same way that you did for your front end. Any time a machine crashes, the load balancer will replace it with a new instance, and any time your servers become too busy, it will spin up additional instances to help with the load.

As you can see, keeping web service machines stateless provides a lot of benefits in terms of both scalability and high availability of your system. The only type of state that is safe to keep on your web service machines are cached objects, which do not need to be synchronized or invalidated in any way. By definition, cache is disposable and can be rebuilt at any point in time, so server failure does not cause any data loss. I will discuss caching in more detail in Chapter 6. Any solution that requires consistency to be propagated across your web service machines will increase your latencies or lead to availability issues. To be sure you don't run into these issues, it is safest to allow your web service machines to store only cached objects that expire based on their absolute Time to Live property. Such objects can be stored in isolation until they expire without the need for your web services to talk to each other.

Any time you need to store any user state on web services, you should look for alternative ways of persisting or distributing that information. Figure 4-5 shows how a stateless service communicates with external data stores, caches, and message queues to get access to persistent data. It is an implementation detail of each of the state-handling components to decide where the state should be persisted. Each of these external persistence stores can be implemented using different technologies suitable for a particular use case, or they could all be satisfied by a single data store.

When building stateless web services, you are going to meet a few common use cases where you will need to share some state between your web service machines.

The first use case is related to security, as your web service is likely going to require clients to pass some authentication token with each web service request.

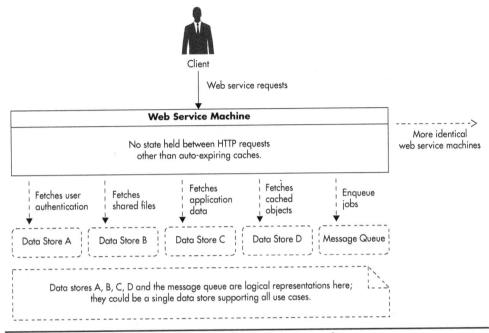

Figure 4-5   *Application state pushed out of web service machines*

That token will have to be validated on the web service side, and client permissions will have to be evaluated in some way to make sure that the user has access to the operation they are attempting to perform. You could cache authentication and authorization details directly on your web service machines, but that could cause problems when changing permissions or blocking accounts, as these objects would need to expire before new permissions could take effect. A better approach is to use a shared in-memory object cache and have each web service machine reach out for the data needed at request time. If not present, data could be fetched from the original data store and placed in the object cache. By having a single central copy of each cached object, you will be able to easily invalidate it when users' permissions change. Figure 4-6 shows how authorization information is being fetched from a shared in-memory object cache. I will discuss object caches in more detail in Chapter 6; for now, let's just say that object cache allows you to map any key (like an authentication token) to an object (like a serialized permissions array).

Another common problem when dealing with stateless web services is how to support resource locking. As I mentioned in Chapter 3, you can use distributed

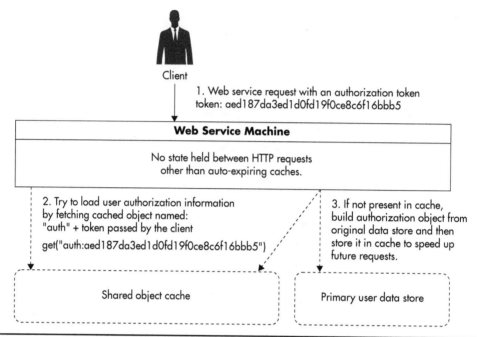

Client

1. Web service request with an authorization token
token: aed187da3ed1d0fd19f0ce8c6f16bbb5

Web Service Machine

No state held between HTTP requests
other than auto-expiring caches.

2. Try to load user authorization information
by fetching cached object named:
"auth" + token passed by the client

get("auth:aed187da3ed1d0fd19f0ce8c6f16bbb5")

3. If not present in cache,
build authorization object from
original data store and then
store it in cache to speed up
future requests.

Shared object cache

Primary user data store

Figure 4-6   *Authorization information fetched from shared object cache*

lock systems like Zookeeper or even build your own simple lock service using a
data store of your choice. To make sure your web services scale well, you should
avoid resource locks for as long as possible and look for alternative ways to
synchronize parallel processes.

Distributed locking is challenging, as each lock requires a remote call and
creates an opportunity for your service to stall or fail. This, in turn, increases your
latency and reduces the number of parallel clients that your web service can serve.
Instead of resource locks, you can sometimes use optimistic concurrency control
where you check the state before the final update rather than acquiring locks.
You can also consider message queues as a way to decouple components and
remove the need for resource locking in the first place (I will discuss queues and
asynchronous processing in more detail in Chapter 7).

HINT

*If you decide to use locks, it is important to acquire them in a consistent order to prevent
deadlocks. For example, if you are locking two user accounts to transfer funds between them,
make sure you always lock them in the same order, such as the account with an alphanumerically
lower account number gets locked first. By using that simple trick, you can prevent deadlocks from
happening and thus increase availability of your service.*

If none of these techniques work for you and you need to use resource locks, it is important to strike a balance between having to acquire a lot of fine-grained locks and having coarse locks that block access to large sets of data. When you acquire a lot of fine-grained locks, you increase latency, as you keep sending requests to the distributed locks service. By having many fine-grained locks, you also risk increasing the complexity and losing clarity as to how locks are being acquired and from where. Different parts of the code acquiring many different locks is a recipe for deadlocks. On the other hand, if you use few coarse locks, you may reduce the latency and risk of deadlocks, but you can hurt your concurrency at the same time, as multiple web service threads can be blocked waiting on the same resource lock. There is no clear rule of thumb here—it is just important to keep the tradeoffs in mind.

> ### HINT
>
> *The key to scalability and efficient resource utilization is to allow each machine to work as independently as possible. For a machine to be able to make progress (perform computation or serve requests), it should depend on as few other machines as possible. Locks are clearly against that concept, as they require machines to talk to each other or to an external system. By using locks, all of your machines become interdependent. If one process becomes slow, anyone else waiting for their locks becomes slow. When one feature breaks, all other features may break. You can use locks in your scheduled batch jobs, crons, and queue workers, but it is best to avoid locks in the request–response life cycle of your web services to prevent availability issues and increase concurrency.*

The last challenge that you can face when building a scalable stateless web service is application-level transactions. Transactions can become difficult to implement, especially if you want to expose transactional guarantees in your web service contract and then coordinate higher-level distributed transactions on top of these services.

A *distributed transaction* is a set of internal service steps and external web service calls that either complete together or fail entirely. It is similar to database transactions, and it has the same motivation—either all of the changes are applied together to create a consistent view of the world, or all of the modifications need to be rolled back to pretend that transaction was never initiated. Distributed transactions have been a subject of study for many decades, and in simple words they are very difficult to scale and coordinate without sacrificing high availability. The most common method of implementing distributed transactions is the 2 Phase Commit (2PC) algorithm.

An example of a distributed transaction would be a web service that creates an order within an online shop. Figure 4-7 shows how such a distributed transaction could be executed. In this example, the OrderService endpoint depends on PaymentService and FulfillmentService. Failure of any of these web services causes OrderService to become unavailable; in addition, all of the collaborating services must maintain persistent connections and application resources for the duration of the transaction to allow rollback in case any components refuse to commit the transaction.

Distributed transactions using 2PCs are notorious for scalability and availability issues. They become increasingly difficult to perform as the number of services involved increases and more resources need to be available throughout the time of the transaction; in addition, the chance of failure increases with each new service. As a simple rule of thumb, I recommend staying away from distributed transactions and consider alternatives instead.

The first alternative to distributed transactions is to not support them at all. It may sound silly, but most startups can live with this type of tradeoff in favor of development speed, availability, and scalability benefits. For example, in a social media website, if you liked someone's update and a part of your action did not propagate to the search index, users would not be able to search for that specific

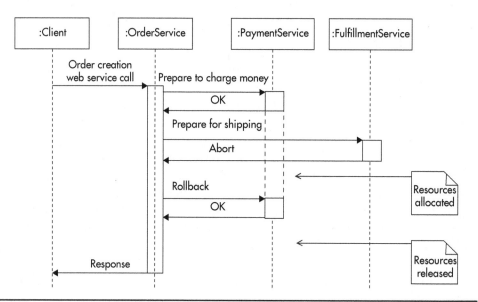

Figure 4-7 *Distributed transaction failure*

update in your event stream. Since the core of your system functionality is not compromised, your company may be fine with such a minor inconsistency in return for the time saved developing it and the costs incurred while trying to scale and maintain the solution.

The second alternative to distributed transactions is to provide a mechanism of compensating transaction. A *compensating transaction* can be used to revert the result of an operation that was issued as part of a larger logical transaction that has failed. Going back to the online store example, your OrderService could issue a request to a PaymentService and then another request to FulfillmentService. Each of these requests would be independent (without underlying transactional support). In case of success, nothing special needs to happen. In case of PaymentService failure, the OrderServcice would simply abort so that FulfillmentService would not receive any requests. Only in the case of PaymentService returning successfully and then FulfillmentService failing would OrderService need to issue an additional PaymentService call to ensure a refund for the previously processed payment. Figure 4-8 shows how such an optimistic approach could be executed.

The benefit of this approach is that web services do not need to wait for one another; they do not need to maintain any state or resources for the duration of the overarching transaction either. Each of the services responds to a single call

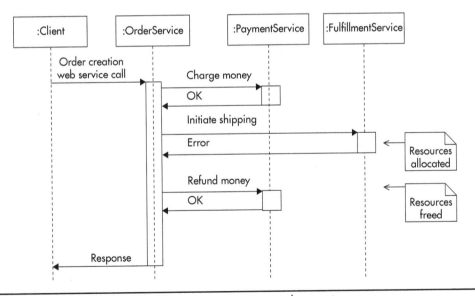

Figure 4-8   *Compensating transaction to correct partial execution*

in isolation. Only the coordinating web service (here the OrderService) becomes responsible for ensuring data consistency among web services. In addition, the compensating transaction can often be processed asynchronously by adding a message into a queue without blocking the client code.

In all cases, I would first question whether transactions or even locking is necessary. In a startup environment, any complexity like this adds to the overall development and support time. If you can get away with something simpler, like making your application handle failures gracefully rather than preventing them at all cost, it is usually a better choice. You should also try to lean back on your data store as much as possible using its transactional support. Most data stores support atomic operations to some degree, which can be used to implement simple "transactions" or exclusive resource access. I will discuss data stores and transactional support in more detail in Chapter 5.

Caching Service Responses

Another important technique of scaling REST web services is to utilize the power of HTTP protocol caching. HTTP caching is a powerful scalability technique for web applications. Being able to apply the same knowledge, skills, and technologies to scale your web services makes HTTP caching so much more valuable. I will discuss HTTP caching in much more detail in Chapter 6, but let's quickly discuss how you can leverage it when building REST web services.

As I mentioned before, REST services utilize all of the HTTP methods (like GET and POST) and when implemented correctly, they should respect the semantics of each of these methods. From a caching perspective, the GET method is the most important one, as GET responses can be cached.

The HTTP protocol requires all GET method calls to be read-only. If a web service request was read-only, then it would not leave anything behind. That in turn would imply that issuing a GET request to a web service or not issuing one would leave the web service in the same state. Since there is no difference between sending a request to a web service or not sending one, responses can be cached by proxies or clients and web service calls can be "skipped" by returning a response from the cache rather than asking the web service for the response.

To take advantage of HTTP caching, you need to make sure that all of your GET method handlers are truly read-only. A GET request to any resource should not cause any state changes or data updates.

A good example of how web applications used to notoriously break this property of the GET method was by using the GET method for state changes. In the early 2000s, it was common to see web applications make changes to the database as a result of a GET request. For example, you would be able to unsubscribe from a mailing list by issuing a GET request to a URL like http://example.com/subscribe?email=artur@ejsmont.org. It might be convenient for the developers, but it would obviously change the state of the application, and there would be a clear difference between sending such a request and not sending it at all.

Nowadays it is rare to see REST web services that would break this rule in such an obvious way; unfortunately, there are other, more subtle ways to get in trouble. For example, in one of the companies I used to work for, we were unable to leverage HTTP caching on our front-end web applications because business intelligence and advertising teams depended on the web server logs to generate their reports and calculate revenue sharing. That meant that even if our web applications were implementing GET methods correctly and all of our GET handlers were read-only, we could not add a layer of caching proxies in front of our web cluster, as it would remove a large part of the incoming traffic, reducing the log entries and skewing the reports.

Another subtle way in which you can break the semantics of GET requests is by using local object caches on your web service machines. For example, in an e-commerce web application you might call a web service to fetch details of a particular product. Your client would issue a GET request to fetch the data. This request would then be routed via a load balancer to one of the web service machines. That machine would load data from the data store, populate its local object cache with the result, and then return a response to the client. If product details were updated soon after the cached object was created, another web service machine might end up with a different version of the product data in its cache. Although both GET handlers were read-only, they did affect the behavior of the web service as a whole, since now, depending on which web service machine you connect to, you might see the old or the new product details as each GET request created a snapshot of the data.

Another important aspect to consider when designing a REST API is which resources require authentication and which do not. REST services usually pass authentication details in request headers. These headers can then be used by the web service to verify permissions and restrict access. The problem with authenticated REST endpoints is that each user might see different data based on their permissions. That means the URL is not enough to produce the response for the particular user. Instead, the HTTP cache would need to include the authentication headers when building the caching key. This cache separation is good if your users should see different data, but it is wasteful if they should actually see the same thing.

HINT

You can implement caching of authenticated REST resources by using HTTP headers like Vary: Authorization in your web service responses. Responses with such headers instruct HTTP caches to store a separate response for each value of the Authorization header (a separate cache for each user).

To truly leverage HTTP caching, you want to make as many of your resources public as possible. Making resources public allows you to have a single cached object for each URL, significantly increasing your cache efficiency and reducing the web service load.

For example, if you were building a social music website (like www.grooveshark .com) where users can listen to music and share their playlists, you could make most of your GET handlers public. Would you need to restrict which users can get details of which album, song, artist, or even playlist? Probably not. By making GET methods public, you could ignore user information in your caching layer, thereby reusing objects much more efficiently.

In the early stages of your startup development, you may not need HTTP caching in your web services layer, but it is worth thinking about. HTTP caching is usually implemented in the web services layer in a similar way to how it is done in the front-end layer. To be able to scale using cache, you would usually deploy reverse proxies between your clients and your web service. That can mean a few different things depending on how your web services are structured and how they are used. Figure 4-9 shows how web services are usually deployed with a reverse proxy between web services and the front-end application.

As your web services layer grows, you may end up with a more complex deployment where each of your web services has a reverse proxy dedicated to cache its results. Depending on the reverse proxy used, you may also have load balancers deployed between reverse proxies and web services to distribute the underlying network traffic and provide quick failure recovery. Figure 4-10 shows how such a deployment might look.

The benefit of such configuration is that now every request passes via a reverse proxy, no matter where it originated from. As your web services layer grows and your system evolves towards a service-oriented architecture, you will benefit more from this mindset. Treating each web service independently and all of its clients in the same way no matter if they live in the web services layer or not promotes decoupling and higher levels of abstraction. Let's now discuss in more detail how web service independence and isolation help scalability.

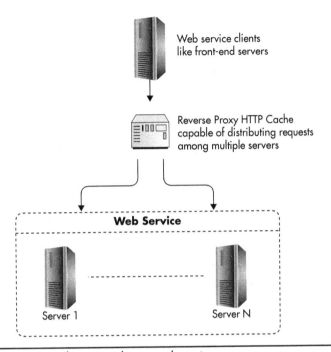

Figure 4-9   *Reverse proxy between clients and services*

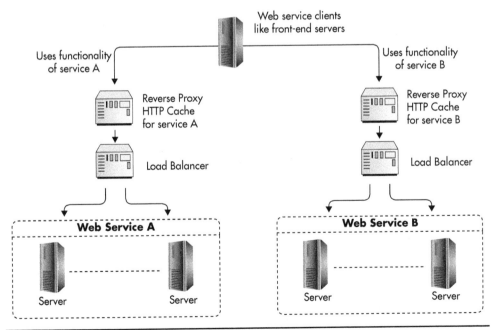

Figure 4-10   *Reverse proxy in front of each web service*

Functional Partitioning

I already mentioned functional partitioning in Chapter 2 as one of the key scalability techniques. At its core, functional partitioning can be thought of as a way to split a large system into a set of smaller, loosely coupled parts so that they can run across more machines rather than having to run on a single, more powerful server. In different areas, functional partitioning may refer to different things. In the context of web services, functional partitioning is a way to split a service into a set of smaller, fairly independent web services, where each web service focuses on a subset of functionality of the overall system.

To explain it better, let's consider an example. If you were to build an e-commerce website, you could build all of the features into a single web service, which would then handle all of the requests. Figure 4-11 shows how your system might look.

Alternatively, you could split the system into smaller, loosely coupled web services, with each one focusing on a narrow area of responsibility. An example of how you could perform such a split is to extract all of the product catalog–related functionality

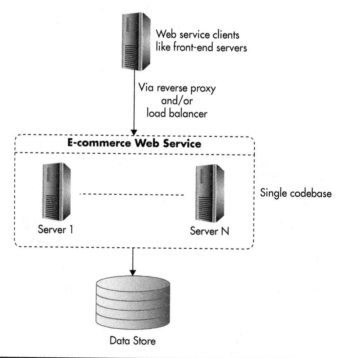

Figure 4-11   *Single service*

and create a separate web service for it called ProductCatalogService. Such a service could allow creation, management, and searching for products; their descriptions; prices; and classifications. In a similar way, you could then extract all of the functionality related to the users, such as managing their accounts, updating credit card details, and printing details of past orders, and create a separate UserProfileService.

Rather than having a single large and potentially closely coupled web service, you would end up with two smaller, more focused, and more independent web services: ProductCatalogService and UserProfileService. This would usually lead to decoupling their infrastructures, their databases, and potentially their engineering teams. In a nutshell, this is what functional partitioning is all about: looking at a system, isolating subsets of functionality that are closely related, and extracting that subset into an independent subsystem.

Figure 4-12 shows how these web services might look. The benefit of functional partitioning is that by having two independent subsystems, you could give them at least twice as much hardware, which can be helpful, especially in the data

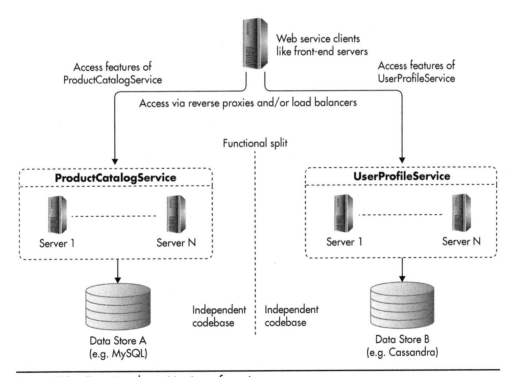

Figure 4-12 *Functional partitioning of services*

layer and especially when you use classical relational database engines, which are difficult to scale.

Since you perform functional partitioning by grouping closely related functionality, there are few dependencies between newly created web services. It may happen that a user-related service refers to some products in the product catalog or that some statistics in a product catalog are derived from the user service data, but most of the time, development and changes can be made in isolation, affecting only one of the services. That allows your technology team to grow, as no one needs to know the entire system any more to be able to make changes, and teams can take ownership of one or more web services but do not need to work on the entire codebase.

Another important effect of functional partitioning is that each of these web services can now be scaled independently. When we think about the ProductCatalogService, it will probably receive substantially more read requests than data updates, as every search and every page view will need to load the data about some products. The UserProfileService, on the other hand, will most likely have a completely different access pattern. Users will only ever want to access their own data (which can help in indexing and distributing the data efficiently), and there may be more writes, as you may want to keep track of which users viewed which products. Finally, your data set may be orders of magnitude larger, as the number of users usually grows faster than the number of products in an online store.

All of these differences in access patterns result in different scalability needs and very different design constraints that apply to each of the services. Does it make sense to use the same caching for both of the services? Does it make sense to use the same type of data store? Are both services equally critical to the business, and is the nature of the data they store the same? Do you need to implement both of these vastly different web services using the same technology stack? It would be best if you could answer "no" to these questions. By having separate web services, you keep more options open; you allow yourself to use the best tool for the job and scale according to the needs of each web service rather than being forced to apply the same pattern across the board.

It may not be necessary in small early-phase startups, but as your system grows and you begin to functionally partition your web services layer, you move closer to the service-oriented architecture, where web services are first-class citizens and where single responsibility, encapsulation, and decoupling are applied on a higher level of abstraction. Rather than on a class or component level, you apply the same design principles on the web service level to allow flexibility, reuse, and maintainability of the overall system.

The main challenge that may be an outcome of performing functional partitioning too early or of creating too many partitions is when new use cases arise that require a combination of data and features present in multiple web services. Going back to our e-commerce example, if you had to create a new RecommendationService, you might realize that it depends on the majority of product catalog data and user profile data to build user-specific recommendation models. In such a case, you may end up having much more work than if both of these services shared a single data store and a single codebase because now RecommendationService will need to integrate with two other web services and treat them as independent entities. Although service integrations may be challenging, functional partitioning is a very important scalability technique.

Summary

Well-designed and well-structured web services can help you in many ways. They can have a positive impact on scalability, on the cost of long-term maintenance, and on the local simplicity of your system, but it would be irresponsible to say that they are a must-have or even that every application can benefit from having a web services layer. Young startups work under great uncertainty and tremendous time pressure, so you need to be more careful not to overengineer and not to waste precious time developing too much upfront. If you need services to integrate with third parties or to support mobile clients, build them from the start, but service-oriented architecture and web services begin to truly shine once your tech team grows above the size of one or two agile teams (more than 10 to 20 engineers).

I encourage you to study more on web services[46,51] on REST and modern approaches to building web services,[20] as well as on SOAP[31] and on service-oriented architecture patterns.

Building scalable web services can be done relatively simply by pushing all of the application state out of the web service machines and caching aggressively. I am sure you are already thinking, "So where do we store all of this state?" or "How do we ensure that we can scale these components as much as we scaled front-end and web services layers? These are both great questions, and we are about to begin answering them as we approach the most exciting and most challenging area for scalability, which is scalability of the data layer.

CHAPTER 5

Data Layer

T raditionally, companies scaled their databases vertically by buying stronger servers, adding random access memory (RAM), installing more hard drives, and hoping that the database engine they used would be able to utilize these resources and scale to their needs. This worked in most cases, and only the largest and most successful companies needed horizontal scalability. All of that changed with the rise of the Internet, social networks, and the globalization of the software industry, as the amounts of data and concurrent users that systems need to support have skyrocketed. Nowadays systems with millions of users and billions of database records are the norm, and software engineers need to have a better understanding of the techniques and tools available to solve these scalability challenges.

In previous chapters we scaled the front-end and web services layers by pushing the state out of our servers so that we could treat them as stateless clones and simply add more servers whenever we needed to scale. Now it is time to tackle the problem of scaling the data layer so that it will be horizontally scalable and so that it will not create a system bottleneck.

Depending on your business needs, required scalability of your application, and your data model, you can use either a traditional relational database engine like MySQL or a more cutting-edge nonrelational data store. Both of these approaches have benefits and drawbacks, and I will try to objectively present both of these as complementary solutions to different application needs. Let's first look at the scalability of relational database engines using the example of a MySQL database.

Scaling with MySQL

MySQL is still the most popular database, and it will take a long time before it becomes irrelevant. Relational databases have been around for decades, and the performance and scalability that can be achieved with MySQL is more than most web startups would ever need. Even though scaling MySQL can be difficult at times and you may need to plan for it from day one, it can be done and dozens of the world's biggest startups are successfully doing it, for example, Facebook,[L35] Tumblr,[L33] and Pintrest.[L31] Let's get started by looking at replication as one of the primary means of scaling MySQL.

Replication

Replication usually refers to a mechanism that allows you to have multiple copies of the same data stored on different machines. Different data stores implement replication in different ways. In the case of MySQL, replication allows you to synchronize the state of two servers, where one of the servers is called a *master* and the other one is called a *slave.* I will discuss different topologies that allow you to synchronize the state of more than two MySQL servers later in this chapter, but the core concept focuses on replicating content between a master and a slave.

When using MySQL replication, your application can connect to a slave to read data from it, but it can modify data only through the master server. All of the data-modifying commands like updates, inserts, deletes, or create table statements must be sent to the master. The master server records all of these statements in a log file called a binlog, together with a timestamp, and it also assigns a sequence number to each statement. Once a statement is written to a binlog, it can then be sent to slave servers.

Figure 5-1 illustrates how statement replication works. First the client connects to the master server and executes a data modification statement. That statement is executed and written to a binlog file. At this stage the master server returns

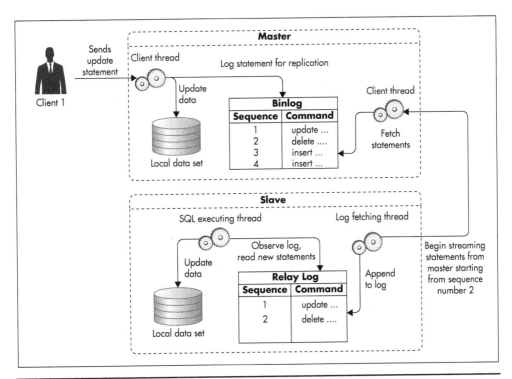

Figure 5-1   *MySQL replication*

a response to the client and continues processing other transactions. At any point in time the slave server can connect to the master server and ask for an incremental update of the master's binlog file. In its request, the slave server provides the sequence number of the last command that it saw. Since all of the commands stored in the binlog file are sorted by sequence number, the master server can quickly locate the right place and begin streaming the binlog file back to the slave server. The slave server then writes all of these statements to its own copy of the master's binlog file, called a relay log. Once a statement is written to the relay log, it is executed on the slave data set, and the offset of the most recently seen command is increased.

An important thing to note here is that MySQL replication is asynchronous. That means that the master server does not wait for slave to get the statements replicated. The master server writes commands to its own binlog, regardless if any slave servers are connected or not. The slave server knows where it left off and makes sure to get the right updates, but the master server does not have to worry about its slaves at all. As soon as a slave server disconnects from the master, the master forgets all about it. The fact that MySQL replication is asynchronous allows for decoupling of the master from its slaves—you can always connect a new slave or disconnect slaves at any point in time without affecting the master.

Because replication is asynchronous and the master does not need to keep track of its slaves, this allows for some interesting topologies. For example, rather than having just a single slave server, you can create multiple slave replicas and distribute read queries among them. In fact, it is a common practice to have two or more slaves for each master server.

Figure 5-2 shows a master server with multiple slave machines. Each of the slave servers keeps track of the last statement that was replicated. They all connect to the master and keep waiting for new events, but they do not interact with each other. Any slave server can be disconnected or connected at any point in time without affecting any other servers.

Having more than one slave machine can be useful for a number of reasons:

► You can distribute read-only statements among more servers, thus sharing the load among more machines. This is scaling by adding clones (explained in Chapter 2) applied to database engines, as you add more copies of the same data to increase your read capacity.

► You can use different slaves for different types of queries. For example, you could use one slave for regular application queries and another slave for slow, long-running reports. By having a separate slave for slow-running queries, you can insulate your application from input/output (I/O)–intensive queries, improving the overall user experience.

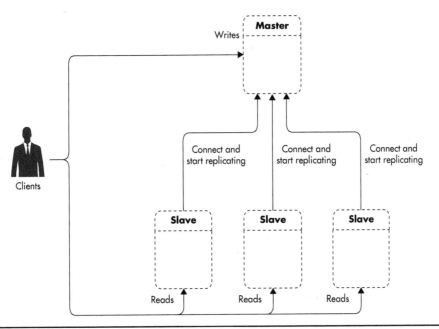

Figure 5-2 *MySQL replication with multiple slaves*

▶ You can use the asynchronous nature of MySQL replication to perform zero-downtime backups. Performing a consistent backup of a slave machine is simple—all you need to do is shut down the MySQL process, copy the data files to your archive location, and start MySQL again. As soon as MySQL starts, it connects to its master and begins catching up on any statements that it might have missed.

▶ If one of your slaves dies, you can simply stop sending requests to that server (taking it out of rotation) until it is rebuilt. Losing a slave is a nonevent, as slaves do not have any information that would not be available via the master or other slaves. MySQL servers do not keep track of each other's availability, so detection of server failure must be performed on the database client side. You can either implement it in your application logic or use a smart proxy/ load balancer that can detect slave failures.

One of the main reasons why people use replication in MySQL and other data stores is to increase availability by reducing the time needed to replace the broken database. When using MySQL replication, you have two main failure scenarios that you need to be ready to recover from: failure of a slave and failure of a master.

Slave failures are usually not a big concern, as they can be handled quickly. All you need to do is stop sending queries to the broken slave to end the outage. You may still have reduced capacity, but the availability of the system is restored as soon as you take the slave server out of rotation. At a later point in time you can rebuild the slave server and add it back into rotation.

> ### HINT
>
> *It is important to remember that rebuilding a MySQL slave is a manual process, and it requires a full backup of the database to be taken from the master or one of the remaining slaves. MySQL does not allow you to bootstrap a slave from an empty database. To be able to start a slave and continue replicating statements from the master, you need a consistent backup of all the data and a sequence number of the last statement that was executed on the database before taking the backup. Once you have a backup and a sequence number, you can start the slave and it will begin catching up with the replication backlog. The older the backup and the busier the database, the longer it will take for the new slave to catch up. In busy databases, it can take hours before a slave manages to replicate all data updates and can be added back into rotation.*

Rebuilding slaves can seem like a lot of trouble, but a scenario that is even more complex to recover from is master failure. MySQL does not support automatic failover or any mechanism of automated promotion of slave to a master. If your master fails, you have a lot of work ahead of you. First, you need to find out which of your slaves is most up to date (which slave has the highest statement sequence number). Then you need to reconfigure it to become a master. If you have more than one slave, you need to make sure that they are identical to your new master by either rebuilding them all from the backup of the new master or by manually tweaking binlog and relay log files to align all servers to the exact same state. Finally, you need to reconfigure all remaining slaves to replicate from the new master. Depending on the details of your configuration, this process may be a bit simpler or a bit more complicated, but it is still a nightmare scenario for most engineers.

The difficulty of recovering from master failure brings us to another interesting replication deployment topology called master-master. In this case you have two servers that could accept writes, as Master A replicates from Master B and Master B replicates from Master A. MySQL replication allows for that type of circular replication, as each statement written to a master's binlog includes the name of the server it was originally written to. This way, any statement that is sent to Server A is replicated to Server B, but then it does not replicate back to Server A, as Server A knows that it already executed that statement.

Figure 5-3 shows what master-master deployment looks like. All writes sent to Master A are recorded in its binlog. Master B replicates these writes to its relay log and executes them on its own copy of the data. Master B writes these statements to its own binlog as well in case other slaves want to replicate them. In a similar way, Master A replicates statements from Master B's binlog by appending them to its own relay log, executing all new statements, and then logging them to its own binlog.

This topology is more complicated, but it can be used for faster master failover and more transparent maintenance. In case of Master A failure, or any time you need to perform long-lasting maintenance, your application can be quickly reconfigured to direct all writes to Master B.

Figure 5-4 shows how you can create two identical server groups with Master A and Master B each having an equal number of slaves. By having the same number of slaves, your application can be running with equal capacity using either of the groups. That, in turn, means that in case of Master A failure, you can quickly fail over to use Master B and its slaves instead.

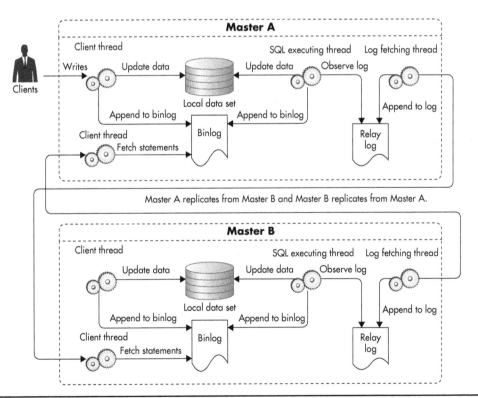

Figure 5-3 *MySQL master-master replication*

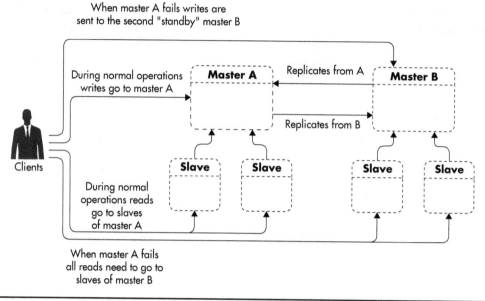

Figure 5-4 *MySQL master-master failover*

Having identical groups of servers in a master-master configuration allows you to switch between groups with minimal downtime. For example, if you need to upgrade your software or hardware on your master databases, you may need to shut down each server for an hour at a time to do the work, but you may be able to do it with just a few seconds of application downtime. To achieve that, you would upgrade one server group at a time. First, you upgrade the standby Master B and its slaves. Then, you stop all the writes coming into the Master A database, which begins the downtime. Then you wait just long enough for all the writes to replicate from Master A to Master B. You can then safely reconfigure your application to direct all writes to Master B, as it has already replicated all previous commands and there is no risk of conflicts or update collisions. By reconfiguring the application, you end the downtime, since reads and writes are accepted again. Finally, you can perform maintenance on Master A and its slaves. Figure 5-5 shows the timing of each of the steps and the total downtime.

Although in theory, it is also possible to write to both servers at the same time, I would advise against it due to a much higher complexity and risk of data inconsistency. It is not safe to simply start sending writes to either of the masters without additional configuration and use case analysis. For example, if you wanted to send writes to both masters at the same time, you would need to use

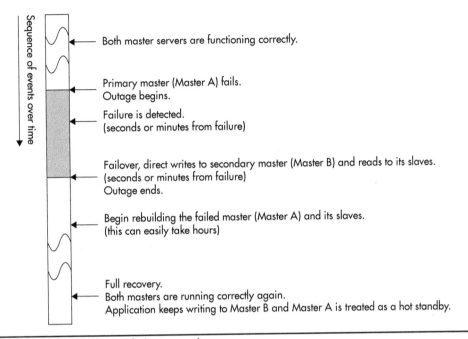

Sequence of events over time

Both master servers are functioning correctly.

Primary master (Master A) fails.
Outage begins.

Failure is detected.
(seconds or minutes from failure)

Failover, direct writes to secondary master (Master B) and reads to its slaves.
(seconds or minutes from failure)
Outage ends.

Begin rebuilding the failed master (Master A) and its slaves.
(this can easily take hours)

Full recovery.
Both masters are running correctly again.
Application keeps writing to Master B and Master A is treated as a hot standby.

Figure 5-5   *Maintenance failover timeline*

auto-increment and UUID() in a specific way to make sure you never end up with the same sequence number being generated on both masters at the same time. You can also run into trouble with data inconsistency. For example, updating the same row on both masters at the same time is a classic race condition leading to data becoming inconsistent between masters. Figure 5-6 shows a sequence of events leading to both master servers having inconsistent data.

Although master-master replication can be useful in increasing the availability of your system, it is not a scalability tool. Even if you took all the precautions and managed to write to both masters at the same time, you would not be able to scale using this technique. There are two main reasons why master-master replication is not a viable scalability technique:

▶ *Both masters have to perform all the writes.* The fact that you distribute writes to both master servers from your application layer does not mean that each of them has less to do. In fact, each of the masters will have to execute every single write statement either coming from your application or coming via the replication. To make it even worse, each master will need to perform

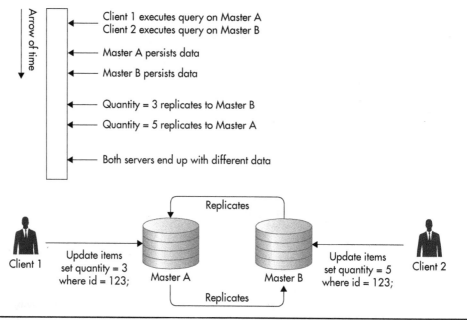

Figure 5-6 *Update collision*

additional I/O to write replicated statements into the relay log. Since each master is also a slave, it writes replicated statements to a separate relay log first and then executes the statement, causing additional disk I/O.

▶ *Both masters have the same data set size.* Since both masters have the exact same data set, both of them will need more memory to hold ever-growing indexes and to keep enough of the data set in cache. As your data set grows, each of your masters needs to grow with it (by being scaled vertically).

In addition to master-master replication, you can use MySQL ring replication, where instead of two master servers, you chain three or more masters together to create a ring. Although that might seem like a great idea, in practice, it is the worst of the replication variants discussed so far. Figure 5-7 shows what that topology looks like.

Not only does ring replication not help you scale writes, as all masters need to execute all the write statements, but it also reduces your availability and makes failure recovery much more difficult. By having more masters, statistically, you

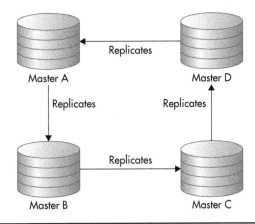

Figure 5-7 *MySQL ring replication*

have a higher chance of one of them failing; at the same time, ring topology makes it more difficult to replace servers and recover from failures correctly.[136]

> *Replication lag* is a measurement of how far behind a particular slave is from its master. Any time you execute a write on the master, your change becomes visible as soon as the transaction commits. Although data is already updated on the master and can be read from there, it cannot be seen on the slave until the statement is replicated and executed there as well. When hosting your system on a decent network (or cloud), your replication lag should be less than a second. That means that any time you write to the master, you should expect your read replicas to have the same change less than a second later.

Another interesting fact is that ring replication significantly increases your replication lag, as each write needs to jump from master to master until it makes a full circle. For example, if the replication lag of each of your servers was 500 ms, your total lag would be 1.5 s in a four-node configuration, as each statement needs to be replicated three times before being visible to all of the servers.

HINT

It is worth pointing out that any master-master or ring topology makes your system much more difficult to reason about, as you lose a single source of truth semantics. In regular master-slave replication, you can always query the master to get the most recent data. There is no way that the master would be behind or that you would read some stale data, with writes being in flight between servers, as all the writes are sent by the application to the same machine. That allows you to be sure that any time you ask the master for data, you will get the most recent version of it. By allowing writes to be sent to multiple masters at the same time, with asynchronous replication in between them, you lose this kind of consistency guarantee. There is no way for you to query the database for the most recent data, as writes propagate asynchronously from each server. No matter which server you ask, there may be an update on its way from the master that cannot be seen yet. That, in turn, prevents the overall consistency of your system. I will discuss the nature and challenges of this type of consistency (called eventual consistency) later in this chapter.

Replication Challenges

The most important thing to remember when scaling using replication is that it is only applicable to scaling reads. When using replication, you will not be able to scale writes of your MySQL database. No matter what topology you use, replication is not the way to scale writes, as all of your writes need to go through a single machine (or through each machine in case of multimaster deployments). Depending on your deployment, it may still make sense to use replication for high availability and other purposes, but it will not help you scale write-heavy applications.

On the other hand, replication is an excellent way of scaling read-heavy applications. If your application does many more reads than writes, replication is a good way to scale. Instead of a single server having to respond to all the queries, you can have many clones sharing the load. You can keep scaling read capacity by simply adding more slaves, and if you ever hit the limit of how many slaves your master can handle, you can use multilevel replication to further distribute the load and keep adding even more slaves. By adding multiple levels of replication, your replication lag increases, as changes need to propagate through more servers, but you can increase read capacity, which may be a reasonable tradeoff. Figure 5-8 shows how you can deploy multiple levels of slaves to further scale the read capacity.

Another thing worth knowing is that replication is a great way to scale the number of concurrently reading clients and the number of read queries per second, but it is not a way to scale the overall data set size. For example, if you wanted to scale your database to support 5,000 concurrent read connections,

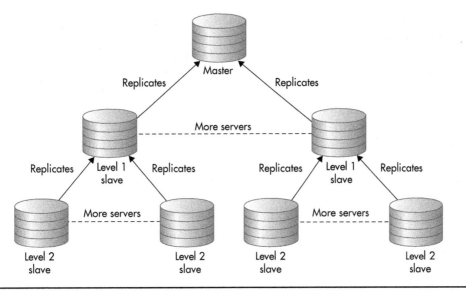

Figure 5-8 *Multilevel MySQL replication*

then adding more slaves or caching more aggressively could be a good way to go. On the other hand, if you wanted to scale your active data set to 5TB, replication would not help you get there. The reason why replication does not help in scaling the data set size is that all of the data must be present on each of the machines. The master and each of its slaves need to have all of the data. That, in turn, means that a single server needs to write, read, index, and search through all of the data contained in your database.

> *Active data set* is all of the data that must be accessed frequently by your application. It is usually difficult to measure the size of the active data set precisely because data stores do not report this type of metric directly. A simple way of thinking about the active data set is to imagine all of the data that your database needs to read from or write to disk within a time window, like an hour, a day, or a week.

It is important to think about your data access patterns and the active data set size, because having too much active data is a common source of scalability issues.

Having a lot of inactive data may increase the size of your database indexes, but if you do not need to access that data repeatedly, it does not put much pressure on your database. Active data, on the other hand, needs to be accessed, so your database can either buffer it in memory or fetch it from disk, which is usually where the bottleneck is. When the active data set is small, the database can buffer most of it (or all of it) in memory. As your active data set grows, your database needs to load more disk blocks because your in-memory buffers are not large enough to contain enough of the active disk blocks. At a certain point, buffers become useless and all that database ends up doing is performing random disk I/O, trying to fetch the disk blocks necessary to complete application requests.

To explain better how an active data set works, let's consider an example. If you had an e-commerce website, you might use tables to store information about each purchase. This type of data is usually accessed frequently right after the purchase and then it becomes less and less relevant as time goes by. Sometimes you may still access older transactions after a few days or weeks to update shipping details or to perform a refund, but after that, the data is pretty much dead except for an occasional report query accessing it. This type of active data set behaves like a time window. It moves with time, but it does not grow aggressively as long as the number of purchases per day does not grow. Figure 5-9 illustrates transactions by their creation time, with data being accessed in the last 48 hours highlighted.

Let's now consider a different example showing an access pattern that could result in an unlimited active data set growth. If you built a website that allowed users to listen to music online, your users would likely come back every day or every week to listen to their music. In such case, no matter how old an account is, the user is still likely to log in and request her playlists on a weekly or daily basis. As the user base grows, the active data set grows, and since there is no natural way of deactivating the data over time, your system needs to be able to sustain the growth of the active data set. I will discuss how to deal with active data set growth later in this chapter, but for now let's remember that replication is not a way to solve this problem.

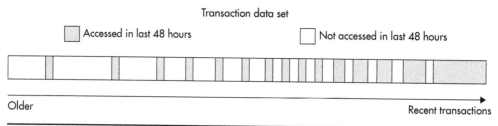

Figure 5-9 *Active and inactive data*

Another thing to remember when working with MySQL replication is that slaves can return stale data. MySQL replication is asynchronous, and any change made on the master needs some time to replicate to its slaves. It is critical to remember that, as you can easily run into timing issues where your code writes to the master and then it performs a read on a slave to fetch the same data. In such a scenario, depending on the replication lag, the delay between requests, and the speed of each server, you may get the freshest data or you may get stale data, as your write may still be replicating to the slave.

During normal operations, the replication lag can be as low as half a second, but it does not mean that you can depend on it to be that low all the time. The reason why replication lag can suddenly increase is that MySQL replication runs as a single thread on slaves. Although the master can process multiple updates in parallel, on slaves, all these statements are executed one at a time. That "gotcha" in MySQL replication is often a source of bugs and outages during database maintenance because a long-running update like an alter table statement blocks replication of all the tables for as long as the statement takes to execute, which can be seconds, minutes, or even hours.

To prevent these timing issues, one approach is to cache the data that has been written on the client side so that you would not need to read the data that you have just written. Alternatively, you can send critical read requests to the master so that they would always result in the most up-to-date data. Finally, you can try to minimize the replication lag to reduce the chance of stale data being read from slaves. For example, to make sure your alter table statements do not block replication, you can issue them on the master with binlog disabled and manually execute them on each slave as well. This way, altering a large table would not block writes to other tables and all servers would end up with the same schema.

It is critical not to underestimate the complexity and cost of MySQL replication, as it can be a serious challenge for less experienced administrators and you need to have a much deeper understanding of MySQL replication and MySQL itself to manage and use replication in a safe manner.

There are many ways in which you can break MySQL replication or end up with inconsistent data. For example, using functions that generate random numbers or executing an update statement with a limit clause may result in a different value written on the master and on its slaves, breaking the consistency of your data. Once your master and your slaves get out of sync, you are in serious trouble, as all of the following update/insert/delete statements may also behave differently on each of the servers because they may be affected by the difference in state. This can result in hard-to-debug problems, ghostlike bugs, and replication repeatedly breaking, as statements execute successfully on the master but then throw errors on the slave, stopping the replication process.

Although some open-source tools like pt-table-checksum or pt-table-sync can help you discover and fix such problems, there is no high-availability autopilot built into MySQL replication. If things break, you are the one who will have to fix them, and it may require a great deal of knowledge, experience, and time to get there.

Considering that managing MySQL replication is fairly involved, it can be a good strategy to use a hosted MySQL solution like Amazon RDS (Amazon Relational Database Service) or Rackspace Cloud Database to reduce the burden. Especially if you work for a young startup and you need to get to market as fast as possible, you may be better off using hosted MySQL rather than learning and doing everything by yourself. Hosted MySQL usually comes with a lot of useful features, such as setting up replication, automated backups, and slave bootstrapping with a click of a button. Some of the providers support more advanced features, such as automated failover to another availability zone, but you may still get into trouble if your replicas get out of sync, so learning more about MySQL would still be needed.

Even though I focused on MySQL replication in this section, a lot of the information covered here applies to other data stores as well. Replication is usually implemented as asynchronous propagation of changes from a single master to one or many slaves. Details of the implementation are usually different, making some of the challenges easier and others harder to overcome, but they all carry the same scalability benefits of distributing read queries among more machines and allowing you to offload slow queries and backups to separate servers. Whether you use replication in MySQL, Redis, MongoDB, or Postgres, you will not be able to scale writes or your data set size using it. Let's now have a look at the second main scalability technique, which is data partitioning, also known as sharding.

Data Partitioning (Sharding)

Data partitioning is one of the three most basic scalability techniques listed in Chapter 2 (next to functional partitioning and scaling by adding clones). The core motivation behind data partitioning is to divide the data set into smaller pieces so that it could be distributed across multiple machines and so that none of the servers would need to deal with the entire data set. By dividing the data set into smaller buckets and assigning each bucket to a single server, servers become independent from one another, as they share nothing (at least in the simple sharding scenario). Without data overlap, each server can make authoritative decisions about data modifications without communication overhead and without affecting availability during partial system failures.

People often refer to data partitioning as *sharding,* and although the exact origin of this term is not clear, some people believe that it originated in the 1990s from Ultima Online. Ultima Online was the first massively multiplayer online role-playing game, and it required so many resources that developers decided to divide the world of the game into isolated, independent servers (also called *shards*). In the world of the game, they explained the existence of these independent parallel worlds using a compelling storyline of a world crystal being shattered, creating alternative realities. Each world was independent, and characters were bound to exist within a single shard without the ability to interact across shards.

Regardless of its origin, sharding can be explained using a metaphor of transporting a sheet of glass. The larger the sheet, the more difficult it is to handle and transport due to its size and weight. As soon as you shatter the glass into small pieces, however, you can transport it more easily. No matter how large the original sheet, you can fill buckets, trucks, or other containers of any size and transport it bit by bit rather than having to deal with it all at once. If the sheet of glass was your data set, then your buckets are servers running your data store, and sharding is the act of breaking the monolithic piece of data into tiny portions so that they can be poured into containers of any size.

Choosing the Sharding Key

The core idea of sharding is to divide the data in some way so that each server would get only a subset of it. At the same time, when you need to access the data to read or write it, you should be able to ask only the server who has the information you need rather than talking to all the servers and trying to figure out who has the data you are interested in. Being able to locate the shard on which the data lives without having to ask all the servers is what sharding keys are used for.

A *Sharding key* is the information that is used to decide which server is responsible for the data that you are looking for. The way a sharding key is used is similar to the way you interact with object caches. To get data out of the cache, you need to know the caching key, as that is the only way to locate the data. A sharding key is similar—to access the data, you need to have the sharding key to find out which server has the data. Once you know which server has the data, you can connect to it and issue your queries.

To illustrate it better, let's consider an example of an e-commerce website again. If you were building a large-scale e-commerce website, you could put all of the user data into a single MySQL database and then host it on a single machine. Figure 5-10 shows how that might look. In this configuration, you do not need to decide which server to talk to, as there is only one server and it contains all of the data.

If you wanted to scale the data size beyond a single server, you could use sharding to distribute it among multiple MySQL database servers. Any time you want to use sharding, you need to find a way to split your data set into independent buckets. For example, since in traditional online stores, users do not need to interact with each other, you could assign each user to one of the shards without sacrificing functionality. By doing this, you can easily distribute your users among many servers, and any time you want to read or write data related to a particular user, you would only need to talk to one of the servers.

Once you decide how to split the data, you then need to select the sharding key. If you shard based on the user, your sharding key would be something that identifies the user, for example, an account ID (also known as a user ID). Once you decide upon the sharding key, you also need to choose an algorithm, which will allow you to map the sharding key value to the actual server number. For the sake of simplicity, let's say that you wanted to have only two shards; in this case, you could allocate all of the users with even user IDs to shard 1 and all of the users with odd user IDs to shard 2. Figure 5-11 shows the process of mapping the user data to the server number.

By performing a split and then selecting the sharding key and a mapping method, your data does not have to live on a single machine any more. Each machine ends up with roughly the same amount of data, as you assign new users to one of the

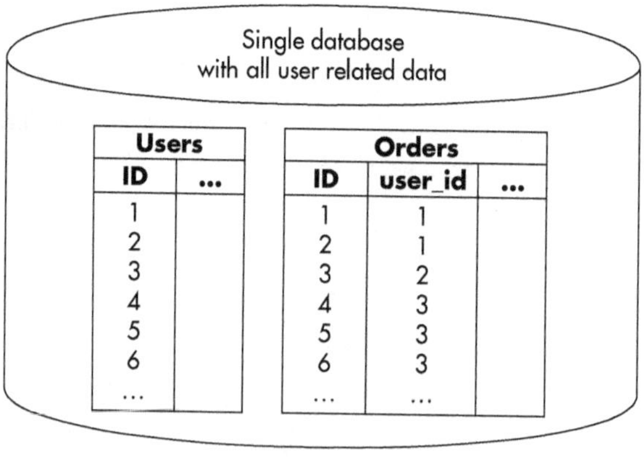

Figure 5-10 *User database without sharding*

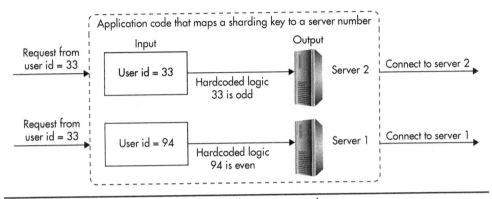

Figure 5-11   *Mapping the sharding key to the server number*

servers based on the user ID. In addition, each piece of data lives on one machine only, making your database servers share nothing and giving them authority over the data that they have.

Figure 5-12 shows how a sharded MySQL database could look. Each user is allocated to a single database server based on the user ID. Any time you want to access a user's data, you would take the user ID and check whether it is odd or even to find out which database server this user belongs to. Once you know the server number, you simply connect to it and perform your database queries as if it was a regular database. In fact, MySQL does not need any special configuration, as it does not know that sharding is applied to the data set. All of the sharding logic lives in your application and the database schema is identical on all of the shards.

Shard 1					Shard 2				
Users		**Orders**			**Users**		**Orders**		
ID	...	ID	user_id	...	ID	...	ID	user_id	...
1		1	1		2		1	2	
3		2	1		4		2	4	
5		3	3		6		3	4	
7		4	3		8		4	4	
9		5	3		10		5	6	
...		6	5		...		6	8	
		...	...				...	...	

Figure 5-12   *User database with sharding*

If you look more closely at Figure 5-12 you may notice that order IDs are not unique across shards. Since IDs are generated using auto_increment and databases do not know anything about one another, you get the same IDs generated on each of the servers. In some cases, this may be acceptable, but if you wanted to have globally unique IDs, you could use auto_increment_increment and auto_increment_offset to make sure that each shard generates different primary keys.

> **HINT**
>
> *Sharding can be implemented in your application layer on top of any data store. All you need to do is find a way to split the data so it could live in separate databases and then find a way to route all of your queries to the right database server. The data store does not need to support sharding for your application to use it, but some data stores provide automatic sharding and data distribution out of the box. I will discuss automatic sharding in more detail later in this chapter.*

I used user ID as the sharding key in this example, as it usually allows you to create many tiny buckets rather than a few large ones. Sharding into a small number of large buckets may not let you distribute the data evenly among multiple machines. For example, if you sharded the data based on the user's country of origin, you would use country_code as your sharding key and then map country_code to a server number. This might look like it gives you the same result, but it does not. If you shard by the country of origin, you are likely to have an uneven distribution of data. Some countries will have a majority of your users and others will have very few, making it harder to ensure equal distribution and load. By splitting your data into large buckets, you can also end up in a situation where one bucket becomes so large that it cannot be handled by a single machine any more. For example, the number of users from the United States can grow beyond the capacity of a single server, defeating the purpose of sharding altogether. Figure 5-13 shows how sharding by country code can cause some servers to be overloaded and others to be underutilized. Although the number of countries is equal, the amount of data is not.

When you perform sharding, you should try to split your data set into buckets of similar size, as this helps to distribute the data evenly among your servers. It is usually not possible to ensure equal size of your data buckets, but as long as your buckets are small and you have a lot of them, your servers will still end up with a pretty good overall data distribution.

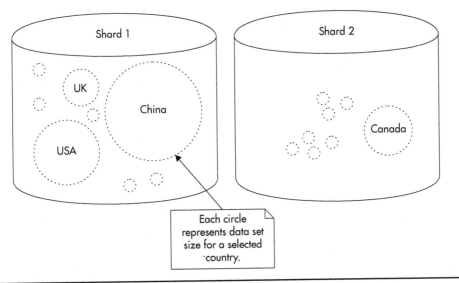

Figure 5-13 *Uneven distribution of data*

Advantages of Sharding

As you can probably already see, the most important advantage of sharding is that when applied correctly, it allows you to scale your database servers horizontally to almost any size.

To have a truly horizontally scalable system, all of your components need to scale horizontally. Without sharding, you are most likely going to hit MySQL scalability limits no matter what you do. Sooner or later, your data size will be too large for a single server to manage or you will get too many concurrent connections for a single server to handle. You are also likely to reach your I/O throughput capacity as you keep reading and writing more data (there is always a limit to how many hard drives you can connect to a single database server).

By using application-level sharding, none of the servers need to have all of the data. This allows you to have multiple MySQL servers, each with a reasonable amount of RAM, hard drives, and central processing units (CPUs) and each of them being responsible for a small subset of the overall data, queries, and read/write throughput. By having multiple servers, you can scale the overall capacity by adding more servers rather than by making each of your servers stronger.

Since sharding splits data into disjointed subsets, you end up with a share-nothing architecture. There is no overhead of communication between servers, and there is no need for cluster-wide synchronization or blocking. Each database server is independent as if it was a regular MySQL instance and it can be managed, optimized, and scaled as a regular MySQL server would be.

Another advantage of sharding is that you can implement it in the application layer and then apply it to any data store, regardless of whether it supports sharding out of the box or not. You can apply sharding to object caches, message queues, nonstructured data stores, or even file systems. Any place that requires lots of data to be persisted, managed, and searched through could benefit from data partitioning to enable scalability.

Challenges of Sharding

Unfortunately, sharding does not come without its costs and challenges. Implementing sharding in your application layer allows you to scale more easily, but it adds a significant amount of work and complexity. Although it might sound like adding a sharding key and routing queries among more machines should be easy to do, in reality, it requires a lot of extra code and makes things much more complex.

One of the most significant limitations that come with application-level sharding is that you cannot execute queries spanning multiple shards. Any time you want to run such a query, you need to execute parts of it on each shard and then somehow merge the results in the application layer. In some cases, that might be easy to do, but in others, it might be prohibitively difficult.

To illustrate it better, let's consider an example. If you had an e-commerce website and you sharded the data across multiple database servers based on the user ID (like we did in previous examples in this chapter), you could easily access data of a particular user, but you would not be able to run queries that span multiple users. If you wanted to find the most popular item in the last seven days, you would need to run your query on each of the shards and then compute the correct result in the application. Even in such a simple scenario, it is very easy to make wrong assumptions and write invalid code, as most of us are not used to working with sharding and disjointed data sets. If all of the data was hosted on a single machine, all you would need to do to get the item with the highest number of sales is run a query similar to Listing 5-1.

Listing 5-1 *Example of a simple GET request*

```
SELECT item_id, SUM(amount) total
FROM orders WHERE order_date > '2014-11-01'
ORDER BY total LIMIT limit 1;
```

Top Sales from Shard A		Top Sales from Shard B	
item_id	Total Sales	item_id	Total Sales
4	13	2	16
5	12	3	14
1	10	5	11
...		...	

Table 5-1   *Summarized Data from Each of the Shards*

With that mind-set, you might assume that all you need to do is run the same query on each of your servers and pick the highest of the values. Unfortunately, that would not guarantee a correct result. If you had two servers and each of them had top sales data, as is shown in Table 5-1, your code would return an incorrect value. Running the query on each of the servers and picking the highest value would result in returning item_id=2, as it had 16 sales on shard B. If you looked at the data more closely, though, you would realize that item_id=5 had a higher overall sales number of 23.

As you can see, dealing with disjointed data sets and trying to execute queries across shards can be tricky. Although Listing 5-1 shows one of the simplest examples imaginable, you may need to fetch a much larger data set from each of the servers and compute the final result in the application layer to guarantee correctness. As your queries become more complex, that can become increasingly difficult, making complex reports a serious challenge.

The term *ACID transaction* refers to a set of transaction properties supported by most relational database engines. A stands for Atomicity, C for Consistency, I for Isolation, and D for Durability. An *atomic* transaction is executed in its entirety. It either completes or is rejected and reverted. *Consistency* guarantees that every transaction transforms the data set from one consistent state to another and that once the transaction is complete, the data conforms to all of the constraints enforced by the data schema. *Isolation* guarantees that transactions can run in parallel without affecting each other. Finally, *durability* guarantees that data is persisted before returning to the client, so that once a transaction is completed it can never be lost, even due to server failure. When people say that a certain data store supports ACID transactions, they mean that each transaction executed by that data store provides all of the ACID guarantees.

Another interesting side effect of distributing data across multiple machines is that you lose the ACID properties of your database as a whole. You can still depend on ACID transactions on each of the shards, but if you needed to make changes across shards, you would lose the ACID properties. Maintaining ACID properties across shards requires you to use distributed transactions, which are complex and expensive to execute (most open-source database engines like MySQL do not even support distributed transactions). For example, if you had to update all of the orders of a particular user, you could do it within the boundaries of a single server, thus taking advantage of ACID transactions. However, if you needed to update all of the orders of a particular item, you would need to send your queries to multiple servers. In such a case, there would be no guarantee that all of them would succeed or all of them would fail. You could successfully execute all of the queries on Shard A, committing the transaction, and then fail to commit your transaction on Shard B. In such a case, you would have no way to roll back queries executed on Shard A, as your transaction had already completed.

Another challenge with sharding in your application layer is that as your data grows, you may need to add more servers (shards). Depending on how you map from sharding key to the server number, it might be surprisingly difficult to add more servers to your sharded deployment.

At the beginning of this section, I explained that the sharding key is used to map to a server number. The simplest way to map the sharding key to the server number is by using a modulo operator. In the first example of this section, I had two shards and I decided to direct users with odd user IDs to Shard A and users with even user IDs to Shard B, which is a modulo 2 mapping.

Modulo(n,x) is the remainder of the division of x by n. It allows you to map any integer number to one of the numbers in range from 0 to n−1. For example, if you had six servers, you would use modulo(6, userId) to calculate the server number based on the user ID.

The problem with modulo-based mapping is that each user is assigned to a particular server based on the total number of servers. As the total number of servers changes, most of the user–server mappings change. For example, if you had three servers, numbered 0, 1, and 2, then user_id=8 would be mapped to the last server as modulo(3,8)=2. If you now added a fourth server, you would have four servers numbered 0, 1, 2, and 3. Executing the same mapping code for the same user_id=8 would return a different result: modulo(4,8)=0.

As you can see, adding a server could become a huge challenge, as you would need to migrate large amounts of data between servers. You would also need to do it without losing track of which user's data should be migrated to which server. When scaling your system horizontally, scaling events should be much cheaper and simpler than that; that is why we need to look for alternatives.

One way to avoid the need to migrate user data and reshard every time you add a server is to keep all of the mappings in a separate database. Rather than computing server number based on an algorithm, we could look up the server number based on the sharding key value. In our e-commerce example, we would need a separate data store with mappings of user_id to server number. Figure 5-14 shows how mappings could be stored in a data store and looked up by the application (mappings could be cached in the application to speed up the mapping code).

The benefit of keeping mapping data in a database is that you can migrate users between shards much more easily. You do not need to migrate all of the data in

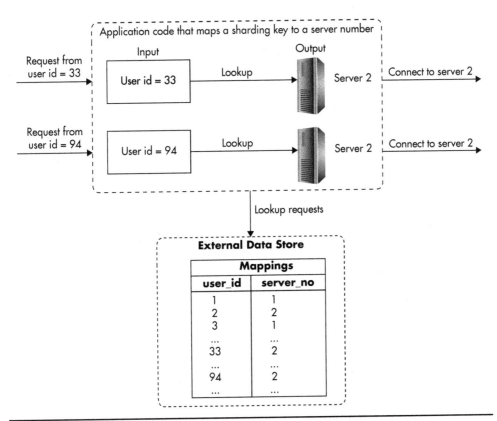

Figure 5-14   *External mapping data store*

one shot, but you can do it incrementally, one account at a time. To migrate a user, you need to lock its account, migrate the data, and then unlock it. You could usually do these migrations at night to reduce the impact on the system, and you could also migrate multiple accounts at the same time, as there is no data overlap.

By keeping mappings in a database, you also benefit from additional flexibility, as you can cherry-pick users and migrate them to the shards of your choice. Depending on the application requirements, you could migrate your largest or busiest clients to separate dedicated database instances to give them more capacity. Conversely, if high activity was not a good thing, you could punish users for consuming too many resources by hosting them together with other noisy users.

Since mapping data needs to be stored somewhere, you could either use MySQL itself to store that data or use an alternative data store. If you wanted to keep mapping data in MySQL, you could deploy a MySQL master server that would be the source of truth for the mapping table and then replicate that data to all of the shards. In this scenario, any time you create a new user, you need to write to the global master. Then the user entry replicates to all of the shards, and you can perform read-only lookups on any of the shards. Figure 5-15 shows how that could be done.

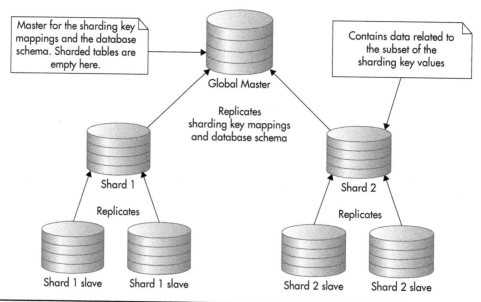

Figure 5-15 *Master of all the shards*

This is a relatively simple approach, as you add one more MySQL instance without introducing any new technologies. Since the mapping data set is small, it should not be a serious challenge to cache most of it in memory and replicate it quickly to all of the shards, but that is assuming you do not create thousands of mappings per second.

Depending on your infrastructure, adding another MySQL instance could be a good idea, but if you already used another highly scalable data store (I will talk about these later in this chapter), you may also consider keeping the mapping data there rather than writing it to all of the shards. Keeping mappings in a separate data store increases the complexity of your system as you need to deploy, manage, and scale yet another data store instance, but if you were already using one, it could be a relatively easy way out.

Luckily, there is one more solution to sharding that reduces the risk of resharding at relatively low cost and with minimal increase of complexity. In this scenario, you use the modulo function to map from the sharding key value to the database number, but each database is just a logical MySQL database rather than a physical machine. First, you decide how many machines you want to start with. Then you forecast how many machines you may realistically need down the road.

For example, you estimate that you will need two servers to start with and you will never need more than 32 machines in total (32 shards). In such a situation, you create 16 databases on each of the physical servers. On Server A you name them db-00 ... db-15 and on Server B you name them db-16 ... db-31. You then deploy the exact same schema to each of these databases so that they are identical. Figure 5-16 shows how such a deployment might look.

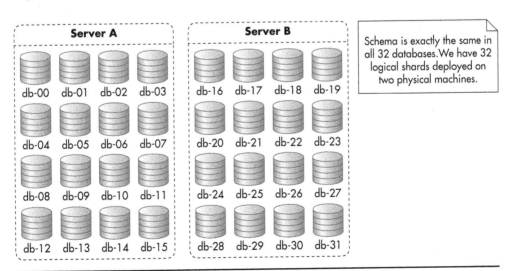

Figure 5-16 *Initial deployment of multidatabase sharded solution*

At the same time, you implement mapping functions in your code that allow you to find the database number and the physical server number based on the sharding key value. You implement a `getDbNumber` function that maps the sharding key value (like a user ID) to the database number (in this case, 32 of them) and `getServerNumber`, which maps the database number to a physical server number (in this case, we have two). Listing 5-2 shows how all of the mapping code would look initially.

Listing 5-2   *Mapping functions*

```
/**
 * Returns a logical database number based on the value of
 * the sharding key.
 * @param int $shardingKey
 * @return int database number
 */
function getDbNumber($shardingKey) {
    return $shardingKey % 32;
}
/**
 * Returns a physical server number based on the db number.
 * @param int $dbNumber
 * @return int physical server number
 */
function getServerNumber($dbNumber) {
    return $dbNumber < 16 ? 0 : 1;
}
```

You can then deploy your application and begin operation. As your database grows and you need to scale out, you simply split your physical servers in two. You take half of the logical database and move it to new hardware. At the same time, you modify your mapping code so that `getServerNumber` would return the correct server number for each logical database number. Figure 5-17 shows how your deployment might look after scaling out to four physical servers.

Although adding multiple databases on each machine is slightly more complicated than a simple sharded deployment, it gives you much more flexibility when it comes to scaling out. Being able to double your capacity by simply copying binary database backups and updating a few lines of code is a huge time saver. It is also much easier and safer to perform, as you do not need to update, insert, or delete any data for the migration to be completed. All you do is move the entire MySQL database from one server to another.

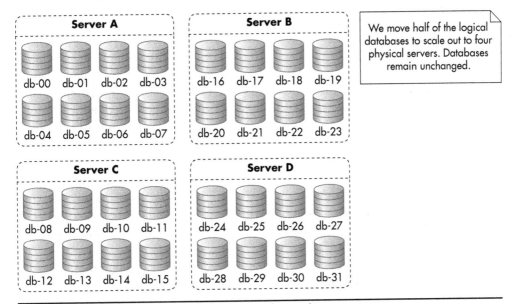

Figure 5-17 *Multidatabase sharded solution after scaling-out event*

Another benefit of this approach is that you can scale out relatively quickly with minimal amount of downtime. With good planning, you should be able to complete such a scaling-out event in less than a couple of minutes downtime. The actual scaling-out procedure might look as follows:

▶ First, you set up your new servers as replicas of your current shards.

▶ Then you need to stop all writes for a brief moment to allow any in-flight updates to replicate.

▶ Once slaves catch up with masters, you disable replication to new servers, as you do not want them to continue replicating the data that they will not be responsible for.

▶ You can then change the configuration of your application to use new servers and allow all traffic.

A challenge that you may face when working with application-level sharding is that it may be harder to generate an identifier that would be unique across all of the shards. Some data stores allow you to generate globally unique IDs, but since MySQL does not natively support sharding, your application may need to enforce these rules as well.

If you do not care how your unique identifiers look, you can use MySQL auto-increment with an offset to ensure that each shard generates different numbers. To do that on a system with two shards, you would set auto_increment_increment=2 and auto_increment_offset=1 on one of them and auto_increment_increment=2 and auto_increment_offset=2 on the other. This way, each time auto-increment is used to generate a new value, it would generate even numbers on one server and odd numbers on the other. By using that trick, you would not be able to ensure that IDs are always increasing across shards, since each server could have a different number of rows, but usually that is not be a serious issue.

Another simple alternative to generating globally unique IDs is to use atomic counters provided by some data stores. For example, if you already use Redis, you could create a counter for each unique identifier. You would then use Redis' INCR command to increase the value of a selected counter and return it in an atomic fashion. This way, you could have multiple clients requesting a new identifier in parallel and each of them would end up with a different value, guaranteeing global uniqueness. You would also ensure that there are no gaps and that each consecutive identifier is bigger than the previous ones.

HINT

An interesting way of overcoming the complexity of application-level sharding is to push most of its challenges onto the cloud hosting provider. A good example of how sharding can be made easier for developers is by using Azure SQL Database Elastic Scale. Azure SQL Database Elastic Scale is a set of libraries and supporting services that take responsibility for sharding, shard management, data migration, mapping, and even cross-shard query execution. Rather than having to implement all of this code and supporting tools yourself, you can use the provided libraries and services to speed up your development and avoid painful surprises. Although the Azure SQL Database is using a custom version of SQL Server (not MySQL), it is worth mentioning it here, as it is a great example of how cloud-hosting providers expand their support for scalability.[13]

As you can see, a lot of challenges come with application-level sharding. Let's now have a quick look at how you could combine replication, sharding, and functional partitioning to enable a MySQL-based system to scale efficiently.

Putting It All Together

As I mentioned earlier, scalability can be boiled down to three underlying techniques: scaling by adding copies of the same thing, functional partitioning, and data partitioning. All of these techniques could be applied to a MySQL-based system to allow it to scale. Imagine again that you are hosting an e-commerce website.

This time, we will look at the bigger picture and we will discuss how different scalability techniques complement each other.

If you were to build an e-commerce system, you could design it in a simple way where you only have one web service containing all of the functionality of the application. You could also have that web service talk to a single MySQL database for all of its persistence needs. In such a simple scenario, your system might look similar to Figure 5-18.

Assuming that your web service was stateless, you could scale the web service machines, but you would not be able to scale your database past a single server. If your application was performing many more reads than writes, you could scale reads by adding read replica servers. These servers would have an exact copy of the data that the master database has, thus allowing you to scale by adding more copies of the same thing. In this configuration, your system might look like Figure 5-19.

Now, if that was not enough to scale your system, you might decide to split it into two functional components by performing functional partitioning. For example,

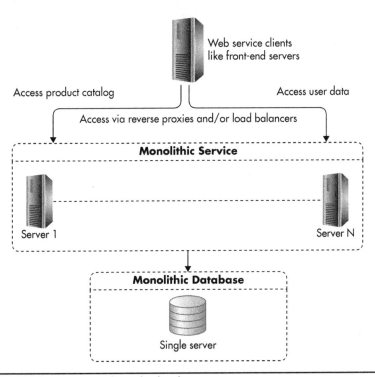

Figure 5-18   *Single service and single database*

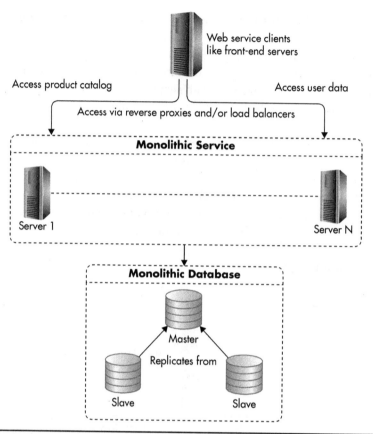

Figure 5-19 *Scaling catalog by adding replicas*

you could decide to store all of the user-centric data on one database and the rest of the data in a separate database. At the same time, you would split the functionality of your web services layer into two independent web services: ProductCatalogService and CustomerService. ProductCatalogService would be responsible for managing and accessing information about products, categories, and promotions and CustomerService would be responsible for user accounts, orders, invoices, and purchase history. After performing functional partitioning, your system might look like Figure 5-20.

By dividing your web service into two highly decoupled services, you could now scale them independently. You could use MySQL replication to scale reads of the ProductCatalogService since the product catalog would be used mainly as a read-only service. Users would search through the data, retrieve product details,

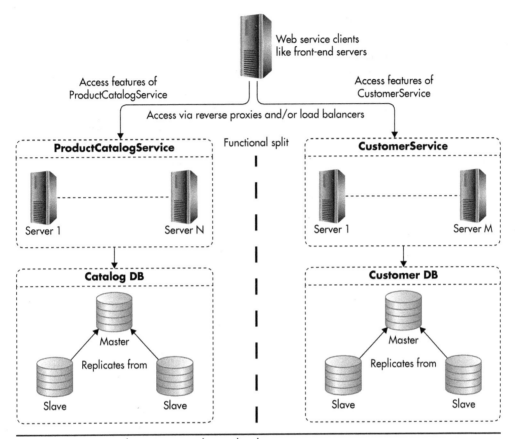

Figure 5-20 *Two web services and two databases*

or list products in different categories, but they would not be allowed to modify any data in the ProductCatalogService. The only people allowed to modify data in the catalog would be your merchants, and these modifications would happen relatively rarely in comparison to all other types of queries.

On the other hand, CustomerService would require much higher write throughput, as most operations related to user data require writes to persist results of user actions. Each operation, such as adding an item to cart, processing a payment, or requesting a refund, would require writes to the database.

Since your product catalog is mainly read-only and the size is relatively small, you might choose to scale it by adding more read replicas (scaling by adding clones). By keeping all of the products in a single database, you would make your search queries simpler, as you would not need to merge query results across shards. On the other hand, since your user data set was much larger and required many more writes, you could scale it by applying sharding (scaling by data partitioning). You would not depend on replication to scale CustomerService, but you might still want to keep one read replica of each shard just for high-availability and backup purposes. Figure 5-21 shows how your system might look.

In this scenario, replication would be implemented using MySQL replication and sharding would be implemented in the application layer. The application would need to store user IDs in cookies or sessions so that every request sent to CustomerService could have the user ID (used as the sharding key). Based on the

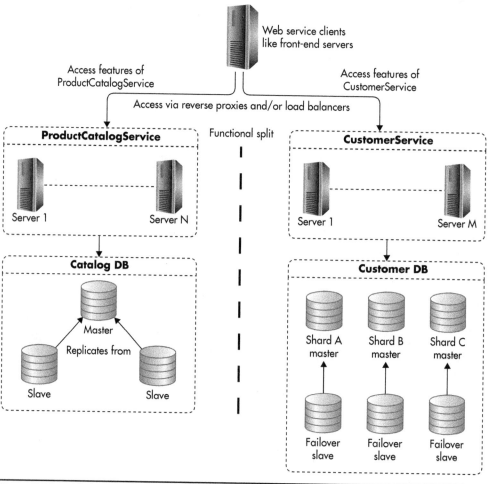

Figure 5-21 *All three techniques applied*

sharding key, the web service could then connect to the correct shard (which is just a regular MySQL database instance) and execute the necessary queries. As you can see, you can mix and match different scalability techniques to help your MySQL-based system grow.

Although application-level sharding is a great way to increase your I/O capacity and allow your application to handle more data, a lot of challenges come with it. Your code becomes much more complex, cross-shard queries are a pain point, and you need to carefully select your sharding key—even then, adding hardware and migrating data can be a challenge.

Replication helps with read throughput and enables higher availability, but it also comes with its own difficulties, especially in terms of ensuring data consistency and recovering from failures. It also forces your application to be aware of replication so that it can handle replication lag correctly and direct queries to the right servers.

Luckily, MySQL and other relational databases are no longer the only way to go when it comes to storing data. Let's now have a look at alternative technologies that can be used as data stores allowing scalability and high availability.

Scaling with NoSQL

Traditionally, scaling relational databases was the main pain point when scaling web applications. As graduates of computer science courses, we were taught for decades that data should be normalized and transactions should be used to enforce data consistency. Some people would go even further, pushing huge parts of their business logic into the database layer so it would execute as stored procedures or triggers directly on the database servers rather than in the application layer. There was a conviction that relational databases were all there was and all there was ever going to be. If you needed a large-scale database, you needed stronger servers and a bunch of costly software licenses, as there were no alternatives.

> *Data normalization* is a process of structuring data so that it is broken into separate tables. As part of the normalization process, people would usually break data down into separate fields, make sure that each row could be identified by a primary key, and that rows in different tables would reference each other rather than having copies of the same

information. Having data in such a form reduces the data size, as there is less redundancy. It also allows for better indexing and searching because data is segregated and smaller in size. Normalization also increases data integrity, as anytime an application needs to update existing data, it only needs to update it in one place (other rows can reference this data, but they would not contain copies of it).

The mind-set that relational database engines were the only way to go began to change in the 2000s with a publication of a few ground-breaking white papers and the increasing popularity of online businesses. Because companies needed to break new scalability records, they needed to look for new, innovative ways to manage the data. Rather than demanding full ACID compliance and expecting databases to run distributed transactions, companies like Amazon, Google, and Facebook decided to build their own simplified data stores. These data stores would not support SQL language, complex stored procedures, or triggers, but what they gave in return was true horizontal scalability and high availability beyond what relational databases could ever offer.

As their platforms proved successful, the world's largest web startups began publishing computer science white papers describing their innovative technologies. A few famous white papers from Google were Google File System,[w44] MapReduce,[w1] and BigTable,[w28] published in early 2000s. These publications were followed by one of the most famous data store publications, *Dynamo*, which was a data store designed solely to support the amazon.com checkout process.[w39] By 2010, principles and design decisions made by these early pioneers made their way into open-source data stores like Cassandra, Redis, MongoDB, Riak, and CouchDB, and the era of NoSQL began.

NoSQL is a broad term used to label many types of data stores that diverge from the traditional relational database model. These data stores usually do not support the SQL language, thus the term NoSQL.

The reason why these new technologies were so successful at handling ever-growing amounts of data was that they were built with scalability in mind and they were making significant tradeoffs to support this scalability.

The mind shift of the NoSQL era is that when you set out to design a data store, you need to first decide what features are most important to you (for example availability, latency, consistency, ease of use, transactional guarantees, or other dimensions of scalability). Once you decide on your priorities you can then make tradeoffs aligned with what is most important. In the same way, when you are choosing an open-source NoSQL data store, you need to first define the priority order of features that you need and then choose a data store that can satisfy most of them rather than hoping to get everything. If you are hoping to find a "better SQL" in NoSQL, you will be disappointed, as all of the NoSQL data stores make significant sacrifices to support their top-priority features and you need to prepare to make these sacrifices yourself if you want to build a horizontally scalable data layer.

Traditionally, making tradeoffs and sacrifices was not really in the nature of database designers until Eric Brewer's famous CAP theorem,[w23–w25] which stated that it was impossible to build a distributed system that would simultaneously guarantee consistency, availability, and partition tolerance. In this theorem, a distributed system consists of nodes (servers) and network connections allowing nodes to talk to each other. Consistency ensures that all of the nodes see the same data at the same time. Availability guarantees that any available node can serve client requests even when other nodes fail. Finally, partition tolerance ensures that the system can operate even in the face of network failures where communication between nodes is impossible.

> **HINT**
>
> CAP is even more difficult to understand, as the way consistency is defined in CAP is different from the way it was traditionally defined in ACID. In CAP, consistency ensures that the same data becomes visible to all of the nodes at the same time, which means that all of the state changes need to be serializable, as if they happened one after another rather than in parallel. That, in turn, requires ways of coordinating across CPUs and servers to make sure that the latest data is returned. In ACID, on the other hand, consistency is more focused on relationships within the data, like foreign keys and uniqueness.

Since all available nodes need to process all incoming requests (availability) and at the same time they all need to respond with the same data (consistency), there is no way for data to propagate among servers in case of network failure. Figure 5-22 shows a hypothetical data store cluster that conflicts with the CAP theorem. In this example, you can see a network failure separating nodes A and B. You can also see that node C has failed and that multiple clients are reading and writing the same data using different nodes.

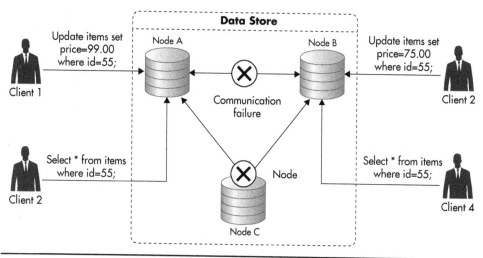

Figure 5-22 *Data store conflicting with the CAP theorem*

The CAP theorem quickly became popular, as it was used as a justification for tradeoffs made by the new NoSQL data store designers. It was popularized under a simplified label, "Consistency, availability, or partition tolerance: pick two," which is not entirely correct, but it opened engineers' eyes to the fact that relational databases with all of their guarantees and features may simply not be able to scale in the way people expected them to. In 2012, Brewer published a white paper titled "CAP 12 Years Later" in which he explained some of the misconceptions about CAP and that tradeoffs are usually made in more subtle ways than sacrificing consistency or high availability altogether. Regardless of its accuracy, the phrase "pick two" became the catchphrase of NoSQL, as it is a powerful way to drive a message that scalable data stores require tradeoffs.

The Rise of Eventual Consistency

As the simplified version of the CAP theorem suggests (pick two), building a distributed data store requires us to relax the guarantees around availability, consistency, or partition tolerance. Some of the NoSQL data stores choose to sacrifice some of the consistency guarantees to make scalability easier. For example, this is what Amazon did with its Dynamo data store.[w39] Rather than enforcing full consistency or trying to aim for distributed transactions, Amazon decided that high availability was the most important thing for their online business. Amazon wanted to make sure that you would never get a blank page in the middle of your browsing session and that your shopping cart would never get lost.

Based on these priorities, Amazon then made a series of sacrifices to support their high-availability and scalability needs. They sacrificed complex queries, simplified the data model, and introduced a concept of eventual consistency instead of trying to implement a globally consistent system.

> *Eventual consistency* is a property of a system where different nodes may have different versions of the data, but where state changes eventually propagate to all of the servers. If you asked a single server for data, you would not be able to tell whether you got the latest data or some older version of it because the server you choose might be lagging behind.

If you asked two servers for the exact same data at the exact same time in a globally consistent system, you would be guaranteed to get the same response. In an eventually consistent system, you cannot make such assumptions. Eventually, consistent systems allow each of the servers to return whatever data they have, even if it is some previous stale version of the data the client is asking for. If you waited long enough, though, each server would eventually catch up and return the latest data.

Figure 5-23 shows a scenario where Client A sends an update to Server 1 of an eventually consistent data store. Immediately after that, Clients B and C

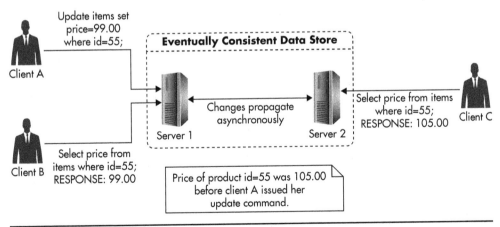

Figure 5-23 *Eventual consistency*

send queries for that data to Servers 1 and 2. Since the data store is eventually consistent, they cannot be sure if they got the latest data. They know that they got data that was valid at some point in time, but there is no way to know whether the data they got was the freshest or not. In this case, Client B got the latest data, but Client C got a stale response because changes made by Client A have not propagated to Server 2 yet. If Client C waited long enough before sending the request to Server 2, it would receive the same data that Client A has written.

Some data stores use eventual consistency as a way to increase high availability. Clients do not have to wait for the entire system to be ready for them to be able to read or write. Servers accept reads and writes at all times, hoping that they will be able to replicate incoming state changes to their peers later on. The downside of such an optimistic write policy is that it can lead to conflicts, since multiple clients can update the same data at the exact same time using different servers. Figure 5-24 shows such a conflict scenario. By the time nodes A and B notice the conflict, clients are already gone. Data store nodes need to reach a consensus on what should happen with the price of item id=55.

There are different ways in which conflicts like this can be resolved. The simplest policy is to accept the most recent write and discard earlier writes. This is usually called "the most recent write wins" and it is appealing due to its simplicity, but it may lead to some data being lost.

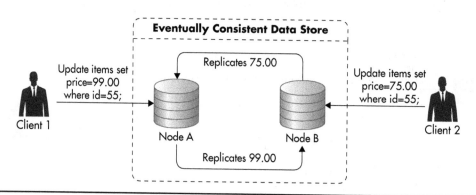

Figure 5-24   *Eventual consistency write conflict*

Alternatively, some data stores like Dynamo push the responsibility for conflict resolution onto its clients. They detect conflicts and keep all of the conflicting values. Any time a client asks for that data, they would then return all of the conflicted versions of the data, letting the client decide how to resolve the conflict. The client can then apply different business rules to resolve each type of conflict in the most graceful way. For example, with the Amazon shopping cart, even if some servers were down, people would be able to keep adding items to their shopping carts. These writes would then be sent to different servers, potentially resulting in multiple versions of each shopping cart. Whenever multiple versions of a shopping cart are discovered by the client code, they are merged by adding all the items from all of the shopping carts rather than having to choose one winning version of the cart. This way, users will never lose an item that was added to a cart, making it easier to buy.

Figure 5-25 shows how client-side conflict resolution might look. The client created a shopping cart using Server A. Because of a temporary network failure, the client could not write to Server A, so it created a new shopping cart for the same user on Server B. After network failure recovery, both nodes A and B ended up with two conflicting versions of the same shopping cart. To cope with the conflict, they each keep both of the versions and return them to the client in consecutive calls. Then it is up to the client code to decide how to resolve the conflict. In this case, the client decided to merge carts by adding both items and saving the updated cart so that there would be no conflicting versions in the data store.

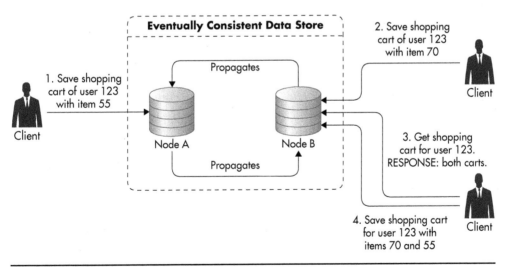

Figure 5-25   *Client-side conflict resolution*

In addition to the conflict resolution mechanisms mentioned earlier, eventually consistent data stores often support ongoing data synchronization to ensure data convergence. Even when you think of a simple example of an eventually consistent system like MySQL replication, where only one server can accept writes, it can be a challenge to keep all of the copies of the data in sync. Even the smallest human error, application bug, or hardware issue could result in the slave having different data from the master. To deal with edge-case scenarios where different servers end up with different data, some NoSQL data stores, like Cassandra, employ additional self-healing strategies.

For example, 10 percent of reads sent to Cassandra nodes trigger a background *read repair* mechanism. As part of this process, after a response is sent to the client, the Cassandra node fetches the requested data from all of the replicas, compares their values, and sends updates back to any node with inconsistent or stale data. Although it might seem like overkill to keep comparing all of the data 10 percent of the time, since each of the replicas can accept writes, it is very easy for data to diverge during any maintenance or network issues. Having a fast way of repairing data adds overhead, but it makes the overall system much more resilient to failures, as clients can read and write data using any of the servers rather than having to wait for a single server to become available.

Eventual consistency is a tradeoff and it is usually much more difficult to reason about an eventually consistent system than a globally consistent one. Whatever you read could be some stale version of the data; whatever you write might overwrite data that you did not expect to be there because you read from a stale copy.

Using an eventually consistent data store does not mean that you can never enforce read-after-write semantics. Some of the eventually consistent systems, like Cassandra, allow clients to fine-tune the guarantees and tradeoffs made by specifying the consistency level of each query independently. Rather than having a global tradeoff affecting all of your queries, you can choose which queries require more consistency and which ones can deal with stale data, gaining more availability and reducing latency of your responses.

> *Quorum consistency* means the majority of the replicas agree on the result. When you write using quorum consistency, the majority of the servers need to confirm that they have persisted your change. Reading using a quorum, on the other hand, means that the majority of the replicas need to respond so that the most up-to-date copy of the data can be found and returned to the client.

A quorum is a good way to trade latency for consistency in eventually consistent stores. You need to wait longer for the majority of the servers to respond, but you get the freshest data. If you write certain data using quorum consistency and then you always read it using quorum consistency, you are guaranteed to always get the most up-to-date data and thus regain the read-after-write semantics.

To explain better how quorum consistency works, let's consider Figure 5-26. In this example, your data is replicated across three nodes. When you write data, you write to at least two nodes (at least two nodes need to confirm persisting your changes before returning the response). That means the failure of Server 2 does not prevent the data store from accepting writes. Later on, when Server 2 recovers and comes back online with stale data, clients would still get the most up-to-date information because their quorum reads would include at least one of the remaining servers, which has the most up-to-date data.

Faster Recovery to Increase Availability

In a similar way in which Dynamo and Cassandra traded some of their consistency guarantees in favor of high availability, other data stores trade some of their high availability for consistency. Rather than guaranteeing that all the clients can read and write all of the time, some data store designers decided to focus more on quick failure recovery rather than sacrificing global consistency.

A good example of such a tradeoff is MongoDB, another popular NoSQL data store. In MongoDB, data is automatically sharded and distributed among multiple

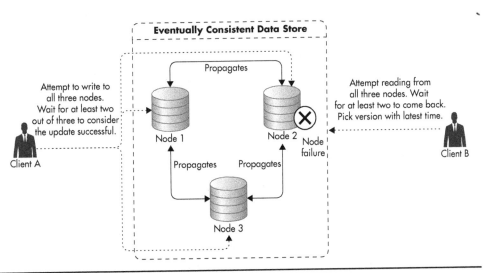

Figure 5-26 *Quorum operations during failure*

servers. Each piece of data belongs to a single server, and anyone who wants to update data needs to talk to the server responsible for that data. That means any time a server becomes unavailable, MongoDB rejects all writes to the data that the failed server was responsible for.

The obvious downside of having a single server responsible for each piece of data is that any time a server fails, some of your client operations begin to fail. To add data redundancy and increase high availability, MongoDB supports replica sets, and it is recommended to set up each of the shards as a replica set. In replica sets, multiple servers share the same data, with a single server being elected as a primary. Whenever the primary node fails, an election process is initiated to decide which of the remaining nodes should take over the primary role. Once the new primary node is elected, replication within the replica set resumes and the new primary node's data is replicated to the remaining nodes. This way, the window of unavailability can be minimized by automatic and prompt failover.

You could now think that things are great—you have a consistent data store and you only risk a minute of downtime when one of your primary nodes fails. The problem with NoSQL data stores is that they are littered with "gotchas" and you cannot assume anything about them without risking painful surprises. It is not because data store designers are evil, but because they have to make tradeoffs that affect all sorts of things in ways you might not expect.

With regard to consistency in MongoDB, things are also more complicated than you might expect. You might have read that MongoDB is a CP data store (favoring consistency and partition tolerance over availability), but the way in which consistency is defined is not what you might expect. Since MongoDB replica sets use asynchronous replication, your writes reach primary nodes and then they replicate asynchronously to secondary nodes. This means that if the primary node failed before your changes got replicated to secondary nodes, your changes would be permanently lost.

Figure 5-27 shows how a primary node failure causes some writes to be lost. In a similar way to how Cassandra allowed you to increase consistency, you can also tell MongoDB to enforce secondary node consistency when you perform a write. But would you not expect that to be the default in a CP system? In practice, enforcing writes to be synchronously replicated to secondary nodes is expensive in MongoDB, as writes are not propagated one by one; rather, the entire replication backlog needs to be flushed and processed by the secondary node for a write to be acknowledged.

Many of the modern NoSQL data stores support automatic failover or failure recovery in one form or another. No matter which NoSQL data store you choose, you need to study it deeply and resist any assumptions, as practice is usually more complicated than the documentation makes it look.

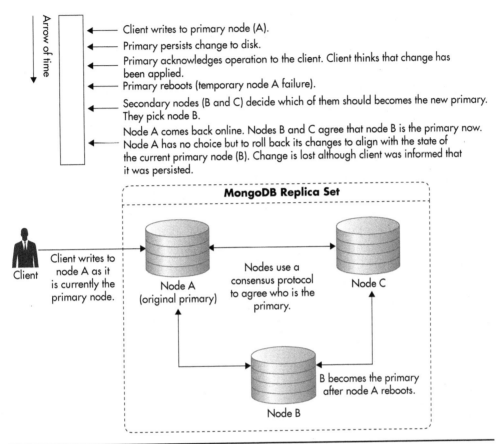

Arrow of time

- Client writes to primary node (A).
- Primary persists change to disk.
- Primary acknowledges operation to the client. Client thinks that change has been applied.
- Primary reboots (temporary node A failure).
- Secondary nodes (B and C) decide which of them should becomes the new primary. They pick node B.
- Node A comes back online. Nodes B and C agree that node B is the primary now. Node A has no choice but to roll back its changes to align with the state of the current primary node (B). Change is lost although client was informed that it was persisted.

MongoDB Replica Set

Client writes to node A as it is currently the primary node.

Client

Node A (original primary)

Nodes use a consensus protocol to agree who is the primary.

Node C

B becomes the primary after node A reboots.

Node B

Figure 5-27   *Update lost due to primary node failure*

Cassandra Topology

NoSQL data stores vary significantly, but they use some common patterns to distribute data among multiple servers, replicate information, and handle failures. Let's have a closer look at Cassandra, which is one of the most popular NoSQL data stores, to see some of these key features.

Cassandra is a data store that was originally built at Facebook and could be seen as a merger of design patterns borrowed from BigTable (developed at Google) and Dynamo (built by Amazon).

The first thing that stands out in the Cassandra architecture is that all of its nodes are functionally equal. Cassandra does not have a single point of failure, and all of its nodes perform the exact same functions. Clients can connect to any of Cassandra's nodes and when they connect to one, that node becomes the client's session coordinator. Clients do not need to know which nodes have what data, nor do they have to be aware of outages, repairing data, or replication. Clients send all of their requests to the session coordinator and the coordinator takes responsibility for all of the internal cluster activities like replication or sharding.

Figure 5-28 shows the topology of a Cassandra cluster. Clients can connect to any of the servers no matter what data they intend to read or write. Clients then issue their queries to the coordinator node they chose without any knowledge about the topology or state of the cluster. Since each of the Cassandra nodes knows the status of all of the other nodes and what data they are responsible for, they can delegate queries to the correct servers. The fact that clients know very little about the topology of the cluster is a great example of decoupling and significantly reduces complexity on the application side.

Although all of the Cassandra nodes have the same function in the cluster, they are not identical. The thing that makes each of the Cassandra nodes unique is the data set that they are responsible for. Cassandra performs data partitioning

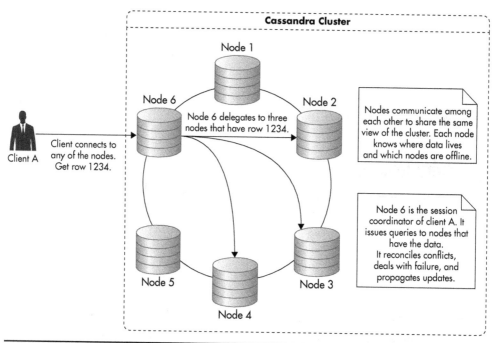

Figure 5-28 *Topology of a Cassandra cluster*

automatically so that each of the nodes gets a subset of the overall data set. None of the servers needs to have all of the data, and Cassandra nodes communicate among one other to make sure they all know where parts of the data live.

Another interesting feature of Cassandra is its data model, which is very different from the relational data model used in databases like MySQL. The Cassandra data model is based on a wide column, similar to Google's BigTable.[w28] In a wide column model, you create tables and then each table can have an unlimited number of rows. Unlike the relational model, tables are not connected, each table lives independently, and Cassandra does not enforce any relationships between tables or rows.

Cassandra tables are also defined in a different way than in relational databases. Different rows may have different columns (fields), and they may live on different servers in the cluster. Rather than defining the schema up front, you dynamically create fields as they are required. This lack of upfront schema design can be a significant advantage, as you can make application changes more rapidly without the need to execute expensive alter table commands any time you want to persist a new type of information.

The flip side of Cassandra's data model simplicity is that you have fewer tools at your disposal when it comes to searching for data. To access data in any of the columns, you need to know which row are you looking for, and to locate the row, you need to know its *row key* (something like a primary key in a relational database).

Cassandra partitions data based on a row key in a similar way to what we did with MySQL sharding earlier in this chapter. When you send your query to your session coordinator, it hashes the row key (which you provided) to a number. Then, based on the number, it can find the partition range that your row key belongs to (the correct shard). Finally, the coordinator looks up which Cassandra server is responsible for that particular partition range and delegates the query to the correct server.

In addition to automatic data partitioning, Cassandra supports a form of replication. It is important to note, though, that in Cassandra, replication is not like we have seen in MySQL. In Cassandra, each copy of the data is equally important and there is no master–slave relationship between servers. In Cassandra, you can specify how many copies of each piece of data you want to keep across the cluster, and session coordinators are responsible for ensuring the correct number of replicas.

Anytime you write data, the coordinator node forwards your query to all of the servers responsible for the corresponding partition range. This way, if any of the servers was down, the remaining servers can still process the query. Queries for failed nodes are buffered and then replayed when servers become available again (that buffering is also called hinted handoff). So although the client connects to a single server and issues a single write request, that request translates to multiple write requests, one for each of the replica holders.

Figure 5-29 shows how a write request might be coordinated in a cluster with the replication factor equal to three when a quorum consistency level was requested. In such a scenario, the coordinator has to wait for at least two nodes to confirm that they have persisted the change before it can return to the client. In this case, it does not matter to the client whether one of the nodes is broken or down for maintenance, because node 6 returns as soon as two of the nodes acknowledge that they have persisted the change (two out of three is the majority of the nodes, which is enough to guarantee quorum-level consistency).

Another extremely valuable feature of Cassandra is how well automated it is and how little administration it requires. For example, replacing a failed node does not require complex backup recovery and replication offset tweaking, as often happens in MySQL. All you need to do to replace a broken server is add a new (blank) one and tell Cassandra which IP address this new node is replacing.

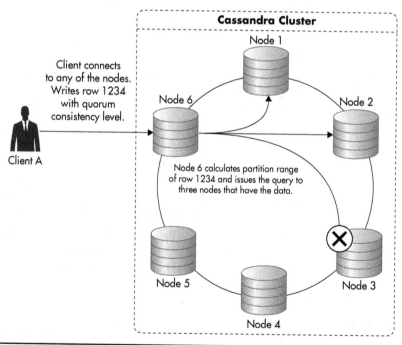

Figure 5-29 *Writing to Cassandra*

All of the data transferring and consistency checking happens automatically in the background. Since each piece of data is stored on multiple servers, the cluster is fully operational throughout the server replacement procedure. Clients can read and write any data they wish even when one server is broken or being replaced. As soon as node recovery is finished, the new node begins processing requests and the cluster goes back to its original capacity.

From a scalability point of view, Cassandra is a truly horizontally scalable data store. The more servers you add, the more read and write capacity you get, and you can easily scale in and out depending on your needs. Since data is sliced into a high number of small partition ranges, Cassandra can distribute data more evenly across the cluster. In addition, since all of the topology is hidden from the clients, Cassandra is free to move data around. As a result, adding new servers is as easy as starting up a new node and telling it to join the cluster. Again, Cassandra takes care of rebalancing the cluster and making sure that the new server gets a fair share of the data.

As of this writing, Cassandra is one of the clear leaders when it comes to ease of management, scalability, and self-healing, but it is important to remember that everything has its price. The main challenges that come with operating Cassandra are that it is heavily specialized, it has a very particular data model, and it is an eventually consistent data store.

You can work around eventual consistency by using quorum reads and writes, but the data model and tradeoffs made by the designers can often come as a surprise. Anything that you might have learned about relational databases is pretty much invalid when you work with NoSQL data stores like Cassandra. It is easy to get started with most NoSQL data stores, but to be able to operate them at scale takes much more experience and understanding of their internal structure than you might expect.

For example, even though you can read in the open-source community that "Cassandra loves writes", deletes are the most expensive type of operation you can perform in Cassandra, which can come as a big surprise. Most people would not expect that deletes would be expensive, but it is a consequence of the design tradeoffs made by Cassandra developers. Cassandra uses append-only data structures, which allows it to write inserts with astonishing efficiency. Data is never overwritten in place and hard disks never have to perform random write operations, greatly increasing write throughput. But that feature, together with the fact that Cassandra is an eventually consistent data store, forces deletes and updates to be internally persisted as inserts as well. As a result, some use cases that add and delete a lot of data can become inefficient because deletes increase the data size rather than reducing it (until the compaction process cleans them up).

A great example of how that can come as a surprise is a common Cassandra anti-pattern of a queue. You could model a simple first-in-first-out queue in Cassandra by using its dynamic columns. You add new entries to the queue by appending new columns, and you remove jobs from the queue by deleting columns. With a small scale and low volume of writes, this solution would seem to work perfectly, but as you keep adding and deleting columns, your performance will begin to degrade dramatically. Although both inserts and deletes are perfectly fine and Cassandra purges old deleted data using its background compaction mechanism, it does not particularly like workloads with such a high rate of deletes (in this case, 50 percent of the operations are deletes).

Without deep knowledge of the strengths, weaknesses, and internals of NoSQL data stores, you can easily paint yourself into a corner. This is not to say that NoSQL is not a good way to go or that Cassandra is not a good data store. Quite the opposite—for some use cases, NoSQL is the best way to go, and Cassandra is one of my favorite NoSQL data stores. The point here is that although NoSQL data stores offer horizontal scalability and great optimizations of certain operations, they are not a silver bullet and they always do it at some cost.

Summary

Scaling the data layer is usually the most challenging area of a web application. You can usually achieve horizontal scalability by carefully designing your application, choosing the right data store, and applying three basic scalability techniques: functional partitioning, replication, and sharding.

No matter which data store you choose or which particular techniques you apply, the critical thing to remember is that data store design is all about tradeoffs. There are no silver bullets, and each application may be better suited for a different data store and a different way of scaling. That is why I would strongly suggest you keep an open mind and try to avoid looking for a golden hammer. Rather than shoehorning every application into a single data store, it is better to realize that all of the data stores have pros and cons and mix and match different technologies based on the use case. Functional partitioning of the web services layer and using different data stores based on the business needs is often referred to as polyglot persistence,[L37] and it is a growing trend among web applications. Although having multiple data store types adds more complexity and increases maintenance costs, it gives more flexibility and allows you to make tradeoffs independently within each of the web services rather than committing to a single data store.

Before you decide to use any of the NoSQL data stores, I suggest reading at least one book about the selected data store and then explicitly search for gotchas, pitfalls, and common problems that people run into when using that technology. To gain more knowledge on data store scalability techniques, I also recommend reading excellent books on MySQL[16] and MongoDB[44] and some of the most famous white papers describing different NoSQL data stores.[w28,w29,w27,w20,w18,w72,w55]

No matter how good our data stores and application designs are, I/O is still a major bottleneck in most systems. Let's move on to caching in the next chapter, as it is one of the easiest strategies to reduce the load put on the data layer.

6

Caching

"The supreme art of war is to subdue the enemy without fighting." –Sun Tzu

Caching, one of the key techniques used to scale web applications, is a critical factor for increasing both performance and scalability at relatively low cost. Caching is fairly simple and can usually be added to an existing application without expensive rearchitecture. In many ways, caching is winning the battle without the fight. It allows you to serve requests without computing responses, enabling you to scale much easier. Its ease makes it a very popular technique, as evidenced by its use in numerous technologies, including central processing unit (CPU) memory caches, hard drive caches, Linux operating system file caches, database query caches, Domain Name System (DNS) client caches, Hypertext Transfer Protocol (HTTP) browser caches, HTTP proxies and reverse proxies, and different types of application object caches. In each case, caching is introduced to reduce the time and resources needed to generate a result. Instead of fetching data from its source or generating a response each time it is requested, caching builds the result once and stores it in cache. Subsequent requests are satisfied by returning the cached result until it expires or is explicitly deleted. Since all cached objects can be rebuilt from the source, they can be purged or lost at any point in time without any consequences. If a cached object is not found, it is simply rebuilt.

Cache Hit Ratio

Cache hit ratio is the single most important metric when it comes to caching. At its core, cache effectiveness depends on how many times you can reuse the same cached response, which is measured as *cache hit ratio*. If you can serve the same cached result to satisfy ten requests on average, your cache hit ratio is 90 percent, because you need to generate each object once instead of ten times. Three main factors affect your cache hit ratio: data set size, space and longevity. Let's take a closer look at each one.

The first force acting on cache hit ratio is the size of your cache key space. Each object in the cache is identified by its cache key, and the only way to locate an object is by performing an exact match on the cache key. For example, if you wanted to cache online store product information for each item, you could use a product ID as the cache key. In other words, the cache key space is the number of all possible cache keys that your application could generate. Statistically, the more unique cache keys your application generates, the less chance you have to reuse any one of them. For example, if you wanted to cache weather forecast data based on a client's Internet Protocol (IP) address, you would have up to 4 billion cache keys possible (this is the number of all possible IP addresses). If you decided to cache the same weather forecast data based on the country of origin of that client, you would end up with just a few hundred possible cache keys (this is the number of countries in the world). Always consider ways to reduce the number of possible cache keys. The fewer cache keys possible, the better for your cache efficiency.

The second factor affecting cache hit ratio is the number of items that you can store in your cache before running out of space. This depends directly on the average size of your objects and the size of your cache. Because caches are usually stored in memory, the space available for cached objects is strictly limited and relatively expensive. If you try to cache more objects than can fit in your cache, you will need to remove older objects before you can add new ones. Replacing (evicting) objects reduces your cache hit ratio, because objects are removed even when they might be able to satisfy future requests. The more objects you can physically fit into your cache, the better your cache hit ratio.

The third factor affecting cache hit ratio is how long, on average, each object can be stored in cache before expiring or being invalidated. In some scenarios, you can cache objects for a predefined amount of time called Time to Live (TTL). For example, caching weather forecast data for 15 minutes should not be a problem. In such a case, you would cache objects with a predefined TTL of 15 minutes. In other use cases, however, you may not be able to risk serving stale data. For example, in an e-commerce system, shop administrators can change product prices at any time and these prices may need to be accurately displayed throughout the site. In such a case, you would need to invalidate cached objects each time the product price changes. Simply put, the longer you can cache your objects for, the higher the chance of reusing each cached object.

Understanding these three basic forces is the key to applying caching efficiently and identifying use cases where caching might be a good idea. Use cases with a high ratio of reads to writes are usually good candidates for caching, as cached objects can be created once and stored for longer periods of time before expiring or becoming invalidated, whereas use cases with data updating very often may render cache useless, as objects in cache may become invalid before they are used again.

In the following sections, I will discuss two main types of caches relevant to web applications: HTTP-based caches and custom object caches. I will then introduce some technologies applicable in each area and some general rules to help you leverage cache more effectively.

Caching Based on HTTP

The HTTP protocol has been around for a long time, and throughout the years a few extensions have been added to the HTTP specification, allowing different parts of the web infrastructure to cache HTTP responses. This makes understanding HTTP caching a bit more difficult, as you can find many different HTTP headers related to caching, and even some Hypertext Markup Language (HTML) metatags. I will describe the key HTTP caching headers later in this section, but before we dive into these details, it is important to note that all of the caching technologies working in the HTTP layer work as read-through caches.

> *Read-through cache* is a caching component that can return cached resources or fetch the data for the client, if the request cannot be satisfied from cache (for example, when cache does not contain the object being requested). That means that the client connects to the read-through cache rather than to the *origin server* that generates the actual response.

Figure 6-1 shows the interactions between the client, the read-through cache, and the origin server. The cache is always meant to be the intermediate (also known as the *proxy*), transparently adding caching functionality to HTTP connections. In Figure 6-1, Client 1 connects to the cache and requests a particular web resource (a page or a Cascading Style Sheet [CSS] file). Then the cache has a chance to "intercept" that request and respond to it using a cached object. Only if the cache does not have a valid cached response, will it connect to the *origin server* itself and forward the client's request. Since the interface of the service and the read-through cache are the same, clients can connect to the service directly (as Client 2 did), bypassing the cache, as read-through cache only works when you connect through it.

Read-through caches are especially attractive because they are transparent to the client. Clients are not able to distinguish whether they received a cached object or not. If a client was able to connect to the origin server directly, it would bypass the cache and get an equally valid response. This pluggable architecture gives a lot of flexibility, allowing you to add layers of caching to the HTTP stack

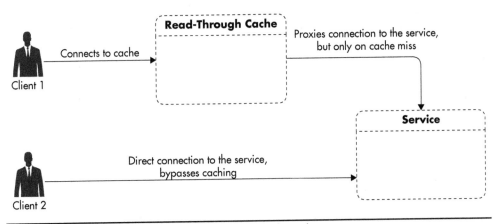

Figure 6-1   *Client interacting with the read-through cache*

without needing to modify any of the clients. In fact, it is common to see multiple HTTP read-through caches chained to one another in a single web request without the client ever being aware of it.

Figure 6-2 shows how chaining HTTP read-through caches might look. I will discuss these caches in more detail later in this chapter, but for now just note that the connection from the client can be intercepted by multiple read-through caches without the client even realizing it. In each step, a proxy can respond to a request using a cached response, or it can forward the request to its source on a cache miss. Let's now have a closer look at how caching can be controlled using HTTP protocol headers.

HTTP Caching Headers

HTTP is a text-based protocol. When your browser requests a page or any other HTTP resource (image, CSS file, or AJAX call), it connects to the HTTP server and sends an HTTP command, like GET, POST, PUT, DELETE, or HEAD, with a set of additional HTTP headers. Most of the HTTP headers are optional, and they can be used to negotiate expected behaviors. For example, a browser can announce that it supports gzip compressed responses, which lets the server decide whether it sends a response in compressed encoding or not. Listing 6-1 shows an example of a simple GET request that a web browser might issue when requesting the uniform resource locator (URL) http://www.example.org/. I have removed unnecessary headers like cookies and user-agent to simplify the example.

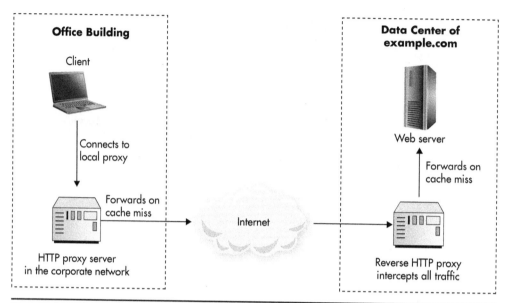

Figure 6-2 *Chain of HTTP read-through caches*

Listing 6-1 *Example of a simple GET request*

```
GET / HTTP/1.1
Host: www.example.org
Accept-Encoding: gzip,deflate
Connection: keep-alive
```

In this example, the browser declares that it supports version 1.1 of the HTTP protocol and compressed data encodings. It also tells the web server what host and what URL it is looking for. Finally, it asks the web server to keep the underlying Transmission Control Protocol/Internet Protocol (TCP/IP) connection open, as it intends to issue more HTTP requests to download further assets like images, CSS files, and JavaScript files.

In response to that request, the web server could reply with something similar to Listing 6-2. Note that the server decided to return a response in compressed encoding using the gzip algorithm, as the client has suggested, but it rejected the request to keep the network connection open (keep-alive header), responding with a (connection: close) response header and closing the connection immediately.

Listing 6-2 *Example of a simple HTTP response*

```
HTTP/1.1 200 OK
Content-Encoding: gzip
Content-Type: text/html; charset=UTF-8
Content-Length: 9381
Connection: close

... response body with contents of the page ...
```

There are dozens of different request headers and corresponding response headers that clients and servers may use, but I will focus only on headers relevant to caching. Caching headers are actually quite difficult to get right, because many different options can be set. To add further complication, some older headers like "Pragma: no-cache" can be interpreted differently by different implementations.

> **HINT**
>
> *You can use the same HTTP headers to control caching of your web pages, static resources like images, and web service responses. The ability to cache web service responses is, in fact, one of the key scalability benefits of REST-ful services. You can always put an HTTP cache between your web service and your clients and leverage the same caching mechanisms that you use for your web pages.*

The first header you need to become familiar with is Cache-Control. Cache-Control was added to the HTTP 1.1 specification and is now supported by most browsers and caching packages. Cache-Control allows you to specify multiple options, as you can see in Listing 6-3.

Listing 6-3 *Example of Cache-Control HTTP header*

```
Cache-Control: no-cache, no-store, max-age=0, must-revalidate
```

The most important Cache-Control options that web servers may include in their responses include

▶ **private** Indicates the result is specific to the user who requested it and the response cannot be served to any other user. In practice, this means that only browsers will be able to cache this response because intermediate caches would not have the knowledge of what identifies a user.

▶ **public**   Indicates the response can be shared between users as long as it has not expired. Note that you cannot specify private and public options together; the response is either public or private.

▶ **no-store**   Indicates the response should not be stored on disks by any of the intermediate caches. In other words, the response can be cached in memory, but it will not be persisted to disk. You should include this option any time your response contains sensitive user information so that neither the browser nor other intermediate caches store this data on disk.

▶ **no-cache**   Indicates the response should not be cached. To be accurate, it states that the cache needs to ask the server whether this response is still valid every time users request the same resource.

▶ **max-age**   Indicates how many seconds this response can be served from the cache before becoming stale (it defines the TTL of the response). This information can be expressed in a few ways, causing potential inconsistency. I recommend not using max-age (it is less backwards compatible) and depend on the Expires HTTP header instead.

▶ **no-transform**   Indicates the response should be served without any modifications. For example, a content delivery network (CDN) provider might transcode images to reduce their size, lowering the quality or changing the compression algorithm.

▶ **must-revalidate**   Indicates that once the response becomes stale, it cannot be returned to clients without revalidation. Although it may seem odd, caches may return stale objects under certain conditions, for example, if the client explicitly allows it or if the cache loses connection to the origin server. By using must-revalidate, you tell caches to stop serving stale responses no matter what. Any time a client asks for a stale object, the cache will then be forced to request it from the origin server.

Note that a cached object is considered *fresh* as long as its expiration time has not passed. Once the expiration time passes, the object becomes *stale,* but it can still be returned to clients if they explicitly allow stale responses. If you want to forbid stale objects from ever being returned to the clients, include the must-revalidate option in the Cache-Control response header. Clients can also include the Cache-Control header in their requests. The Cache-Control header is rarely used by the clients and it has slightly different semantics when included in the request. For example, the max-age option included in the requests tells caches that the client cannot accept objects that are older than max-age seconds, even if these objects were still considered fresh by the cache.

Another HTTP header that is relevant to caching is the Expires header, which allows you to specify an absolute point in time when the object becomes stale. Listing 6-4 shows an example of how it can be used.

Listing 6-4   *Example of Expires HTTP header*

```
Expires: Sat, 23 Jul 2015 13:14:28 GMT
```

Unfortunately, as you can already see, some of the functionality controlled by the Cache-Control header overlaps that of other HTTP headers. Expiration time of the web response can be defined either by Cache-Control: max-age=600 or by setting an absolute expiration time using the Expires header. Including both of these headers in the response is redundant and leads to confusion and potentially inconsistent behavior. For that reason, I recommend deciding which headers you want to use and sticking to them, rather than including all possible headers in your responses.

Another important header is Vary. The purpose of that header is to tell caches that you may need to generate multiple variations of the response based on some HTTP request headers. Listing 6-5 shows the most common Vary header indicating that you may return responses encoded in different ways depending on the Accept-Encoding header that the client sends to your web server. Some clients who accept gzip encoding will get a compressed response, whereas others who cannot support gzip will get an uncompressed response.

Listing 6-5   *Example of Vary HTTP header*

```
Vary: Accept-Encoding
```

There are a few more HTTP headers related to caching that allow for conditional download of resources and revalidation, but they are beyond the scope of this book. Those headers include Age, Last-Modified, If-Modified-Since, and Etag and they may be studied separately. Let's now turn to a few examples of common caching scenarios.

The first and best scenario is allowing your clients to cache a response forever. This is a very important technique, and you want to apply it for all of your static content (like images, CSS, or JavaScript files). Static content files should be considered immutable, and whenever you need to make a change to the contents of such a file, you should publish it under a new URL. For example, when you deploy a new version of your web application, you can bundle and minify all of your CSS files and include a timestamp or a hash of the contents of the file in the URL, as in http://example.org/files/css/css_a8dbcf212c59dad68dd5e9786d6f6b8a.css.

> ### HINT
>
> *Bundling CSS and JS files and publishing them under unique URLs gives you two important benefits: your static files can be cached forever by any caches (browsers, proxies, and CDN servers), and you can have multiple versions of the same file available to your clients at any point in time. This allows you to maximize your cache hit ratio and makes deploying new code much easier. If you deployed a new version of the JavaScript file by replacing an existing URL, some clients who have an old version of the HTML page might load the new JavaScript file and get errors. By releasing new versions of static files under new URLs, you guarantee that users can always download compatible versions of HTML, CSS, and JavaScript files.*

Even though you could cache static files forever, you should not set the Expires header more than one year into the future (the HTTP specification does not permit setting beyond that). Listing 6-6 shows an example of HTTP headers for a static file allowing for it to be cached for up to one year (counting from July 23, 2015). This example also allows caches to reuse the same cached object between different users, and it makes sure that compressed and uncompressed objects are cached independently, preventing any encoding errors.

Listing 6-6 *Example of HTTP headers for static files*

```
Cache-Control: public, no-transform
Expires: Sat, 23 Jul 2015 13:14:28 GMT
Vary: Accept-Encoding
```

The second most common scenario is the worst case—when you want to make sure that the HTTP response is never stored, cached, or reused for any users. To do this, you can use response headers as shown in Listing 6-7. Note that I used another HTTP header here (Pragma: no-cache) to make sure that older clients can understand my intent of not caching the response.

Listing 6-7 *Example of HTTP headers of noncacheable content*

```
Cache-Control: no-cache, no-store, max-age=0, must-revalidate
Expires: Fri, 01 Jan 1990 00:00:00 GMT
Pragma: no-cache
```

A last use case is for situations where you want the same user to reuse a piece of content, but at the same time you do not want other users to share the cached response. For example, if your website allowed users to log in, you may want to display the user's profile name in the top-right corner of the page together with a link to his or her profile page. In such a scenario, the body of the page contains user-specific data, so you cannot reuse the same response for different users. You can still use the full page cache, but it will have to be a private cache to ensure that users see their own personalized pages. Listing 6-8 shows the HTTP headers allowing web browsers to cache the response for a limited amount of time (for example, ten minutes from July 23, 2015, 13:04:28 GMT).

Listing 6-8   *Example of HTTP headers of short-lived full page cache*

```
Cache-Control: private, must-revalidate
Expires: Sat, 23 Jul 2015 13:14:28 GMT
Vary: Accept-Encoding
```

The last thing worth noting here is that in addition to HTTP caching headers, you can find some HTML metatags that seem to control web page caching. Listing 6-9 shows some of these metatags.

Listing 6-9   *Cache-related HTML metatags to avoid*

```
<meta http-equiv="cache-control" content="max-age=0" />
<meta http-equiv="cache-control" content="no-cache" />
<meta http-equiv="expires" content="Tue, 01 Jan 1990 1:00:00 GMT" />
<meta http-equiv="pragma" content="no-cache" />
```

It is best to avoid these metatags altogether, as they do not work for intermediate caches and they may be a source of confusion, especially for less experienced engineers. It is best to control caching using HTTP headers alone and do so with minimal redundancy. Now that we have discussed how HTTP caching can be implemented, let's have a look at different types of caches that can be used to increase performance and scalability of your websites.

Types of HTTP Cache Technologies

The HTTP protocol gives a lot of flexibility in deploying caches between the web client and the web server. There are many ways in which you can leverage

HTTP-based caches, and usually it is fairly easy to plug them into existing applications. There are four main types of HTTP caches: browser cache, caching proxies, reverse proxies, and CDNs. Most of them do not have to be scaled by you, as they are controlled by the user's devices or third-party networks. I will discuss scalability of HTTP-based caches later in this chapter, but first let's discuss each of these HTTP cache types.

Browser Cache

The first and most common type of cache is the caching layer built into all modern web browsers called *browser cache.* Browsers have built-in caching capabilities to reduce the number of requests sent out. These usually use a combination of memory and local files. Whenever an HTTP request is about to be sent, the browser can check the cache for a valid version of the resource. If the item is present in cache and is still fresh, the browser can reuse it without ever sending an HTTP request.

Figure 6-3 shows a developer's toolbar shipped as part of the Google Chrome web browser. In the sequence of web resources being downloaded on the first page load, you can see that the time needed to load the HTML was 582 ms, after which a CSS file was downloaded along with a few images, each taking approximately 300 ms to download.

If HTTP headers returned by the web server allow the web browser to cache these responses, it is able to significantly speed up the page load and save our servers a lot of work rendering and sending these files. Figure 6-4 shows the same page load sequence, but this time with most of the resources being served directly from browser cache. Even though the page itself needs a long time to be verified, all the images and CSS files are served from cache without any network delay.

Name Path	Method	Status Text	Size Content	Time Latency	Timeline		
						2.00 s	3.00 s
blog/	GET	304 Not Modified	250 B 42.2 KB	582 ms 580 ms			
css_16313eece98bb8a23cbf0491df0... /blog/sites/default/files/css	GET	304 Not Modified	238 B 91.0 KB	293 ms 291 ms			
scalability-rules.jpg /blog/sites/default/files	GET	304 Not Modified	238 B 8.9 KB	297 ms 296 ms			
Software%20Architecture%20for%2... /blog/sites/default/files	GET	304 Not Modified	238 B 5.5 KB	305 ms 303 ms			
soa-patterns.jpg /blog/sites/default/files	GET	304 Not Modified	238 B 6.3 KB	326 ms 325 ms			
host-in-the-cloud-cover.jpg /blog/sites/default/files	GET	304 Not Modified	238 B 5.6 KB	368 ms 367 ms			

Figure 6-3 *Sequence of resources downloaded on first visit*

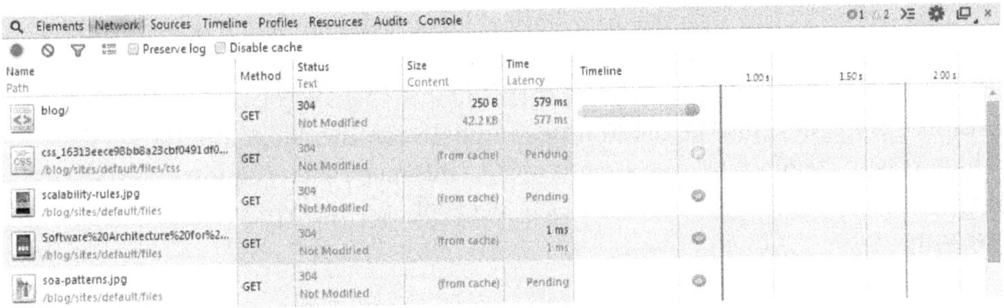

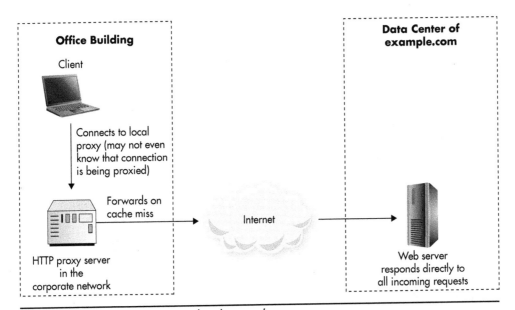

Name Path	Method	Status Text	Size Content	Time Latency	Timeline
blog/	GET	304 Not Modified	250 B 42.2 KB	579 ms 577 ms	
css_16313eece98bb8a23cbf0491df0... /blog/sites/default/files/css	GET	304 Not Modified	(from cache)	Pending	
scalability-rules.jpg /blog/sites/default/files	GET	304 Not Modified	(from cache)	Pending	
Software%20Architecture%20for%2... /blog/sites/default/files	GET	304 Not Modified	(from cache)	1 ms 1 ms	
soa-patterns.jpg /blog/sites/default/files	GET	304 Not Modified	(from cache)	Pending	

Figure 6-4 *Sequence of resources downloaded on consecutive visit*

Caching Proxies

The second type of caching HTTP technology is a *caching proxy*. A caching proxy is a server, usually installed in a local corporate network or by the Internet service provider (ISP). It is a read-through cache used to reduce the amount of traffic generated by the users of the network by reusing responses between users of the network. The larger the network, the larger the potential saving—that is why it was quite common among ISPs to install transparent caching proxies and route all of the HTTP traffic through them to cache as many web requests as possible. Figure 6-5 shows how a transparent caching proxy can be installed within a local network.

Figure 6-5 *HTTP proxy server in local network*

In recent years, the practice of installing local proxy servers has become less popular as bandwidth has become cheaper and as it becomes more popular for websites to serve their resources solely over the Secure Sockets Layer (SSL) protocol. SSL encrypts the communication between the client and the server, which is why caching proxies are not able to intercept such requests, as they do not have the necessary certificates to decrypt and encrypt messages being exchanged.

Reverse Proxy

A *reverse proxy* works in the exactly same way as a regular caching proxy, but the intent is to place a reverse proxy in your own data center to reduce the load put on your own web servers. Figure 6-6 shows a reverse proxy deployed in the data center, together with web servers, caching responses from your web servers.

For some applications, reverse proxies are an excellent way to scale. If you can use full page caching, you can significantly reduce the number of requests coming to your web servers. Using reverse proxies can also give you more flexibility because you can override HTTP headers and better control which requests are being cached and for how long. Finally, reverse proxies are an excellent way to speed up your web services layer. You can often put a layer of reverse proxy servers between your front-end web application servers and your web service machines. Figure 6-7 shows how you can scale a cluster of REST-ful web services

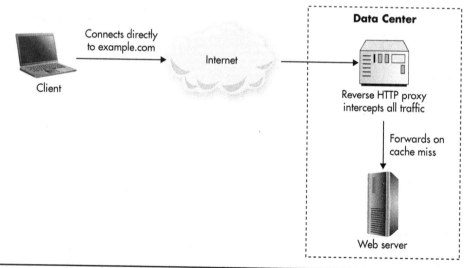

Figure 6-6   *Reverse proxy*

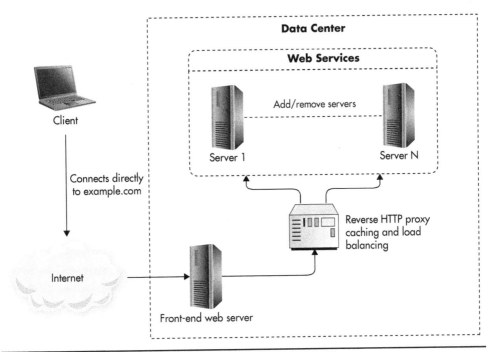

Figure 6-7   *Reverse proxy in front of web services cluster*

by simply reducing the number of requests that need to be served. Even if you were not able to cache all of your endpoints, caching web service responses can be a useful technique.

Content Delivery Networks

A content delivery network (CDN) is a distributed network of cache servers that work in a similar way as caching proxies. They depend on the same HTTP headers, but they are controlled by the CDN service provider. As your web application grows larger, it becomes very beneficial to use a CDN provider. By using a CDN, you reduce the load put on your servers, you save on network bandwidth, and you improve the user experience by pushing content closer to your users. CDN providers usually have dozens of data centers located all around the world, which allows them to serve cached results from the closest cache server, thereby decreasing the network latency. Web applications would typically use CDN to cache their static files like images, CSS, JavaScript, videos, or Portable Document File (PDF) documents. You can implement it easily by creating a "static" subdomain (for example, s.example.org) and generating URLs for all of your static files using this domain. Then, you configure the CDN provider to accept these requests on your behalf and point DNS for s.example.org to the CDN provider. Any time CDN fails to serve a piece of content from its cache, it forwards the request to your web servers (*origin servers*) and caches the response for subsequent users. Figure 6-8 shows how CDN can be used to cache static files.

You can also configure some CDN providers to serve both static and dynamic content of your website so that clients never connect to your data center directly; they always go through the cache servers belonging to the CDN provider. This technique has some benefits. For example, the provider can mitigate distributed denial of service attacks (as CloudFlare does). It can also lead to further reduction of web requests sent to your origin servers, as dynamic content (even private content) can now be cached by the CDN. Figure 6-9 shows how you can configure Amazon CloudFront to deliver both static and dynamic content for you.

Now that we have gone through the different types of caches, let's see how we can scale each type as our website traffic grows.

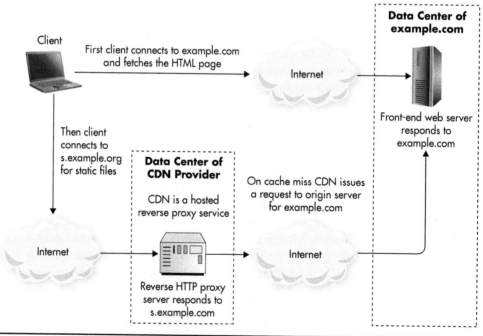

Figure 6-8 *CDN configured for static files*

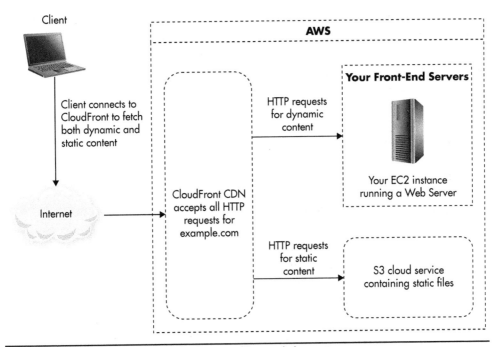

Figure 6-9   *CDN configured for both static files and dynamic content*

Scaling HTTP Caches

One reason HTTP-based caching is so attractive is that you can usually push the load off your own servers onto machines managed by third parties that are closer to your users. Any request served from browser cache, a third-party caching proxy, or a CDN is a request that never got to your web servers, ultimately reducing the stress on your infrastructure. At the same time, requests served from HTTP caches are satisfied faster than your web servers could ever do it, making HTTP-based caching even more valuable.

As mentioned before, do not worry about the scalability of browser caches or third-party proxy servers; they are out of your control. When it comes to CDN providers, you do not have to worry about scalability either, as CDN providers scale transparently, charging you flat fees per million requests or per GB of data transferred. Usually, the prices per unit decrease as you scale out, making them even more cost effective. This leaves you to manage only reverse proxy servers. If you use these, you need to manage and scale them yourself.

There are many open-source reverse proxy solutions on the market, including Nginx, Varnish, Squid, Apache mod_proxy, and Apache Traffic Server. If you are hosted in a private data center, you may also be able to use a built-in reverse proxy functionality provided by some of the hardware load balancers.

For most young startups, a single reverse proxy should be able to handle the incoming traffic, as both hardware reverse proxies and leading open-source ones (Nginx or Varnish) can handle more than 10,000 requests per second from a single machine. As such, it is usually more important to decide what to cache and for how long rather than how to scale reverse proxies themselves. To be able to scale the reverse proxy layer efficiently, you need to focus on your cache hit ratio first. It is affected by the same three factors mentioned at the beginning of the chapter, and in the context of reverse proxies, they translate to the following:

▶ **Cache key space**   Describes how many distinct URLs your reverse proxies will observe in a period of time (let's say in an hour). The more distinct URLs are served, the more memory or storage you need on each reverse proxy to be able to serve a significant portion of traffic from cache. Avoid caching responses that depend on the user (for example, that contain the user ID in the URL). These types of responses can easily pollute your cache with objects that cannot be reused.

▶ **Average response TTL**   Describes how long each response can be cached. The longer you cache objects, the more chance you have to reuse them. Always try to cache objects permanently. If you cannot cache objects forever, try to negotiate the longest acceptable cache TTL with your business stakeholders.

▶ **Average size of cached object**   Affects how much memory or storage your reverse proxies will need to be able to store the most commonly accessed objects. Average size of cached object is the most difficult to control, but you should still keep it in mind because there are some techniques that help you "shrink" your objects. For example, CSS files and JavaScript files can be minified and HTML can be preprocessed to remove redundant white spaces and comments during the template-rendering phase.

It is worth pointing out that you do not have to worry much about cache servers becoming full by setting a long TTL, as in-memory caches use algorithms designed to evict rarely accessed objects and reclaim space. The most commonly used algorithm is Least Recently Used (LRU), which allows the cache server to eventually remove rarely accessed objects and keep "hot" items in memory to maximize cache hit ratio.

Once you verify that you are caching objects for as long as possible and that you only cache things that can be efficiently reused, you can start thinking of scaling out your reverse proxy layer. You are most likely going to reach either the concurrency limit or throughput limit. Both of these problems can be mitigated easily by deploying multiple reverse proxies in parallel and distributing traffic among them.

Figure 6-10 shows a deployment scenario where two layers of reverse proxies are used. The first layer is deployed directly behind a load balancer, which distributes the traffic among the reverse proxies. The second layer is positioned

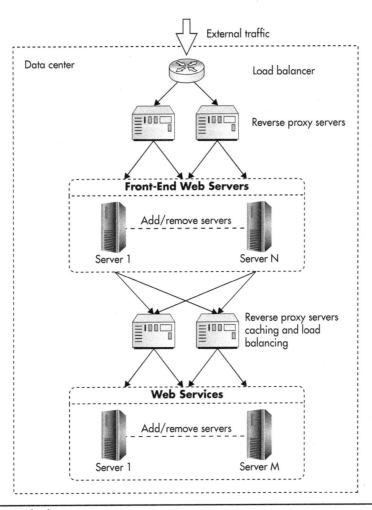

Figure 6-10 *Multiple reverse proxy servers*

between the front-end web servers and web service machines. In this case, front-end web servers are configured to pick a random reverse proxy on each request. Once your stack grows even larger, it makes sense to deploy a load balancer in front of the second reverse proxy layer as well to make configuration changes more transparent and isolated. Luckily, it is unlikely that you would need such a complicated deployment; usually, reverse proxies in front of the front-end web application are unnecessary, and it is more convenient to push that responsibility onto the CDN.

HINT

If you are using HTTP caching correctly, adding more reverse proxies and running them in parallel should not cause problems. The HTTP protocol does not require synchronization between HTTP caches, and it does not guarantee that all of the client's requests are routed through the same physical networks. Each HTTP request can be sent in a separate TCP/IP connection and can be routed through a different set of intermediate caches. Clients have to work under these constraints and accept inconsistent responses or use cache revalidation.

No matter what reverse proxy technology you choose, you can use the same deployment pattern of multiple reverse proxies running in parallel because the underlying behavior is exactly the same. Each proxy is an independent clone, sharing nothing with its siblings, which is why choice of reverse proxy technology is not that important when you think of scalability. For general use cases, I recommend using Nginx or a hardware reverse proxy, as they have superior performance and feature sets. A few Nginx features that are especially worth mentioning are

▶ Nginx uses solely asynchronous processing, which allows it to proxy tens of thousands of concurrent connections with a very low per-connection overhead.

▶ Nginx is also a FastCGI server, which means that you can run your web application on the same web server stack as your reverse proxies.

▶ Nginx can act as a load balancer; it supports multiple forwarding algorithms and many advanced features, such as SPDY, WebSockets, and throttling. Nginx can also be configured to override headers, which can be used to apply HTTP caching to web applications that do not implement caching headers correctly or to override their caching policies.

▶ Nginx is well established with an active community. As of 2013, it is reported to serve over 15% of the Internet (source Netcraft).

If you are hosting your data center yourself and have a hardware load balancer, I recommend using it as a reverse proxy as well to reduce the number of components in your stack. In all other cases, I recommend investigating available open-source reverse proxy technologies like Nginx, Varnish, or Apache Traffic Server; selecting one; and scaling it out by adding more clones.

Finally, you can also scale reverse proxies vertically by giving them more memory or switching their persistent storage to solid-state drive (SSD). This technique is especially useful when the pool of fresh cached objects becomes much larger than the working memory of your cache servers. To increase your hit ratio, you can extend the size of your cache storage to hundreds of GB by switching to file system storage rather than depending solely on the shared memory. By using SSD drives, you will be able to serve these responses at least ten times faster than if you used regular (spinning disc) hard drives due to the much faster random access times of SSD drives. At the same time, since cache data is meant to be disposable, you do not have to worry much about limited SSD lifetimes or sudden power failure–related SSD corruptions.[w73]

Caching Application Objects

After HTTP-based caches, the second most important caching component in a web application stack is usually a custom object cache. Object caches are used in a different way than HTTP caches because they are *cache-aside* rather than *read-through* caches. In the case of cache-aside caches, the application needs to be aware of the existence of the object cache, and it actively uses it to store and retrieve objects rather than the cache being transparently positioned between the application and its data sources (which happens with read-through cache).

Cache-aside cache is seen by the application as an independent key-value data store. Application code would usually ask the object cache if the needed object is available and, if so, it would retrieve and use the cached object. If the required object is not present or has expired, the application would then do whatever was necessary to build the object from scratch. It would usually contact its primary data sources to assemble the object and then save it back in the object cache for future use. Figure 6-11 shows how cache-aside lives "on the side" and how the application communicates directly with its data sources rather than communicating through the cache.

Similar to other types of caches, the main motivation for using object cache is to save the time and resources needed to create application objects from scratch. All of the object cache types discussed in this section can be imagined

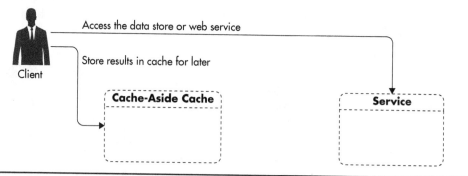

Figure 6-11 *Cache-aside cache*

as key-value stores with support of object expiration, and they usually support a simplistic programming interface, allowing you to get, set, and delete objects based on the unique key string. Let's now have a closer look at different types of object caches and their benefits and drawbacks.

Common Types of Object Caches

As was the case for the HTTP caches we discussed earlier in this chapter, there are many different ways application object caches can be deployed. The actual technologies used may depend on the technology stack used, but the concepts remain similar.

Client-Side Caches

Let's first look at the local storage located directly in the client's device. Years ago, it was impossible for JavaScript to store information on the client's machine, but now, most of the modern web browsers support the web storage specification, allowing JavaScript to store application data directly on the user's device. Even though web storage allows a web application to use a limited amount of space (usually up to 5MB to 25MB of data), it is a great way to speed up web applications and reduce the pressure put on your infrastructure. It is even more valuable, as it can be safely used to store user-specific information because web storage is isolated to a single device.

Listing 6-10 shows how easy it is to store an object in web storage. Web storage works as a key-value store. To store an object, you provide a unique identifier, called the *key,* and the string of bytes that you want to be persisted (called the *value*).

Listing 6-10 *JavaScript code storing objects in web storage*

```
var preferences = {/* data object to be stored */};
localStorage.setItem('preferences', JSON.stringify(preferences));
```

Web storage persists the data permanently so it can be accessed in the future even if the user decides to close the browser or restart the computer. Users are able to clean the web storage data using their browser settings, so you should keep that in mind and use web storage as a cache rather than as a reliable data store. Whenever you want to access the *value* stored in web storage you simply request it using the same *key* that you used when persisting it. Listing 6-11 shows how you can retrieve objects from web storage using JavaScript.

Listing 6-11 *JavaScript code accessing previously persisted object*

```
var cachedData = localStorage.getItem('preferences');
var preferences = JSON.parse(cachedData);
```

Local device storage becomes even more important when you are developing single-page applications (SPAs), as these applications run much more code within the user's browser and perform more asynchronous web requests (AJAX). In particular, if you are developing an SPA for mobile devices (for example, using Sencha Touch framework), you should always integrate a local storage solution to cache web service responses and reduce the number of requests that you need to send to your web servers. Similarly to web storage, you can store data directly on the client's device when developing native mobile applications. In this case, the technologies are different, but the theory of operation is similar. When using local device storage, it is important to remember that it is isolated from your data center, which makes it impossible for your servers to remove/invalidate cached objects directly. Anytime you use web storage or similar client-side storage, you need to include the code responsible for cache refresh and invalidation in your front-end JavaScript code. For example, imagine you were developing a mobile SPA that would allow users to see restaurants within walking distance from their current location. Since it is a mobile application, you might want to speed up the application loading time or reduce its data usage by using local storage. You could do that by showing the user their last search results whenever the application is opened rather than showing a blank screen when waiting for global positioning system (GPS) location and search results.

To execute this, you could save each search result in web storage, together with the user's coordinates and a timestamp; then on load time, you could simply show the last search results by loading it from web storage. At the same time, you could compare a user's location and current time to the coordinates of their previous search. If the user's location has changed significantly—let's say they moved by more than 200 meters or they have not opened the application for more than a day—you could update the user interface to indicate an update is in progress and then issue a new asynchronous request to your server to load new data. This way, your users can see something immediately, making the application seem more responsive; at the same time, you reduce the number of unnecessary requests sent to your servers in case users are opening their apps a few times on their way to the restaurant.

Caches Co-located with Code

Another important type of object cache is one located directly on your web servers. Whether you develop a front-end web application or a web service, you can usually benefit from local cache. Local cache is usually implemented in one of the following ways:

▶ *Objects are cached directly in the application's memory.* The application creates a pool for cached objects and never releases memory allocated for them. In this case, there is virtually no overhead when accessing cached objects, as they are stored directly in the memory of the application process in the native format of the executing code. There is no need to copy, transfer, or encode these objects; they can be accessed directly. This method applies to all programming languages.

▶ *Objects are stored in shared memory segments so that multiple processes running on the same machine could access them.* In this approach, there is still very little overhead, as shared memory access is almost as fast as local process memory. The implementation may add some overhead, but it can be still considered insignificant. For example, in PHP, storing objects in shared memory forces object serialization, which adds a slight overhead but allows all processes running on the same server to share the cached objects pool. This method is less common, as it is not applicable in multithreaded environments like Java, where all execution threads run within a single process.

▶ *A caching server is deployed on each web server as a separate application.* In this scenario, each web server has an instance of a caching server running locally, but it must still use the caching server's interface to interact with the cache rather than accessing shared memory directly. This method is more common in tiny web applications where you start off with a single web server and you deploy your cache (like Memcached or Redis) on the same machine as your web application, mainly to save on hosting costs and network latencies. The benefit of this approach is that your application is ready to talk to an external caching server—it just happens to run on the same machine as your web application, making it trivial to move your cache to a dedicated cluster without the need to modify the application code.

Each of these approaches boils down to the same concept of having an object cache locally on the server where your application code executes. The main benefit of caching objects directly on your application servers is the speed at which they can be persistent and accessed. Since objects are stored in memory on the same server, they can be accessed orders of magnitude faster than if you had to fetch them from a remote server. Table 6-1 shows the orders of magnitude of latencies introduced by accessing local memory, disk, and remote network calls.

An additional benefit of local application cache is the simplicity of development and deployment. Rather than coordinating between servers, deploying additional components, and then managing them during deployments, local cache is usually nothing more than a bit of extra memory allocated by the application process. Local caches are not synchronized or replicated between servers, which also makes things faster and simpler, as you do not have to worry about locking and network latencies. By having identical and independent local caches on

Operation Type	Approximate Time
Time to access local memory	100 ns
SSD disk seek	100,000 ns
Time of a network packet round trip within the same data center	500,000 ns
Disk seek (non-SSD)	10,000,000 ns
Read 1MB sequentially from network	10,000,000 ns
Read 1MB sequentially from disk (non-SSD)	30,000,000 ns
Time of a network packet round trip across Atlantic	150,000,000 ns
How many nanoseconds in a single second	1,000,000,000 ns

Table 6-1 *Approximate Latencies when Accessing Different Resources*

each server, you also make your web cluster easier to scale by adding clones (as described in Chapters 2 and 3) because your web servers are interchangeable yet independent from one another.

Unfortunately, there are some drawbacks to local application caches. Most importantly, each application server will likely end up caching the same objects, causing a lot of duplication between your servers. That is caused by the fact that caches located on your application servers do not share any information, nor are they synchronized in any way. If you dedicate 1GB of memory for object cache on each of your web servers, you realistically end up with a total of 1GB of memory across your cluster, no matter how many servers you have, as each web server will be bound to that limit, duplicating content that may be stored in other caches. Depending on your use case, this can be a serious limitation, as you cannot easily scale the size of your cache.

Another very important limitation of local server caches is that they cannot be kept consistent and you cannot remove objects from such a cache efficiently. For example, if you were building an e-commerce website and you were to cache product information, you might need to remove these cached objects any time the product price changes. Unfortunately, if you cache objects on multiple machines without any synchronization or coordination, you will not be able to remove objects from these caches without building overly complex solutions (like publishing messages to your web servers to remove certain objects from cache).

Distributed Object Caches

The last common type of cache relevant to web applications is a distributed object cache. The main difference between this type and local server cache is that interacting with a distributed object cache usually requires a network round trip to the cache server. On the plus side, distributed object caches offer much better scalability than local application caches. Distributed object caches usually work as simple key-value stores, allowing clients to store data in the cache for a limited amount of time, after which the object is automatically removed by the cache server (object expires). There are many open-source products available, with Redis and Memcached being the most popular ones in the web space. There are commercial alternatives worth considering as well, like Terracotta Server Array or Oracle Coherence, but I would recommend a simple open-source solution for most startup use cases.

Interacting with distributed cache servers is simple, and most caching servers have client libraries for all common programming languages. Listing 6-12 shows the simplicity of caching interfaces. All you need to specify is the server you want to connect to, the key of the value you want to store, and TTL (in seconds) after which the object should be removed from the cache.

Listing 6-12 *PHP code caching user count for five minutes in Memcached*

```
$m = new Memcached();
$m->addServer('10.0.0.1', 11211); //set cache server IP
$m->set('userCount', 123, 600); // set data
```

Storing objects in remote cache servers (like Redis or Memcached) has a few advantages. Most importantly, you can scale these solutions much better. We will look at this in more detail in the next section, but for now, let's say that you can scale simply by adding more servers to the cache cluster. By adding servers, you can scale both the throughput and overall memory pool of your cache. By using a distributed cache, you can also efficiently remove objects from the cache, allowing for cache invalidation on source data changes. As I explained earlier, in some cases, you need to remove objects from cache as soon as the data changes. Having a distributed cache makes such *cache invalidation* (cache object removal) easier, as all you need to do is connect to your cache and request object removal.

Using dedicated cache servers is also a good way to push responsibility out of your applications, as cache servers are nothing other than data stores and they often support a variety of features. For example, Redis allows for data persistence, replication, and efficient implementation of distributed counters, lists, and object sets. Caches are also heavily optimized when it comes to memory management, and they take care of things like object expiration and evictions.

> **HINT**
>
> Cache servers usually use the LRU algorithm to decide which objects should be removed from cache once they reach a memory limit. Any time you want to store a new object in the cache, the cache server checks if there is enough memory to add it in. If there is no space left, it removes the objects that were least recently used to make enough space for your new object. By using LRU cache, you never have to worry about deleting items from cache—they just expire or get removed once more "popular" objects arrive.

Distributed caches are usually deployed on separate clusters of servers, giving them more operating memory than other machines would need. Figure 6-12 shows how cache servers are usually deployed—in a separate cluster of machines accessible from both front-end and web service machines.

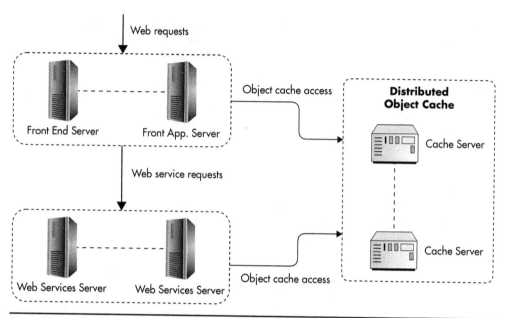

Figure 6-12 *Common distributed cache deployment*

Even though distributed caches are powerful scalability tools and are relatively simple in structure, adding them to your system adds a certain amount of complexity and management overhead. Even if you use cloud-hosted Redis or Memcached, you may not need to worry about deployments and server management, but you still need to understand and monitor them to be able to use them efficiently. Whenever deploying new caches, start as small as possible. Redis is a very efficient cache server, and a single machine can support tens of thousands of operations per second, allowing you to grow to reasonable traffic without the need to scale it at all. As long as throughput is not a problem, scale vertically by adding more memory rather than trying to implement a more complex deployment with replication or data partitioning. When your system grows larger and becomes more popular, you may need to scale above a single node. Let's now have a closer look at how you can scale your object caches.

Scaling Object Caches

When it comes to scaling your object caches, the techniques depend on the location and type of your cache. For example, client-side caches like web browser storage cannot be scaled, as there is no way to affect the amount of memory that browsers allow you to use. The value of web storage comes with the fact that users have their own cache. You can keep adding users, and you do not have to scale the client-side caches to store their user-specific data.

The web server local caches are usually scaled by falling back to the file system, as there is no other way to distribute or grow cache that, by definition, lives on a single server. In some scenarios, you may have a very large data pool where each cached object can be cached for a long period of time but objects are accessed relatively rarely. In such a scenario, it may be a good idea to use the local file system of your web servers to store cached objects as serialized files rather than storing them in the memory of the shared cache cluster. Accessing cached objects stored on the file system is slower, but it does not require remote connections, so that web server becomes more independent and insulated from the other subsystems' failures. File-based caches can also be cheaper because the disk storage is much cheaper than operating memory and you do not have to create a separate cluster just for the shared object cache. Given the rising popularity of SSD drives, file system–based caches may be a cheap and fast random access memory (RAM) alternative.

When it comes to distributed object caches, you may scale in different ways depending on the technology used, but usually data partitioning (explained in Chapters 2 and 5) is the best way to go, as it allows you to scale the throughput and the overall memory pool of your cluster. Some technologies, like Oracle Coherence, support data partitioning out of the box, but most open-source solutions (like Memcached and Redis) are simpler than that and rely on client-side data partitioning.

If you decide to use Memcached as your object cache, the situation is quite simple. You can use the libMemcached client library's built-in features to partition the data among multiple servers. Rather than having to implement it in your code, you can simply tell the client library that you have multiple Memcached servers. Listing 6-13 shows how easy it is to declare multiple servers as a single Memcached cluster using a native PHP client that uses libMemcached under the hood to talk to Memcached servers.

Listing 6-13 *Declaring multiple Memcached servers as a single cluster*

```php
<?php
$cache = new Memcached();
$cache->setOption(Memcached::OPT_LIBKETAMA_COMPATIBLE, true);
$cache->addServers(array(
    array('cache1.example.com', 11211),
```

```
        array('cache2.example.com', 11211),
        array('cache3.example.com', 11211)
));
```

By declaring a Memcached cluster, your data will be automatically distributed among the cache servers using a consistent hashing algorithm. Any time you issue a GET or SET command, the Memcached client library will hash the cache key that you want to access and then map it to one of the servers. Once the client finds out which server is responsible for that particular cache key, it will send the request to that particular server only so that other servers in the cluster do not have to participate in the operation. This is an example of the share-nothing approach, as each cache object is assigned to a single server without any redundancy or coordination between cache servers.

Figure 6-13 illustrates how consistent hashing is implemented. First, all possible cache keys are represented as a range of numbers, with the beginning and end joined to create a circle. Then you place all of your servers on the circle, an equal distance from one another. Then you declare that each server is responsible for the cache keys sitting between it and the next server (moving clockwise along the circle). This way, by knowing the cache key and how many servers you have in the cluster, you can always find out which server is responsible for the data you are looking for.

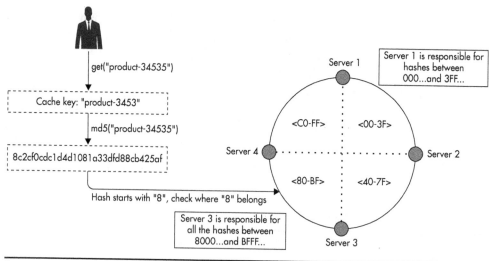

Figure 6-13 *Cache partitioning using consistent hashing*

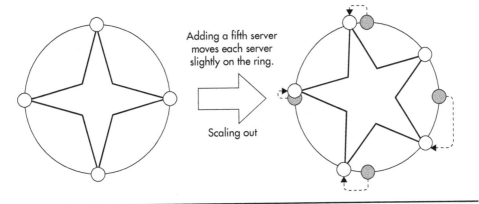

Figure 6-14 *Scaling cache cluster using consistent hashing*

To scale your cache cluster horizontally, you need to be able to add servers to the cluster, and this is where consistent hashing really shines. Since each server is responsible for a part of the key space on the ring, adding a new server to the cluster causes each server to move slightly on the ring. This way, only a small subset of the cache keys get reassigned between servers, causing a relatively small cache-miss wave. Figure 6-14 shows how server positions change when you scale from a four-server cluster to a five-server cluster.

If you used a naïve approach like using a modulo function to map a cache key to the server numbers, each time you added or removed a server from the cluster, most of your cache keys would be reassigned, effectively purging your entire cache. The Memcached client for PHP is not the only client library supporting consistent hashing. In fact, there are many open-source libraries that you can use in your application layer if your cache driver does not support consistent hashing out of the box.

> **HINT**
>
> *To understand caching even better, it is good to think of cache as a large hash map. The reason caches can locate items so fast is that they use hashing functions to determine the "bucket" in which a cached object should live. This way, no matter how large the cache is, getting and setting values can be performed in constant time.*

Another alternative approach to scaling object caches is to use data replication or a combination of data partitioning and data replication. Some object caches, like Redis, allow for master-slave replication deployments, which can be helpful in some scenarios. For example, if one of your cache keys became so "hot" that all of the application servers needed to fetch it concurrently, you could benefit from read replicas. Rather than all clients needing the cached object connecting to a single server, you could scale the cluster by adding read-only replicas of each node in the cluster (see Chapter 2). Figure 6-15 shows how you could deploy read-only replicas of each cache server to scale the read throughput and allow a higher level of concurrency.

It is worth mentioning that if you were hosting your web application on Amazon, you could either deploy your own caching servers on EC2 instances or use Amazon Elastic Cache. Unfortunately, Elastic Cache is not as smart as you might expect, as it is basically a hosted cache cluster and the only real benefit of it is that you do not have to manage the servers or worry about failure-recovery scenarios. When you create an Elastic Cache cluster, you can choose whether you want to use Memcached or Redis, and you can also pick how many servers you want and how much capacity you need per server. It is important to remember that you will still need to distribute the load across the cache servers in your client code because Elastic Cache does not add transparent partitioning or automatic scalability. In a similar way, you can create cache clusters using other

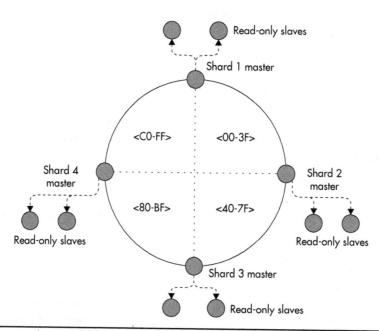

Figure 6-15 *Scaling cache cluster using data partitioning and replication*

cloud-hosting providers. For example, Azure lets you deploy a managed Redis instance with replication and automatic failover in a matter of a few clicks.

Object caches are in general easier to scale than data stores, and usually simple data partitioning and/or replication is enough to scale your clusters horizontally. When you consider that all of the data stored in object caches is, by definition, disposable, the consistency and persistence constraints can be relaxed, allowing for simpler scalability. Now that we have discussed different types of caches and their scalability techniques, let's move on to some general rules of thumb that may be helpful when designing scalable web applications.

Caching Rules of Thumb

How difficult caching is depends on the application needs and how we use it. It's important to know the most common types of caches and how to scale them. In this section, we will discuss where to focus and prioritize your caching efforts to get the biggest bang for the buck. We will also discuss some techniques that can help you reuse cached objects and some pitfalls to watch out for. Let's get to it.

Cache High Up the Call Stack

One of the most important things to remember about caching is that the higher up the call stack you can cache, the more resources you can save. To illustrate it a bit better, let's consider Figure 6-16. It shows how the call stack of an average web request might look and roughly how much can you save by caching on each layer. Treat the percentage of the resources saved on Figure 6-16 as a simplified rule of thumb. In reality, every system will have a different distribution of resources consumed by each layer.

First, your client requests a page or a resource. If that resource is available in one of the HTTP caches (browser, local proxy) or can be satisfied from local storage, then your servers will not even see the request, saving you 100 percent of the resources. If that fails, your second best choice is to serve the HTTP request directly from reverse proxy or CDN, as in such a case you incur just a couple percentage points of the cost needed to generate the full response.

When a request makes it to your web server, you may still have a chance to use a custom object cache and serve the entire response without ever calling your web services. In case you need to call the web services, you may also be able to get the response from a reverse proxy living between your web application and your web services. Only when that fails as well will your web services get involved in

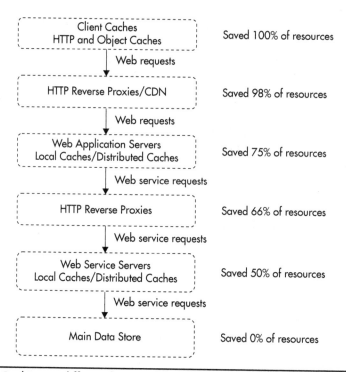

Figure 6-16 *Caching in different layers of the stack*

serving the request. Here again, you may be able to use object caches and satisfy the request without the need to involve the data stores. Only when all of this fails will you need to query the data stores or search engines to retrieve the data needed by the user.

The same principle applies within your application code. If you can cache an entire page fragment, you will save more time and resources than caching just the database query that was used to render this page fragment. As you can see, avoiding the web requests reaching your servers is the ultimate goal, but even when it is not possible, you should still try to cache as high up the call stack as you can.

Reuse Cache Among Users

Another important thing to remember when working with caching is to always try to reuse the same cached object for as many requests/users as you can. Caching objects that are never requested again is simply a waste of time and resources.

To illustrate it better, let's consider an example. Imagine you are building a mobile application that allows users to find restaurants near their current location. The main use case would be for the user to see a list of restaurants within walking distance so they could pick the restaurant they like and quickly have something to eat. A simple implementation of that application could check the GPS coordinates, build a query string containing the user's current location, and request the list of nearby restaurants from the application server. The request to the web application programming interface (API) could resemble Listing 6-14.

Listing 6-14   *Request for lat: -33.880381, lon: 151.209146*

```
GET /restaurants/search?lat=-33.880381&lon=151.209146
```

The problem with this approach is that request parameters will be different for almost every single request. Even walking just a few steps will change the GPS location, making the URL different and rendering your cache completely useless.

A better approach to this problem would be to round the GPS location to three decimal places so that each person within the same street block could reuse the same search result. Instead of having billions of possible locations within the city limits, you reduce the number of possible locations and increase your chances of serving responses from cache. Since the URL does not contain user-specific data and is not personalized, there is no reason why you should not reuse the entire HTTP response by adding public HTTP caching headers.

If you were serving restaurants in Sydney and you decide to round the latitude and longitude to three decimal places, you would reduce the number of possible user locations to less than one million. Having just one million possible responses would let you cache them efficiently in a reverse proxy layer (or even a dynamic content CDN). Because restaurant details are unlikely to change rapidly, you should be able to cache service responses for hours without causing any business impact, increasing your cache hit ratio even further. Listing 6-15 shows how the structure of the URL remains the same and just the request arguments have changed, reducing the number of possible URLs being requested.

Listing 6-15   *Request for lat: -33.867, lon: 151.207*

```
GET /restaurants/search?lat=-33.867&lon=151.207
```

This principle of reusing the same data for many users applies to many more scenarios. You have to look for ways that would let you return the same result multiple times rather than generating it from scratch. If it is not possible to cache entire pages, maybe it is possible to cache page fragments or use some other trick to reduce the number of possible cache keys (as in my restaurant finder example). The point is, you need to maximize the cache hit ratio, and you can only do it by increasing your cache pool, extending the TTL of your objects, and decreasing the number of potential cache keys.

Where to Start Caching?

If you ever find yourself supporting an existing web application that does not have enough caching, you have to ask yourself, "Where do I start? What are the most important queries to be cached? What pages are worth caching? What services need to be cached the most?" As with any type of optimization, to be successful, you need to prioritize based on a strict and simple metric rather than depending on your gut feeling. To prioritize what needs to be cached, use a simple metric of aggregated time spent generating a particular type of response. You can calculate the aggregated time spent in the following way:

aggregated time spent = time spent per request * number of requests

This allows you to find out which pages (or resources) are the most valuable when it comes to caching. For example, in one of my previous jobs I worked on a website with fairly high levels of traffic. We wanted to scale and improve performance at the same time, so we began looking for opportunities to cache more aggressively. To decide where to start, I used a Google Analytics report and correlated traffic stats for the top 20 pages with the average time needed to render each of these pages. Then I created a ranking based on the overall value, similar to Table 6-2.

Value Rank	Page	Avg. Seconds	Requests per Hour	Aggregated Time Spent
1	/	0.55	700000	385000
2	/somePage	1.1	100000	110000
3	/otherPage	0.84	57000	47880

Table 6-2   *Page Ranks Based on Potential Gain from Caching*

If you look closely at Table 6-2 you can see that improving performance of the home page by 5 ms gives more overall saving than improving performance of the second most valuable page by 10 ms. If I went with my gut feeling, I would most likely start optimizing and caching in all the wrong places, wasting a lot of valuable time. By having a simple metric and a ranking of pages to tackle, I managed to focus my attention on the most important pages, resulting in a significant capacity increase.

Cache Invalidation Is Difficult

"There are only two hard things in computer science: cache invalidation and naming things and off-by-one errors." –Phil Karlton

The last rule of thumb is that cache invalidation becomes difficult very quickly. When you initially develop a simple site, it may seem easy. Cache invalidation is simply removing objects from cache once the source data changes to avoid using stale objects. You add an object to cache, and any time the data changes, you go back to the cache and remove the stale object. Simple, right? Well, unfortunately, it is often much more complicated than that. Cache invalidation is difficult because cached objects are usually a result of computation that takes multiple data sources as its input. That, in turn, means that whenever any of these data sources changes, you should invalidate all of the cached objects that have used it as input. To make it even more difficult, each piece of content may have multiple representations, in which case all of them would have to be removed from cache.

To better illustrate this problem, let's consider an example of an e-commerce website. If you used object caches aggressively, you could cache all of the search queries that you send to the data store. You would cache query results for paginated product lists, keyword searches, category pages, and product pages. If you wanted to keep all of the data in your cache consistent, any time a product's details change, you would have to invalidate all of the cached objects that contain that product. In other words you would need to invalidate the query results for all of the queries, including not just the product page, but also all of the other lists and search results that included this product. But how will you find all the search results that might have contained a product without running all of these queries? How will you construct the cache keys for all the category listings and find the right page offset on all paginated lists to invalidate just the right objects? Well, that is exactly the problem—there is no easy way to do that.

The best alternative to cache invalidation is to set a short TTL on your cached objects so that data will not be stale for too long. It works most of the time, but it is not always sufficient. In cases where your business does not allow data inconsistency, you may also consider caching partial results and going to the data source for the missing "critical" information. For example, if your business required you to always display the exact price and stock availability, you could still cache most of the product information and complex query results. The only extra work that you would need to do is fetch the exact stock and price for each item from the main data store before the rendering results. Although such a "hybrid" solution is not perfect, it reduces the number of complex queries that your data store needs to process and trades them for a set of much simpler "WHERE product_id IN (....)" queries.

Advanced cache invalidation techniques are beyond the scope of this book, but if you are interested in learning more about them, I recommend reading two white papers published in recent years. The first one[w6] explains a clever algorithm for query subspace invalidation, where you create "groups" of items to be invalidated. The second one[w62] describes how Facebook invalidates cache entries by adding cache keys to their MySQL replication logs. This allows them to replicate cache invalidation commands across data centers and ensures cache invalidation after a data store update.

Due to their temporary nature, caching issues are usually difficult to reproduce and debug. Although cache invalidation algorithms are interesting to learn, I do not recommend implementing them unless absolutely necessary. I recommend avoiding cache invalidation altogether for as long as possible and using TTL-based expiration instead. In most cases, short TTL or a hybrid solution, where you load critical data on the fly, is enough to satisfy the business needs.

Summary

Caching is one of the most important scalability techniques, as it allows you to increase your capacity at relatively low cost, and you can usually add it to your system at a later stage without the need to significantly rearchitect your system. If you can reuse the same result for multiple users or, even better, satisfy the response without the request ever reaching your servers, that is when you see caching at its best.

I strongly recommend getting very familiar with caching techniques and technologies available on the market, as caching is heavily used by most large-scale websites. This includes general HTTP caching knowledge[42] and caching in the context of REST-ful web services,[46] in addition to learning how versatile Redis can be.[50]

Caching is one of the oldest scalability techniques with plenty of use cases. Let's now move on to a much more novel concept that has been gaining popularity in recent years: asynchronous processing.

Asynchronous Processing

Asynchronous processing and messaging technologies introduce many new concepts and a completely different way of thinking about software. Instead of telling the system what to do step by step, we break down the work into smaller pieces and let it decide the optimal execution order. As a result, things become much more dynamic, but also more unpredictable.

When applied wisely, asynchronous processing and messaging can be very powerful tools in scaling applications and increasing their fault tolerance. However, getting used to them can take some time. In this chapter, I will explain the core concepts behind message queues, event-driven architecture, and asynchronous processing. I will discuss the benefits and the "gotchas," as well as some of the technologies that can be useful on your journey to asynchronous processing.

By the time you reach the end of the chapter, you should have a good understanding of how messaging and asynchronous processing work. I also hope you'll be excited about event-driven architecture, an interesting field gaining popularity in recent years.

Core Concepts

Before we dive into asynchronous processing, let's first start with a brief explanation of synchronous processing and how the two differ. Let's now look at some examples to explain the difference between synchronous and asynchronous processing.

Synchronous processing is the more traditional way of software execution. In synchronous processing, the caller sends a request to get something done and waits for the response before continuing its own work. The caller usually depends on the result of the operation and cannot continue without it. The caller can be a function calling another function, a thread, or even a process sending a request to another process. It can also be an application or a system sending requests to a remote server. The key point is that in all these cases, the caller has to *wait* for the response before continuing its execution.

Asynchronous processing, in a nutshell, is about issuing requests that do not block your execution. In the asynchronous model, the caller never waits idle for responses from services it depends upon. Requests are sent and processing continues without ever being blocked.

Synchronous Example

Let's discuss synchronous processing using an object-oriented programming example of an EmailService. Imagine we have an EmailService interface with a single method, sendEmail, which accepts EmailMessage objects and sends e-mails. In Listing 7-1, you can see how the EmailMessage and EmailService interfaces might look. I do not show the implementation of the service on purpose, because the interface is all that client code should care about.

Listing 7-1   *Simple EmailService and EmailMessage interfaces*

```
Interface EmailMessage {
    public function getSubject();
    public function getTextBody();
    public function getHtmlBody();
    public function getFromEmail();
    public function getToEmail();
    public function getReplyToEmail();
}
Interface EmailService {
    /**
     * Sends an email message
     *
     * @param EmailMessage $email
     * @throws Exception
     * @return void
     */
    public function sendEmail(EmailMessage $email);
}
```

Whenever you wish to send out an e-mail, you obtain an instance of EmailService and invoke the sendEmail method on it. Then the EmailService implementation can do whatever is necessary to get the job done. For example, it could have an SmtpEmailAdapter allowing it to send e-mails over the Simple Mail Transport Protocol (SMTP) protocol. Figure 7-1 shows how the sequence of calls might appear.

The important thing to realize here is that your code has to wait for the e-mail service to complete its task. It means that your code is waiting for the service to resolve Internet Protocol (IP) addresses, establish network connections, and send the e-mail to a remote SMTP server. You also wait for the message to be encoded and all its attachments to be transferred. This process can easily take a few seconds depending on the speed of the SMTP server, network connection, and size of

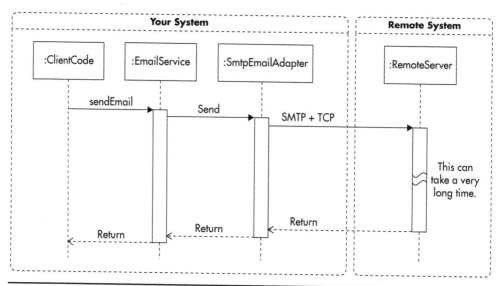

Figure 7-1 *Synchronous invocation*

the message. In this context, synchronous processing means that your code has to synchronize its processing with the remote server and all of your processing pauses for the time necessary to complete the sendMail method. Having to stop execution to wait for a response in such a way is also called *blocking*.

Blocking occurs when your code has to wait for an external operation to finish. Blocking can happen when you read something from a hard drive because the operating system needs time to fetch the data for you. Blocking can also occur when you wait for a user's input, for example, an automated teller machine (ATM) waiting for you to take your credit card before giving you the money. Blocking can also occur when you synchronize multiple processes/threads to avoid race conditions.

Blocking I/O means blocking input/output. This term is used to describe blocking read and write operations on resources like hard drives, network connections, and user interfaces. Blocking I/O occurs most often when interacting with hard drives and network connections. For example, opening a Transmission Control Protocol/Internet Protocol (TCP/IP) network connection to a remote server can be a blocking operation (depending on your programming model). In such a case, your thread blocks on a synchronous call to open the connection.

Synchronous processing makes it hard to build responsive applications because there is no way to guarantee how long it will take for a blocking operation to complete. Every time you perform a blocking operation, your execution thread is blocked. Blocked threads consume resources without making progress. In some cases, it may take a few milliseconds, but in others, it may take several seconds before you get the result or even find out about a failure.

It is especially dangerous to block user interactions, as users become impatient very quickly. Whenever a web application "freezes" for a second or two, users tend to reload the page, click the back button, or simply abandon the application. Users of a corporate web application that provides business-critical processes are more forgiving because they have to get their job done; they do not have much choice but to wait. On the other hand, users clicking around the Web on their way to work have no tolerance for waiting, and you are likely to lose them if your application forces them to wait.

To visualize how synchronous processing affects perceived performance, let's look at Figure 7-2. This diagram shows how all blocking operations happen one after another in a sequence.

The more blocking operations you perform, the slower your system becomes, as all this execution time adds up. If sending e-mail takes 100 ms and updating a database takes 20 ms, then your overall execution time has to be at least 120 ms because in this implementation, operations cannot happen in parallel.

Now that we have explained what synchronous processing looks like, let's go through the same example for asynchronous processing.

Asynchronous Example

In a pure fire-and-forget model, client code has no idea what happens with the request. The client can finish its own job without even knowing if the request was processed or not. Asynchronous processing does not always have to be purely fire-and-forget, however, as it can allow for the results of the asynchronous call to be consumed by the caller using callbacks.

> A *callback* is a construct of asynchronous processing where the caller does not block while waiting for the result of the operation, but provides a mechanism to be notified once the operation is finished. A callback is a function, an object, or an endpoint that gets invoked whenever the asynchronous call is completed. For example, if an asynchronous operation fails, callback allows the caller to handle the error condition. Callbacks are especially common in user interface environments, as they allow slow tasks to execute in the background, parallel to user interactions.

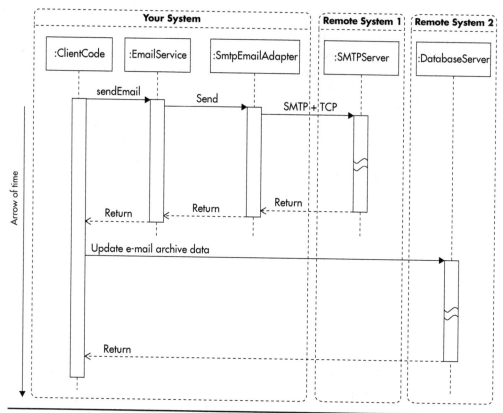

Figure 7-2 *Multiple synchronous operations: adding up of execution times*

Let's go back the EmailService example and imagine an alternative implementation that is split into two independent components. We still use the EmailService interface to send e-mails from the client code, but there is a message queue buffering requests and a back-end process that sends e-mails. Figure 7-3 shows how the invocation could look in this scenario. As we can see, your code does not have to wait for the message delivery. Your code waits only for the message to be inserted into a message queue.

Your code does not know if the e-mail can be delivered successfully, as by the time your code finishes, the e-mail is not even sent yet. It may be just added into the queue or somewhere on its way to the SMTP server. This is an example of asynchronous processing in its *fire-and-forget* form.

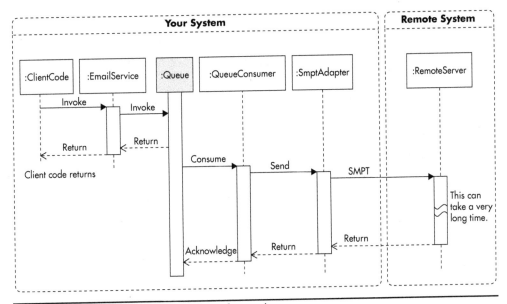

Figure 7-3 *Asynchronous processing of e-mail message*

Another important thing to notice here is that we can have independent threads. Client code can execute in a separate process and add messages to the queue at any point in time. On the other hand, the message queue consumer, who sends out e-mails, can work in a separate process and at a different rate. The message consumer could even be shut down or crash and the client code would not know the difference, as long as it can add messages into the queue.

If we wanted to handle results of e-mails being sent by EmailService, we could provide a web service endpoint or other way of notification (some form of callback). This way, every time an SMTP request fails or a bounced e-mail is detected, we could be notified. We could then implement callback functionality that would handle these notifications. For example, we could update the database record of each e-mail sent by marking it as successfully sent or as being bounced back. Based on these statuses, we could then inform our users of failures. Naturally, callback could handle failure and success notifications in any other way depending on the business needs. In Figure 7-4, we can see how the sequence diagram might appear once we include callback functionality. Client code can continue its execution without blocking, but at the same time, it can handle different results of e-mail delivery by providing a callback.

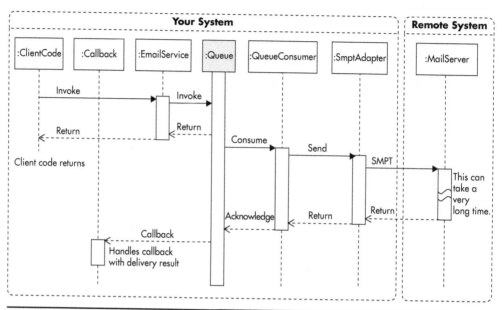

Figure 7-4 *Asynchronous call with a callback*

This diagram is a great simplification of the actual implementation, but we can see that it already becomes much more complicated than the synchronous version from Figure 7-1. Figure 7-4 looks much more complicated because instead of a single application, we effectively decoupled parts of the call sequence into separate applications. Instead of all the steps happening within a single execution thread, we can have ClientCode, Callback, Queue, and QueueConsumer execute in separate threads. They could also execute on different servers as different processes.

To make it easier to work with asynchronous processing, it is important to provide good frameworks and abstraction layers hiding routing and dispatching of asynchronous calls and callbacks. AJAX is a good example of how asynchronous processing can be made simple to use. If an e-mail message was triggered from JavaScript running in the browser, we could handle its results by providing a callback function declared in place. Listing 7-2 shows an example of the sendEmail invocation with a callback function passed as an argument.

Listing 7-2 *Invocation of sendEmail function with a callback function declared in place*

```
// messageRow variable is declared before and
// it is bound to UI element on the screen
emailService.sendEmail(message, function(error){
    if(error){
        // modify UI by accessing messageRow
        messageRow.markAsFailed(error);
    }else{
        // modify UI by accessing messageRow
        messageRow.markAsDelivered();
    }
});
```

The trick here is that JavaScript anonymous functions capture the variable scope in which they are declared. This way, even when the outer function returns, the callback can execute at a later stage, still having access to all the variables defined in the outer scope. This transparent scope inheritance of JavaScript makes it easy to declare callback functions in a concise way.

Finally, let's consider how asynchronous processing affects perceived performance of the application. Figure 7-5 shows how asynchronous calls are executed. Parallel execution of client code and remote calls can be achieved within a single execution thread. As soon as the sendEmail method returns, client code can allow the user to interact with the page elements. Parallel processing is "emulated" by JavaScript's event loop, allowing us to perform Nonblocking I/O and achieve the illusion of multithreaded processing.

> *Nonblocking I/O* refers to input/output operations that do not block the client code's execution. When using nonblocking I/O libraries, your code does not wait while you read data from disk or write to a network socket. Any time you make a nonblocking I/O call, you provide a callback function, which becomes responsible for handling the output of the operation.

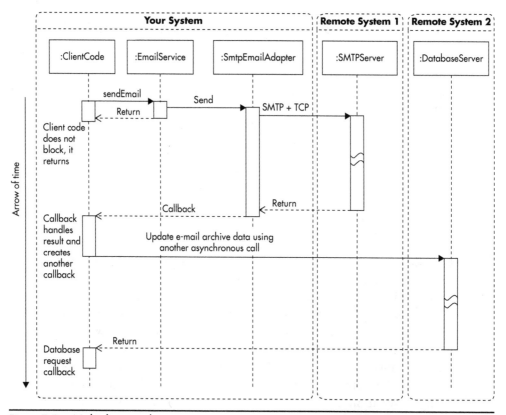

Figure 7-5 *Multiple asynchronous operations: execution time hidden from user*

In this case, we create the illusion of instant e-mail delivery. As soon as the user clicks a button, the sendEmail function is called and asynchronous processing begins. The user can be instantly notified that e-mail has been accepted and that she can continue with her work. Even if sending e-mail takes 100 ms and updating the database takes another 20 ms, the user does not have to wait for these steps to happen. If necessary, when the callback code executes, it can notify the user whether her message was delivered.

We have discussed the core concepts of the synchronous and asynchronous models, but let's further simplify this complicated subject with a quick analogy.

Shopping Analogy

To simplify it even further, you can think of synchronous processing as if you were shopping at a fish market. You approach a vendor, ask for a fish, and wait.

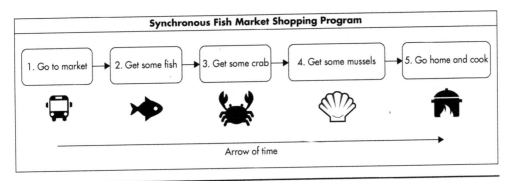

Figure 7-6 *Synchronous shopping scenario*

The vendor wraps the fish for you and asks if you need anything else. You can either ask for more seafood or pay and go to the next stand. No matter how many things you have to buy, you are buying one thing at a time. You need your fish before you go to the next vendor to get some fresh crab. Figure 7-6 shows such a scenario. Why a fish market? you ask. Just to make it more fun and easier to remember.

Continuing our shopping analogy, asynchronous shopping is more like ordering online. Figure 7-7 shows how a sequence of events could look when you order books online. When you place your order, you provide a callback endpoint (the shipping address). Once you submit your request, you get on with your life. In the meantime, the website notifies vendors to send you the books. Whenever books

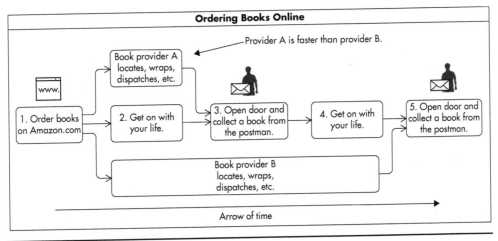

Figure 7-7 *Asynchronous shopping scenario*

arrive at your home, you have an opportunity to handle the result of your order using your callback functionality (steps 3 and 5). You could collect the books yourself or have someone in your family do it for you. The core difference is that no matter how long it takes to ship the books, you do not have to wait motionless for the books to arrive; you can do other things. It also means that multiple providers can now fulfill parts of your order in parallel without synchronizing on each step.

In addition, if you decided to order the books as a gift for a friend, you would not need to handle the response at all and your order would become a fire-and-forget request.

From a scalability point of view, the main difference between these two approaches is that more agents (processes, threads, or independent systems) can work in parallel at any point in time. This, in turn, means that you can execute each agent on a separate central processing unit (CPU) or even on a separate server.

Message Queues

Now that we have discussed the basic concepts of synchronous and asynchronous processing, let's have a look at message queues. Message queues are a great tool for achieving asynchronous processing and they can be used in applications that are built in a synchronous fashion. Even if your application or programming language runtime does not support asynchronous processing, you can use message queues to achieve asynchronous processing.

> A *message queue* is a component that buffers and distributes asynchronous requests. In the message queue context, messages are assumed to be one-way, fire-and-forget requests. You can think of a message as a piece of XML or JSON with all of the data that is needed to perform the requested operation. Messages are created by message producers and then buffered by the message queue. Finally, they are delivered to message consumers who perform the asynchronous action on behalf of the producer.

Message producers and consumers in scalable systems usually run as separate processes or separate execution threads. Producers and consumers are often hosted on different servers and can be implemented in different technologies to allow further flexibility. Producers and consumers can work independently of each other, and they are coupled only by the message format and message queue location. Figure 7-8 shows how producers create messages and send them to the message queue. Independently of producers, the message queue arranges messages in a sequence to be delivered to consumers. Consumers can then consume messages from the message queue.

This is a very abstract view of a message queue. We do not care here about the message queue implementation, how producers send their messages, or how consumers receive messages. At this level of abstraction, we just want to see the overall flow of messages and that producers and consumers are separated from each other by the message queue.

The separation of producers and consumers using a queue gives us the benefit of nonblocking communication between producer and consumer. Producers do not have to wait for the consumer to become available. The producer's execution thread does not have to block until the consumer is ready to accept another piece of work. Instead, producers submit job requests to the queue, which can be done faster, as there is no processing involved.

Another benefit of this separation is that now producers and consumers can be scaled separately. This means that we can add more producers at any time without overloading the system. Messages that cannot be consumed fast enough will just begin to line up in the message queue. We can also scale consumers separately, as now they can be hosted on separate machines and the number of consumers can grow independently of producers. An important feature of the diagram in Figure 7-8 is that there are three distinct responsibilities: producers, message queue, and consumers. Let's now look at each responsibility in more detail.

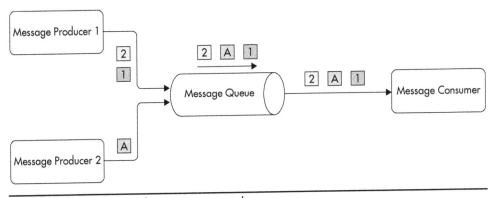

Figure 7-8 *Message producers, queue, and consumers*

Message Producers

Message producers are parts of the client code that initiate asynchronous processing. In message queue–based processing, producers have very little responsibility—all they have to do is create a valid message and send it to the message queue. It is up to the application developer to decide where producers should execute and when they should publish their messages.

> Producing a message is referred to as *publishing* or *message publishing*. *Message producer* and *message publisher* are basically synonyms and can be used interchangeably.

Applications often have multiple producers, publishing the same type of message in different parts of the codebase. All of these messages get queued up together and processed asynchronously.

Going back to our EmailService example, if the e-mail service was implemented with message queues, then producers would be instances of client code that want to send e-mails. Producers could live in the code handling new account creation, purchase confirmation, or reset password. Any time you want to send an e-mail, you would produce a message and add it to the queue. Producers could be implemented in any technology as long as they can locate the message queue and add a valid message to it. Listing 7-3 shows how a sample message could appear. The message format becomes the contract between producers and consumers, so it is important to define it well and validate it strictly.

Listing 7-3 *Custom message format; contract between producers and consumers*

```xml
<?xml version="1.0"?>
<emails>
    <message>
        <type>NEW-ACCOUNT</type>
        <from>some@guy.com</from>
        <to>your@client.org</to>
        <subject>Welcome to Our.Service.Com</subject>
        <textBody>
            Contents of the message.
        </textBody>
```

```
        <htmlBody>
            &lt;h1&gt;Contents of the html.&lt;/h1&gt;
        </htmlBody>
    </message>
</emails>
```

Using a platform-independent format like XML or JSON allows for producers and consumers to be implemented in different technologies and work independently of one another. You could have some PHP code creating e-mails whenever a user subscribes to a new account. You could also have a back-end system written in Java that sends e-mails for every purchase that is processed. Both of these producers could create XML messages and send them to the queue. Producers would not have to wait for e-mails to be delivered; they would simply assume that e-mails will be delivered at some point in time.

> **HINT**
>
> *Not having to know how consumers are implemented, what technologies they use, or even if they are available are signs of strong decoupling (which is a very good thing).*

As we said before, message producers have a lot of freedom and there is not much responsibility on their end.

Let's now take a closer look at the message queue itself.

Message Broker

The core component of message queue–based asynchronous processing is the queue itself. It is the place where messages are sent and buffered for consumers. A message queue can be implemented in many different ways. It could be as simple as a shared folder with an application allowing you to read and write files to and from it. It could be a component backed by a SQL database (as many homegrown message queues are), or it could be a dedicated message broker that takes care of accepting, routing, persisting, and delivering messages. The message queue could also be a simple thread running within the same application process.

Since the message queue is a distinct component that can have more responsibilities, like permissions control, routing, or failure recovery, it is often implemented as an independent application. In such a case, it is usually referred to as a message broker or message-oriented middleware.

A *message broker* is a specialized application designed for fast and flexible message queuing, routing, and delivery. Brokers are the more sophisticated way of implementing message queues and usually provide a lot of specialized functionality out of the box. Message brokers are also optimized for high concurrency and high throughput because being able to enqueue messages fast is one of their key responsibilities. A message broker may be referred to as message-oriented middleware (MOM) or enterprise service bus (ESB), depending on the technology used. They all serve similar purpose, with MOM and ESB usually taking even more responsibilities.

A message broker has more responsibilities than producers do. It is the element decoupling producers from consumers. The main responsibility of the message queue is to be available at all times for producers and to accept their messages. It is also responsible for buffering messages and allowing consumers to consume relevant messages. Message brokers are applications, similar to web application containers or database engines. Brokers usually do not require any custom code; they are configured, not customized. Message brokers are often simpler than relational database engines, which allows them to reach higher throughput and scale well.

Because brokers are distinct components, they have their own requirements and limitations when it comes to scalability. Unfortunately, adding a message broker increases infrastructure complexity and requires us to be able to use and scale it appropriately. We will discuss the benefits and drawbacks of using message brokers in a following section, but let's look at message consumers first.

Message Consumers

Finally, we come to the last component: message consumer. The main responsibility of the message consumer is to receive and process messages from the message queue. Message consumers are implemented by application developers, and they are the components that do the actual asynchronous request processing.

Going back to our EmailSevice example, the consumer would be the code responsible for picking up messages from the queue and sending them to remote mail servers using SMTP. Message consumers, similar to producers, can be implemented in different technologies, modified independently, and run on different servers.

To achieve a high level of decoupling, consumers should not know anything about producers. They should only depend on valid messages coming out of the queue. If we manage to follow that rule, we turn consumers into a lower service layer, and the dependency becomes unidirectional. Producers depend on some work to be done by "some message consumer," but consumers have no dependency on producers whatsoever.

Message consumers are usually deployed on separate servers to scale them independently of message producers and add extra hardware capacity to the system. The two most common ways of implementing consumers are a "cron-like" and a "daemon-like" approach.

A *cron-like consumer* connects periodically to the queue and checks the status of the queue. If there are messages, it consumes them and stops when the queue is empty or after consuming a certain amount of messages. This model is common in scripting languages where you do not have a persistently running application container, such as PHP, Ruby, or Perl. Cron-like is also referred to as a pull model because the consumer pulls messages from the queue. It can also be used if messages are added to the queue rarely or if network connectivity is unreliable. For example, a mobile application may try to pull the queue from time to time, assuming that connection may be lost at any point in time.

A *daemon-like consumer* runs constantly in an infinite loop, and it usually has a permanent connection to the message broker. Instead of checking the status of the queue periodically, it simply blocks on the socket read operation. This means that the consumer is waiting idly until messages are pushed by the message broker into the connection. This model is more common in languages with persistent application containers, such as Java, C#, and Node.js. This is also referred to as a push model because messages are pushed by the message broker onto the consumer as fast as the consumer can keep processing them.

Neither of these approaches is better or worse; they are just different methods of solving the same problem of reading messages from the queue and processing them.

In addition to different execution models, message consumers can use different subscription methods. Message brokers usually allow consumers to specify what messages they are interested in. It is possible to read messages directly from a named queue or to use more advanced routing methods. The availability of different routing methods may depend on which message broker you decide to use, but they usually support the following routing methods: direct worker queue, publish/subscribe, and custom routing rules.[12,24]

Let's quickly look at each message routing method.

Direct Worker Queue Method

In this delivery model, the consumers and producers only have to know the name of the queue. Each message produced by producers is added to a single work queue. The queue is located by name, and multiple producers can publish to it at any point in time. On the other side of the queue, you can have one or more consumers competing for messages. Each message arriving to the queue is routed to only one consumer. This way, each consumer sees only a subset of messages. Figure 7-9 shows the structure of the direct worker queue.

This routing model is well suited for the distribution of time-consuming tasks across multiple worker machines. It is best if consumers are stateless and uniform; then replacement of failed nodes becomes as easy as adding a new worker node. Scaling becomes trivial as well, as all we have to do is add more worker machines to increase the overall consumer throughput. Please note that consumers can scale independently of producers.

Good examples of this model include sending out e-mails, processing videos, resizing images, or uploading content to third-party web services.

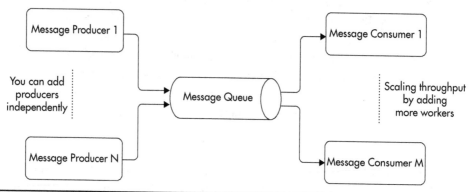

Figure 7-9   *Direct worker queue*

Publish/Subscribe Method

In the publish/subscribe model, messages can be delivered to more than one consumer. Producers publish messages to a topic, not a queue. Messages arriving to a topic are then cloned for each consumer that has a declared subscription to that topic. If there are no consumers at the time of publishing, messages can be discarded altogether (though this behavior may depend on the configuration of the message broker).

Consumers using the publish/subscribe model have to connect to the message broker and declare which topics they are interested in. Whenever a new message is published to a topic, it is cloned for each consumer subscribing to it. Each consumer then receives a copy of the message into their private queue. Each consumer can then consume messages independently from other consumers, as it has a private queue with copies of all the messages that were published to the selected topic.

Figure 7-10 shows how messages published to a topic are routed to separate queues, each belonging to a different consumer.

A good example of this routing model is to publish a message for every purchase. Your e-commerce application could publish a message to a topic each time a purchase is confirmed. Then you could create multiple consumers performing different actions whenever a purchase message is published. You could have a consumer that notifies shipping providers and a different consumer that processes loyalty program rules and allocates reward points. You would also have a way to add more functionality in the future without the need to ever change existing publishers or consumers. If you needed to add a consumer that sends out a purchase confirmation e-mail with a PDF invoice, you would simply deploy a new consumer and subscribe to the same topic.

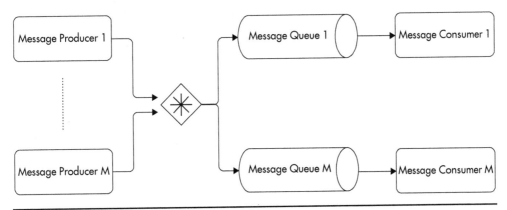

Figure 7-10   *Publish/subscribe queue model*

The publish/subscribe model is a flexible pattern of messaging. It is also a variation of a generic design pattern called observer[1,7] used to decouple components and to promote the open-closed principle (described in Chapter 2). To make it more flexible and scalable, most brokers allow for competing consumers, in which case multiple consumers subscribe to the same queue and messages are distributed among them, rather than a single consumer having to process all of the messages.

Custom Routing Rules

Some message brokers may also support different forms of custom routing, where a consumer can decide in a more flexible way what messages should be routed to its queue. For example, in RabbitMQ you can use a concept of bindings to create flexible routing rules (based on text pattern matching).[12] In ActiveMQ you can use the Camel extension to create more advanced routing rules.[25]

Logging and alerting are good examples of custom routing based on pattern matching. You could create a "Logger Queue" that accepts all log messages and an "Alert Queue" that receives copies of all critical errors and all Severity 1 support tickets. Then you could have a "File Logger" consumer that would simply write all messages from the "Logger Queue" to a file. You could also have an "Alert Generator" consumer that would read all messages routed to the "Alert Queue" and generate operator notifications. Figure 7-11 shows such a configuration.

The idea behind custom routing is to increase flexibility of what message consumers can subscribe to. By having more flexibility in the message broker, your system can adapt to new requirements using configuration changes rather than having to change the code of existing producers and consumers.

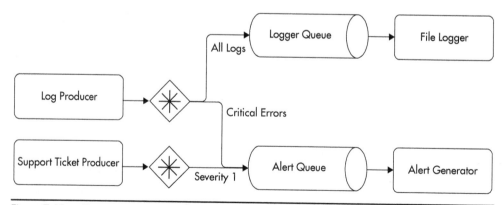

Figure 7-11   *Custom routing configuration*

These are the most common routing methods, but I encourage you to read documentation for your message broker or check out some of the books on messaging.[12,24,25] Now that we've covered the most important concepts of asynchronous processing and messaging, let's have a quick look at different messaging protocols and then at the infrastructure to see where message brokers belong.

Messaging Protocols

A messaging protocol defines how client libraries connect to a message broker and how messages are transmitted. Protocols can be binary or text based, they can specify just minimal functionality, or they can describe in details hundreds of features. You should be familiar with the messaging protocols used to transport messages from producers to consumers. As an application developer, you will probably not have to develop your own implementation of any messaging protocol, but it is best to understand the properties of each protocol so that you can choose the best fit for your project. Here, we will look at the three most common protocols in the open-source world: AMQP, STOMP, and JMS.

AMQP (Advanced Message Queuing Protocol) is a well-defined contract for publishing, consuming, and transferring messages, and best of all, it is an industry standard. It is more advanced than STOMP, and it is aimed at enterprise integration and interoperability. Since it is a standardized protocol accepted by OASIS (Organization for the Advancement of Structured Information Standards),[w54] integration between different messaging vendors, consumers, and publishers is easier. AMQP includes a lot of features in the protocol specification itself, so things like reliable messaging, delivery guarantees, transactions, and other advanced features are guaranteed to be implemented in the same way by all supporting libraries and servers. Most modern programming languages have stable AMQP clients, and as of this writing both RabbitMQ and ActiveMQ support AMQP as a communication protocol. Considering all of its benefits, I would recommend AMQP as a messaging protocol whenever it is possible.

STOMP (Streaming Text-Oriented Messaging Protocol), on the other hand, is a truly minimalist protocol. In fact, simplicity is one of its main advantages. STOMP is a stateless, text-based protocol similar to HTTP. It supports fewer than a dozen operations, so implementation and debugging of libraries are much easier. It also means that the protocol layer does not add much performance overhead. What can be unpleasant about STOMP is that advanced features have to be implemented as extensions using custom headers, and as a result, interoperability can be limited because there is no standard way of doing certain things. A good example of impaired interoperability is message prefetch count. It allows the consumer to declare how many messages they want to receive from the server without having to acknowledge them. Prefetch is a great way of increasing throughput because messages are received in batches instead of one message at a time. Although both RabbitMQ and ActiveMQ support this feature, they both implement it using different custom STOMP headers. If you talk to ActiveMQ, you have to specify it using the "activemq.prefetchSize" header; when talking to RabbitMQ, you have to set the "prefetch-count" header instead. Obviously, this does not let you create a universal STOMP client library supporting the prefetch feature, as your library will need to know how to negotiate it with every type of message broker, and what is even worse, your code will have to know whether it is talking to RabbitMQ or ActiveMQ. Even though this is a simplistic example, it should demonstrate how important standards are and how difficult it may become to integrate your software using nonstandardized protocols.

The last protocol, JMS (Java Message Service), is a Java messaging standard widely adopted across Java-based application servers and libraries. Even though JMS provides a good feature set and is popular, unfortunately, it is a purely Java standard and your ability to integrate with non-JVM (Java Virtual Machine)–based technologies will be very limited. If you develop purely in Java or JVM-based languages like Groovy or Scala, JMS can actually be a good protocol for you. If you have to integrate with different platforms, though, you may be better off using AMQP or STOMP, as they have implementations for all popular languages.

From a scalability point of view, protocols used to transfer messages are not really a concern, so you should make your choice based on the feature set and availability of the tools and libraries for your programming languages.

Messaging Infrastructure

So far we have discussed message queues, brokers, producers, and consumers. We have also described some of the most common messaging protocols. Let's take a step back now to see how messaging components affect our system infrastructure.

We first looked at infrastructure in Chapter 1. Figure 7-12 shows that same infrastructure from Chapter 1, but with message brokers highlighted for better clarity. The message queuing systems are usually accessible from both front-end and back-end sides of your system. You would usually produce messages in the front end and then consume them in the back end, but it does not have to be this way. Some applications could consume messages in the front end. For example, an online chat application could consume messages to notify the user as soon as a new message arrives in her mailbox. How you use the message broker ultimately depends on your needs and your use cases—it is just another tool in your toolbox.

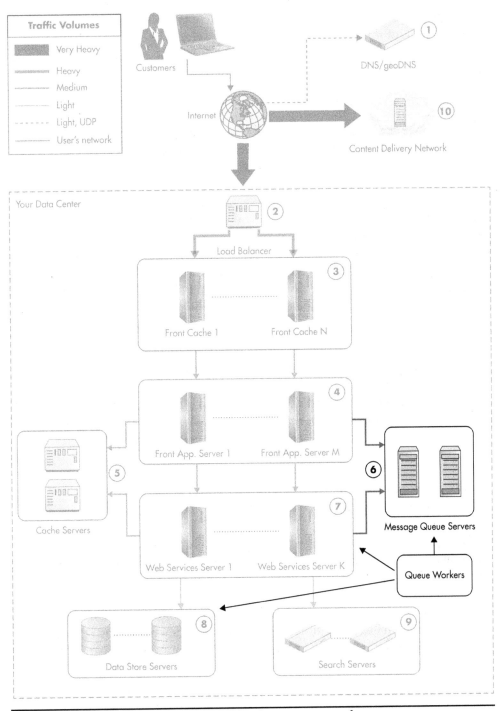

Traffic Volumes

- Very Heavy
- Heavy
- Medium
- Light
- Light, UDP
- User's network

Figure 7-12   *Message brokers and queue workers in system infrastructure*

In Figure 7-12, servers dedicated to message consumers are labeled "Queue Workers." It is common to see entire clusters of servers dedicated solely to message processing. These machines are often called queue workers, as their sole purpose is to perform work based on queue messages.

> **HINT**
>
> *If you hosted your servers in the cloud, like Amazon EC2 or another virtualization provider, you could easily select different types of server instances for the queue workers cluster depending on what their bottleneck is (memory, I/O, or CPU).*

It is best to isolate queue workers into a separate set of servers so their scalability would not depend on the scalability of other components. The more independent and encapsulated the workers, the less impact and dependency on the rest of the system. An important thing to remember here is that queue worker machines should be stateless just like web application servers and web service machines. Workers should get all of their data from the queue and external persistence stores. Then machine failures and scaling out will not be a problem.

> **HINT**
>
> *You may need to use other services to save and retrieve state from to keep your queue workers stateless. For example, if your workers are transcoding videos, your message producer should upload the video binary file into a distributed persistence store (like S3 or a shared FTP, SAN, or NAS). Then it should publish a message to the queue with location of the binary so that any queue worker machine could process the message without having to keep local state.*

By having queue workers stateless and isolated to a separate set of machines, you will be able to scale them horizontally by simply adding more servers. Failures will have no impact on you either because new workers can always be added to replace broken ones.

Usually, message brokers provide some built-in functionality for horizontal scalability,[12,25] but each broker may have its own gotchas and scalability limitations. There are limitations on the total throughput of a single queue because messages passing through the queue need to be delivered to all connected subscribers. As long as your application is able to distribute messages across multiple queues using simple application-level sharding, you should be able to scale messaging brokers horizontally by adding more message broker servers.

If you require throughput of thousands or tens of thousands of messages per second, RabbitMQ or ActiveMQ should work fine out of the box. If you plan for hundreds of thousands of messages per second, you may need to add custom sharding mechanisms into your application to spread the load among multiple broker instances.

Surprisingly, even in using a cloud-based messaging platform like Microsoft Azure Queues, you may hit scalability limits. For example, as of this writing, Microsoft Azure Queues has a throughput limitation of 2,000 messages per second, per queue,[L1] which is a lot. Another Azure product called Service Bus Queues has a hard limit of 100 concurrent connections to a single queue. Depending on your needs, this may be irrelevant, but you simply cannot assume that infinite scalability is available, unless you do some research. Before committing to a messaging solution, always check the most current pricing, required infrastructure, and out-of-the-box scalability guarantees.

> ### HINT
>
> *You can think of a message broker as if it was a very "dumb" SQL database engine—an engine that does not allow updates, and the only operation you can perform is to add an item to the end of a table and pop an item from the beginning of a table. A message broker can also be a stand-alone application or an embedded one. It can be connected to using standard protocols and shared libraries. A message broker is just an abstraction of adding messages to the queues and routing them to consumers.*

Before you decide which message broker to choose and whether you really have to worry about the broker's scalability in the first place, prepare the following metrics for your application:

▶ Number of messages published per second

▶ Average message size

▶ Number of messages consumed per second (this can be much higher than publishing rate, as multiple consumers may be subscribed to receive copies of the same message)

▶ Number of concurrent publishers

▶ Number of concurrent consumers

▶ If message persistence is needed (no message loss during message broker crash)

▶ If message acknowledgment is needed (no message loss during consumer crash)

With these metrics, you have an informed approach to discuss your scalability needs with vendors and/or the open-source community. We will look at a few message brokers later in this chapter and discuss their impact on scalability, but before we do that, let's review the benefits of messaging and motivation for adding this extra complexity to our systems.

Benefits of Message Queues

So far, we have looked at the core concepts and terminology of asynchronous processing and message queues, and you've likely deduced that they don't come for free. You will now need to learn, deploy, optimize, and scale your message queues. Adding new components to your stack usually increases the overall complexity of your system. Since it is so much work, why should you bother? There are a number of benefits to using message queues:

► Enabling asynchronous processing

► Easier scalability

► Evening out traffic spikes

► Isolating failures and self-healing

► Decoupling

In addition to giving you these benefits, message queues are a specific type of technology. Once you become familiar with them and integrate them into your system, you will find many use cases where a message queue is a perfect fit, making things easier and faster.

Enabling Asynchronous Processing

One of the most visible benefits of using a message queue is the fact that it gives us a way to defer processing of time-consuming tasks without blocking our clients. The message broker becomes our door to the world of asynchronous processing. Anything that is slow or unpredictable is a candidate for asynchronous processing. The only requirement is that you have to find a way to continue execution without having the result of the slow operation.

Good use cases for a message queue could be

▶ **Interacting with remote servers**   If your application performs operations on remote servers, you might benefit from deferring these steps via a queue. For example, if you had an e-commerce platform, you might allow users to create marketing campaigns advertising their products. In such a case, you could let users select which items should be promoted and add requests to the queue so that users would not have to wait for remote service calls to finish. In the background, your system could contact multiple advertising providers like Google AdWords and set up marketing campaigns.

▶ **Low-value processing in the critical path**   Every application has some critical paths or features that have to work all the time as a matter of top priority. In an e-commerce website, it may be the ability to place orders, search for products, and process payments. It is a common requirement that critical paths have to work 24/7 no matter what else breaks. After all, what kind of e-commerce is it if you cannot place orders or pay for goods? Under such constraints, integrating with a new recommendation engine in checkout could introduce a new point of failure. It could also slow down the checkout process itself. Instead of synchronously sending orders to the recommendation system, you could enqueue them and have them processed asynchronously by an independent component.

▶ **Resource intensive work**   Most CPU- or I/O-hungry processing like transcoding videos, resizing images, building PDFs, or generating reports are good candidates for a queue-based workflow instead of running synchronously to users' interactions.

▶ **Independent processing of high- and low-priority jobs**   For example, you could have separate queues dedicated to top-tier customers (high-urgency tasks) and others for low-value customers (less urgent tasks). You could then dedicate more resources to these high-value jobs and protect them from spikes of low-value tasks.

Message queues enable your application to operate in an asynchronous way, but it only adds value if your application is not built in an asynchronous way to begin with. If you developed in an environment like Node.js, which is built with asynchronous processing at its core, you will not benefit from a message broker that much. A message broker does not make already asynchronous systems more asynchronous. What is good about message brokers is that they allow you to easily introduce asynchronous processing to other platforms, like those that are synchronous by nature (C, Java, PHP, Ruby).

Easier Scalability

Applications using message brokers are usually easier to scale due to the nature of deferred processing. Since you produce messages as fire-and-forget requests, for expensive tasks you can publish requests from multiple servers in parallel. You can also process messages in parallel on multiple back-end servers. You can run multiple physical servers dedicated to message queue consumers, and it is usually easy to keep adding more machines as your workload increases.

A good example of parallel back-end processing could be a service resizing images and videos. Figure 7-13 shows how such an application could be assembled. Your front-end application uploads files to a network attached storage (NAS) (1) and then publishes a message for each file to be processed (2). Messages get buffered in the message queue and get picked up by workers at a later stage (3). Each worker consumes a message from a queue and begins the resizing process (which may take some time to complete). Once the file is processed, it can be uploaded back to NAS (4). Workers could also publish a new message to a separate queue to indicate that work has been completed. In such configuration, you can easily add or remove back-end servers whenever demand changes.

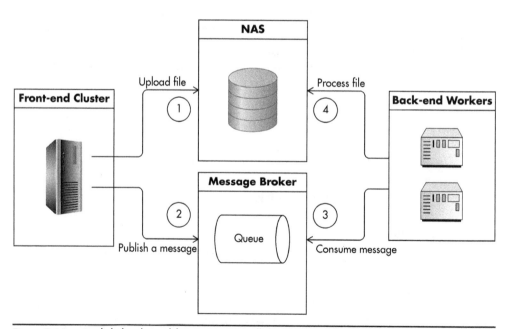

Figure 7-13   *Scalability by adding more parallel queue workers*

As you can see, by adding more message consumers, we can increase our overall throughput. No matter what the constraint on our queue worker nodes is (disk, memory, CPU, external latency), we can process more messages by simply adding more back-end servers. What gives us even more flexibility is that adding servers does not require publisher configuration changes. Consumers simply connect to the message broker and begin consuming messages; producers do not have to know how many consumers are there or where are they hosted.

Even if you used Node.js or Erlang, which are asynchronous by nature, you would still benefit from using queues as a way to share the workload among multiple servers.

Evening Out Traffic Spikes

Another advantage of using message queues is that they allow you to transparently even out traffic spikes. By using a message broker, you should be able to keep accepting requests at high rates even at times of increased traffic. Even if your publishing generates messages much faster than consumers can keep up with, you can keep enqueueing messages, and publishers do not have to be affected by a temporary capacity problem on the consumer's side.

If your front-end application produces messages to be consumed by the back-end cluster, the more traffic you get in the front end, the more messages you will be publishing to the queues. Since front-end code does not have to wait for slow operations to complete, there is no impact on the front-end user. Even if you produce messages faster than consumers can keep processing them, messages still get enqueued quickly. The only impact of the traffic spike is that it takes longer before each message gets processed, because messages "sit" longer in the queues. Figure 7-14 shows how queue consumers work at their full capacity as long as there are messages to be processed. Even when the front-end application produces messages above capacity limits, messages can still be enqueued quickly and processed over time. After the traffic spike is over, consumers eventually catch up with the messages and "drain the queues."

This property of evening out spikes increases your availability. Your system is less likely to go down even if you are not able to fully process all of the incoming requests right away. Soon after the spike is over, the system automatically recovers to its normal status.

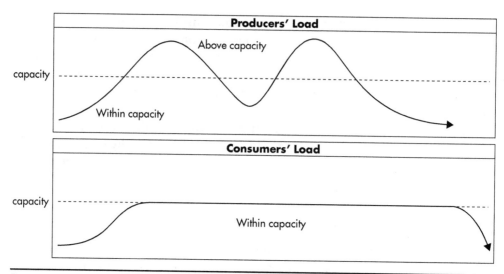

Figure 7-14 *Consumers process messages at their full capacity, but don't get overwhelmed.*

Isolating Failures and Self-Healing

As was already discussed, message queues allow us to remove functionality from critical paths and to insulate producers from consumers, making a system more robust and fault tolerant. The message broker isolates failures of different parts of your system because publishers do not depend directly on consumers being available. Publishers are not affected by failures happening on the consumers' side of the queue. Symmetrically, consumers can keep doing their work even if publishers experience technical issues. As long as there are messages in the queue, consumers are not affected in any way by the producers' failures.

The fact that consumers' availability does not affect producers allows us to stop message processing at any time. This means that we can perform maintenance and deployments on back-end servers at any time. We can simply restart, remove, or add servers without affecting producers' availability, which simplifies deployments and server management.

Finally, having multiple queue worker servers makes the system more tolerant to failures and allows it to heal itself to some extent. If you have multiple workers, a hardware failure can be dealt with as a matter of low priority. Instead of breaking the entire application whenever a back-end server goes offline, all that we experience is reduced throughput, but there is no reduction of availability. Reduced throughput of asynchronous tasks is usually invisible to the user, so there is no consumer impact. To recover from failure, you simply add a server replacement and the system "heals" itself automatically by slowly catching up with the queues and draining messages over time.

Surviving failures and self-healing are some of the most important features of truly horizontally scalable systems.

Decoupling

Message queues allow us to achieve some of the highest degrees of decoupling, which can have big impact on the application architecture. I already explained the benefits of decoupling on its own in Chapter 2, but I want to emphasize here how much message queues promote decoupling.

As I mentioned earlier in this chapter, using a message broker allows us to isolate message producers from message consumers. We can have multiple producers publishing messages, and we can also have multiple consumers processing messages, but they never talk to one another directly. They do not even have to know about each other at all.

> **HINT**
>
> *Whenever we can separate two components to a degree that they do not know about each other's existence, we have achieved a high degree of decoupling.*

Ideally, we should strive to create publishers that do not care who is consuming their messages or how. All that publishers need to know is the format of the message and where to publish it. On the other hand, consumers can become oblivious as to who publishes messages and why. Consumers can focus solely on processing messages from the queue. Figure 7-15 shows how producers and consumers become unaware of one another. It is best if they do not know what is on the other side of the queue.

Such a high level of decoupling, by use of an intermediate message broker, makes it easier to develop consumers and producers independently. They can even be developed by different teams using different technologies. Because message brokers use standard protocols and messages themselves can be encoded using standards like JSON or XML, message brokers can become an integration point between completely independent applications.

> **HINT**
>
> *You can think of a queue as a border. Whatever happens on the other side of that border should be an implementation detail, not known to the code at hand. The queue becomes your single point of interaction and the message format becomes your contract.*

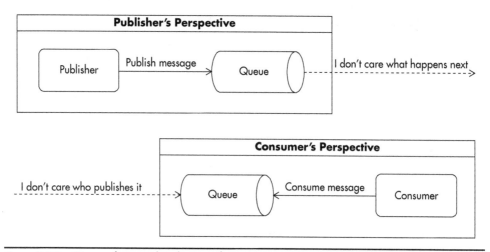

Figure 7-15 *Decoupling and isolation of message producers and consumers*

Although message queues offer great benefits, remember there is no golden hammer. In the following section, let's consider some of the common challenges related to messaging.

Message Queue–Related Challenges

As with most technologies, messaging comes with its own set of challenges and costs. Some of the common difficulties and pitfalls you may encounter when working with message queues and asynchronous processing include no message ordering, message requeueing, race conditions, and increased complexity. Let's look at each in more detail.

No Message Ordering

The first significant challenge developers face when working with message queues at scale is simply that message ordering is not guaranteed. This is caused by the fact that messages are processed in parallel and there is no synchronization between consumers. Each consumer works on a single message at a time and has no knowledge of other consumers running in parallel to it (which is a good thing). Since your consumers are running in parallel and any of them can become slow or even crash at any point in time, it is difficult to prevent messages from being occasionally delivered out of order.

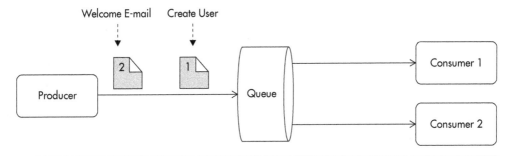

Figure 7-16   *Producer creates two messages related to the same user.*

It is difficult to explain messages being consumed out of order, so let's use a sequence of diagrams. For the sake of simplicity, let's look at a synthetic example of producers sending multiple message types to a shared queue. Figure 7-16 shows a producer publishing two messages. The first message is sent to create a new user account, and the second message is published to send the user a welcome e-mail. Notice that there are two concurrently running message consumers working in parallel on the same message queue.

Each message has an equal chance of being sent to either one of the consumers, as they both arrive at the same logical queue. It is easy to imagine a scenario where each message is sent to a different consumer, as in Figure 7-17. Now, the order of these messages being processed depends on how fast each consumer is and how much time it takes to complete task1 and task2. Either the account can be created first or the e-mail can be created first. The problem that becomes visible here is that e-mail creation could fail if there was no user account present first. It is a classic example of a race condition, as execution of these two tasks in parallel without synchronization may produce incorrect results, depending on the ordering.

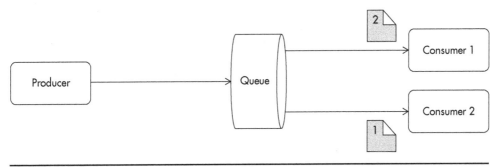

Figure 7-17   *Each consumer receives one of the two messages.*

To make things worse, there is another possible failure scenario. Consumer 2 can become unavailable or simply crash. In such a situation, messages that were sent to that consumer may have to be returned to the queue and sent to other consumers. Requeueing messages is a strategy used by many message brokers, as it is assumed that the message has not been fully processed until it is "acknowledged" by the consumer. Figure 7-18 shows how a message could be requeued and how it could be delivered out of order to consumer 1.

If that was not bad enough, there is an additional difficulty in this failure scenario. There is no guarantee that consumer 2 did not process the message before the failure occurred. Consumer 2 might have already sent out an e-mail and crashed just before sending the message acknowledgment back to the message broker. In such a situation, message 1 would actually be processed twice.

Fortunately, there are things we can do to make the message ordering problem disappear. Here are three common ways to solve the ordering problem:

▶ *Limit the number of consumers to a single thread per queue.* Some message queues guarantee ordered delivery (First In First Out [FIFO]) as long as you consume messages one at a time by a single client. Unfortunately, this is not a scalable solution and not all messaging systems support it.

▶ *Build the system to assume that messages can arrive in random order.* This may be either easy or difficult depending on the system and on the requirements, but seems the best way out. In the previous example, we could achieve it by changing who publishes which messages. If the front end published a create-account message, then consumer 1 could publish an email-customer message once the account has been created. In this case, message ordering is forced by the application-level workflow. If we decided to go down this route, we would need to make sure that all of our engineers understood the constraints. Otherwise, incorrect message ordering may come as a bitter surprise.

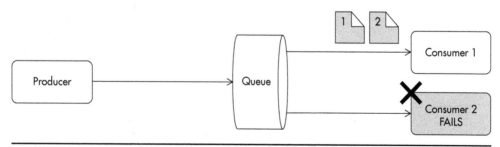

Figure 7-18 *Consumer failure causes message to be passed on to another worker.*

▶ *Use a messaging broker that supports partial message ordering guarantee. This is the case with ActiveMQ's message groups, for example.*

It is best to depend on the message broker to deliver messages in the right order by using a partial message guarantee (ActiveMQ) or topic partitioning (Kafka).[w52] If your broker does not support such functionality, you will need to ensure that your application can handle messages being processed in an unpredictable order.

Partial message ordering is a clever mechanism provided by ActiveMQ called message groups. Messages can be published with a special "label" called a message group ID. The group ID is defined by the application developer (for example, it could be a customer ID). Then all messages belonging to the same group are guaranteed to be consumed in the same order they were produced. Figure 7-19 shows how messages belonging to different groups get queued up separately for different consumers. Whenever a message with a new group ID gets published, the message broker maps the new group ID to one of the existing consumers. From then on, all the messages belonging to the same group are delivered to the same consumer. This may cause other consumers to wait idly without messages as the message broker routes messages based on the mapping rather than random distribution. In our example, if both account creation and e-mail notification messages were published with the same message group ID, they would be guaranteed to be processed in the same order they were published.

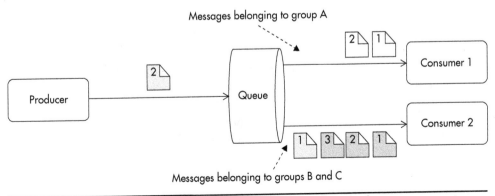

Figure 7-19 *Message groups get assigned to consumers when the first message arrives.*

Message ordering is a serious issue to consider when architecting a message-based application, and RabbitMQ, ActiveMQ, and Amazon SQS messaging platform cannot guarantee global message ordering with parallel workers. In fact, Amazon SQS is known for unpredictable ordering of messages because their infrastructure is heavily distributed and ordering of messages is not supported. You can learn more about some interesting ways of dealing with message ordering.[w14,w52]

Message Requeueing

As previously mentioned, messages can be requeued in some failure scenarios. Dealing with this problem can be easy or difficult, depending on the application needs. A strategy worth considering is to depend on at-least-once delivery instead of exactly-once delivery. By allowing messages to be delivered to your consumers more than once, you make your system more robust and reduce constraints put on the message queue and its workers. For this approach to work, you need to make all of your consumers idempotent, which may be difficult or even impossible in some cases.

> An *idempotent consumer* is a consumer that can process the same message multiple times without affecting the final result. An example of an idempotent operation would be setting a price to $55. An example of a nonidempotent operation would be to "increase price by $5." The difference is that increasing the price by $5 twice would increase it by a total of $10. Processing such a message twice affects the final result. In contrast, setting the price to $55 once or twice leaves the system in the same state.

Unfortunately, making all consumers idempotent may not be an easy thing to do. Sending e-mails is, by nature, not an idempotent operation, because sending two e-mails to the customer does not produce the same result as sending just a single e-mail. Adding an extra layer of tracking and persistence could help, but it would add a lot of complexity and may not be able to handle all of the failure scenarios. Instead, make consumers idempotent whenever it is practical, but remember that enforcing it across the system may not always be worth the effort.

Finally, idempotent consumers may be more sensitive to messages being processed out of order. If we had two messages, one to set the product's price to $55 and another one to set the price of the same product to $60, we could end up with different results based on their processing order. Having two nonidempotent consumers increasing the price by $5 each would be sensitive to message requeueing (redelivery), but not to out-of-order delivery.

Race Conditions Become More Likely

One of the biggest challenges related to asynchronous systems is that things that would happen in a well-defined order in a traditional programming model can suddenly happen in a much more unexpected order. As a result, the asynchronous programming is more unpredictable by nature and more prone to race conditions, as work is broken down into much smaller chunks and there are more possible orders of execution.

Since asynchronous calls are made in a nonblocking way, message producers can continue execution without waiting for the results of the asynchronous call. Different message consumers may also execute in a different order because there is no built-in synchronization mechanism. Different parts of an asynchronous system, especially a distributed one, can have different throughput, causing uneven latency in message propagation throughout the system.

Especially when a system is under heavy load, during failure conditions and deployments, code execution may become slower in different parts of the system. This, in turn, makes things more likely to happen in unexpected order. Some consumers may get their messages much later than others, causing hard-to-reproduce bugs.

> **HINT**
>
> *You could say that asynchronous programming is programming without a call stack.[w11] Things simply execute as soon as they are able to, instead of traditional step-by-step programming.*

The increased risk of race conditions is mainly caused by the message-ordering issue discussed earlier. Get into a habit of careful code review, with an explicit search for race conditions and out-of-order processing bugs. Doing so will increase your chance of mitigating issues and building more robust solutions. The less you assume about the state of an asynchronous system, the better.

Risk of Increased Complexity

Systems built as hybrids of traditional imperative and message-oriented code can become more complex because their message flow is not explicitly declared anywhere. When you look at the producer, there is no way of telling where the consumers are or what they do. When you look at the consumer, you cannot be sure under what conditions messages are published. As the system grows and messaging is added ad hoc through the code, without considering the overall architecture, it may become more and more difficult to understand the dependencies.

When integrating applications using a message broker, you must be very diligent in documenting dependencies and the overarching message flow. Remember the discussion about levels of abstraction and how you should be able to build the mental picture of the system (Chapter 2). Without good documentation of the message routes and visibility of how the messages flow through the system, you may increase the complexity and make it much harder for developers to understand how the system works.

Keep things simple and automate documentation creation so it will be generated based on the code itself. If you manage to keep documentation of your messaging in sync with your code, you should be able to find your way through the dependencies.

Message Queue–Related Anti-Patterns

In addition to message queue–related challenges, I would like to highlight a few common design anti-patterns. Engineers tend to think alike, and they often create similar solutions to similar problems. When the solution proves to be successful over and over again, we call it a pattern, but when the solution is repeatedly difficult to maintain or extend, we call it an anti-pattern. A typical anti-pattern is a solution that seems like a good idea at first, but the longer you use it, the more issues you discover with it. By getting familiar with anti-patterns, you should be able to easily avoid them in the future—it is like getting a vaccination against a common design bug.

Treating the Message Queue as a TCP Socket

Some message brokers allow you to create return channels. A return channel becomes a way for the consumer to send a message back to the producer. If you use it a lot, you may end up with an application that is more synchronous than asynchronous. Ideally, you would want your messages to be truly one-way requests (fire-and-forget). Opening a response channel and waiting for response messages makes messaging components more coupled and undermines some of the benefits of messaging. Response channels may also mean that failures of different components on different sides of the message broker may have an impact on one another. When building scalable systems, avoid return channels, as they usually lead to synchronous processing and excessive resource consumption.

Treating Message Queue as a Database

You should not allow random access to elements of the queue. You should not allow deleting messages or updating them, as this will lead to increased complexity. It is best to think of a message queue as an append-only stream (FIFO). It is most common to see such deformations when the message queue is built on top of a relational database or NoSQL engine because this allows secondary indexes and random access to messages. Using random access to modify and delete messages may prevent you from scaling out and migrating to a different messaging broker.

If you have to delete or update messages in flight (when they are in the middle of the queue), you are probably doing something wrong or applying messaging to a wrong use case.

Coupling Message Producers with Consumers

As I mentioned before, it is best to avoid explicit dependency between producers and consumers. You should not hardcode class names or expect messages to be produced or consumed by any particular piece of code. It is best to think of the message broker as being the endpoint and the message body as being the contract. There should be no assumptions or any additional knowledge necessary. If something is not declared explicitly in the message contract, it should be an implementation detail, and it should not matter to the other side of the contract.

For example, a flawed implementation I saw involved serializing an entire object and adding it to the message body. This meant that the consumer had to have this particular class available, and it was not able to process the message without executing the serialized object's code. Even worse, it meant that the consumer had to be implemented in the same technology as the producer and its deployment had to be coordinated to prevent class mismatches. Messages should not have "logic" or executable code within. Messages should be a data transfer object[10] or simply put, a string of bytes that can be written and read by both consumer and producer.

Treat the format of the message as a contract that both sides need to understand, and disallow any other type of coupling.

Lack of Poison Message Handling

When working with message queues you have to be able to handle broken messages and bugs in consumer code. A common anti-pattern is to assume that messages are always valid. A message of death (also known as a poison message) is a message that causes a consumer to crash or fail in some unexpected way. If your messaging system is not able to handle such cases gracefully, you can freeze your entire message-processing pipeline, as every time a consumer crashes, the broker will requeue the message and resend it to another consumer. Even with auto-respawning consumer processes, you would freeze the pipeline, as all of your consumers would keep crashing and reprocessing the same message for infinity.

To prevent that scenario, you need to plan for failures. You have to assume that components of your messaging platform will crash, go offline, stall, and fail in unexpected ways. You also have to assume that messages may be corrupt or even malicious. Assuming that everything would work as expected is the quickest way to building an unavailable system.

> ### HINT
>
> Hope for the best, prepare for the worst.

You can deal with a poison message in different ways depending on which message broker you use. In ActiveMQ you can use dead-letter queue policies out of the box.[25] All you need to do is set limits for your messages, and they will be automatically removed from the queue after a certain number of failures. If you use Amazon SQS, you can implement poison message handling in your own code by using an approximate delivery counter. Every time a message is redelivered, SQS increments its approximate delivery counter so that your application could easily recognize messages of death and route them to a custom dead-letter queue or simply discard them. Similarly, in RabbitMQ you get a boolean flag telling you if a message has been delivered before, which could be used to build a dead-letter queue functionality. Unfortunately, it is not as simple to use as having a counter or an out-of-the-box functionality.

Whenever you use message queues, you simply have to implement poison message handling.

Quick Comparison of Selected Messaging Platforms

Choosing a message broker is similar to choosing a database management system. Most of them work for most use cases, but it always pays to know what you are dealing with before making a commitment. This section is a quick overview of three most common message brokers: Amazon Simple Queue Service (SQS), RabbitMQ, and ActiveMQ.

Unfortunately, there is no way to recommend a messaging platform without knowing details of the application use cases, so you may have to do some more research before making your final decision. I recommend reading more[25,12,L1–L3] to learn specific details about selected platforms. Here, let's focus on the strengths and best use cases of each platform, which should empower you with the knowledge necessary to begin your own selection.

Amazon Simple Queue Service

Amazon SQS is known for its simplicity and pragmatic approach. SQS is a cloud-based service provided by Amazon with a public application programming interface (API) and software development kit (SDK) libraries available for most programming languages. It is hosted and managed by Amazon, and users are charged pro rata for the amount of messages they publish and amount of service calls they issue.

If you are hosting your application on Amazon EC2, Amazon SQS, which is a hosted messaging platform, is certainly worth considering. The main benefit of using SQS is that you do not have to manage anything yourself. You do not have to scale it, you do not need to hire additional experts, you do not need to worry about failures. You do not even need to pay for additional virtual server instances that would need to run your message brokers. SQS takes care of the infrastructure, availability, and scalability, making sure that messages can be published and consumed all the time.

If you work for a startup following the Lean Startup methodology, you should consider leveraging SQS to your advantage. Lean Startup advocates minimal viable product (MVP) development and a quick feedback loop.[30,9] If SQS functionality is enough for your needs, you benefit in the following ways:

▶ Deliver your MVP faster because there is no setup, no configuration, no maintenance, no surprises.

▶ Focus on the product and customers instead of spending time on the infrastructure and resolving technical issues.

▶ Save money by using SQS rather than managing message brokers yourself.

Saving time and money in early development stages (first 6 to 12 months) is critical, because your startup may change direction very rapidly. Startup reality is so unpredictable that a few months after the MVP release, you may realize that you don't need the messaging component at all, and then all the time invested into it would become a waste!

If you do not prioritize every dollar and every minute spent, your startup may run out of money before ever finding product-market fit (offering the right service to the right people). SQS is often a great fit for early-stage startups, as it has the lowest up-front time and money cost.

> ### HINT
>
> *Any up-front cost, whether it is money or time, may become a waste. The higher the chance of changes, the higher the risk of investment becoming a waste.*

To demonstrate the competitiveness of Amazon SQS, let's have a look at a simple cost comparison. To deploy a highly available message broker using ActiveMQ or RabbitMQ, you will need at least two servers. If you are using Amazon EC2, at the time of writing, two medium-sized reserved instances would cost you roughly $2,000 a year. In comparison, if you used SQS and needed, on average, four requests per message, you would be able to publish and process one billion messages per year for the same amount of money. That is 32 messages per second, on average, throughout the entire year.

In addition, by using SQS you can save hours needed to develop, deploy, manage, upgrade, and configure your own message brokers, which can easily add up to thousands of dollars per year. Even if you assumed that initial time effort to get message brokers set up and integrated would take you a week of up-front work, plus an hour a week of ongoing maintenance effort, you would end up with at least two weeks of time spent looking after your broker rather than looking after your customers' needs.

Simply put, if you don't expect large message volumes, or you don't know what to expect at all, you are better off using SQS. SQS offers just the most basic functionality, so even if you decide to use your own messaging broker later on, you should have no problems migrating away from it. All you need to do when integrating with SQS is to make sure your publishers and consumers are not coupled directly to SQS SDK code. I recommend using thin wrappers and your own interfaces together with design patterns like Dependency Injection, Factory, façade, and Strategy.[1,7,10] Figure 7-20 shows how your infrastructure becomes simplified by removing custom messaging brokers and using SQS.

When it comes to scalability, SQS performs very well. It scales automatically according to your needs and provides really impressive throughput without any preparation or capacity planning. You should be able to publish and consume tens of thousands of messages per second, per queue (assuming multiple

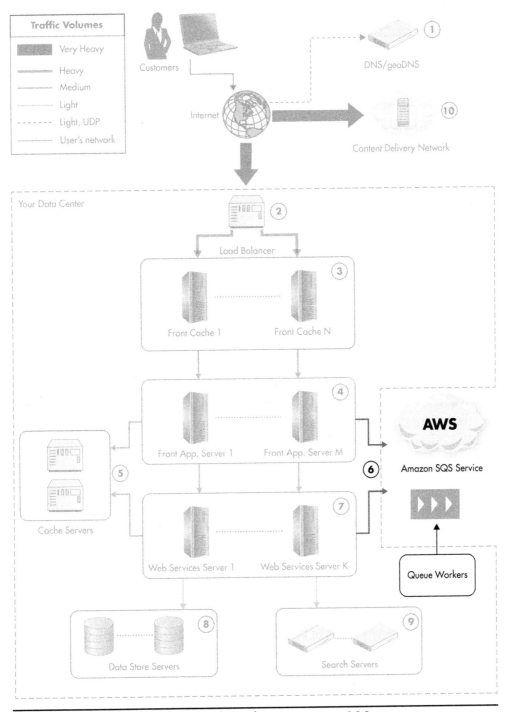

Traffic Volumes

Very Heavy
Heavy
Medium
Light
Light, UDP
User's network

Customers

DNS/geoDNS ①

Internet

Content Delivery Network ⑩

Your Data Center

② Load Balancer

③ Front Cache 1 .... Front Cache N

④ Front App. Server 1 .... Front App. Server M

AWS

⑥ Amazon SQS Service

⑤ Cache Servers

⑦ Web Services Server 1 .... Web Services Server K

Queue Workers

⑧ Data Store Servers

⑨ Search Servers

Figure 7-20 *Simplified infrastructure depending on Amazon SQS*

concurrent clients). Adding more queues, producers, and consumers should allow you to scale without limits.

It is important to remember that SQS is not a golden hammer, though. It scales well, but it has its limitations. Let's quickly discuss its disadvantages.

First of all, Amazon had to sacrifice some features and guarantees to be able to scale SQS easily. Some of the features missing in SQS are that it does not provide any complex routing mechanisms and is less flexible than RabbitMQ or ActiveMQ.[12,25,L3] If you decide to use SQS, you will not be able to deploy your own logic into it or modify it in any way, as it is a hosted service. You either use it as is, or you don't use it at all.

Second, SQS has limits on message size, and you may be charged extra if you publish messages with large bodies (tens of kilobytes).

Another important thing to remember is that messages will be delivered out of order using SQS and that you may see occasional redeliveries. Even if you have a single producer, single queue, and single consumer, there is no message-ordering guarantee whatsoever.

Finally, you pay per service call, which means that polling for nonexisting messages counts as a service call; it also means that sending thousands of messages per second may become more expensive than using your own message broker.

If your company is a well-established business and you are not dealing with a huge amount of uncertainty, it may be worth performing a deeper analysis of available platforms and choose a self-managed messaging broker, which could give you more flexibility and advanced features. Although SQS is great from a scalability and up-front cost point of view, it has a very limited feature set. Let's see now what self-managed brokers can offer.

RabbitMQ

RabbitMQ is a high-performance platform created initially for financial institutions. It provides a lot of valuable features out of the box, it is relatively simple to operate, and it is extremely flexible. Flexibility is actually the thing that makes RabbitMQ really stand out.

RabbitMQ supports two main messaging protocols—AMQP and STOMP— and it is designed as a generic-purpose messaging platform, without preferences towards Java or any other programming language.

The most attractive feature of RabbitMQ is the ability to dynamically configure routes and completely decouple publishers from consumers. In regular messaging, the consumer has to be coupled by a queue name or a topic name. This means that different parts of the system have to be aware of one another to some extent.

In RabbitMQ, publishers and consumers are completely separated because they interact with separate endpoint types. RabbitMQ introduces a concept of an exchange.

An *exchange* is just an abstract named endpoint to which publishers address their messages. Publishers do not have to know topic names or queue names as they publish messages to exchanges. Consumers, on the other hand, consume messages from queues.

Publishers have to know the location of the message broker and the name of the exchange, but they do not have to know anything else. Once a message is published to an exchange, RabbitMQ applies routing rules and sends copies of the message to all applicable queues. Once messages appear in queues, consumers can consume them without knowing anything about exchanges.

Figure 7-21 shows how RabbitMQ takes care of routing and insulates publishers from consumers, both physically and logically. The trick is that routing rules can be defined externally using a web administration interface, AMQP protocol, or RabbitMQ's REST API. You can declare routing rules in the publisher's or consumer's code, but you are not required to do so. Your routing configuration can be managed externally by a separate set of components.

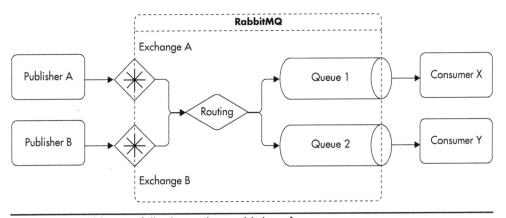

Figure 7-21   *RabbitMQ fully decoupling publishers from consumers*

If you think about message routing this way, you move closer towards service-oriented architecture (SOA). In SOA, you create highly decoupled and autonomous services that are fairly generic and that can be wired together to build more complex applications using service orchestration and service policies.[31] In the context of RabbitMQ, you can think of it as an external component that can be used to decide which parts of the system should communicate with each other and how messages should flow throughout the queues. The important thing about RabbitMQ routing is that you can change these routing rules remotely, and you can do it on the fly, without the need to restart any components.

It is worth noting that RabbitMQ can provide complex routing based on custom routing key patterns and simpler schemas like direct queue publishing and publish/subscribe.

Another important benefit of using RabbitMQ is that you can fully configure, monitor, and control the message broker using its remote REST API. You can use it to create any of the internal resources like hosts, nodes, queues, exchanges, users, and routing rules. Basically, you can dynamically reconfigure any aspect of the message broker without the need to restart anything or run custom code on the broker machine. To make things even better, the REST API provided by RabbitMQ is really well structured and documented. Figure 7-22 shows RabbitMQ's self-documenting endpoint, so you don't even need to search for the documentation of the API version you are running to learn all about it.

GET	PUT	DELETE	POST	Path	Description
X				/api/overview	Various random bits of information that describe the whole system.
X				/api/connections	A list of all open connections.
X		X		/api/connections/name	An individual connection. DELETEing it will close the connection.
X				/api/channels	A list of all open channels.
X				/api/channels/channel	Details about an individual channel.
X				/api/exchanges	A list of all exchanges.
X				/api/exchanges/vhost	A list of all exchanges in a given virtual host.
X	X	X		/api/exchanges/vhost/name	An individual exchange. To PUT an exchange, you will need a body looking something like this: {"type":"direct","auto_delete":false,"durable":true,"arguments":[]}
X				/api/exchanges/vhost/name/bindings	A list of all bindings on a given exchange.
X				/api/queues	A list of all queues.
X				/api/queues/vhost	A list of all queues in a given virtual host.

Figure 7-22 *Fragment of RabbitMQ REST API documentation within the endpoint*

When it comes to feature comparison, RabbitMQ is much richer than SQS and supports more flexible routing than ActiveMQ. On the other hand, it does miss a few nice-to-have features like scheduled message delivery. The only important drawbacks of RabbitMQ are the lack of partial message ordering and poor poison message support.

From a scalability point of view, RabbitMQ is similar to ActiveMQ. Its performance is comparable to ActiveMQ as well. It supports different clustering and replication topologies, but unfortunately, it does not scale horizontally out of the box, and you would need to partition your messages across multiple brokers to be able to scale horizontally. It is not very difficult, but it is not as easy as when using SQS, which simply does it for you.

If you are not hosted on Amazon EC2 or you need more flexibility, RabbitMQ is a good option for a message broker. If you are using scripting languages like PHP, Python, Ruby, or Node.js, RabbitMQ will allow you to leverage its flexibility and configure it at runtime using AMQP and RabbitMQ's REST API.

ActiveMQ

The last message broker I would like to introduce is ActiveMQ. Its functionality is similar to RabbitMQ and it has similar performance and scalability abilities. The main difference is that it is written in Java and it can be run as an embedded message broker within your application. This offers some advantages and may be an important decision factor if you develop mainly in Java. Let's go through some of the ActiveMQ strengths first and then discuss some of its drawbacks.

Being able to run your application code within the message broker or run the message broker within your application process allows you to use the same code on both sides of the border. It also allows you to achieve much lower latency because publishing messages within the same Java process is basically a memory copy operation, which is orders of magnitude faster than sending data over a network.

ActiveMQ does not provide advanced message routing like RabbitMQ, but you can achieve the same level of sophistication by using Camel. Camel is an integration framework designed to implement enterprise integration patterns,[10,31–32] and it is a great tool in extending ActiveMQ capabilities. Camel allows you to define routes, filters, and message processors using XML configuration and allows you to wire your own implementations of different components. If you decide to use Camel, you will add extra technology to your stack, increasing the complexity, but you will gain many advanced messaging features.

In addition to being Java based, ActiveMQ implements a common messaging interface called JMS (Java Message Service) and allows the creation of plugins, written also in Java.

Finally, ActiveMQ implements message groups mentioned earlier, which allow you to partially guarantee ordered message delivery. This feature is quite unique and neither RabbitMQ nor SQS has anything like that. If you desperately need FIFO-style messaging, you may want to use ActiveMQ.

We went through some of the most important strengths of ActiveMQ, so now it is time to mention some of its drawbacks.

First, ActiveMQ has much less flexible routing than RabbitMQ. You could use Camel, but if you are not developing in Java, it would add to the burden for your team. Also, Camel is not a simple technology to use, and I would recommend using it only if you have some experienced engineers on the team. There are a few features allowing you to build direct worker queues and persistent fan-out queues, but you don't have the ability to route messages based on more complex criteria.

The second major drawback in comparison to RabbitMQ is that ActiveMQ cannot be fully controlled using its remote API. In contrast, RabbitMQ can be fully configured and monitored using a REST API. When dealing with ActiveMQ, you can control some aspects of the message broker using the JMX (Java Management Extensions) protocol, but it is not something you would like to use when developing in languages other than Java.

Finally, ActiveMQ can be sensitive to large spikes of messages being published. It happened to me multiple times during load tests that ActiveMQ would simply crash when being overwhelmed by high message rates for extended periods of time. Although it is a stable platform, it does not have access to low-level functions like memory allocation and I/O control because it runs within JVM. It is still possible to run out of memory and crash the broker if you publish too many messages too fast.

Final Comparison Notes

Comparing ActiveMQ and RabbitMQ based on Google Trends,[14] we can see that RabbitMQ has gained a lot of popularity in recent years and both message brokers are pretty much going head to head now (as of this writing). Figure 7-23 shows ActiveMQ and RabbitMQ over the course of the last five years.

These trends may also be caused by the fact that RabbitMQ was acquired by SpringSource, which is one of the top players in the world of Java, and that ActiveMQ is being redeveloped from scratch under a new name, Apollo.

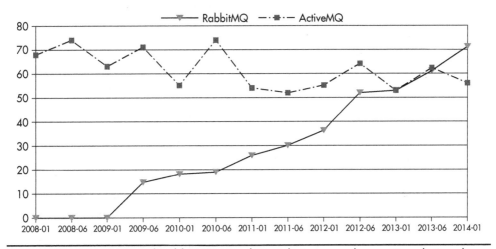

Figure 7-23 *ActiveMQ and RabbitMQ search popularity according to Google Trends*

Another way to compare brokers is by looking at their high-availability focus and how they handle extreme conditions. In this comparison, ActiveMQ scores the worst of all three systems. It is relatively easy to stall or even crash ActiveMQ by simply publishing messages faster than they can be routed or persisted. Initially, ActiveMQ buffers messages in memory, but as soon as you run out of RAM, it either stalls or crashes completely.

RabbitMQ performs better in such a scenario, as it has a built-in *backpressure* feature. If messages are published faster than they can be processed or persisted, RabbitMQ begins to throttle producers to avoid message loss and running out of memory. The benefit of that approach is increased stability and reliability, but it can cause unexpected delays on the publisher side, as publishing messages slows down significantly whenever backpressure is triggered.

In this comparison, SQS performs better than both ActiveMQ and RabbitMQ, as it supports very high throughput and Amazon is responsible for enforcing high availability of the service. Although SQS is a hosted platform, you can still experience throttling in some rare situations and you need to make sure that your publishers can handle failures correctly. You do not have to worry about crashing brokers, recovery procedures, or scalability of SQS, though, as it is managed by Amazon.

No matter which of the three technologies you choose, throughput is always finite and the best way to scale is by partitioning messages among multiple broker instances (or queues in the case of SQS).

If you decide to use SQS, you should be able to publish tens of thousands of messages per second, per queue, which is more than enough for most startups. If you find yourself reaching that limit, you would need to create multiple queue instances and distribute messages among them to scale out your overall throughput. Since SQS does not preserve message ordering and has very few advanced features, distributing messages among multiple SQS queues should be as easy as picking one of the queues at random and publishing messages to it. On the consumer side, you would need similar numbers of consumers subscribing to each of the queues and similar hardware resources to provide even consumer power.

If you decide to use ActiveMQ or RabbitMQ, your throughput per machine is going to depend on many factors. Primarily you will be limited by CPU and RAM of machines used (hardware or virtual servers), average message size, message fan-out ratio (how many queues/customers each message is delivered to), and whether your messages are persisted to disk or not. Regardless of how many messages per second you can process using a single broker instance, as you need to scale out, your brokers need to be able to scale out horizontally as well.

As I mentioned before, neither ActiveMQ nor RabbitMQ supports horizontal scalability out of the box, and you will need to implement application-level partitioning to distribute messages among multiple broker instances. You would do it in a similar way as you would deal with application-level data partitioning described in Chapter 5. You would deploy multiple brokers and distribute messages among them. Each broker would have the exact same configuration with the same queues (or exchanges and routing). Each of the brokers would also have a pool of dedicated customers.

If you use ActiveMQ and depend on its message groups for partial message ordering, you would need to use the message group ID as a sharding key so that all of the messages would be published to the same broker, allowing it to enforce ordering. Otherwise, assuming no message-ordering guarantees, you could select brokers at random when publishing messages because from the publisher's point of view, each of them would be functionally equal.

Messaging platforms are too complex to capture all their differences and gotchas on just a few pages. Having said that, you will need to get to know your tools before you can make really well-informed choices. In this section, I only mentioned the most popular messaging platforms, but there are more message brokers out there to choose from. I believe messaging is still an undervalued technology and it is worth getting to know more platforms. I recommend starting the process by reading about RabbitMQ[12] and ActiveMQ,[25] as well as a fantastic paper on Kafka.[w52]

Introduction to Event-Driven Architecture

We have gone a long way since the beginning of this chapter, but there is one more exciting concept I would like to introduce, which is event-driven architecture (EDA). In this section I will explain the core difference between the traditional programming model and EDA. I will also present some of its benefits and how you can use it within a larger non-EDA system.

First of all, to understand EDA, you need to stop thinking about software in terms of requests and responses. Instead, you have to think about components announcing things that have already happened. This subtle difference in the way you think about interactions has a profound impact on the architecture and scalability. Let's start off slowly by defining some basic terms and comparing how EDA is different from the traditional request/response model.

Event-driven architecture (EDA) is an architecture style where most interactions between different components are realized by announcing events that have already happened instead of requesting work to be done. On the consumer side, EDA is about responding to events that have happened somewhere in the system or outside of it. EDA consumers do not behave as services; they do not do things for others. They just react to things happening elsewhere.

An event is an object or a message that indicates something has happened. For example, an event could be announced or emitted whenever an order in an online store has been placed. In such case, an event would probably contain information about the buyer and items purchased. An event is an entity holding the data necessary to describe what has happened. It does not have any logic; instead, it is best to think of an event as a piece data describing something that has happened in the real world or within the application.

So far the difference between EDA and messaging can still be quite blurry. Let's have a closer look at the differences between the following interaction patterns: request/response, messaging, and EDA.

Request/Response Interaction

This is the traditional model, resembling the synchronous method or function invocation in traditional programming languages like C or Java. A caller sends a request and waits for the receiver to process the message and return with a response. I described this model in detail earlier in this chapter, so we won't go into more detail here. The important things to remember are that the caller has to be able to locate the receiver, it has to know the receiver's contract, and it is temporally coupled to the receiver.

> *Temporal coupling* is another term for synchronous invocation and means that caller cannot continue without the response from the receiver. This dependency on the receiver to finish its work is where coupling comes from. In other words, the weakest link in the entire call stack dictates the overall latency. (You can read more about temporal coupling.[w10,31])

In the case of request/response interactions, the contract includes the location of the service, the definition of the request message, and the definition of the response message. Clients of the service need to know at least this much to be able to use the service. Knowing things about the service implies coupling, as we discussed it in Chapter 2—the more you need to know about a component, the stronger is your coupling to it.

Direct Worker Queue Interaction

In this interaction model, the caller publishes messages into the queue or a topic for consumers to react to. Even though this is much more similar to the event-driven model, it still leaves opportunities for closer coupling. In this model, the caller would usually send a message to a queue named something like OrderProcessingQueue, indicating that the caller knows what needs to be done next (an order needs to be processed).

The good side of this approach is that it is asynchronous and there is no temporal coupling between the producer and consumer. Unfortunately, it usually happens that the producer knows something about the consumer and that the message sent to the queue is still a request to do something. If the producer knows what has to be done, it is still coupled to the service doing the actual work—it may not be coupled by the contract, but it is still coupled logically.

In the case of queue-based interaction, the contract consists of the queue location, the definition of the message sent to the queue, and quite often, the expectation about the result of the message being processed. As I already mentioned, there is no temporal coupling and since we are not expecting a response, we also reduce the contract's scope because the response message is not part of it any more.

Event-Based Interaction

Finally, we get to the event-driven interaction model, where the event publisher has no idea about any consumers being present. The event publisher creates an instance of an event, for example, NewOrderCreated, and announces it to the event-driven framework. The framework can use an ESB, it can be a built-in component, or it can even use a messaging broker like RabbitMQ. The important thing is that events can be published without having to know their destination. Event publishers do not care who reacts or how they react to events.

By its nature, all event-driven interactions are asynchronous, and it is assumed that the publisher continues without needing to know anything about consumers.

The main advantage of this approach is that you can achieve a very high level of decoupling. Your producers and consumers do not have to know each other. Since the event-driven framework wires consumers and producers together, producers do not need to know where to publish their event—they just announce them. On the other hand, consumers do not need to know how to get to the events they are interested in either—they just declare which types of events they are interested in, and the event-driven framework is responsible for routing them to the consumer.

It is worth pointing out that the contract between producer and consumers is reduced to just the event message definition. There are no endpoints, so there is no need to know their locations. Also, since the publisher does not expect responses, the contract does not include them either. All that publishers and consumers have in common is the format and meaning of the event message.

To visualize it better, let's consider two more diagrams. Figure 7-24 shows how the client and service are coupled to each other in the request/response interaction model. It shows all the pieces of information that the client and service need to share to be able to work together. The total size of the contract is called the contract surface area.

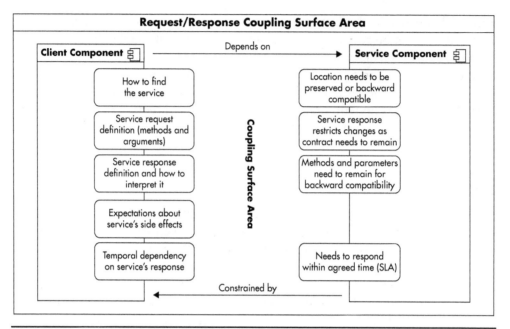

Figure 7-24 *Coupling surface area between the service and its clients*

Contract Surface Area is the measurement of coupling. The more information components need to know about each other to collaborate, the higher the surface area. The term comes from diagrams and UML modeling as the more lines you have between two components, the stronger the coupling.

In the Request/Response interaction model clients are coupled to the service in many ways. They need to be able to locate the service and understand its messages. Contract of the service includes both request and response messages. The client is also coupled temporally, as it has to wait for the service to respond. Finally, clients often assume a lot about the service's methods. For example, clients of the createUser service method could assume that a user object gets created somewhere in the service's database.

On the other side of the contract, the service does not have an easy job adapting to changing business needs as it needs to keep the contract intact. The service is coupled to its clients by every action that it ever exposed and by every piece of information included in request or response messages ever exposed. The service is also responsible for supporting agreed SLA (Service Layer Agreement) which means responding quickly and not going offline too often. Finally service is constrained by the way it is exposed to its clients, which may prevent you from partitioning the service into smaller services to scale better.

In comparison, Figure 7-25 shows EDA interactions. We can see that many coupling factors are removed and that the overall coupling surface area is much smaller. Components do not have to know much about each other, and the only point of coupling is the event definition itself. Both the publisher and consumer have to establish a shared understanding of the event type body and its meaning. In addition, the event consumer may be constrained by the event message, because if certain data was not included in the event definition, the consumer may need to consult a shared source of truth, or it may not have access to a piece of information at all.

In a purely EDA, all the interactions are based on events. This leads to an interesting conclusion that if all of the interactions are asynchronous and all the interactions are carried out using events, you could use events to re-create the state of the entire system by simply replaying events. This is exactly what event sourcing allows us to do.[L6–L7,24]

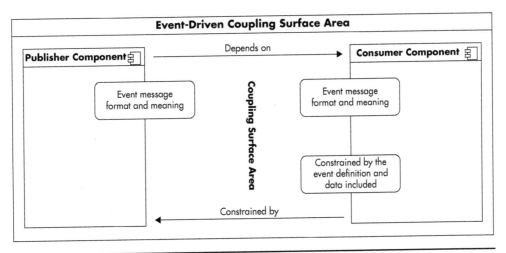

Figure 7-25 *Coupling surface area between EDA components*

Event sourcing is a technique where every change to the application state is persisted in the form of an event. Events are usually stored on disk in the form of event log files or some data store. At the same time, an application is built of event consumers, which process events passed to them. As a result, you can restore the system to an old state (for example, using a daily snapshot) and replay events to reach the same end state.

I have seen EDA with event sourcing in action handling 150,000 concurrently connected clients performing transactions with financial ramifications. If there was ever a crash, the entire system could be recovered to the most recent consistent state by replaying the event log. It also allowed engineers to copy the event log and debug live issues in the development environment by simply replaying the event logs. It was a very cool sight.

In fact, asynchronous replication of distributed systems is often done in a similar way. For example, MySQL replication is done in a similar way, as every data modification is recorded in the binary log right after the change is made on the master server. Since all state changes are in the binary log, the state of the slave replica server can be synchronized by replaying the binary log.[16] The only difference is that consumers of these events are replicating slaves. Having all events persisted in a log means that you can add a new event consumer and process historical events, so it would look like it was running from the beginning of time.

The important limitation of event sourcing is the need for a centralized state and event log. To be able to reconstruct the state of the application based on event log alone, you need to be processing them in the same order. You could say that you need to assume a Newtonian perception of time with an absolute ordering of events and a global "now." Unfortunately, in distributed systems that are spanning the globe, it becomes much harder because events may be happening simultaneously on different servers in different parts of the world. You can read more about the complexity of event sourcing and reasoning about time, [L7,39] but for simplicity, you can just remember that event sourcing requires sequential processing of all events.

Whether you use event sourcing or not, you can still benefit from EDA and you can benefit from it even in pre-existing systems. If you are building a new application from scratch, you have more freedom of choice regarding which parts should be developed in EDA style, but even if you are maintaining or extending an existing application, there are many cases where EDA will come in handy. The only trick is to start thinking of the software in terms of events. If you want to add new functionality and existing components do not have to know the results of the operation, you have a candidate for an event-driven workflow.

For example, you could develop a core of your online shopping cart in a traditional way and then extend it by publishing events from the core of the system. By publishing events, you would not make the core depend on external components, you would not jeopardize its availability or responsiveness, yet you could add new features by adding new event consumers later on. The EDA approach would also let you scale out, as you could host different event consumers on different servers.

Summary

We covered a lot of material in this chapter, discussing asynchronous processing, messaging, different brokers, and EDA. To cover these topics in depth would warrant a book dedicated to each. Our discussion here has been simple and fairly high level. The subject matter is quite different from the traditional programming model, but it is really worth learning. The important thing to remember is that messaging, EDA, and asynchronous processing are just tools. They can be great when applied to the right problem, but they can also be a nightmare to work with when forced into the wrong place.

You should come away from this chapter with a better understanding of the value of asynchronous processing in the context of scalability and having gained enough background to explore these topics on your own. All of the concepts presented in this chapter are quite simple and there is nothing to be intimidated by, but it can take some time before you feel that you fully understand the reasoning behind them. Different ways of explaining the same thing may work better for different people, so I strongly encourage you to read more on the subjects. I recommend reading a few books[31–32,24–27,12] and articles.[L6,w10–w11]

Asynchronous processing is still underinvested. High-profile players like VMware (RabbitMQ, Spring AMQP), LinkedIn (Kafka), and Twitter (Storm) are entering the stage. Platforms like Erlang and Node.js are also gaining popularity because distributed systems are built differently now. Monolithic enterprise servers with distributed transactions, locking, and synchronous processing seem to be fading into the past. We are moving into an era of lightweight, innovative, and highly parallel technologies, and startups should be investing in these types of solutions. EDA and asynchronous processing are going through their renaissance, and they are most likely going to become even more popular, so learning about them now is a good investment for every engineer.

structuring your data, indexing it efficiently, and being able to perform more complex searches over it is a serious challenge. As the size of your data set grows from gigabytes to terabytes, it becomes increasingly difficult to find the data you are looking for efficiently. Any time you read, update, delete, or even insert new data, your applications and data stores need to perform searches to be able to locate the right rows (or data structures) that need to be read and written. To be able to understand better how to search through billions of records efficiently, you first need to get familiar with how indexes work.

Introduction to Indexing

Being able to index data efficiently is a critical skill when working with scalable websites. Even if you do not intend to be an expert in this field, you need to have a basic understanding of how indexes and searching work to be able to work with ever-growing data sets.

Let's consider an example to explain how indexes and searching work. Let's say that you had personal data of a billion users and you needed to search through it quickly (I use a billion records to make scalability issues more apparent here, but you will face similar problems on smaller data sets as well). If the data set contained first names, last names, e-mail addresses, gender, date of birth, and an account number (user ID), in such a case your data could look similar to Table 8-1.

If your data was not indexed in any way, you would not be able to quickly find users based on any criteria. The only way to find a user would be to scan the entire data set, row by row. If you had a billion users and wanted to check if a particular e-mail address was in your database, you would need to perform up to a billion comparisons. In the worst-case scenario, when a user was not in your data set, you would need to perform one billion comparisons (as you cannot be sure that user is not there until you check all of the rows). It would also take you, on average, half a

User ID	First Name	Last Name	E-mail	Gender	Date of Birth
135	John	Doe	jdoe@example.com	Male	10/23/86
70	Richard	Roe	richard@example.org	Male	02/18/75
260	Marry	Moe	moemarry@example.info	Female	01/15/74
...	...	...	...	...	...

Table 8-1 *Sample of Test User Data Set*

billion comparisons to find a user that exists in your database, because some users would live closer to the beginning and others closer to the end of the data set.

A *full table scan* is often the term used for this type of search, as you need to scan the entire data set to find the row that you are looking for. As you can imagine, that type of search is expensive. You need to load all of the data from disk into memory to be able to perform comparisons and check if the row at hand is the one you are looking for. A full table scan is pretty much the worst-case scenario when it comes to searching, as it has $O(n)$ cost.

> *Big O notation* is a way to compare algorithms and estimate their cost. In simple terms, Big O notation tells you how the amount of work changes as the size of the input changes. Imagine that *n* is the number of rows in your data set (the size) and the Big O notation expression estimates the cost of executing your algorithm over that data set. When you see the expression $O(n)$, it means that doubling the size of the data set roughly doubles the cost of the algorithm execution. When you see the expression $O(n^2)$, it means that as your data set doubles in size, the cost grows quadratically (much faster than linear).

Because a full table scan has a linear cost, it is not an efficient way to search large data sets. A common way to speed up searching is to create an index on the data that you are going to search upon. For example, if you wanted to search for users based on their e-mail address, you would create an index on the e-mail address field.

In a simplified way, you can think of an index as a lookup data structure, just like a book index. To build a book index, you sort terms (keywords) in alphabetic order and map each of them to a page number. When readers want to find pages referring to a particular term, they can quickly locate the term in the index and find page numbers that they should look at. Figure 8-1 shows how data is structured in a book index.

There are two important properties of an index:

▶ An index is structured and sorted in a specific way, optimized for particular types of searches. For example, a book index can answer questions like "What pages refer to the term sharding?" but it cannot answer questions like "What pages refer to more than one term?" Although both questions refer to locations of terms in the book, a book index is not optimized to answer the second question efficiently.

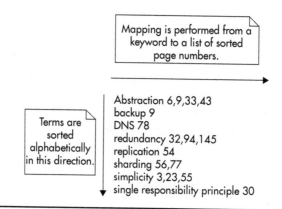

Figure 8-1   *Book index structure*

▶ The data set is reduced in size because the index is much smaller in size than the overall body of text so that the index can be loaded and processed faster. A 400-page book may have an index of just a few pages. That makes searching for terms faster, as there is less content to search through.

The reason why most indexes are sorted is that searching through a sorted data set can be performed much faster than through an unsorted one. A good example of a simple and fast searching algorithm is the *binary search* algorithm. When using a binary search algorithm, you don't scan the data set from the beginning to the end, but you "jump around," skipping large numbers of items. The algorithm takes a range of sorted values and performs four simple steps until the value is found:

1.   You look at the middle item of the data set to see if the value is equal, greater to, or smaller than what you are searching for.

2.   If the value is equal, you found the item you were looking for.

3.   If the value is greater than what you are looking for, you continue searching through the smaller items. You go back to step 1 with the data set reduced by half.

4.   If the value is smaller than what you are looking for, you continue searching through the larger items. You go back to step 1 with the data set reduced by half.

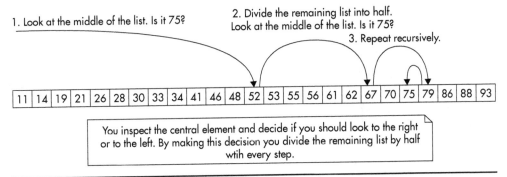

Figure 8-2   *Searching for number 75 using binary search*

Figure 8-2 shows how binary search works on a sequence of sorted numbers. As you can see, you did not have to investigate all of the numbers.

The brilliance of searching using this method is that with every comparison you reduce the number of items left by half. This in turn allows you to narrow down your search rapidly. If you had a billion user IDs, you would only need to perform, on average, 30 comparisons to find what you are looking for! If you remember, a full table scan would take, on average, half a billion comparisons to locate a row. The binary search algorithm has a Big O notation cost of $O(log_2 n)$, which is much lower than the $O(n)$ cost of a full table scan.

It is worth getting familiar with Big O notation, as applying the right algorithms and data structures becomes more important as your data set grows. Some of the most common Big O notation expressions are $O(n\text{\textasciicircum}2)$, $(n*log(n))$, $O(n)$, $O(log(n))$, and $O(1)$. Figure 8-3 shows a comparison of these curves, with the horizontal axis being the data set size and the vertical axis showing the relative computation cost. As you can see, the computational complexity of $O(n\text{\textasciicircum}2)$ grows very rapidly, causing even small data sets to become an issue. On the other hand, $O(log(n))$ grows so slowly that you can barely notice it on the graph. In comparison to the other curves, $O(log(n))$ looks more like a constant time $O(1)$ than anything else, making it very effective for large data sets.

Indexes are great for searching, but unfortunately, they add some overhead. Maintaining indexes requires you to keep additional data structures with sorted lists of items, and as the data set grows, these data structures can become large and costly. In this example, indexing 1 billion user IDs could grow to a monstrous 16GB of data. Assuming that you used 64-bit integers, you would need to store 8 bytes for the user ID and 8 bytes for the data offset for every single user. At such scale, adding indexes needs to be well thought out and planned, as having too

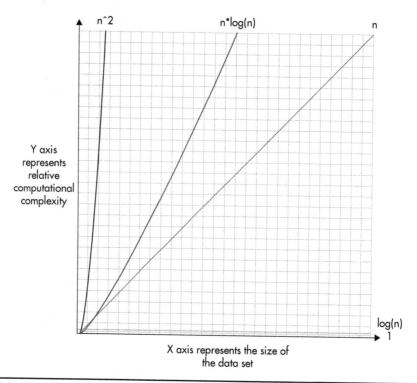

Y axis represents relative computational complexity

X axis represents the size of the data set

Figure 8-3   *Big O notation curves*

many indexes can cost you a great amount of memory and I/O (the data stored in the index needs to be read from the disk and written to it as well).

To make it even more expensive, indexing text fields like e-mail addresses takes more space because the data being indexed is "longer" than 8 bytes. On average, e-mail addresses are around 20 bytes long, making indexes even larger.

Considering that indexes add overhead, it is important to know what data is worth indexing and what is not. To make these decisions, you need to look at the queries that you intend to perform on your data and the cardinality of each field.

Cardinality is a number of unique values stored in a particular field. Fields with high cardinality are good candidates for indexes, as they allow you to reduce the data set to a very small number of rows.

To explain better how to estimate cardinality, let's take a look at the example data set again. The following are all of the fields with estimated cardinality:

▶ **gender**   In most databases, there would be only two genders available, giving us very low cardinality (cardinality ~ 2). Although you can find databases with more genders (like transsexual male), the overall cardinality would still be very low (a few dozen at best).

▶ **date of birth**   Assuming that your users were mostly under 80 years old and over 10 years old, you end up with up to 25,000 unique dates (cardinality ~ 25000). Although 25,000 dates seems like a lot, you will still end up with tens or hundreds of thousands of users born on each day, assuming that distribution of users is not equal and you have more 20-year-old users than 70-year-old ones.

▶ **first name**   Depending on the mixture of origins, you might have tens of thousands of unique first names (cardinality ~ tens of thousands).

▶ **last name**   This is similar to first names (cardinality ~ tens of thousands).

▶ **email address**   If e-mail addresses were used to uniquely identify accounts in your system, you would have cardinality equal to the total number of rows (cardinality = 1 billion). Even if you did not enforce e-mail address uniqueness, they would have few duplicates, giving you a very high cardinality.

▶ **user id**   Since user IDs are unique, the cardinality would also be 1 billion (cardinality = 1 billion).

The reason why low-cardinality fields are bad candidates for indexes is that they do not narrow down the search enough. After traversing the index, you still have a lot of rows left to inspect. Figure 8-4 shows two indexes visualized as sorted lists. The first index contains user IDs and the location of each row in the data set. The second index contains the gender of each user and reference to the data set.

Both of the indexes shown in Figure 8-4 are sorted and optimized for different types of searches. Index A is optimized to search for users based on their user ID, and index B is optimized to search for users based on their gender.

The key point here is that searching for a match on the indexed field is fast, as you can skip large numbers of rows, just as the binary search algorithm does. As soon as you find a match, though, you can no longer narrow down the search efficiently. All you can do is inspect all remaining rows, one by one. In this example, when you find a match using index A, you get a single item; in comparison, when you find a match using index B, you get half a billion items.

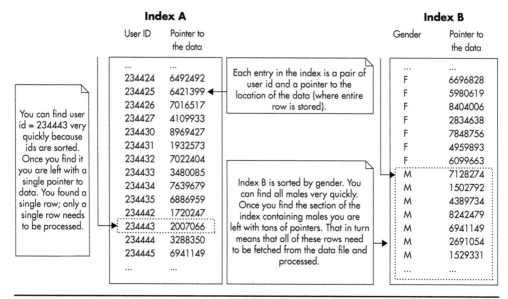

Figure 8-4   *Field cardinality and index efficiency*

The cardinality of a field is not the only thing that affects index performance. Another important factor is the item distribution. If you were indexing a field where some values were present in just a single item and others were present in millions of records, then performance of the index would vary greatly depending on which value you look for. For example, if you indexed a date of birth field, you are likely going to end up with a bell curve distribution of users. You may have a single user born on October 4, 1923, and a million users born on October 4, 1993. In this case, searching for users born on October 4, 1923, will narrow down the search to a single row. Searching for users born on October 4, 1993, will result in a million items left to inspect and process, making the index less efficient.

Luckily, indexing a single field and ending up with a million items is not the only thing you can do. Even when cardinality or distribution of values on a single field is not great, you can create indexes that have more than one field, allowing you to use the second field to narrow down your search further.

> A *compound index,* also known as a *composite index,* is an index that contains more than one field. You can use compound indexes to increase search efficiency where cardinality or distribution of values of individual fields is not good enough.

If you use compound indexes, in addition to deciding which fields to index, you need to decide in what order they should be indexed. When you create a compound index, you effectively create a sorted list ordered by multiple columns. It is just as if you sorted data by multiple columns in Excel or Google Docs. Depending on the order of columns in the compound index, the sorting of data changes. Figure 8-5 shows two indexes: index A (indexing first name, last name, and date of birth) and index B (indexing last name, first name, and date of birth).

Index A

First Name	Last Name	DOB	Pointer to the Data
CHARLES	LEE	12-Jan-1985	6492492
DAVID	LEE	14-Aug-1984	6421399
DONALD	JACKSON	19-Mar-1986	7016517
FRANK	GARCIA	6-Dec-1978	8969427
FRANK	GARCIA	16-Jun-1981	1932573
FRANK	LEE	11-Sep-1980	6886959
GARY	GARCIA	8-Apr-1984	6099663
GARY	GARCIA	7-Oct-1986	2007066
GARY	**LEE**	**28-Mar-1986**	3480085
GARY	**LEE**	2-Sep-1986	6941149
JAMES	THOMAS	22-Oct-1982	7022404
JOHN	JACKSON	2-Dec-1983	7639679
JOSEPH	THOMAS	3-Apr-1985	1720247
LARRY	ANDERSON	9-Jan-1984	8242479
LARRY	LEE	14-Apr-1981	4959893
MARK	JACKSON	7-Aug-1985	2691054
ROBERT	JACKSON	13-Dec-1983	8404006
SCOTT	ANDERSON	9-Mar-1978	2834638
THOMAS	ANDERSON	7-Nov-1985	7848756

Index B

Last Name	First Name	DOB	Pointer to the Data
ANDERSON	LARRY	9-Jan-1984	8242479
ANDERSON	SCOTT	9-Mar-1978	2834638
ANDERSON	THOMAS	7-Nov-1985	7848756
GARCIA	FRANK	6-Dec-1978	8969427
GARCIA	FRANK	16-Jun-1981	1932573
GARCIA	GARY	8-Apr-1984	6099663
GARCIA	GARY	7-Oct-1986	2007066
JACKSON	DONALD	19-Mar-1986	7016517
JACKSON	JOHN	2-Dec-1983	7639679
JACKSON	MARK	7-Aug-1985	2691054
JACKSON	ROBERT	13-Dec-1983	8404006
LEE	CHARLES	12-Jan-1985	6492492
LEE	DAVID	14-Aug-1984	6421399
LEE	FRANK	11-Sep-1980	6886959
LEE	**GARY**	**28-Mar-1986**	3480085
LEE	**GARY**	2-Sep-1986	6941149
LEE	LARRY	14-Apr-1981	4959893
THOMAS	JAMES	22-Oct-1982	7022404
THOMAS	JOSEPH	3-Apr-1985	1720247

Figure 8-5 *Ordering of columns in a compound index*

The most important thing to understand here is that indexes A and B are optimized for different types of queries. They are similar, but they are not equal, and you need to know exactly what types of searches you are going to perform to choose which one is better for your application.

Using index A, you can efficiently answer the following queries:

▶ get all users where first name = Gary

▶ get all users where first name = Gary and last name = Lee

▶ get all users where first name = Gary and last name = Lee and date of birth = March 28, 1986

Using index B, you can efficiently answer the following queries:

▶ get all users where last name = Lee

▶ get all users where last name = Lee and first name = Gary

▶ get all users where last name = Lee and first name = Gary and date of birth = March 28, 1986

As you might have noticed, queries 2 and 3 in both cases can be executed efficiently using either one of the indexes. The order of matching values would be different in each case, but it would result in the same number of rows being found and both indexes would likely have comparable performance.

To make it more interesting, although both indexes A and B contain date of birth, it is impossible to efficiently search for users born on April 8, 1984, without knowing their first and last names. To be able to search through index A, you need to have a first name that you want to look for. Similarly, if you want to search through index B, you need to have the user's last name. Only when you know the exact value of the leftmost column can you narrow down your search by providing additional information for the second and third columns.

Understanding the indexing basics presented in this section is absolutely critical to being able to design and implement scalable web applications. In particular, if you want to use NoSQL data stores, you need to stop thinking of data as if it were stored in tables and think of it as if it were stored in indexes. Let's explore this idea in more detail and see how you can optimize your data model for fast access despite large data size.

Modeling Data

When you use NoSQL data stores, you need to get used to thinking of data as if it were an index.

The main challenge when designing and building the data layer of a scalable web application is identifying access patterns and modeling your data based on these access patterns. Data normalization and simple rules of thumb learned from relational databases are not enough when working with terabytes of data. Huge data sets and the technical limitations of data stores will force you to design your data model much more carefully and consider use cases over the data relationships.

To be able to scale your data layer, you need to analyze your access patterns and use cases, select a data store, and then design the data model. To make it more challenging, you need to keep the data model as flexible as possible to allow for future extensions. At the same time, you want to optimize it for fast access to keep up with the growth of the data size.

These two forces often conflict, as optimizing the data model usually reduces the flexibility; conversely, increasing flexibility often leads to worse performance and scalability. In the following subsections we will discuss some NoSQL modeling techniques and concrete NoSQL data model examples to better explain how it is done in practice and what tradeoffs you need to prepare yourself for. Let's start by looking at NoSQL data modeling.

NoSQL Data Modeling

If you used relational databases before, you are likely familiar with the process of data modeling. When designing a relational database schema, you would usually start by looking at the data itself. You would ask yourself, "What is the data that I need to store?" You would then go through all of the bits of information that need to be persisted and isolate entities (database tables). You would then decide which pieces of information should be stored in which table. You would also create relationships between tables using foreign keys. You would then iterate over the schema design, trying to reduce the amount of redundant data and circular relationships.

As a result of this process, you would usually end up with a normalized and flexible database schema that could be used to answer almost any type of question using SQL queries. You would usually finish this process without thinking much about particular features or what feature would need to execute what types of queries. Your schema would be designed mainly based on the data itself, not queries or use cases. Later on, as you implement your application and new types of queries are needed, you would create new indexes to speed up these queries, but the data schema would usually remain unchanged, as it would be flexible enough to handle any type of query.

Unfortunately, that process of design and normalization focused on data does not work when applied to NoSQL data stores. NoSQL data stores trade data model flexibility (and ability to perform joins) for scalability, so you need to find a different approach.

To be able to model data in NoSQL data stores and access it efficiently, you need to change the way you design your schema. Rather than starting with data in mind, you need to start with queries in mind. I would argue that designing a data model in the NoSQL world is more difficult than it is in the relational database world. Once you optimize your data model for particular types of queries, you usually lose the ability to perform other types of queries. Designing a NoSQL data model is much more about tradeoffs and data layout optimization than it is about normalization.

When designing a data model for a NoSQL data store, you want to identify all the queries and access patterns first. Only once you understand how your data will be accessed can you move on to identifying key pieces of data and looking for ways to structure it so that you could execute all of your query types efficiently.

For example, if you were designing an e-commerce website using a relational database, you might not think much about how data would be queried. You might decide to have separate tables for products, product categories, and product reviews. Figure 8-6 shows how your data model might look.

If you were designing the same type of e-commerce website and you had to support millions of products with millions of user actions per hour, you might decide to use a NoSQL data store to help you scale the system. You would then have to model your data around your main queries rather than using a generic normalized model.

For example, if your most important queries were to load a product page to display all of the product-related metadata like name, image URL, price, categories it belongs to, and average user ranking, you might optimize your data model for this use case rather than keeping it normalized. Figure 8-7 shows an alternative data model with example documents in each of the collections.

By grouping most of the data into the product entity, you would be able to request all of that data with a single document access. You would not need to join tables, query multiple servers, or traverse multiple indexes. Rendering a product page could then be achieved by a single index lookup and fetching of a single

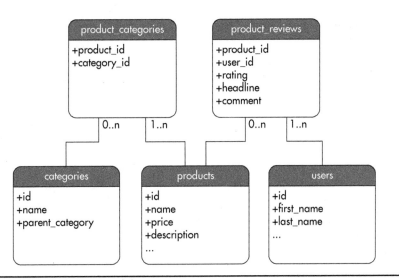

Figure 8-6 *Relational data model*

Collection of users

```
{
  "id": 4234,
  "userName": "Sam",
  "email": "sam@example.org",
  "yearOfBirth": 1981,
  ...
}
...
```

Collection of products

```
{
  "id": 6329103,
  "name": "Digital wall clock",
  "price": 59.95,
  "description": "...",
  "thumbnail": "http://example.org/img/6329103.jpg",
  "categories": ["clocks", "kitchen", "electronics"],
  "categoryIds": [4123, 53452, 342],
  "avgRating": 3.75,
  "recentComments": [
    {
      "id": 6523123,
      "userId": 4234,
      "userName": "Sam",
      "rating": 5,
      "comment": "That is the coolest clock I ever had."
    }
    ...
  ]
}
...
```

Collection of product reviews

```
{
  "id": 6523123,
  "product": {
    "id": 6329103,
    "name": "Digital wall clock",
    "price": 59.95,
    "thumbnail": "http://example.org/img/6329103.jpg"
  },
  "user": {
    "id": 4234,
    "userName": "Sam"
  },
  "rating": 5,
  "comment": "That is the coolest clock I ever had."
}
...
```

Figure 8-7 *Nonrelational data model*

document. Depending on the data store used, you might also shard data based on the product ID so that queries regarding different products could be sent to different servers, increasing your overall capacity.

There are considerable benefits and drawbacks of data denormalization and modeling with queries in mind. Your main benefit is performance and ability to efficiently access data despite a huge data set. By using a single index and a single "table," you minimize the number of disk operations, reducing the I/O pressure, which is usually the main bottleneck in the data layer.

On the other hand, denormalization introduces data redundancy. In this example, in the normalized model (with SQL tables), category names live in a separate table and each product is joined to its categories by a product_categories table. This way, category metadata is stored once and product metadata is stored once (product_categories contains references only). In the denormalized approach (NoSQL-like), each product has a list of category names embedded. Categories do not exist by themselves—they are part of product metadata. That leads to data redundancy and, what is more important here, makes updating data much more difficult. If you needed to change a product category name, you would need to update all of the products that belong to that category, as category names are stored within each product. That could be extremely costly, especially if you did not have an index allowing you to find all products belonging to a particular category. In such a scenario, you would need to perform a full table scan and inspect all of the products just to update a category name.

> ### *HINT*
>
> *Flexibility is one of the most important attributes of good architecture. To quote Robert C. Martin again, "Good architecture maximizes the number of decisions not made." By denormalizing data and optimizing for certain access patterns, you are making a tradeoff. You sacrifice some flexibility for the sake of performance and scalability. It is critical to be aware of these tradeoffs and make them very carefully.*

As you can see, denormalization is a double-edged sword. It helps us optimize and scale, but it can be restricting and it can make future changes much more difficult. It can also easily lead to a situation where there is no efficient way to search for data and you need to perform costly full table scans. It can also lead to situations where you need to build additional "tables" and add even more redundancy to be able to access data efficiently.

Regardless of the drawbacks, data modeling focused on access patterns and use cases is what you need to get used to if you decide to use NoSQL data stores. As mentioned in Chapter 5, NoSQL data stores are more specialized than relational database engines and they require different data models. In general, NoSQL data stores do not support joins and data has to be grouped and indexed based on the access patterns rather than based on the meaning of the data itself.

Although NoSQL data stores are evolving very fast and there are dozens of open-source projects out there, the most commonly used NoSQL data stores can be broadly categorized based on their data model into three categories:

▶ **Key-value data stores**   These data stores support only the most simplistic access patterns. To access data, you need to provide the key under which data was stored. Key-value stores have a limited programming interface— basically all you can do is set or get objects based on their key. Key-value stores usually do not support any indexes or sorting (other than the primary key). At the same time, they have the least complexity and they can implement automatic sharding based on the key, as each value is independent and the only way to access values is by providing their keys. They are good for fast one-to-one lookups, but they are impractical when you need sorted lists of objects or when you need to model relationships between objects. Examples of key-value stores are Dynamo and Riak. Memcached is also a form of a key-value data store, but it does not persist data, which makes it more of a key-value cache than a data store. Another data store that is sometimes used as a key-value store is Redis, but it has more to offer than just key-value mappings.

▶ **Wide columnar data stores**   These data stores allow you to model data as if it was a compound index. Data modeling is still a challenge, as it is quite different from relational databases, but it is much more practical because you can build sorted lists. There is no concept of a join, so denormalization is a standard practice, but in return wide columnar stores scale very well. They usually provide data partitioning and horizontal scalability out of the box. They are a good choice for huge data sets like user-generated content, event streams, and sensory data. Examples of wide columnar data stores are BigTable, Cassandra, and HBase.

▶ **Document-oriented data stores**   These data stores allow more complex objects to be stored and indexed by the data store. Document-based data stores use a concept of a document as the most basic building block in their data model. Documents are data structures that can contain arrays, maps, and nested structures just as a JSON or XML document would. Although documents have flexible schemas (you can add and remove fields at will on a per-document basis), document data stores usually allow for more complex indexes to be added to collections of documents. Document stores usually offer a fairly rich data model, and they are a good use case for systems where data is difficult to fit into a predefined schema (where it is hard to create a SQL-like normalized model) and at the same time where scalability is required. Examples of document-oriented data stores are MongoDB, CouchDB, and Couchbase.

There are other types of NoSQL data stores like graph databases and object stores, but they are still much less popular. Going into more detail about each of these data store types is outside the scope of this book, especially because the NoSQL data store market is very fragmented, with each of the data stores evolving in a slightly different direction to satisfy specialized niche needs.

Instead of trying to cover all of the possible data stores, let's have a look at a couple of data model examples to see how NoSQL modeling works in practice.

Wide Column Storage Example

Consider an example where you needed to build an online auction website similar in concept to eBay. If you were to design the data model using the relational database approach, you would begin by looking for entities and normalize the model. As I mentioned before, in the NoSQL world, you need to start by looking at what queries you are going to perform, not just what data you are going to store.

Let's say that you had the following list of use cases that need to be satisfied:

1. Users need to be able to sign up and log in.

2. Logged-in users can view auction details by viewing the item auction page.

3. The item auction page contains product information like title, description, and images.

4. The item auction page also includes a list of bids with the names of users who placed them and the prices they offered.

5. Users need to be able to change their user name.

6. Users can view the history of bids of other users by viewing their profile pages. The user profile page contains details about the user like name and reputation score.

7. The user profile page shows a list of items that the user placed bids on. Each bid displays the name of the item, a link to the item auction page, and a price that the user offered.

8. Your system needs to support hundreds of millions of users and tens of millions of products with millions of bids each.

After looking at the use cases, you might decide to use a wide columnar data store like Cassandra. By using Cassandra, you can leverage its high availability and automated horizontal scalability. You just need to find a good way to model these use cases to make sure that you can satisfy the business needs.

The Cassandra data model is often represented as a table with an unlimited number of rows and a nearly unlimited number of arbitrary columns, where each row can have different columns, and column names can be made up on the spot (there is no table definition or strict schema and columns are dynamically created as you add fields to the row). Figure 8-8 shows how the Cassandra table is usually illustrated.

Each row has a row key, which is a primary key and at the same time a sharding key of the table. The row key is a string—it uniquely identifies a single row and it is automatically indexed by Cassandra. Rows are distributed among different servers based on the row key, so all of the data that needs to be accessed together in a single read needs to be stored within a single row. Figure 8-8 also shows that rows are indexed based on the row key and columns are indexed based on a column name.

The way Cassandra organizes and sorts data in tables is similar to the way compound indexes work. Any time you want to access data, you need to provide a row key and then column name, as both of these are indexed. Because columns

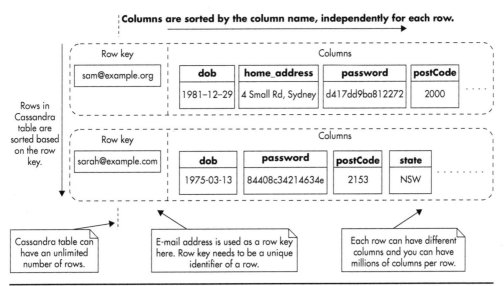

Figure 8-8   *Fragments of two rows in a Cassandra table*

are stored in sorted order, you can perform fast scans on column names to retrieve neighboring columns. Since every row lives on its own and there is no table schema definition, there is no way to efficiently select multiple rows based on a particular column value.

You could visualize a Cassandra table as if it was a compound index. Figure 8-9 shows how you could define this model in a relational database like MySQL. The index would contain a row key as the first field and then column name as the second field. Values would contain actual values from Cassandra fields so that you would not need to load data from another location.

As I mentioned before, indexes are optimized for access based on the fields that are indexed. When you want to access data based on a row key and a column name, Cassandra can locate the data quickly, as it traverses an index and does not need to perform any table scans. The problem with this approach is that queries that do not look for a particular row key and column may be inefficient because they require expensive scans.

HINT

Many NoSQL data modeling techniques can be boiled down to building compound indexes so that data can be located efficiently. As a result, queries that can use the index perform very well, but queries that do not use the index require a full table scan.

Going back to the example of an online auction website, you could model users in Cassandra by creating a users table. You could use the user's e-mail address (or

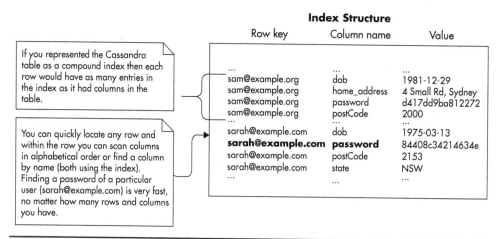

Figure 8-9 *Cassandra table represented as if it were a compound index*

user name) as a row key of the users table so that you could find users efficiently when they are logging in to the system. To make sure you always have the user's row key, you could then store it in the user's HTTP session or encrypted cookies for the duration of the visit.

You would then store user attributes like first name, last name, phone number, and hashed password in separate columns of the users table. Since there is no predefined column schema in Cassandra, some users might have additional columns like billing address, shipping address, or contact preference settings.

HINT

Any time you want to query the users table, you should do it for a particular user to avoid expensive table scans. As I mentioned before, Cassandra tables behave like compound indexes. The row key is the first field of that "index," so you always need to provide it to be able to search for data efficiently. You can also provide column names or column name ranges to find individual attributes. The column name is the second field of the "compound index" and providing it improves search speed even further.

In a similar way, you could model auction items. Each item would be uniquely identified by a row key as its ID. Columns would represent item attributes like title, image URLs, description, and classification. Figure 8-10 shows how both the users table and items table might look. By having these two tables, you can efficiently find any item or user by their row key.

To satisfy more use cases, you would also need to store information about which users placed bids on which items. To be able to execute all of these queries efficiently, you would need to store this information in a way that is optimized for two access patterns:

▶ Get all bids of a particular item (use case 4)

▶ Get all bids of a particular user (use case 7)

To allow these access patterns, you need to create two additional "indexes": one indexing bids by item ID and the second one indexing bids by user ID. As of this writing Cassandra does not allow you to index selected columns, so you need to create two additional Cassandra tables to provide these indexes. You could create one table called item_bids to store bids per item and a second table called user_bids to store bids per user.

Alternatively, you could use another feature of Cassandra called column families to avoid creating additional tables. By using column families, you would

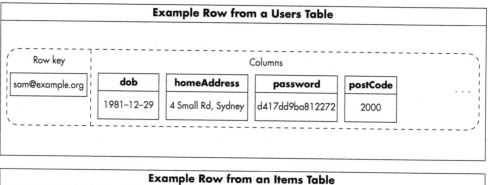

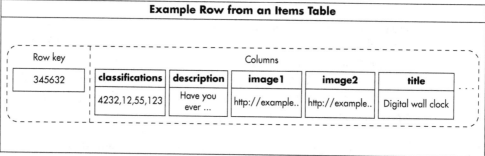

Figure 8-10 *User and item tables*

still end up with denormalized and duplicated data, so for simplicity's sake I decided to use separate tables in this example. Any time a user places a bid, your web application needs to write to both of these data structures to keep both of these "indexes" in sync. Luckily, Cassandra is optimized for writes and writing to multiple tables is not a concern from a scalability or performance point of view.

Figure 8-11 shows how these two tables might look. If you take a closer look at the user_bids table, you may notice that column names contain timestamps and item IDs. By using this trick, you can store bids sorted by time and display them on the user's profile page in chronological order.

By storing data in this way you are able to write into these tables very efficiently. Any time you need to place a bid, you would serialize bid data and simply issue two commands:

▶ set data under column named "$time|$item_id" for a row "$user_email" in table user_bids

▶ set data under column named "$time|$user_email" for a row "$item_id" in table item_bids

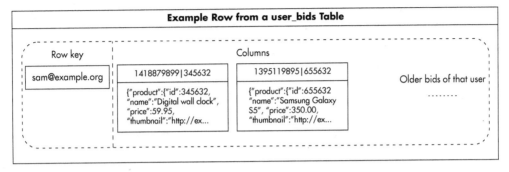

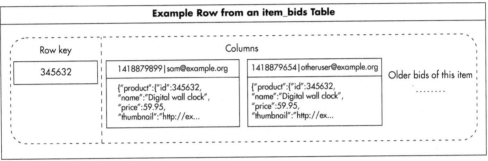

Figure 8-11   *Tables storing bids based on item and user*

Cassandra is an eventually consistent store, so issuing writes this way ensures that you never miss any writes. Even if some writes are delayed, they still end up in the same order on all servers. No matter how long it takes for such a command to reach each server, data is always inserted into the right place and stored in the same order. In addition, order of command execution on each server becomes irrelevant, and you can issue the same command multiple times without affecting the end result (making these commands idempotent).

It is also worth noting here that bid data would be denormalized and redundant, as shown in Listing 8-1. You would set the same data in both user_bids and item_bids tables. Serialized bid data would contain enough information about the product and the bidding user so that you would not need to fetch additional values from other tables to render bids on the user's profile page or item detail pages. This data demineralization would allow you to render an item page with a single query on the item table and a single column scan on the item_bids table. In a similar way, you could render the user's profile page by a single query to the users table and a single column scan on the user_bids table.

Listing 8-1 *Serialized bid data stored in column values*

```
{
    "product": {
        "id": 345632,
        "name": "Digital wall clock",
        "price": 59.95,
        "thumbnail": "http://example.org/img/6329103.jpg"
    },
    "user": {
        "email": "sam@example.org",
        "name": "Sam",
        "avatar": "http://example.org/img/fe6e3424rwe.jpg"
    },
    "timestamp": 1418879899
}
```

Once you think your data model is complete, it is critical to validate it against the list of known use cases. This way, you can ensure that your data model can, in fact, support all of the access patterns necessary. In this example, you could go over the following use cases:

▶ To create an account and log in (use case 1), you would use e-mail address as a row key to locate the user's row efficiently. In the same way, you could detect whether an account for a given e-mail address exists or not.

▶ Loading the item auction page (use cases 2, 3, and 4) would be performed by looking up the item by ID and then loading the most recent bids from the item_bids table. Cassandra allows fetching multiple columns starting from any selected column name, so bids could be loaded in chronological order. Each item bid contains all the data needed to render the page fragment and no further queries are necessary.

▶ Loading the user page (use cases 6 and 7) would work in a similar way. You would fetch user metadata from the users table based on the e-mail address and then fetch the most recent bids from the user_bids table.

▶ Updating the user name is an interesting use case (use case 5), as user names are stored in all of their bids in both user_bids and item_bids tables. Updating the user name would have to be an offline process because it requires much more data manipulation. Any time a user decides to update his or her user name, you would need to add a job to a queue and defer execution to an offline process. You would be able to find all of the bids made by the user using the user_bids table. You would then need to load each of these bids, unserialize them, change the embedded user name, and save them back. By loading each bid from the user_bids table, you would also find its timestamp and item ID. That, in turn, would allow you to issue an additional SET command to overwrite the same bid metadata in the item_bids table.

▶   Storing billions of bids, hundreds of millions of users, and millions of items (user case 8) would be possible because of Cassandra's auto-sharding functionality and careful selection of row keys. By using user ID and an item ID as row keys, you are able to partition data into small chunks and distribute it evenly among a large number of servers. No auction item would receive more than a million bids and no user would have more than thousands or hundreds of thousands of bids. This way, data could be partitioned and distributed efficiently among as many servers as was necessary.

There are a few more tradeoffs that are worth pointing out here. By structuring data in a form of a "compound index," you gain the ability to answer certain types of queries very quickly. By denormalizing the bid's data, you gain performance and help scalability. By serializing all the bid data and saving it as a single value, you avoid joins, as all the data needed to render bid page fragments are present in the serialized bid object.

On the other hand, denormalization of a bid's data makes it much more difficult and time consuming to make changes to redundant data. By structuring data as if it were an index, you optimize for certain types of queries. This, in turn, makes some types of queries perform exceptionally well, but all others become prohibitively inefficient.

Finding a flexible data model that supports all known access patterns and provides maximal flexibility is the real challenge of NoSQL. For example, using the data model presented in this example, you cannot efficiently find items with the highest number of bids or the highest price. There is no "index" that would allow you to efficiently find this data, so you would need to perform a full table scan to get these answers. To make things worse, there is no easy way to add an index to a Cassandra table. You would need to denormalize it further by adding new columns or tables.

An alternative way to deal with the NoSQL indexing challenge is to use a dedicated search engine for more complex queries rather than trying to satisfy all use cases with a single data store. Let's now have a quick look at search engines and see how they can complement a data layer of a scalable web application.

Search Engines

Nearly every web application needs to perform complex search queries nowadays. For example, e-commerce platforms need to allow users to search for products based on arbitrary combinations of criteria like category, price range, brand, availability, or location. To make things even more difficult, users can also search for arbitrary words or phrases and apply sorting according to their own preferences.

Whether you use relational databases or NoSQL data stores, searching through large data sets with such flexibility is going to be a significant challenge even if you apply the best modeling practices and use the best technologies available on the market.

Allowing users to perform such wide ranges of queries requires either building dozens of indexes optimized for different types of searches or using a dedicated search engine. Before deciding whether you need a dedicated search engine, let's start with a quick introduction to search engines to understand better what they do and how they do it.

Introduction to Search Engines

You can think of search engines as data stores specializing in searching through text and other data types. As a result, they make different types of tradeoffs than relational databases or NoSQL data stores do. For example, consistency and write performance may be much less important to them than being able to perform complex searches very fast. They may also have different needs when it comes to memory consumption and I/O throughput as they optimize for specific interaction patterns.

Before you begin using dedicated search engines, it is worth understanding how full text search works itself. The core concept behind full text search and modern search engines is an inverted index.

> An *inverted index* is a type of index that allows you to search for phrases or individual words (full text search).

The types of indexes that we discussed so far required you to search for an exact value match or for a value prefix. For example, if you built an index on a text field containing movie titles, you could efficiently find rows with a title equal to "It's a Wonderful Life." Some index types would also allow you to efficiently search for all titles starting with a prefix "It's a Wonderful," but they would not let you search for individual words in a text field. If your user typed in "Wonderful Life," he or she would not find the "It's a Wonderful Life" record unless you used a full text search (an inverted index). Using an inverted index allows you to search for any of the words contained in the text field, regardless of their location and order. For example, you could search for "Life Wonderful" or "It's a Life" and still find the "It's a Wonderful Life" record.

When you index a piece of text like "The Silence of the Lambs" using an inverted index, it is first broken down into tokens (like words). Then each of the tokens can be preprocessed to improve search performance. For example, all words may be lowercased, plural forms changed to singular, and duplicates removed from the list. As a result, you may end up with a smaller list of unique tokens like "the," "silence," "of," "lamb."

Once you extract all the tokens, you then use them as if they were keywords in a book index. Rather than adding a movie title in its entirety into the index, you add each word independently with a pointer to the document that contained it. Figure 8-12 shows the structure of a simplistic inverted index.

As shown in Figure 8-12, document IDs next to each token are in sorted order to allow a fast search within a list and, more importantly, merging of lists. Any time you want to find documents containing particular words, you first find these words in the dictionary and then merge their posting lists.

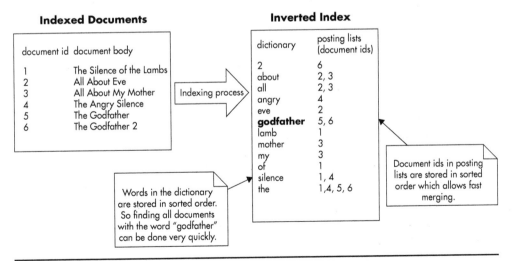

Figure 8-12 *Inverted index structure*

HINT

The structure of an inverted index looks just like a book index. It is a sorted list of words (tokens) and each word points to a sorted list of page numbers (document IDs).

Searching for a phrase ("silence" AND "lamb") requires you to merge posting lists of these two words by finding an intersection. Searching for words ("silence" OR "lamb") requires you to merge two lists by finding a union. In both cases, merging can be performed efficiently because lists of document IDs are stored in sorted order. Searching for phrases (AND queries) is slightly less expensive, as you can skip more document IDs and the resulting merged list is usually shorter than in the case of OR queries. In both cases, though, searching is still expensive and carries an $O(n)$ time complexity (where n is the length of posting lists).

Understanding how an inverted index works may help to understand why OR conditions are especially expensive in a full text search and why search engines need so much memory to operate. With millions of documents, each containing thousands of words, an inverted index grows in size faster than a normal index would because each word in each document must be indexed.

Understanding how different types of indexes work will also help you design more efficient NoSQL data models, as NoSQL data modeling is closer to designing indexes than designing relational schemas. In fact, Cassandra was initially used at Facebook to implement an inverted index and allow searching through the messages inbox.[w27] Having said that, I would not recommend implementing a full text search engine from scratch, as it would be very expensive. Instead, I would recommend using a general-purpose search engine as an additional piece of your infrastructure. Let's have a quick look at a common search engine integration pattern.

Using a Dedicated Search Engine

As I mentioned before, search engines are data stores specializing in searching. They are especially good at full text searching, but they also allow you to index other data types and perform complex search queries efficiently. Any time you need to build a rich search functionality over a large data set, you should consider using a search engine.

A good place to see how complex searching features can become is to look at used car listings websites. Some of these websites have hundreds of thousands of cars for sale at a time, which forces them to provide much more advanced searching criteria (otherwise, users would be flooded with irrelevant offers). As a result, you can find advanced search forms with literally dozens of fields. You can search for anything from free text, mark, model, min/max price, min/max mileage, fuel type, transmission type, horsepower, and color to accessories like electric mirrors and heated seats. To make things even more complicated, once you execute your search, you want to display facets to users to allow them to narrow down their search even further by selecting additional filters rather than having to start from scratch.

Complex search functionality like this is where dedicated search engines really shine. Rather than having to implement complex and inefficient solutions yourself in your application, you are much better off by using a search engine. There are a few popular search engines out there: search engines as a service, like Amazon CloudSearch and Azure Search, and open-source products, like Elasticsearch, Solr, and Sphinx.

If you decide to use a hosted service, you benefit significantly from not having to operate, scale, and manage these components yourself. Search engines, especially the cutting-edge ones, can be quite difficult to scale and operate in production, unless you have engineers experienced with this particular technology. You may sacrifice some flexibility and some of the edge-case features, but you reduce your time to market and the complexity of your operations.

Going into the details of how to configure, scale, and operate search engines is beyond the scope of this book, but let's have a quick look at how you could integrate with one of them. For example, if you decided to use Elasticsearch as a search engine for your used car sales website, you would need to deploy it in your data center and index all of your cars in it. Indexing cars using Elasticsearch would be quite simple since Elasticsearch does not require any predefined schema. You would simply need to generate JSON documents for each car and post them to be indexed by Elasticsearch. In addition, to keep the search index in sync with your primary data store, you would need to refresh the documents indexed in Elasticsearch any time car metadata changes.

HINT

A common pattern for indexing data in a search engine is to use a job queue (especially since search engines are near real time anyway). Anytime anyone modifies car metadata, they submit an asynchronous message for this particular car to be reindexed. At a later stage, a queue worker picks up the message from the queue, builds up the JSON document with all the information, and posts to the search engine to overwrite previous data.

Figure 8-13 shows how a search engine deployment could look. All of the searches would be executed by the search engine. Search results could then be enriched by real-time data coming from the main data store (if it was absolutely necessary).

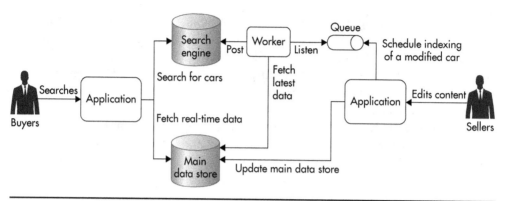

Figure 8-13 *Inverted index structure*

On the other hand, people editing their car listings would write directly to the main data store and refresh the search index via a queue and an asynchronous indexing worker process.

By having all of your cars indexed by Elasticsearch, you could then start issuing complex queries like "Get all cars mentioning 'quick sale' made by Toyota between 2000 and 2005 with electric windows and tagged as special offer. Then sort it all by price and product facets like location, model, and color."

Search engines are an important tool in the NoSQL web stack toolbelt, and I strongly recommend getting familiar with at least a couple of platforms to be able to choose and use them efficiently.

Summary

Being able to search for data efficiently can be a serious challenge. The key things to take away from this chapter are that data should be stored in a way that is optimized for specific access patterns and that indexes are the primary tool for making search scalable.

It is also important to remember that NoSQL brings a new way of thinking about data. You identify your main use cases and access patterns and derive the data model out of this knowledge rather than structuring data in a generic way. It may also require dedicated search engines, to complement your infrastructure and deal with the most complex search scenarios.

Explore searching, indexing, and data modeling in more detail.[16,19,w27–w28,w47–w48,w71] Searching for data was the last purely technical chapter of this book; let's now have a look at some other dimensions of scalability in the context of web startups.

Other Dimensions
of Scalability

The majority of this book is dedicated to technical details of designing and building scalable web applications, as these subjects are the main areas of focus for software engineers. In reality, building scalable systems is more than just writing code. Some of the other dimensions of scalability that you need to pay attention to are

▶ **Scaling operations**   How many servers can you run in production? Once you deploy your system to hundreds of servers, you need to be able to manage them efficiently. If you need to hire an additional sysadmin every time you add 20 web servers to your stack, you are not going to be able to scale fast or cheap.

▶ **Scaling your own impact**   How much value for your customers and your company can you personally generate? As your startup grows, your individual impact should grow with it. You should be more efficient and able to increase your personal contributions by expanding your responsibilities and advising your business leaders.

▶ **Scaling the engineering department**   How many engineers can your startup hire before becoming inefficient? As your company grows, you need to be able to hire more engineers and increase the size of your engineering department without reducing their productivity. That means developing the right culture and structuring your teams and systems in a way that allows parallel development and collaboration at scale.

As you become more senior, you should be able to appreciate these additional facets of scalability. For your applications to be truly scalable, you need to be able to scale the size of your teams, the number of servers you support, and your own personal productivity, minimizing the costs (time and money) at the same time. Let's now discuss some of the ways in which you can help your startup scale.

Scaling Productivity through Automation

"If you want something to happen, ask.
If you want it to happen often, automate it." – Ivan Kirigin

A big part of startup philosophy is to scale the value of your company exponentially over time while keeping your costs growing at a much slower rate. That means that the cost of serving the first ten million users should be higher than the cost of serving the second ten million users. Although that may be counterintuitive, the cost of capacity unit should decrease over time. That means your company has to become more efficient as it grows. The cost per user or per transaction or per checkout (or whatever you measure) should decrease as you grow in size.

Modern technology startups manage to achieve incredible customer-to-employee ratios, where tiny technical teams support products used by tens or even hundreds of millions of users. This efficiency constraint makes scalability even more challenging, as it means that you need to design and build systems that become more efficient as they grow. To achieve this level of efficiency, you need to automate everything you can. Let's have a look at some common areas that can be automated to increase efficiency.

Testing

Testing is the first thing that you should automate when building a scalable web application. Although it took over a decade for businesses and engineers to appreciate automated testing, it is finally becoming a de facto standard of our industry. The main reason why automated testing is a sound investment is that the overall cost of manual testing grows much faster over time than the overall cost of automated testing.

Figure 9-1 shows the overall cost of manual and automated testing. If you decide to depend on manual testing alone, you do not have any up-front investments. You hire testers and they test your application before every release. Initially, the cost is small, but it stacks up very fast. Every time you build a new feature, you need to test that feature, as well as all the previously released features, to make sure that your changes did not break anything else. That, in turn, means that the cost of testing each release is higher than testing any of the previous releases (you become less efficient over time). It also takes longer and longer to release new versions of software because testing cycles become longer as your system grows in size.

Automated testing requires an up-front investment, as you need to set up your automated testing suites and deploy continuous integration servers, but it is much cheaper going forward. Once you are done with initial setup, you only create tests for new features. You do not need to spend time on regression testing existing features because this does not cost you anything. As a result, you become more efficient over time because with every release, the ratio of code being tested by existing tests to the new code (which requires tests to be created) increases. Eventually, you reach a break-even point where the overall cost of automated testing is lower than manual testing.

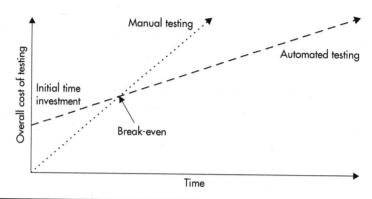

Figure 9-1 *Overall cost of manual and automated testing*

Although it is difficult to measure the costs and benefits of automated testing, I would expect a startup to reach the break-even point after three to six months of development. The benefits of automated testing depend on the volatility of your business, the number of "pivots" (when you decide to change the focus of your business), the size of your team, and the tolerance for defects.

In addition to the time and money spent, automated tests bring confidence to your team and allow you to make rapid changes and refactor aggressively, which is a great advantage when working for a startup. By using automated tests and continuous integration, you can also speed up your development cycles. You do not need to spend days or weeks hardening and testing your code before releasing it. By having a suite of automated tests, you can integrate early and release more often, making you more responsive to market needs.

> **HINT**
>
> With the safety net of automated tests, your teams can become what Robert C. Martin calls fearless engineers. Fearless engineers are not afraid to make changes. They control their software and they have legitimate confidence that bugs are detected before they make their way into production.

Depending on the languages and technologies you work with, you may use different tools to automate your tests. First of all, you want the majority of your tests to be unit tests, which can execute without other components being deployed. Unit tests are the fastest to execute and cheapest to maintain. They don't cause false positives, and they are easy to debug and fix when making changes.

In addition, you may want to have integration tests, which span multiple components, and some end-to-end tests, which test entire applications via their public interfaces. Two tools that are worth recommending for end-to-end tests are Jmeter and Selenium. Jmeter is great at testing low-level Hypertext Transfer Protocol (HTTP) web services, HTTP redirects, headers, and cookies and it is also a great tool for performance and load testing. Selenium, on the other hand, allows you to remotely control a browser from within your tests. As a result, you can create test cases for complex scenarios like login, purchase, or subscription. Using Selenium, you can automate anything that a manual tester would do and plug it into your automated test suites.

Once you automate your tests, you gain a solid foundation to automate your entire build deployment and release process. Let's have a look at how you can expand automation in these areas.

Build and Deployment

The next step in increasing your efficiency is to automate your entire build, test, and deployment process. Manual deployments are a time sink in the same way manual testing is. As the number of servers and services grows, more people need to be involved, more servers and services need to be coordinated, and it becomes more difficult to execute a successful deployment. As it becomes more difficult and complex to release software, releases take longer and testing/integration cycles become longer as well. As a result, your releases become larger because more code is developed between releases, leading to even larger and more complex releases. Figure 9-2 shows the vicious cycle of manual releases and the positive cycle of automated releases.

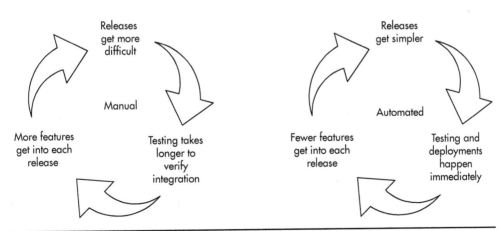

Figure 9-2 *Manual deployments vs. automated deployments*

The best practice, as of this writing, to break the vicious cycle of manual releases is to automate the entire build, test, and deployment process by adopting continuous integration, delivery, and deployment.

Continuous integration is the first step of the automation evolution. It allows your engineers to commit to a common branch and have automated tests executed on that shared codebase any time that changes are made. Writing automated tests and committing to a shared branch allows your engineers to detect integration issues early. You reduce time spent on merging long-living branches and the effort needed to coordinate releases. By having a stable integration branch with all tests passing (as they are executed for every commit on the integration server), you can deploy to production at any point in time. Continuous integration does not span onto deployment—it only ensures that code can be built and packaged and that tests pass for every commit.

Continuous delivery is the second step in the automation evolution. In addition to running unit tests and building software packages, the continuous delivery pipeline deploys your software to a set of test environments (usually called dev, testing, or staging). A critical feature of that process is that software is built, assembled, and deployed in a reproducible way without any human interaction. That means that any time engineers make a commit to any of the repositories, a set of new builds is triggered; software is deployed to the dev, test, or staging environment; and additional end-to-end test suites are executed to verify correctness of the wider system. As a result, it becomes a business decision whether to deploy code to production or not rather than being an engineering/ testing team's decision. Once the change makes its way through the continuous delivery pipeline, it is ready to be deployed to production. At this stage of evolution, deployment to production usually uses the same automated scripts as deployment to staging environments, and it can be done by a click of a button or issuing a single command, regardless of the complexity of the infrastructure and number of servers.

Continuous deployment is the final stage of the deployment pipeline evolution, where code is tested, built, deployed, and pushed to production without any human interaction. That means that every commit to the shared branch triggers a deployment to production servers without humans being involved. Deployments become cheap and can occur multiple times a day rather than once every couple of weeks.

Figure 9-3 shows an example of a continuous deployment pipeline. It also shows which areas are automated by continuous integration, delivery, and deployment, respectively. Ideally, software would move automatically through the entire pipeline, so that a commit on the integration branch would trigger tests

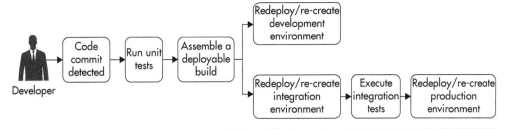

Figure 9-3 *Example of a continuous deployment pipeline*

to be executed and a build assembled. Then code would be deployed to dev and testing environments. Automated end-to-end tests would be executed against the testing environment. If all these steps were successful, code would be immediately deployed to production servers, ending the continuous deployment pipeline.

While working in different companies over the years, I have witnessed deployments of various sizes and various degrees of automation. For example, in one of the teams that I have worked with, it would take three people up to four hours per week to release software. That is a combined cost of over 300 man-hours per year. That equates to one of our engineers doing nothing but releasing software for two months straight. On the other end of the spectrum, I have seen people deploy software to production with every commit, where a release cycle takes 15 minutes from commit to code being in production.

> ### HINT
>
> *Testing and deployments have to be automated if you want to scale. If you need to do more than click a button to create a build, run tests, and deploy software to production, you need to automate further.*

The number of tools and platforms that help implement continuous deployment has been increasing in recent years, but it is still a fairly involved process to set up a full-stack, continuous deployment pipeline. Setting up a continuous deployment pipeline is challenging because it requires skills from both ends of DevOps. You need to have Dev's knowledge of the code and testing tools and Ops' expertise in setting up servers and deploying software and managing configurations.

Your best bet is to make sure that you have an experienced DevOps engineer on your team to avoid frustration and speed up the initial setup. If you have to learn how to build a continuous deployment pipeline yourself, I would recommend using Jenkins (which is an open-source product) or Atlassian Bamboo (which is a commercial product but with a great feature set) as the tool controlling the pipeline.

In addition to configuring the continuous deployment tool (for example, using Jenkins), you will need to decide how to manage configuration of your servers. The goal is to store server configuration in the source control system to be able to re-create servers at any point in time and track changes. If you want to manage servers at scale, it is absolutely critical to manage their configuration using specialized tools like Chef or Puppet so that you can build server definitions and then create identical instances of these servers at will.

> ### HINT
>
> *Having to control more than a dozen servers manually or allowing your servers' configurations to diverge from one another is a recipe for disaster. Each server type (like a database server or a web server) should have a server definition created using a configuration management tool. This definition should then be used to create all of the instances of a particular server type, ensuring that each and every one of them is identical. By following this process, you can scale the number of servers without affecting the overall management cost. Whether you need to deploy a single server or a hundred servers, your overhead of building a server definition is constant, and deploying to more servers is just a matter of creating more server instances of a particular type.*

Once you have server definitions and the continuous deployment tool configured, you are ready to deploy automatically to your servers. To achieve that, you may need to write some custom scripts that will know which servers need to be redeployed in what order. You may also need additional commands, such as purging caches, restarting web servers, or taking servers out of a load balancer.

To be able to deploy to production, your continuous deployment pipeline (and custom scripts) may need to be integrated with your cloud hosting provider to allow server images to be created (for example, Amazon Machine Image [AMI]), new server instances to be built, and servers to be added or removed from load balancers. There is no single right way of doing it, and depending on your infrastructure, skills, and preferences, you may opt for one way or another. For example, if you were hosting your stack on Amazon, you might want to use AMI images for your deployments to also allow auto-scaling and automated server replacement. In such a case, your continuous deployment pipeline might look as follows:

1. Developer commits code to a master branch.

2. Continuous deployment tool is notified by a github web hook.

3. The pipeline starts by checking out the code. Then unit tests are executed; the build is assembled; and test results, documentation, and other artifacts are zipped and pushed to permanent storage (like Amazon S3).

4. On success, a new server instance is created using Amazon API to build a new server image. The instance is restored using the most recent production AMI image for that cluster (let's say a web service cluster).

5. The instance is then upgraded using configuration management tools to bring its packages up to date and to deploy the latest version of your application. This way, you perform installation, configuration, and dependency assembly only once.

6. Once the instance is ready, you take a snapshot of it as a new AMI image so that it can be used later to create new server instances.

7. As the next step in the pipeline, you deploy the newly created server image in the testing/staging cluster and verify its correctness using end-to-end tests like Selenium or Jmeter.

8. In the next step, you mark the newly created AMI image as production ready and move on to production deployment.

9. You can then redeploy the production web service cluster by updating the load balancer and taking servers out of rotation, one by one, or by doubling the capacity and killing the old instances. Either way, deployment is performed by the Elastic Load Balancer by re-creating all server instances from scratch using the newly created AMI image.

Having a continuous deployment pipeline like this allows you to deliver software extremely fast. You can deploy new features multiple times a day and quickly validate your ideas by running A/B tests on your users rather than having to wait weeks for customer feedback.

The only question that may still remain is "How do you make sure that things don't break if every commit goes straight to production?" To address this concern, it is best to use a combination of continuous deployment best practices:

►   Write unit tests for all of your code. Your code coverage should be at least 85 percent to give you a high stability and confidence level.

►   Create end-to-end test cases for all critical paths like sign up, purchase, adding an item to a shopping cart, logging in, or subscribing to a newsletter. Use a tool like Selenium so that you can quickly verify that the most important parts of your system are actually working before deploying code to production hosts.

►   Use *feature toggles* to enable and disable selected features instantly. A feature in hidden mode is not visible to the general audience, and disabled features are not visible at all. By using feature toggles, you can quickly disable a new broken feature without redeploying any servers.

▶ Use A/B tests and feature toggles to test new features on a small subset of users. By rolling out features in a hidden mode and enabling them for a small group of users (let's say, 2 percent of users), you can test them with less risk. During the A/B testing phase, you can also gather business-level metrics to see whether a new feature is used by users and whether it improves your metrics (for example, increased engagement or user spending).

▶ Use a wide range of monitoring tools, embed metrics into all of your applications, and configure alerts on critical metrics so that you will be the first to know whenever things break.

Following these best practices will help you implement a continuous deployment pipeline and push changes to production faster without increasing the risk of failures, but no matter how well you test your code, your servers will occasionally fail and you need to be able to handle these failures fast and efficiently. To be able to scale your operations, it is absolutely critical to automate monitoring and alerting. Let's now have a closer look at how it could be achieved.

Monitoring and Alerting

The main motivation to automate monitoring and alerting of your systems is to increase your availability by reducing mean time to recovery (MTTR). It may seem like a luxury to have automated monitoring, failure detection, and alerting when you run two servers in production, but as the number of servers grows, it becomes absolutely critical to be able to run your operations efficiently. Mean time to recovery is a combination of four components:

MTTR = Time to discover + Time to respond + Time to investigate + Time to fix

Time to discover is the time needed for your business to realize there is a problem with the system. In small companies, failures are often reported by customers or when employees notice that something broke. As a result, things can be broken for hours or even days before anyone reports a problem, resulting in poor user experience and terrible availability metrics. By using automated monitoring, you should be able to reduce the time to discovery to a few minutes.

The second component of MTTR is *time to respond*. Again, in small companies, it can take hours before the right person responds to the problem. People may not know who to call, they may not have private phone numbers, engineers being called may not have their laptops or passwords necessary to log in to the right servers, or they may just have their phones turned off. As a result, time to respond is unpredictable and it can easily take a few hours before the right person can start looking at a problem. As your company grows, your operations team needs to automate failure notifications so that production issues can be escalated to the right people and so that they can be ready to respond to critical problems within minutes. In addition to automated alerting, you need to develop procedures to define who is on call on which days and how they should react to different types of issues. By implementing clear procedures and automated alerting, you should be able to reduce the time to respond to tens of minutes rather than hours.

The last component of MTTR that you can reduce by monitoring is *time to investigate*, as *time to fix* is independent from monitoring and alerting. In small companies, when things break, engineers start logging into production servers, tailing logs, and trying to figure out what exactly broke. In many cases, it is a data store or an external system failure causing alerts through complex knock-on effects, and finding a root cause by traversing logs on dozens of servers can be a very time-consuming process.

To speed up debugging and maintain a clear picture of your "battlefield," you can introduce metrics and log aggregation. By monitoring internals of your system, you can quickly identify components that are slow or failing. You can also deduce knock-on effects by correlating different metrics. Finally, by aggregating logs, you can quickly search for log entries related to the issue at hand, reducing time to investigate even further.

In addition to reducing MTTR, collecting different types of metrics can help you see trends and gain insight into your business. To get the most out of your monitoring configuration, you should collect four different types of metrics:

- ▶ **Operating system metrics**   These allow you to see the status of your hardware, network infrastructure, and operating systems. On this level, you collect information like CPU load, memory statistics, number of processes running, network connections, and disk I/O. These metrics are mainly for system admins and DevOps people to estimate capacity and debug performance problems.

- ▶ **Generic server metrics**   These are all of the metrics that you can get from standard web servers, application containers, databases, message queues, and cache servers. In this level you collect metrics such as the number of database transactions per second, time spent waiting for locks, number of web requests per second, the number of messages in the deepest queue, or a cache hit ratio of your object cache server. These metrics help you gain a much deeper insight into the bottlenecks of each of your components.

▶ **Application metrics**   These are metrics that your application publishes to measure performance and gain insight into what is happening within the application. Examples of application-level metrics can be calls to external systems like databases, object caches, third-party services, and data stores. With every external call, you would want to keep track of the error rate, number of calls, and time it took to execute the call. By having these types of metrics, you can quickly see where the bottlenecks are in your systems, which services are slow, and what the trends of capacity are. On this level, you may also want to collect metrics such as how long it takes for each web service endpoint to generate a response or how often different features are used. The main purpose of these metrics is to allow engineers to understand what their code is doing and what pressures it is facing.

▶ **Business metrics**   These are metrics that track business events. For example, you may track dollars spent, user account creation, the number of items added to shopping carts, or the number of user logins per minute. The value of such metrics from an engineer's point of view is that they allow you to verify within seconds whether you have a consumer-affecting problem or not. You can also use them to translate production issues into business impact, like dollars lost or user login failure count. By knowing the business impact of your issues, you can escalate more efficiently and verify recovery of critical systems by observing user activity.

Operating web applications at scale without metrics in each of the four categories mentioned earlier is like driving blind. In fact, I would argue that every single service you deploy to production should publish metrics so that you can diagnose and operate it at scale. Let's now have a look at how monitoring can be done in practice.

Monitoring and alerting are usually implemented by installing a monitoring agent on each of your servers. Each agent is then configured to collect metrics about that server and all of its services. Depending on the role of the server, the agent could have plugins installed to collect metrics from different sources, such as database processes, message queues, application servers, and caches. Each monitoring agent would usually aggregate dozens, hundreds, or even thousands of metrics. Periodically (for example, every minute or every five minutes), the agent would publish its metrics to a central monitoring service, which is usually a cloud service or an internally deployed monitoring server.

Once metrics are published to the monitoring service, they can be recorded so that dashboards and graphs can be drawn. At the same time, the monitoring service can watch the rate of change and values of each of these metrics, and alerts can be sent whenever safety thresholds are breached. For example, you can send a text message to your engineers on call if the number of open connections to your database reaches a certain level (as it may indicate that database queries execute too slowly and connections keep piling up as a result).

By having metrics pushed to a central monitoring service from all of your servers, you can visualize them per server or per server group. That also allows you to set alerts per server or per cluster of servers. For example, you could monitor free disk space per server because some servers may run out of disk space faster than others. On the other hand, when monitoring the number of open database connections to your replication slaves, you might be interested in a sum of all the connections across the entire cluster to see the higher-level picture of your system, regardless of which machines are out of rotation or in maintenance.

In addition to metrics gathering via internal monitoring agents and the monitoring service, you can use an external service level agreement (SLA) monitoring service. The advantage of using a third-party SLA monitoring service is that it connects to your services from external networks just like your customers would. As a result, it can detect network outages, routing/virtual private network (VPN) configuration issues, Domain Name Service (DNS) problems, load balancer configuration problems, Secure Sockets Layer (SSL) certificate expiration, and other issues that may be impossible to detect from within your own networks. In addition, some of the SLA monitoring services allow you to measure performance of your services from different locations on the planet and using different devices (simulating mobile network and low-bandwidth connections). As a result, they can provide you with an ocean of valuable data points, allowing you to optimize your user experience and alert on additional types of failures.

Figure 9-4 shows how monitoring and alerting could be implemented. You would have monitoring agents deployed across all of your servers, metrics being pushed to a central monitoring service, and alerting rules being configured within the monitoring service. In addition, an external SLA monitoring service could be utilized to watch performance and availability from the client's point of view.

As you can imagine, quite a few different components need to be put in place for such a comprehensive monitoring setup to work. You need to install your monitoring agents with plugins for all possible types of services that you want to monitor. You also need to be able to publish arbitrary metrics from your application code to monitor application and business metrics. Then you need to configure all of these agents to publish data to the aggregations service, and on

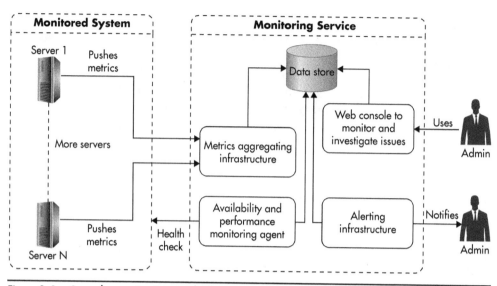

Figure 9-4   *Sample monitoring and alerting configuration*

the service side you need to configure graphs, thresholds, alerts, and dashboards. Getting it all to work together and managing all these components at scale can be quite a lot of work—that is why I recommend using a third-party, cloud-based monitoring service rather than deploying your own solution.

The best monitoring service I have seen so far (as of 2014) is Datadog, and I would strongly recommend testing it before committing to a different solution.[L5] Some of its advantages are the feature set, ease of integration, and ease of use. Datadog provides plugins to monitor dozens of different open-source servers so that you would not need to develop custom code to monitor things like data stores, message queues, and web servers. In addition, it provides a simple application programming interface (API) and client libraries, so you can start publishing custom metrics from within your application code in a matter of minutes. Finally, it has a user-friendly user interface (UI), allowing you to configure graphs, dashboards thresholds, and alerts with minimal effort.

The competition in monitoring space has been increasing in recent years, and there are quite a few good alternatives that you might want to look at, with Stackdriver, New Relic, and Server Density, to name a few. Some of these providers, like Server Density, provide external SLA monitoring as part of their offering; others don't. If you need a separate provider for external SLA monitoring, I recommend looking at Pingdom, Moniris, and Keynote.

With monitoring, alerting, and on-call procedures, you should be able to reduce MTTR to tens of minutes. If you wanted to reduce the time needed to investigate and debug issues even further, you might also want to implement a log aggregation and indexing solution.

Log Aggregation

When working with small applications, which run on just a couple of servers, log aggregation is not really necessary. Things usually break on the same server, and you usually have just a handful of log files to tail or grep through to find the root cause of an issue. Unfortunately, as your system grows and the number of servers goes into the dozens (and then the hundreds), you lose the ability to manually search through logs. Even with as few as ten servers it becomes impossible to tail, grep through, and correlate events happening across all of the log files on all of these servers simultaneously. Requests to your front-end layer may cascade to dozens of web service calls, and searching through all of the logs on all the machines becomes a serious challenge. To be able to search through logs and effectively debug problems, you need a way to collect all of your logs in a central location. There are a few common ways of solving this.

First of all, you can log to a data store directly rather than logging to files. The good side of this approach is that you do not have to move the logs once they are written, but the downside is that all of your components become dependent on the availability and performance of the logging data store. Because of this additional coupling, logging directly to a data store is not recommended.

A better alternative is to write to local log files and then have these logs shipped to a centralized log service. In its simplest form, you install log-forwarding agents on each of your servers and configure them to stream logs to a central log server. The main benefit of this approach is its simplicity, as all you need is a log server and log-forwarding agents installed on each of your servers.

There are quite a few open-source products that allow you to stream logs to a centralized log server, and a good example of such a product is Fluentd. Fluentd is easy to work with; it is robust, scalable, and offers a wide range of features. Your log-forwarding agents can tail multiple log files, perform complex filtering and transformations, and then forward logs to a central log server. In addition to having all of the log files on a single server, you can merge events from different sources and standardize time formats to a single time zone, as dealing with logs in multiple time zones and formats can be frustrating.

Streaming all of your logs to a central server is an improvement, but if you store your logs in flat files, it is still going to be time consuming to search through them.

The more logs you have, the slower it will become to perform searches. Depending on your needs, you may want to go a step further and use a log-indexing platform to speed up your searches and make log data more available across your company.

Figure 9-5 shows how a complete log aggregation deployment might look. You install a log-forwarding agent on each of your servers with a configuration telling it which logs to forward, how to filter and transform the log events, and where to send them. Then the logs are streamed to a set of search engine servers, where they are persisted and indexed so that you can search through them efficiently. In addition, a log-processing platform provides you with a web-based interface to make searching through logs easier.

Deploying and managing a set of components to allow log aggregation and indexing is a fair amount of work, and I recommend using a hosted solution whenever it is possible and affordable. As of this writing, one of the most famous and most attractive solutions on the market is Splunk, but unfortunately, it is quite expensive and not all startups will get enough value from it to justify the cost. Some cloud vendors have a basic solution for log aggregation, like Amazon CloudWatch Logs or Azure Diagnostics, but they may not provide you with enough flexibility. You can also consider an independent hosted log-processing service like Loggy, which provides good functionality regardless of your hosting platform.

If sharing your application logs with third parties or running third-party agents on your servers is not an option, you might need to go for a self-hosted, open-source solution. In such a case, I recommend looking at Logstash, which is a feature-rich and scalable log-indexing platform. Logstash uses its own

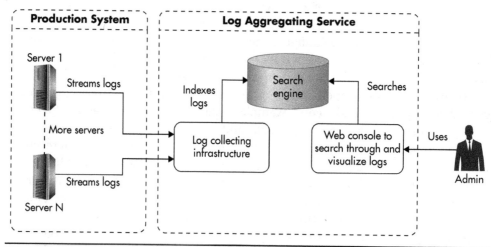

Figure 9-5   *Sample log aggregation workflow*

log-forwarding agents to ship logs to the Elasticsearch search engine. It also comes with a web interface called Kibana to let you perform free text searches and visualize your logs in near real time. The only downside of using Logstash is that you need to learn how to configure and operate it. Although the Logstash platform is a solid piece of software, it is not simple. Even a simple deployment requires a lot of configuration steps,[L8–L9] and without an experienced sysadmin, it may become more of a burden than a benefit to manage it yourself.

Having automated testing, configuration management, deployments, monitoring, alerting, and keeping all of your logs in a central location should enable you to operate web applications at scale. Let's now have a look at what can you do to scale your own personal productivity as your startup grows.

Scaling Yourself

The main reason why startups are so attractive is the hope to achieve exponential growth. Growing fast and efficiently is what allows investors and founders to make a profit. To enable this exponential growth, your startup needs you to become more efficient as it grows as well. You need to become more productive and generate more value for your customers and for your business as you go along. Let's discuss some of the challenges that you may face when working in a startup and how you could approach them to maximize your own productivity and happiness.

Overtime Is Not a Way to Scale

Working under a lot of pressure with limited resources, tight deadlines, and under extreme uncertainty can be nerve wracking, and this is exactly what web startups feel like. Startups are an explosive cocktail of emotions. They are challenging, exhausting, and very rewarding at the same time, but you need to be careful not to fall into a blind race, as working can easily become a thoughtless compulsion.

At first, getting more done by working longer hours feels natural. You push yourself a bit more, work a few extra hours every day, or work over the weekends. It feels like the right thing to do and it feels like a relatively small sacrifice to make, as you are full of energy, motivation, hope, and belief in your future. In addition, it feels good to be needed and to be the hero who saves the day. After all, if working harder is what it takes, then why not do it?

The problem is that in the long run, working overtime is a terrible strategy to scale your productivity. As you work longer hours for extended periods of time, your mental capacity decreases; your creativity drops; and your attention span, field of vision, and ability to make decisions all degrade. In addition, you are likely going to become more cynical, angry, or irritable. You will resent people who work less than you do; you will feel helpless or depressed in the face of an ever-growing pile of work. You may even begin to hate what you used to love doing or feel anxious, with the only way to repress this anxiety being to work even harder. All of these are symptoms of burnout.

Burnout is your archenemy when working for a startup, as it sneaks upon you slowly and by the time it hits you, you are completely blind to it, making you fall even deeper into its grip. It is like a vicious cycle—you work harder, get more tired, you can't see ways to work smarter, and as a result you end up working even harder. Everyone experiences burnout slightly differently, but from my experience, it is a terrible state to be in and it takes months to fully recover. Again, based on my own experiences, you can expect significant burnout after anything from three to nine months of excessive work (working under high pressure for over 45 to 60 hours a week).

Figure 9-6 shows how productivity changes over time when working excessively. Initially, you experience increased productivity, as you perform at full capacity for more hours. Shortly after that, your productivity begins to decline, diminishing the benefit of working overtime. Finally, if you let it go on for too long, your productivity becomes marginal. You can't get anything meaningful done even though you spend endless hours working, and eventually you have to give up on the project or quit.

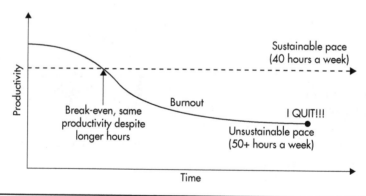

Figure 9-6 *Productivity over time*

HINT

If you are working for a startup, chances are that you are already experiencing burnout. The bad news is that there is no quick and easy cure for it. Working less, exercising more, and spending time with friends and family helps, but recovering fully this way takes months. A quicker way is to take a long holiday (three to six weeks) or leave the project altogether and take a couple of months of light work. It can take a lot of focus and a couple of burnouts in your lifetime before you learn how to recognize early symptoms and how to prevent it altogether by managing yourself.

Rather than continually falling into cycles of hyperproductivity and crashes, it is more efficient and healthier to maintain a more sustainable level of effort. Every person has different limits, depending on their motivation, internal energy, engagement, and personality, but from my personal experience, working more than 50 hours per week is dangerous, and working more than 60 hours per week leads to burnout in a matter of months.

Your time is one of the most precious and nontransferable values you have. You are spending it at a constant rate of 60 minutes per hour, and there is no way to scale beyond that. Instead of trying to work longer hours, you need to find ways to generate more value for your customers, business, and peers within the safety zone of 40 hours per week. Although it may sound like an empty slogan, you truly need to learn to work smarter, not harder.

Managing Yourself

A good way to look at the problem of maximizing your own productivity is to look at your workload as if you were managing a project and all of your potential tasks were parts of this project. When managing a project, you have three "levers" allowing you to balance the project: scope, cost, and time.

Anytime you increase or decrease the scope, cost, or deadline, the remaining two variables need to be adjusted to reach a balance. As you add more work, you need to spend more resources or extend deadlines. As you reduce the time available to deliver your project, you need to reduce scope or add resources. Finally, as you reduce available resources, you need to either cut the scope or extend your deadlines.

Figure 9-7 shows the project management triangle with a few extra notes to help you memorize some of the coping strategies. The first thing that you need to do is to accept the fact that managing a project is about making tradeoffs. You spend more time or money or do less work. It is as simple as that. When you

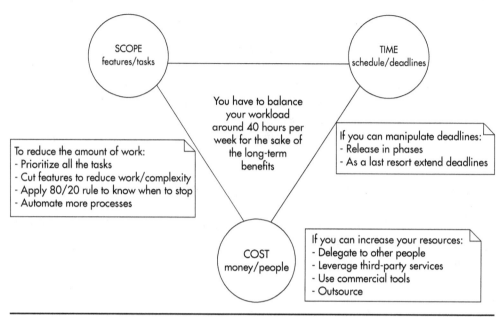

Figure 9-7   *Project management levers*

start thinking about work this way, you may be able to find ways to balance your project without working overtime.

> ### HINT
>
> *It is important to consider the role of quality in this context. I would suggest that building automated tests and ensuring high-quality code is part of the scope of each feature. You should not try to reduce scope by sacrificing quality if you want to maintain efficiency over the long term. In a way, sacrificing the quality of your code is like borrowing money from Tony Soprano. It may seem like a good idea when you are in a rush and under pressure, but sooner or later you will have to start repaying the vig (excessive weekly interest on a loan).*

Let's have a closer look at how you can influence the amount of work, cost, and deadlines to make your own workload more sustainable.

Influencing the Scope

"Without data, you're just another person with an opinion." –W. Edwards Deming

Influencing the scope of work is usually the easiest way to balance your workload, and it is also an area where the most significant savings can be made. The first step to get better at managing your own workload is to understand that any time you get a new task or an existing task increases in size, you need to reevaluate deadlines, increase available resources, or cut scope elsewhere.

Anything that you decide to do takes time, and by doing one thing you will have less time for the remaining tasks. It may sound obvious, but learning how to prioritize tasks based on their cost and value is the most important skill in managing scope. After all, one of the most important things for a startup to survive is making sure you are building the right stuff. To prioritize tasks efficiently, you need to know their value and their cost. You can then prioritize them based on their relative value/cost ratio.

Task priority = (value of that task) / (overall cost of that task)

The cost component of the equation is usually estimated quite accurately by estimating the time needed to complete the task. Even for larger projects that include financial costs (buy more servers or get additional services), people are usually good at coming up with relatively accurate estimates. The real difficulties begin when you try to estimate the value of each task, as most of the time, people do it based solely on their personal gut feeling rather than past experience or actual data.

This inability to evaluate the true value of features is what leads most companies to develop things that nobody needs. I have witnessed people working their hands to the bone on features that made absolutely no difference, just because they bought into a vision based on someone's gut feeling without any data or critical validation. In fact, following a vision without validating it is probably one of the most common reasons for startup failures. That is why gathering data and making decisions based on experiments is what the Lean Startup movement is advocating. By designing experiments, gathering data, and making decisions based on this data, you can reduce the risk of building things that nobody needs.

> ### HINT
>
> *Following your gut feeling might be a great way to go if you are Richard Branson or Warren Buffett, but in reality, most of us are not. That is why most decisions should be made based on data, not gut feeling.*

Changing the decision-making culture of your startup may be difficult, and it is beyond the scope of this book, but I strongly recommend reading more about the Lean Startup philosophy.[30,9] Even if you are not able to change the way decisions are made in your organization, you should collect metrics, talk to your customers, run A/B tests, and try to help your business people make sure that you are not building unnecessary things.

Another way to reduce the scope of your work is to follow the 80/20 rule and know when to stop doing things rather than compulsively working for marginal gain. The 80/20 rule is an observation that 80 percent of the value is generated by 20 percent of the effort. Surprisingly, the 80/20 rule applies in many areas of software development:

▶ 80 percent of the features can be built in 20 percent of the overall time.

▶ 80 percent of code coverage can be achieved in 20 percent of the overall time.

▶ 80 percent of users use only 20 percent of the features; in fact, studies show that in many systems almost half of the features are never used.[L10]

▶ 80 percent of the documentation value is in 20 percent of its text.

▶ 80 percent of the bugs come from 20 percent of the code.

▶ 80 percent of the code changes are made in 20 percent of the codebase.

Although the 80/20 rule is a simplification, by realizing it, you can reduce the time spent on gold plating and make sure that you stop working on the task as soon as it is "complete enough" rather than trying to reach the 100 percent, regardless of the cost. Applying the 80/20 rule is about being pragmatic and considering the cost of your work. You can apply the 80/20 rule in many ways; here are some ideas of how you could apply the 80/20 mind-set to reduce the amount of work that needs to be done:

▶ Negotiate with your stakeholders to reduce the scope of new features to 80 percent and delay the most expensive/difficult parts to future releases. By getting the base functionality out early, you can gather A/B test results before investing more time in their "full" implementation. The minimum viable product mentality can be applied to any feature, and in some cases, it is all that your customers really need.

▶ Keep functionality minimalistic and simple as long as possible. Use A/B testing any time you add new features to make sure that they are used and that they generate the expected value. Code that is not used is a form of technical debt, and features that are not used should be removed to reduce that debt. Remember that less is more, especially in a startup.

▶ Make sure that you implement only the code that is absolutely necessary without adding nice-to-have parameters, classes, and methods. All this "you ain't gonna need it" code needs to be tested, documented, understood, and managed. Less is more!

- ▶ Strive for 85 percent to 90 percent code coverage rather than going for 100 percent coverage at all costs. Some areas of code may be much more difficult to test than others, and the cost of testing this remaining 10 percent may be more than it is worth.

- ▶ When creating documentation, focus on critical information and the high-level picture rather than documenting everything imaginable. Draw more diagrams, as images are truly worth a thousand words. If you feel that your documentation is complete, you have most likely wasted 80 percent of the time!

- ▶ Don't fix it if it ain't broke. Refactor parts of your codebase as you need to modify them, but allow old code to just sit there if it does not need to be changed. Why would you want to refactor a class that no one touched for months? Just to feel better? I know that it sounds harsh, but doing things like that is a compulsion and you simply can't afford to do that in a startup.

- ▶ Always try to distinguish whether a task at hand belongs to the "I have to do it" or "I want to do it" category, as the second one is a source of huge amounts of extra work. Engineers love to learn and they love to build software—that makes us biased towards building rather than reusing and towards trying new things rather than doing what we already know. As a result, we tend to chase the newest, coolest technologies, frameworks, and patterns rather than using the best tool for the job. In addition, we are smart enough to be able to justify our choices and fool ourselves into believing that the choice we made is truly the best option there is for our company. Practicing self-awareness and watching out for these biases should help you reduce the amount of unnecessary work.

- ▶ Don't scale or optimize until you absolutely have to, and remember that even when you think you have to, you may be falling into an "I want to do it" trap. You should not build horizontal scalability into every project you work on, as most of the time it will be a waste of time. It is estimated that 90 percent of startups that get seed funding fail. The same statistic applies to startups that go through accelerators. Out of the remaining 10 percent that survive, the majority never need to scale beyond a dozen servers, not to mention horizontal scalability. If you work for a startup, you should plan for scalability, but defer complexity and time investments for as long as you can so you can focus on more urgent needs, like making sure that you are building a product that your customers really need.

It is especially difficult for engineers to manage scope, as engineers are passionate and optimistic people. We want to get everything done, we want it all to be perfect, and we truly believe it can all be done by tomorrow afternoon. We wish our UIs were beautiful, back ends were optimized, data was consistent, and code was clean. Unfortunately, unless you have unlimited resources or years of time to muck around, you will have to make sacrifices and sometimes you will need to let go of some things for the sake of more important tasks. Be pragmatic.

Influencing the Cost

Another way to balance your workload and allow your startup to scale is to learn how to increase the costs to reduce the amount of work. You can reduce the scope of your own work by delegating tasks and responsibilities to other people, tools, or third-party companies. If you have too much work to do, all of the work truly needs to be done, nothing else can be automated, and deadlines cannot be postponed, you should start looking for ways to delegate.

By delegating tasks to other members of your team, you increase the scalability of your department. If you are the only person who can do a certain task, you are the bottleneck and a single point of failure. By having multiple people on the team equally capable of performing a particular task, work can be distributed more evenly among more people and you stop being the bottleneck. In addition, by having more people working on the same problem, you increase the chances of breakthroughs and innovation in this area. For example, your peer may find a way to automate or optimize part of the workflow that you would never think of.

To be able to easily delegate tasks and responsibilities to other team members, you need to make sure that people are familiar with different tasks and different parts of the application. For that reason, you need to actively share knowledge within the team and collaborate more closely. Here are some of the practices that help in sharing knowledge and responsibility for a project:

- ▶ **Pair programming** This is a practice where two engineers work together on a single task. Although it may seem inefficient, pair programming leads to higher-quality designs, fewer bugs, and much closer collaboration. I would not recommend practicing pair programming all the time, but one day a week may be a great way to share knowledge, develop a shared understanding of the system, and agree on best practices. It is also a great way to mentor more junior members of the team, as they can see firsthand how senior engineers think and how they solve problems.

- ▶ **Ad hoc design sessions** These are spontaneous discussions involving whiteboards or pen and paper to discuss problems, brainstorm ideas, and come up with a better solution.

▶ **Ongoing code reviews**   This is a practice of reviewing each other's code. Although code reviews may be associated mainly with code quality, they are a powerful way to increase collaboration and knowledge sharing. Reviewing each other's code allows engineers not only to provide feedback and enforce best practices, it is also a great way for engineers to stay up to date with changes being made.

Another way to reduce the workload by increasing costs is by buying the services of third-party companies or using commercial tools. A good example of scaling your throughput by third parties is by using third-party monitoring and alerting tools. If you wanted to develop a monitoring and alerting system yourself, it might take you months to get anything useful and scalable built. However, if you decided to deploy an open-source alternative, you might only need days to get it up and running, but you would still incur some ongoing management time costs. If you decided to sign up with a third party, on the other hand, you could convert the time cost of developing and managing the service into a dollars cost. By using a third-party monitoring service, you drastically reduce the initial time cost and trade ongoing time cost for an ongoing money cost. In a similar way, you can reduce your workload or increase your productivity by using more sophisticated commercial tools, hosted data stores, caches, workflow engines, and video conferencing services.

HINT

Engineers love to build software. This love for building new things makes us biased towards developing rather than reusing. Developing things like monitoring services, analytics and alerting platforms, frameworks, or even data stores is just another form of reinventing the wheel. Before you jump into implementation, you should always check what can be used for free and what can be bought.

Although reducing the workload by increasing cost is usually beyond an engineer's pay grade, it is something that can be presented to the business leaders. Not having to do the work at all is a way to scale, as it allows you to keep 100 percent focused on your customers' needs.

Influencing the Schedule

The last of the three levers of project management that you may be able to affect is the schedule. In a similar way as with costs, it may be out of your direct control to decide which features can be released by when, but you can usually affect the schedule to some degree by providing feedback to your business leaders. Most of the time, both deadlines and the order of features being released are negotiable and subject to cost considerations. On a very rare occasion you may face a hard deadline when your company schedules a media campaign that cannot be canceled or when your company signs a contract forcing you to deliver on time, but most of the time, things are flexible.

To be absolutely clear, I am not trying to say that you should extend deadlines, as delaying releases is usually a bad idea and it hurts your company. What I am trying to say is that when working in a startup, you are much closer to the decision-making people and you can have a much bigger impact on what gets shipped and when. Rather than passively listening for commands, you should actively provide feedback to your business leaders, letting them know which features are cheap and quick to build and which ones are expensive or risky. As a result, they may understand the costs better and prioritize tasks more accurately.

In addition to providing constant feedback, I recommend releasing in smaller chunks. By reducing the size of each release, you can gain consumer feedback more quickly and decide whether you should keep building what you intended to build or if you should change the direction and build something different. Rapid learning is what Lean Startup methodology is all about. You release often, you gather feedback and data, and then you figure out what your next move is going to be rather than trying to plan it all up front. By developing the product in small pieces, you reduce the risk and the cost of making mistakes, which are an inevitable part of working for a startup.

For example, if you were extending an e-commerce platform to allow external merchants to build their own online stores, you might simply come up with a list of features, plan execution, and then work on that plan for three or six months before releasing it to your customers. By working for three months without any customer feedback, you work as if you were suspended in a vacuum. There is no way of knowing whether your customers will like your features; there is also no way of knowing what other features merchants might need. The larger the release cycle, the higher the risk of building things that customers don't need.

A better way of approaching such a scenario would be to release a minimal management console as soon as possible and then add features based on your customer feedback. By releasing more quickly, you give yourself an opportunity to interview your customers, run surveys, collect A/B testing data, and ultimately learn. Then, based on this additional information, you can further refine your feature set without the need to implement everything up front. By breaking larger features into smaller pieces, you can also leverage the 80/20 rule, as you will often discover that what you have already built is enough for your customers and further phases of development on a particular feature may not be needed any more.

In addition to splitting features into smaller chunks, you may experiment with *mocks,* which are especially helpful in early phases of startup development. A *mock* is a feature that is not really implemented, but presented to users to measure their engagement and validate whether this feature is needed or not.

For example, if you wanted to implement an artificial intelligence algorithm that would automatically tag product pictures uploaded by your merchants, you might need months or years to complete the implementation. Instead of doing that, you could resort to a mock to run a quick and cheap experiment. You could start by selecting a sample of random products in your database. You would then ask your employees to tag the selected images rather than using actual artificial intelligence software. Finally, you could interview your merchants and run A/B tests to measure the impact on search engine optimization and user engagement. By using such a mock and collecting data, your startup could learn more about the true value of the feature in a very quick time (a matter of weeks); then based on this, you could decide whether it is worth building the feature or whether you should build something different.

Depending on your role and the company you are working for, it may be easier to control the scope, costs, or schedules. By looking for tradeoffs and providing feedback to your business leaders, you should be able to balance your workload more efficiently and hopefully avoid working overtime.

Scaling Agile Teams

The final aspect of scalability that I would like to highlight is the challenge of scaling agile teams. As your organization grows, you will need to hire more engineers, managers, product owners, and system administrators to be able to grow your product. Unfortunately, scaling agile is difficult, as you cannot scale an agile team by simply adding people to it. Things that work in teams of eight people do not work as well in larger teams consisting of dozens or hundreds of people.

Adding More People

A good example of things that don't scale linearly as your team grows is communication. When working in a team of five, you can always get up to speed on what is happening; what changes are being made; what requirements have been discussed; and what designs, standards, and practices were chosen. As you keep adding people to the team, the number of communication paths grows very rapidly, making it impractical for everyone to stay up to date with everyone else at the same time. Figure 9-8 shows how the number of communication paths grows with the size of the team.

A common way out of this problem is to create a set of smaller teams of four to nine people and to give each of the teams a set of distinct responsibilities based on their functions. You can have a team of testers, a team of system administrators, a few teams of programmers focusing on different areas, and you can sometimes even see teams of project managers and product owners. It may seem like a good idea to grow this way, but what you inevitably end up with is a culture of handoffs, politics, finger pointing, and hostility among what becomes a set of opposing camps.

The reason why this approach does not work efficiently is that teams are created based on their job function, not an area of product development. As a result, your development and deployment life cycle becomes a pipeline of handoffs where people at every stage care about their own point of view rather than considering the overarching goals. In companies like that, product owners pass requirements to engineers, who then write code and hand over features to testers and sysadmins. Whenever things go wrong, finger pointing begins, stronger and stricter procedures are developed, and progress becomes even more difficult to make as everyone wants to save their own skin.

Luckily, there is a better way to scale software engineering teams: by removing monopolies and creating cross-functional teams.[L11] Rather than having teams consisting of only testers or only programmers, you should build teams around products or services. For example, you can have a dedicated team maintaining a checkout functionality, with a designer, web developer, a sysadmin, three

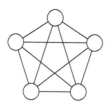

5 people on the team
10 communication paths

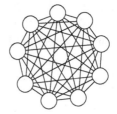

9 people on the team
36 communication paths

Figure 9-8 *Number of communication paths*

back-end engineers, and a couple of front-end ones. As a result, such a team can autonomously design, develop, and deploy features. Ideally, such a team could also gather feedback, analyze metrics, and lead the development of the checkout "product" without having to wait for anyone else.

By reducing dependencies between teams and giving them more autonomy, progress can be made independently. When you think of it, scalability on the organization level is similar to the scalability of your applications. You need to be able to add more workers (servers) to distribute the work among them. Following this analogy, to maximize throughput, your workers need to be able to make decisions locally so that they do not have to wait for other workers. In addition, they need to have the skills, tools, and authority (code and data) to execute with minimal communication overhead.

This model of scaling technology departments by building cross-functional teams can be especially successful in startups embracing service-oriented architecture (or micro-services), as you design your system as a set of loosely coupled UIs and web services, which can then be developed and deployed independently by separate teams. It is best to have teams responsible for an end-to-end product, like a "checkout experience," including UI, front end, back end, and data stores, but as your applications grow, you may need to create a dedicated team handling the checkout UI and another managing a checkout web service. By splitting the team in two, you can have more people working on the checkout product, but at the same time, you create cross-team dependencies, which can make it more difficult to make progress, as UI guys need to wait for service changes.

Procedures and Innovation

Another important part of scaling your engineering department is to get the right balance among procedures, standards, and autonomy of your teams. As your organization grows, you may want to develop certain procedures to make sure that your organization is aligned and everybody follows best practices. For example, you may require all teams to have an on-call roster to ensure 24-hour support for production issues. You may want every service to have a business continuity plan to be able to recover quickly in case of major disasters and failures. You may also want to develop certain coding standards, documentation standards, branching strategies, agile processes, review processes, automation requirements, schema modeling guidelines, audit trail requirements, testing best practices, and much, much more.

An important thing to keep in mind is that as you develop all of these standards and procedures, you benefit from them, but at the same time, you sacrifice some of your team's autonomy, flexibility, and ability to innovate.

For example, you may develop a process mandating that every product that goes into production needs to have data replication and a secondary hot standby environment for business continuity. It may be a great idea if all of your systems require 99.999 percent availability, but at the same time, it may slow your teams down significantly. Rather than developing and deploying a lightweight MVP service within a couple of weeks, your people may need to spend an additional month making that service robust enough to be able to meet your business continuity requirements. In some cases, it may be a good thing, but at the same time, it will make experimentation and learning much more expensive, as you will be forced to treat all of your use cases in the same way, regardless of their true requirements.

Procedures and standards are an important part of growing up as a company, but you need to keep them lean and flexible so that they do not have an adverse effect on your productivity, agility, and your culture.

Culture of Alignment

The last, but not least, important facet of scaling technology organizations is to align your teams on common goals and build a good engineering culture. Without alignment, every team will do their own thing. They will lead products in different directions, they will focus on different priorities, and they will ultimately clash against each other as they try to achieve conflicting goals. Anything that you can do as an engineer, a leader, or a business person to align your teams is going to magnify the momentum and increase the overall productivity of your startup.

Figure 9-9 shows how you can visualize alignment across your technology department. When your teams are unaligned, they all pull in different directions. As a result, the overall direction of movement is undefined and uncoordinated. In comparison, by making everyone pull in the same direction, you magnify their strengths, as they do not have to fight each other's conflicting interests.

To align your teams more closely, you can start by developing a culture of humility, respect, and trust, where every engineer's motto is that "we are all in this together." To be a good team player, the benefit of the company should always come before the benefit of a team, and the benefit of the team should always come before the benefit of an individual.

Whether you are a CTO, a manager, or an engineer, you can always influence the culture by aiming to work together, learning about others' needs, seeking compromises, and trying to understand others' points of view. A good engineering

Unaligned Teams   **Aligned Teams**

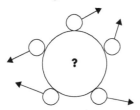   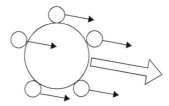

Every team pulls in their   When all of your teams
own direction. As a result   pull in the same direction
you are not moving much.   you move without
                                        resistance.

Figure 9-9   *Effects of alignment*

culture is built on foundations of mutual respect, trust, and mindfulness.[L11,11] Without a good culture, you end up in a vicious cycle of hiring ever worse engineers, getting bogged down with politics and egos, and fighting obstructionism.

For people to be productive, healthy, and happy, you need to create an environment where everyone can feel safe and accepted, and where people get support from their peers. The good news is that it is in everyone's capacity to ignite and foster a good engineering culture. You do not have to be a CEO to do this.

Summary

As I have learned over the years, scalability is a deep and difficult subject. I have covered a lot of different topics in this book and although I have just scratched the surface of many of these subjects, I believe that it will help you build a holistic picture of scalability and inspire you to learn more about it.

If you are passionate about scalability from the organizational point of view, I strongly recommend that you learn more about the Lean Startup mentality,[30,9] building a good engineering culture,[11] and automating processes.[4] Each of these subjects is deep as an ocean by itself, and covering it all in this chapter would not be possible.

On a personal level, my final piece of advice to you is to remain pragmatic and never stop learning. Building software, and especially scalable software, is a game of tradeoffs, and there is never a single right way to do things. Learn as much as you can and then decide for yourself what rules are worth following and when to break them.

A

References

References noted in italics are not directly quoted within this book, but they contribute to the greater body of knowledge about Web Scalability and are recommended as further reading.

Books

1. Robert Cecil Martin (2002) Agile Software Development, Principles, Patterns, and Practices

2. Eric Evans (2003) Domain-Driven Design: Tackling Complexity in the Heart of Software

3. Dean Leffingwell, Don Widrig (2010) Agile Software Requirements: Lean Requirements Practices for Teams, Programs, and the Enterprise

4. John Allspaw, Jesse Robbins (2010) Web Operations: Keeping the Data on Time

5. Diomidis Spinellis, Georgios Gousios (2009) Beautiful Architecture: Leading Thinkers Reveal the Hidden Beauty in Software Design

6. *John Allspaw (2008) The Art of Capacity Planning: Scaling Web Resources*

7. Erich Gamma, Richard Helm, Ralph Johnson, John Vlissides (1994) Design Patterns: Elements of Reusable Object-Oriented Software

8. Steve Souders (2009) Even Faster Web Sites: Performance Best Practices for Web Developers

9. Curt Hibbs, Steve Jewett, Mike Sullivan (2009) The Art of Lean Software Development

10. Martin Fowler (2002) Patterns of Enterprise Application Architecture

11. Brian Fitzpatrick, Ben Collins-Sussman (2012) Team Geek

12. Alvaro Videla, Jason Williams (2012) RabbitMQ in Action: Distributed Messaging for Everyone

13. *Ian Molyneaux (2009) The Art of Application Performance Testing: Help for Programmers and Quality Assurance*

14. Gary Mak (2008) Spring Recipes: A Problem-Solution Approach

15. *Chad Fowler (2009) The Passionate Programmer: Creating a Remarkable Career in Software Development*

16. Jeremy Zawodny, Derek Balling (2004) High Performance MySQL: Optimization, Backups, Replication, Load Balancing & More

17. *Ivo Jansch (2008) PHP|Architect's Guide to Enterprise PHP Development*

18. Paul Allen, Joseph Bambara (2007) Sun Certified Enterprise Architect for Java EE Study Guide

19. Thomas Cormen, Charles Leiserson, Ronald Rivest, Clifford Stein (2003) Introduction to Algorithms

20. David Chappell, Tyler Jewell (2002) Java Web Services

21. *Vivek Chopra, Sing Li, Jeff Genender (2007) Professional Apache Tomcat 6*

22. Glen Smith, Peter Ledbrook (2009) Grails in Action

23. Chuck Lam (2010) Hadoop in Action

24. Opher Etzion, Peter Niblett (2011) Event Processing in Action

25. Bruce Snyder, Dejan Bosanac, Rob Davies (2011) ActiveMQ in Action

26. *Henry Liu (2009) Software Performance and Scalability: A Quantitative Approach*

27. Bill Wilder (2012) Cloud Architecture Patterns

28. John Arundel (2013) Puppet 3 Beginner's Guide

29. Jeffrey Barr (2010) Host Your Web Site in the Cloud: Amazon Web Services Made Easy

30. Eric Ries (2011) The Lean Startup

31. Arnon Rotem-Gal-Oz (2012) SOA Patterns

32. Gregor Hohpe, Bobby Woolf (2003) Enterprise Integration Patterns: Designing, Building, and Deploying Messaging Solutions

33. David S. Linthicum (2009) Cloud Computing and SOA Convergence in Your Enterprise: A Step-by-Step Guide

34. Bashar Abdul-Jawad (2008) Groovy and Grails Recipes

35. Charles Bell, Mats Kindahl, Lars Thalmann (2010) MySQL High Availability

36. Eric Freeman, Elisabeth Robson, Bert Bates, Kathy Sierra (2004) Head First Design Patterns

37. Robert C. Martin (2008) Clean Code: A Handbook of Agile Software Craftsmanship

38. *Steve McConnell (2004) Code Complete, Second Edition*

39. Dominic Betts, Julián Domínguez, Grigori Melnik, Fernando Simonazzi, Mani Subramanian, Microsoft (2012) Exploring CQRS and Event Sourcing A Journey into High Scalability, Availability, and Maintainability with Windows Azure; http://msdn.microsoft.com/en-us/library/jj554200.aspx

40. Frederick Brooks (1995) The Mythical Man-Month: Essays on Software Engineering

41. Martin L. Abbott, Michael T. Fisher (2009) The Art of Scalability: Scalable Web Architecture, Processes, and Organizations for the Modern Enterprise

42. Duane Wessels (2001) Web Caching

43. Martin Abbott, Michael Fisher (2011) Scalability Rules: 50 Principles for Scaling Web Sites

44. Kyle Banker (2011) MongoDB in Action

45. Joel Spolsky (2004) Joel on Software

46. Jim Webber, Savas Parastatidis, Ian Robinson (2010) REST in Practice

47. Flavio Junqueira, Benjamin Reed (2013) ZooKeeper

48. Peter Membrey, David Hows, Eelco Plugge (2012) Practical Load Balancing: Ride the Performance Tiger

49. Steve Souders (2007) High Performance Web Sites

50. Josiah L. Carlson (2013) Redis in Action

51. Martin Kalin (2013) Java Web Services: Up and Running, 2nd Edition

White Papers

w1. Jeffrey Dean, Sanjay Ghemawat (2004) MapReduce: Simplied Data Processing on Large Clusters
http://static.usenix.org/event/osdi04/tech/full_papers/dean/dean.pdf

w2. Floris Engelbertink, Harald Vogt (2010) How to Save on Software Maintenance Costs
http://www.omnext.net/downloads/Whitepaper_Omnext.pdf

w3. Zhenmin Li, Shan Lu, Suvda Myagmar, and Yuanyuan Zhou, Member (2006) CP-Miner: Finding Copy-Paste and Related Bugs in Large-Scale Software Code
http://pages.cs.wisc.edu/~shanlu/paper/TSE-CPMiner.pdf

w4.   Angela Lozano, Michel Wermelinger (2010) Tracking Clones' Imprint
http://released.info.ucl.ac.be/pmwiki/uploads/Publications/
TrackingClonesImprint/clonesImprint.pdf

w5.   NASA Office of Chief Engineer (2009) NASA Study on Flight Software
Complexity
http://www.nasa.gov/pdf/418878main_FSWC_Final_Report.pdf

w6.   Jakub Łopuszanski (2013) Algorithm for Invalidation of Cached Results of
Queries to a Single Table
http://vanisoft.pl/~lopuszanski/public/cache_invalidation.pdf

w7.   Google, Inc. (2012) Spanner: Google's Globally-Distributed Database
http://static.googleusercontent.com/external_content/untrusted_dlcp/
research.google.com/en/us/archive/spanner-osdi2012.pdf

w8.   *Solarflare (2012) Cisco and Solarflare Achieve Dramatic Latency Reduction
for Interactive Web Applications with Couchbase, a NoSQL Database
http://www.cisco.com/en/US/prod/collateral/switches/ps9441/ps9670/white_
paper_c11-708169.pdf*

w9.   *Couchbase (2013) Dealing with Memcached Challenges
http://www.couchbase.com/sites/default/files/uploads/all/whitepapers/
Couchbase_Whitepaper_Dealing_with_Memcached_Challenges.pdf*

w10. Gregor Hohpe (2006) Programming Without a Call Stack: Event-Driven
Architectures
http://www.eaipatterns.com/docs/EDA.pdf

w11. Matt Welsh (2000) The Staged Event-Driven Architecture for Highly-
Concurrent Server Applications
http://www.eecs.harvard.edu/~mdw/papers/quals-seda.pdf

w12. *Raja Appuswamy, Christos Gkantsidis, Dushyanth Narayanan, Orion
Hodson, Antony Rowstron (2013) Nobody Ever Got Fired for Buying a Cluster
http://research.microsoft.com/pubs/179615/msrtr-2013-2.pdf*

w13. *Dushyanth Narayanan, Eno Thereska, Austin Donnelly, Sameh Elnikety,
Antony Rowstron (2009) Migrating Server Storage to SSDs: Analysis of
Tradeoffs
http://citeseerx.ist.psu.edu/viewdoc/download?doi=10.1.1.150.2362&rep=rep
1&type=pdf*

w14. Jiri Simsa, Randy Bryant, Garth Gibson, Jason Hickey (2013) Scalable
Dynamic Partial Order Reduction
http://www.pdl.cmu.edu/PDL-FTP/Storage/scalablePOR.pdf

w15. Ariel Rabkin, Randy Katz (2012) How Hadoop Clusters Break
http://www.cs.princeton.edu/~asrabkin/papers/software12.pdf

w16. *Peter Bailis, Shivaram Venkataraman, Michael J. Franklin, Joseph M. Hellerstein, Ion Stoica (2012) Probabilistically Bounded Staleness for Practical Partial Quorums*
http://arxiv.org/pdf/1204.6082.pdf

w17. *Tim Kraska, Gene Pang, Michael J. Franklin, Samuel Madden (2013) MDCC: Multi-Data Center Consistency*
http://arxiv.org/pdf/1203.6049.pdf

w18. Google, Inc. (2011) Megastore: Providing Scalable, Highly Available Storage for Interactive Services
http://pdos.csail.mit.edu/6.824-2012/papers/jbaker-megastore.pdf

w19. *Brenda M. Michelson (2006) Event-Driven Architecture Overview*
http://www.omg.org/soa/Uploaded%20Docs/EDA/bda2-2-06cc.pdf

w20. Facebook Data Infrastructure Team (2010) Hive: A Petabyte Scale Data Warehouse Using Hadoop
http://people.cs.kuleuven.be/~bettina.berendt/teaching/2010-11-2ndsemester/ctdb/petabyte_facebook.pdf

w21. *Ian Foster, Yong Zhao, Ioan Raicu, Shiyong Lu (2008) Cloud Computing and Grid Computing 360-Degree Compared*
http://arxiv.org/ftp/arxiv/papers/0901/0901.0131.pdf

w22. *Daniel J. Abadi (2012) Consistency Tradeoffs in Modern Distributed Database System Design*
http://cs-www.cs.yale.edu/homes/dna/papers/abadi-pacelc.pdf

w23. Peter Bailis, Alan Fekete, Ali Ghodsi, Joseph M. Hellerstein, Ion Stoica (2013) HAT, not CAP: Highly Available Transactions
http://arxiv.org/pdf/1302.0309.pdf

w24. Stephan Muller (2012) The CAP-Theorem & Yahoo's PNUTS
http://www.math.hu-berlin.de/~muellste/CAP-PNUTS-Text.pdf

w25. Eric Brewer (2012) CAP Tvelve Years Later: How the "Rules" Have Changed
http://www.realtechsupport.org/UB/NP/Numeracy_CAP+12Years_2012.pdf

w26. *Microsoft Research (2012) Cloud Types for Eventual Consistency*
http://research.microsoft.com/pubs/163842/final-with-color.pdf

w27. Avinash Lakshman, Prashant Malik (2009) Cassandra: A Decentralized Structured Storage System
http://www.cs.cornell.edu/projects/ladis2009/papers/lakshman-ladis2009.pdf

w28. Fay Chang, Jeffrey Dean, Sanjay Ghemawat, Wilson C. Hsieh, Deborah A. Wallach, Mike Burrows, Tushar Chandra, Andrew Fikes, Robert E. Gruber (2006) Bigtable: A Distributed Storage System for Structured Data http://static.usenix.org/events/osdi06/tech/chang/chang_html/?em_x=22

w29. Ryan Thompson, T.C. Friel (2013) The Sustainability of Cloud Storage http://sais.aisnet.org/2013/ThompsonFriel.pdf

w30. *Edward P. Holden, Jai W. Kang (2011) Databases in the Cloud: A Status Report http://sigite2011.sigite.org/wp-content/uploads/2011/10/session11-paper02.pdf*

w31. *Azza Abouzeid, Kamil Bajda-Pawlikowski, Daniel Abadi, Avi Silberschatz, Alexander Rasin (2009) HadoopDB: An Architectural Hybrid of MapReduce and DBMS Technologies for Analytical Workloads http://www-master.ufr-info-p6.jussieu.fr/2009/Ext/naacke/grbd2010/extra/exposes2010/C3_VLDB09_HadoopDB.pdf*

w32. *Brian Holcomb (2013) NoSQL Database in the Cloud: Riak on AWS http://media.amazonwebservices.com/AWS_NoSQL_Riak.pdf*

w33. *Miles Ward (2013) NoSQL Database in the Cloud: MongoDB on AWS http://media.amazonwebservices.com/AWS_NoSQL_MongoDB.pdf*

w34. Matt Tavis, Philip Fitzsimons (2012) Web Application Hosting in the AWS Cloud Best Practices http://media.amazonwebservices.com/AWS_Web_Hosting_Best_Practices.pdf

w35. Jinesh Varia (2011) Architecting for the Cloud: Best Practices http://media.amazonwebservices.com/AWS_Cloud_Best_Practices.pdf

w36. Jeff Barr, Attila Narin, and Jinesh Varia (2011) Building Fault-Tolerant Applications on AWS http://media.amazonwebservices.com/AWS_Building_Fault_Tolerant_Applications.pdf

w37. *Amazon Web Services (2010) AWS Security Best Practices http://media.amazonwebservices.com/Whitepaper_Security_Best_Practices_2010.pdf*

w38. Jinesh Varia (2008) Cloud Architectures http://media.amazonwebservices.com/AWS_Cloud_Architectures.pdf

w39. Amazon.com (2007) Dynamo: Amazon's Highly Available Key-Value Store http://www.read.seas.harvard.edu/~kohler/class/cs239-w08/decandia07dynamo.pdf

w40. *Edward Curry, Desmond Chambers, Gerard Lyons (2004) Extending Message-Oriented Middleware Using Interception http://www.edwardcurry.org/web_publications/curry_DEBS_04.pdf*

w41. *Sharma Chakravarthy, Raman Adaikkalavan (2007) Ubiquitous Nature of Event-Driven Approaches: A Retrospective View http://drops.dagstuhl.de/opus/volltexte/2007/1150/pdf/07191. ChakravarthySharma.Paper.1150.pdf*

w42. Daniel Ford, Francois Labelle, Florentina Popovici, Google (2010) Availability in Globally Distributed Storage Systems http://static.googleusercontent.com/external_content/untrusted_dlcp/ research.google.com/en//pubs/archive/36737.pdf

w43. *Daniel Peng, Frank Dabek, Google (2010) Large-Scale Incremental Processing Using Distributed Transactions and Notifications http://static.googleusercontent.com/external_content/untrusted_dlcp/ research.google.com/en//pubs/archive/36726.pdf*

w44. Sanjay Ghemawat, Howard Gobioff, Shun-Tak Leung, Google (2003) The Google File System http://static.googleusercontent.com/external_content/untrusted_dlcp/ research.google.com/en//archive/gfs-sosp2003.pdf

w45. *Grzegorz Malewicz, Matthew H. Austern, Aart J. C. Bik, James C. Dehnert, Ilan Horn, Naty Leiser, Grzegorz Czajkowski, Google (2010) Pregel: A System for Large-Scale Graph Processing http://kowshik.github.io/JPregel/pregel_paper.pdf*

w46. *Sergey Melnik, Andrey Gubarev, Jing Jing Long, Geoffrey Romer, Shiva Shivakumar, Matt Tolton, Theo Vassilakis, Google (2010) Dremel: Interactive Analysis of Web-Scale Datasets http://static.googleusercontent.com/external_content/untrusted_dlcp/ research.google.com/en//pubs/archive/36632.pdf*

w47. Sergey Brin, Lawrence Page, Google (1998) The Anatomy of a Large-Scale Hypertextual Web Search Engine http://ilpubs.stanford.edu:8090/361/1/1998-8.pdf

w48. Luiz André Barroso, Jeffrey Dean, Urs Hölzle, Google (2003) Websearch for a Planet: The Google Cluster Architecture http://www.eecs.harvard.edu/~dbrooks/cs246-fall2004/google.pdf

w49. *Mike Burrows, Google, Inc. (2006) The Chubby Lock Service for Loosely-Coupled Distributed Systems http://static.googleusercontent.com/external_content/untrusted_dlcp/ research.google.com/en//archive/chubby-osdi06.pdf*

w50. *Raymond Cheng, Will Scott, Paul Ellenbogen, Arvind Krishnamurthy, Thomas Anderson (2013) Radiatus: Strong User Isolation for Scalable Web Applications*
http://www.cs.washington.edu/education/grad/UW-CSE-13-11-01.PDF

w51. *Yahoo! Research (2010) Feeding Frenzy: Selectively Materializing Users' Event Feeds.*

w52. LinkedIn (2011) Kafka: A Distributed Messaging System for Log Processing
http://research.microsoft.com/en-us/um/people/srikanth/netdb11/netdb11papers/netdb11-final12.pdf

w53. *LinkedIn (2013) Using Set Cover to Optimize a Large-Scale Low Latency Distributed Graph*
http://0b4af6cdc2f0c5998459-c0245c5c937c5dedcca3f1764ecc9b2f.r43.cf2.rackcdn.com/11567-hotcloud13-wang.pdf

w54. AMQP.org (2011) AMQP v1.0 Specification
http://www.amqp.org/sites/amqp.org/files/amqp.pdf

w55. DataStax (2014) Apache Cassandra 2.0 Documentation
http://www.datastax.com/documentation/cassandra/2.0/pdf/cassandra20.pdf

w56. *DataStax (2014) CQL for Cassandra 2.0 Documentation*
http://www.datastax.com/documentation/cql/3.1/pdf/cql31.pdf

w57. George Candea, Armando Fox from Stanford University (2003) Crash-Only Software
https://www.usenix.org/legacy/events/hotos03/tech/full_papers/candea/candea.pdf

w58. Konstantin V. Shvachko (2010) HDFS Scalability: The Limits to Growth
https://www.usenix.org/legacy/publications/login/2010-04/openpdfs/shvachko.pdf

w59. *Google, Inc. (2013) MillWheel: Fault-Tolerant Stream Processing at Internet Scale*
http://static.googleusercontent.com/media/research.google.com/en/us/pubs/archive/41378.pdf

w60. *Google, Inc. (2010) FlumeJava: Easy, Efficient Data-Parallel Pipelines*
http://pages.cs.wisc.edu/~akella/CS838/F12/838-CloudPapers/FlumeJava.pdf

w61. Ranjit Noronha, Dhabaleswar K. Panda (2008) IMCa: A High Performance Caching Front-End for GlusterFS on InfiniBand
http://nowlab.cse.ohio-state.edu/publications/conf-papers/2008/noronha-icpp08.pdf

w62. Facebook (2013) Scaling Memcache at Facebook
https://www.usenix.org/system/files/conference/nsdi13/nsdi13-final170_
update.pdf&sa=U&ei=gWJjU97pOeqxsQSDkYDAAg&ved=0CBsQFj
AA&usg=AFQjCNGMeuWne9ywncbgux_XiZW6lQWHNw

w63. *Intel (2012) Enhancing the Scalability of Memcached*
https://software.intel.com/sites/default/files/m/0/b/6/1/d/45675-
memcached_05172012.pdf

w64. *Yahoo! (2010) ZooKeeper: Wait-Free Coordination for Internet-Scale Systems*
https://www.usenix.org/legacy/event/usenix10/tech/full_papers/Hunt.pdf

w65. *University of Washington (2011) Scalable Consistency in Scatter*
http://homes.cs.washington.edu/~arvind/papers/scatter.pdf

w66. *James Cipar, Greg Ganger, Kimberly Keeton, Charles B. Morrey III, Craig A. N.*
Soules, Alistair Veitch (2012) LazyBase: Trading Freshness for Performance in
a Scalable Database
http://www.pdl.cmu.edu/PDL-FTP/Database/euro166-cipar.pdf

w67. *Hyeontaek Lim, Bin Fan, David G. Andersen, Michael Kaminsky (2011) SILT:*
A Memory-Efficient, High-Performance Key-Value Store
https://www.cs.cmu.edu/~dga/papers/silt-sosp2011.pdf

w68. *Wyatt Lloyd, Michael J. Freedman, Michael Kaminsky, David G. Andersen*
(2011) Don't Settle for Eventual: Scalable Causal Consistency for Wide-Area
Storage with COPS
http://sns.cs.princeton.edu/docs/cops-sosp11.pdf

w69. *Microsoft (2007) Dryad: Distributed Data-Parallel Programs from Sequential*
Building Blocks
http://www.cs.cmu.edu/~./15712/papers/isard07.pdf

w70. *Facebook (2013) TAO: Facebook's Distributed Data Store for the Social Graph*
https://www.cs.cmu.edu/~pavlo/courses/fall2013/static/papers/11730-atc13-
bronson.pdf

w71. Facebook (2013) Unicorn: A System for Searching the Social Graph
http://db.disi.unitn.eu/pages/VLDBProgram/pdf/industry/p871-curtiss.pdf

w72. Google (2014) Mesa: Geo-Replicated, Near Real-Time, Scalable Data
Warehousing
http://static.googleusercontent.com/media/research.google.com/en/us/
pubs/archive/42851.pdf

w73. The Ohio State University (2013) Understanding the Robustness of SSDs
under Power Fault
https://www.usenix.org/system/files/conference/fast13/fast13-final80.pdf

Appendix: References **373**

w74. Philippe Flajolet, Éric Fusy, Olivier Gandouet, Frédéric Meunier (2007)
HyperLogLog: The Analysis of a Near-Optimal Cardinality Estimation
Algorithm
http://algo.inria.fr/flajolet/Publications/FlFuGaMe07.pdf

w75. *Google, Inc. (2013) HyperLogLog in Practice: Algorithmic Engineering of a
State of the Art Cardinality Estimation Algorithm
http://static.googleusercontent.com/media/research.google.com/en//pubs/
archive/40671.pdf*

w76. Martin Fowler (2004) Inversion of Control Containers and the Dependency
Injection Pattern
https://blog.itu.dk/MMAD-F2013/files/2013/02/3-inversion-of-control-
containers-and-the-dependency-injection-pattern.pdf

w77. Martin Thompson, Dave Farley, Michael Barker, Patricia Gee, Andrew
Stewart (2011) Disruptor: High Performance Alternative to Bounded Queues
for Exchanging Data Between Concurrent Threads
http://disruptor.googlecode.com/files/Disruptor-1.0.pdf

w78. *Pat Helland (2009) Building on Quicksand
http://blogs.msdn.com/cfs-file.ashx/__key/communityserver-components-
postattachments/00-09-20-52-14/BuildingOnQuicksand_2D00_
V3_2D00_081212h_2D00_pdf.pdf*

w79. *Mark Slee, Aditya Agarwal, Marc Kwiatkowski, Facebook (2007) Thrift:
Scalable Cross-Language Services Implementation
http://thrift.apache.org/static/files/thrift-20070401.pdf*

Talks

t1. Robert C. Martin (2011) Keynote Speech of Ruby Midwest: Architecture the
Lost Years

t2. *Renat Khasanshyn (2012) CouchConf San Francisco
http://www.couchbase.com/presentations/benchmarking-couchbase*

t3. *Google, Inc. (2012) F1: The Fault-Tolerant Distributed RDBMS Supporting
Google's Ad Business
http://static.googleusercontent.com/external_content/untrusted_dlcp/
research.google.com/en//pubs/archive/38125.pdf*

t4. *Andy Parsons (2013) Lessons on Scaling Rapidly-Growing Startups in the Cloud
http://java.dzone.com/articles/lessons-scaling-rapidly*

t5. *Sean Cribbs (2012) Fear No More: Embrace Eventual Consistency*
*http://qconsf.com/sf2012/dl/qcon-sanfran-2012/slides/SeanCribbs_*
FearNoMoreEmbraceEventualConsistency.pdf

t6. *Robert Hodges (2013) State of the Art for MySQL Multi-Master Replication*
http://www.percona.com/live/mysql-conference-2013/sites/default/files/
slides/mysql-multi-master-state-of-art-2013-04-24_0.pdf

t7. *Jay Patel (2013)*
http://www.slideshare.net/jaykumarpatel/cassandra-data-modeling-best-
practices

Links

L1. Windows Azure Queues and Windows Azure Service Bus Queues:
Compared and Contrasted
http://msdn.microsoft.com/en-us/library/windowsazure/hh767287.aspx

L2. Thomas Bayer (2013) Broker Wars
http://www.predic8.com/activemq-hornetq-rabbitmq-apollo-qpid-
comparison.htm

L3. Amazon SQS Documentation
http://aws.amazon.com/documentation/sqs/

L4. Google Trends of ActiveMQ and RabbitMQ Searches
http://www.google.com/trends/explore?q=activemq%2C+rabbitmq%2C+z
eromq%2C+hornetq#q=activemq%2C%20rabbitmq&date=7%2F2008%20
61m&cmpt=q

L5. Datadog
https://www.datadoghq.com/product/

L6. Martin Fowler (2011) The LMAX Architecture
http://martinfowler.com/articles/lmax.html

L7. Martin Fowler (2005) Event Sourcing
http://martinfowler.com/eaaDev/EventSourcing.html

L8. Mitchell Anicas (2014) How to Use Logstash and Kibana to Centralize Logs
on Ubuntu 14.04
https://www.digitalocean.com/community/tutorials/how-to-use-logstash-
and-kibana-to-centralize-and-visualize-logs-on-ubuntu-14-04

L9. Logstash (2013) Introduction
http://logstash.net/docs/1.4.2/tutorials/getting-started-with-logstash

L10. Luu Duong's Blog (2009) Applying the "80-20 Rule" with The Standish
Group's Statistics on Software Usage
http://luuduong.com/blog/archive/2009/03/04/applying-the-quot8020-
rulequot-with-the-standish-groups-software-usage.aspx

L11. Spotify (2014) Spotify Engineering Culture
https://labs.spotify.com/2014/03/27/spotify-engineering-culture-part-1/

L12. *The Netflix Tech Blog (2010) Chaos Monkey Released into the Wild*
http://techblog.netflix.com/2012/07/chaos-monkey-released-into-wild.html

L13. Azure SQL Database Elastic Scale Overview
http://azure.microsoft.com/en-us/documentation/articles/sql-database-
elastic-scale-introduction/

L14. *The Netflix Tech Blog (2013) Astyanax Update*
http://techblog.netflix.com/2013/12/astyanax-update.html

L15. Red Hat Storage Server NAS Takes on Lustre, NetApp
http://www.theregister.co.uk/2012/06/27/redhat_storage_server_2_launch/

L16. Zookeeper
http://zookeeper.apache.org/

L17. Curator
http://curator.apache.org/

L18. Amazon API (2012) Elastic Load Balancer LB Cookie Stickiness
http://docs.aws.amazon.com/ElasticLoadBalancing/latest/APIReference/
API_CreateLBCookieStickinessPolicy.html

L19. F5 DevCentral (2013) Back to Basics: The Many Faces of Load Balancing
Persistence
https://devcentral.f5.com/articles/back-to-basics-the-many-faces-of-load-
balancing-persistence

L20. Amazon (2013) Creating Latency Resource Record Sets
http://docs.aws.amazon.com/Route53/latest/DeveloperGuide/
CreatingLatencyRRSets.html

L21. Amazon (2012) Multi-Region Latency Based Routing Now Available for AWS
http://aws.amazon.com/blogs/aws/latency-based-multi-region-routing-
now-available-for-aws/

L22. Amazon (2014) Two New Edge Locations for CloudFront and Route 53
http://aws.amazon.com/blogs/aws/two-new-edge-locations-for-cloudfront-and-route-53-taipei-and-rio-de-janeiro/

L23. Wikipedia, List of Managed DNS Providers
http://en.wikipedia.org/wiki/List_of_managed_DNS_providers

L24. Cloudharmony blog (2012) Comparison and Analysis of Managed DNS Providers
http://blog.cloudharmony.com/2012/08/comparison-and-analysis-of-managed-dns.html

L25. Citrix (2013) Citrix NetScaler
http://www.citrix.com/content/dam/citrix/en_us/documents/products-solutions/netscaler-data-sheet.pdf

L26. F5 Networks (2013) Comparative Performance Report
http://www.f5.com/pdf/reports/F5-comparative-performance-report-ADC-2013.pdf

L27. statisticshowto.com, Misleading Graphs: Real Life Examples
http://www.statisticshowto.com/misleading-graphs/

L28. Gernot Heiser (2010) Systems Benchmarking Crimes
http://www.cse.unsw.edu.au/~gernot/benchmarking-crimes.html

L29. *Amazon, Auto-scaling Documentation*
http://docs.aws.amazon.com/AutoScaling/latest/DeveloperGuide/USBasicSetup-Console.html

L30. *Amazon, Auto-scaling Documentation*
http://docs.aws.amazon.com/AutoScaling/latest/DeveloperGuide/as-register-lbs-with-asg.html

L31. highscalability.com (2013) Scaling Pinterest: From 0 to 10s of Billions of Page Views a Month in Two Years
http://highscalability.com/blog/2013/4/15/scaling-pinterest-from-0-to-10s-of-billions-of-page-views-a.html

L32. highscalability.com (2010) 7 Lessons Learned While Building Reddit to 270 Million Page Views a Month
http://highscalability.com/blog/2010/5/17/7-lessons-learned-while-building-reddit-to-270-million-page.html

L33. highscalability.com (2012) Tumblr Architecture: 15 Billion Page Views a Month and Harder to Scale Than Twitter
http://highscalability.com/blog/2012/2/13/tumblr-architecture-15-billion-page-views-a-month-and-harder.html

L34. Charles Bretana via stackoverflow.com (2009) Does Anyone Have a Good Analogy for Dependency Injection? http://stackoverflow.com/questions/424457/does-anyone-have-a-good-analogy-for-dependency-injection

L35. highscalability.com (2010) Facebook at 13 Million Queries Per Second Recommends: Minimize Request Variance http://highscalability.com/blog/2010/11/4/facebook-at-13-million-queries-per-second-recommends-minimiz.html

L36. www.percona.com (2014) MySQL Ring Replication: Why It Is a Bad Option http://www.percona.com/blog/2014/10/07/mysql-ring-replication-why-it-is-a-bad-option/

L37. Pramod Sadalage, Martin Fowler (2012) Introduction to Polyglot Persistence: Using Different Data Storage Technologies for Varying Data Storage Needs http://www.informit.com/articles/article.aspx?p=1930511

L38. *Fangjin Yang (2012) Fast, Cheap, and 98% Right: Cardinality Estimation for Big Data http://druid.io/blog/2012/05/04/fast-cheap-and-98-right-cardinality-estimation-for-big-data.html*

L39. *Stripe, API Libraries https://stripe.com/docs/libraries*

Index

A

A/B tests, 340, 352
abstraction
    avoiding overengineering, 40–41
    promoting simplicity, 38–40
    reducing coupling on higher levels of, 44–46
access patterns
    data modeling focus on, 314, 316–317
    denormalizing/optimizing for, 316
    identifying/modeling data based on, 313
    in NoSQL data stores, 317–318
    wide column storage example, 321, 324–325
account ID (user ID)
    in binary search, 307
    in full table scans, 305
    implementing sharding key, 172–174,
        188–189
    partitioning search data, 325
    search optimization, 309–310
ACID (Atomicity, Consistency, Isolation,
    Durability) transaction, 177, 178
active data set size, 167–168
ActiveMQ
    advanced routing rules, 264
    comparing messaging platforms, 286, 288,
        292–294
    load handling, 269
    messaging protocols, 265–266
    ordering messages, 280
    overview of, 291–292
    partial message ordering guarantee, 279
    poison message handling, 284
ad hoc design sessions, 354
administration, Cassandra, 202–203
Advanced Message Queuing Protocol (AMQP),
    265, 288–289
agent, monitoring, 342
agile teams, scaling
    adding more people, 357–359
    culture of alignment, 360–361

    overview of, 357
    procedures and innovation, 359–360
AJAX
    front-end applications with, 29
    local device storage for SPAs, 229
    simplifying asynchronous processing,
        252–253
alerts
    automating, 340–345
    automating build and deployment, 340
    custom routing rules for, 264
alignment, culture of, 361–362
alter table statements, MySQL replication, 169
Amazon
    CloudFront, 17, 117–119, 222–223
    CloudSearch, 329
    CloudWatch, 116, 118
    CloudWatch Logs, 346
    Dynamo. *See* Dynamo data store
    Elastic Cache, 238–239
    RDS (Relational Database Service), 170
    Route 53 service, 101–103, 117–119
Amazon EC2 (Elastic Compute Cloud)
    auto-scaling, 115–116
    AWS web deployment, 117–119
    deploying own caching servers, 238–239
    load balancer. *See* Amazon ELB
        (Elastic Load Balancer)
    queue workers, 268
Amazon ELB (Elastic Load Balancer)
    automating build and deployment, 339
    auto-scaling, 116–118
    as hosted service, 106–107
    stateless web service machines and, 140
Amazon Machine Image (AMI), 115, 339
Amazon SQS (Simple Queue Service)
    comparing messaging platforms, 293–294
    disadvantages of, 288
    message ordering problem, 280, 288
    overview of, 285–288
    poison message handling, 284

CPSIA information can be obtained
at www.ICGtesting.com
Printed in the USA
FSHW022250080921
84486FS